BETWEEN INDIAN AND WHITE WORLDS

BETWEEN INDIAN AND WHITE WORLDS

THE CULTURAL BROKER

EDITED BY

MARGARET CONNELL SZASZ

UNIVERSITY OF OKLAHOMA PRESS : NORMAN AND LONDON

ALSO BY MARGARET CONNELL SZASZ

Education and the American Indian: The Road to Self-Determination
(Albuquerque, 1974; 1977, 2nd ed.)

Indian Education in the American Colonies, 1607–1783 (Albuquerque, 1988)

Library of Congress Cataloging-in-Publication Data

Between Indian and white worlds : the cultural broker / edited by
Margaret Connell Szasz.
    p. cm.
Includes bibliographical references and index.
ISBN 0-8061-2595-0 (alk. paper)
    1. Indians of North America—Government relations.
2. Intercultural communication—North America. 3. Indians of North
America—Cultural assimilation. 4. Indians of North America—
Biography. I. Szasz, Margaret.
E91.B48   1994
305.897—dc20   93-41717
                                           CIP

This book is published with the generous assistance of Edith Gaylord
Harper.

Parts of chapter 11, "Jesse Rowlodge: Southern Arapaho as Political
Intermediary," by Donald J. Berthrong, were previously published in
American Indian Quarterly and appear here by permission.

The paper in this book meets the guidelines for permanence and
durability of the Committee on Production Guidelines for Book Longevity of the Council on Library Resources, Inc. ∞

1 2 3 4 5 6 7 8 9 10

To my parents

CONTENTS

List of Illustrations ix

Acknowledgments xi

Introduction 3
  Margaret Connell Szasz

PART ONE: Brokers of the Colonial World 21

 1. The Ways and Words of the Other: Diego de Vargas
  and Cultural Brokers in Late Seventeenth-Century
  New Mexico
   John L. Kessell 25

 2. "Faithful, Knowing, and Prudent": Andrew Montour as
  Interpreter and Cultural Broker, 1740–1772
   Nancy L. Hagedorn 44

 3. Samson Occom: Mohegan as Spiritual Intermediary
   Margaret Connell Szasz 61

PART TWO: Brokers of an Expanding Republic 79

 4. Red-Head's Domain: William Clark's Indian Brokerage
   James P. Ronda 81

 5. An Alternative Missionary Style: Evan Jones and
  John B. Jones Among the Cherokees
   William G. McLoughlin 98

6. American Indian School Pupils as Cultural Brokers:
    Cherokee Girls at Brainerd Mission, 1828–1829
        Michael C. Coleman   122

PART THREE: Brokers for the Wild West   137

7. Helen Hunt Jackson as Power Broker
        Valerie Sherer Mathes   141

8. Interpreting the Wild West, 1883–1914
        L. G. Moses   158

9. Female Native Teachers in Southeast Alaska:
    Sarah Dickinson, Tillie Paul, and Frances Willard
        Victoria Wyatt   179

10. Three Cultural Brokers in the Context of
    Edward S. Curtis's *The North American Indian*
        Mick Gidley   197

PART FOUR: Twentieth-Century Brokers   217

11. Jesse Rowlodge: Southern Arapaho as Political
    Intermediary
        Donald J. Berthrong   223

12. D'Arcy McNickle: Living a Broker's Life
        Dorothy R. Parker   240

13. Speaking Their Language: Robert W. Young and
    the Navajos
        Peter Iverson   255

14. Pablita Velarde: The Pueblo Artist as Cultural Broker
        Sally Hyer   273

Conclusion   294
        Margaret Connell Szasz

Notes   301
Bibliography   347
The Contributors   367
Index   371

ILLUSTRATIONS

FIGURES

Communicating with the Full Moon,
by Pablita Velarde   *frontispiece*

Diego de Vargas   28

Taos Pueblo, by Henry R. Poore   38

Diego de Vargas's summons for Pecos fighting men, 1696   40

Wahu Toya, an aged Pecos Indian, 1880   42

Johnson Hall, where Andrew Montour frequently
interpreted   54

The Reverend Samson Occom (1723–1792)   62

The Reverend Samson Occom—a portrait from the 1760s   70

Andrew Jackson peace medal, dated 1829   85

Helen Hunt Jackson   143

Mission Indians at home, Saboba   151

Ramona Lubo   155

Buffalo Bill's Wild West Show troupe, 1893   160

Two members of William Cody's World's Fair troupe,
ca. 1893   169

Autographed photo from Buffalo Bill to Red Shirt   173

Indian Village at the Pacific Southwest Exposition, 1928   176

Edward S. Curtis and George Hunt filming in Kwakiutl
country, ca. 1912   205

A. B. Upshaw, 1906   210

Jesse Rowlodge, 1958   238

D'Arcy McNickle   243

Robert W. Young   257

Dressing a Young Woman for Her First Ceremonial Dance,
by Pablita Velarde   283

Communicating with the Full Moon, by Pablita Velarde   290

MAPS

Cultural brokers: areas of influence   4

Pueblo language groups   29

Cherokee lands in the West   101

The Cherokee Nation, 1819–1838   103

Southern California Mission Indian villages during
the 1880s   149

ACKNOWLEDGMENTS

THE idea for this book began to germinate in the mid-1980s when I was living in Exeter, England, so I would like to thank my colleagues at the University of Exeter, including B. A. Turner, Richard Maltby, and especially Mick Gidley. Gidley was the catalyst for the conference "'Culture Brokers' in the History of Indian/White Relations," held in London at the Institute of United States Studies in 1986. Participants in that conference who spurred my thinking on the subject included Peter J. Parish, then director of the institute, Jacqueline Fear, David Murray, and Gidley.

Their disputatious assessment of brokerage eventually led to another discussion of the subject at Northern Arizona University, where I spoke for a lecture series sponsored by the Center for Colorado Plateau Studies and arranged by L. G. Moses and Cathy Trotta. I appreciate their providing me with the opportunity to explore further dimensions of this theme. More recently, I was the recipient of the Snead Wertheim Lectureship in History and Anthropology at the University of New Mexico. I am grateful to the donors of that lectureship, James Snead and Jerry Wertheim, because they enabled me to reconstruct yet another version of my thoughts on cultural intermediaries, which I delivered as a lecture to the university.

My colleagues in the Department of History at the University of New Mexico have helped to refine my thoughts on brokers; among them are John Kessell, Dan Feller, Richard Etulain, Bill Dabney, Carol Lovato, and Mel Yazawa. I am also indebted to William T.

Hagan and Grayson Noley, who offered comments on my study of Samson Occom at the Western History Association Conference held in 1989.

I further refined my thoughts on cultural brokers during a teaching exchange at the University of Aberdeen, Scotland, in 1991–1992, where participation in the History Departmental Research Seminar organized by Till Geiger, discussions with colleagues David Ditchburn, Grant Simpson, William Pike, Paul Dukes, Rosemary Tysack, and Roy C. Bridges, along with lively tutorial sessions with the students in the "Red Indian" History course, offered a wide range of perspectives on cultural intermediaries. The typing skills and gracious assistance of Sandra Williams of the University of Aberdeen were invaluable.

Carol Cooperrider's cartographic skills are clearly evident in the map "Cultural Brokers: Areas of Influence." John N. Drayton, Barbara Siegemund-Broka, and others at the University of Oklahoma Press have offered able guidance in the process of crafting this study.

I am grateful to Nancy O. Lurie for her provocative ideas and warm support. I would also like to thank my contributors, who have borne with patience and good humor my many requests and have expanded my perception of intermediaries. I am especially indebted to William G. McLoughlin, whose death has left a void in the profession, but whose heritage will continue to enlarge our understanding. My family, Eric, Chris, Scott, and Maria, have listened patiently to the theme of cultural intermediaries over these eight years. And Ferenc M. Szasz has again served as chief critic and supporter in immeasurable ways.

MARGARET CONNELL SZASZ

Albuquerque, New Mexico

BETWEEN INDIAN AND WHITE WORLDS

INTRODUCTION

MARGARET CONNELL SZASZ

IN his narrative *The Dancing Healers* (1988), Carl A. Hammersch-lag, a Yale-trained psychiatrist, confessed that he had "learned many steps from many dancers." "We are always patients, and sometimes we are healers," he wrote. "We move from being one to being the other." After working among American Indians in the Southwest for two decades, Hammerschlag could speak to the theme of cultural intermediaries. He had become one.[1]

Hammerschlag's interpretation of cultures had thrust him into that frontier region where cultural borders rub together, where cultural intermediaries—the people between the borders—juggle the ways of different societies with apparent ease. Cultural borders are a universal phenomenon. They emerge wherever cultures encounter each other. One only needs to live on the continent of Europe or within a nationalistic region of Britain, such as Scotland, to become aware of the universality of abrasiveness along cultural borders. For intermediaries or cultural brokers, however, these borders have become pathways that link peoples rather than barriers that separate them.

At a recent academic conference in Louisville, Kentucky, a small group of scholars of America's native people gathered in a hotel conference room late one afternoon. When they pulled their chairs together to form a large circle, one of them remarked, "If we had a drum, we could have our own powwow." An academic gathering with a largely non-Indian audience might seem an unlikely place for a powwow. But for these cultural intermediaries, the possibility

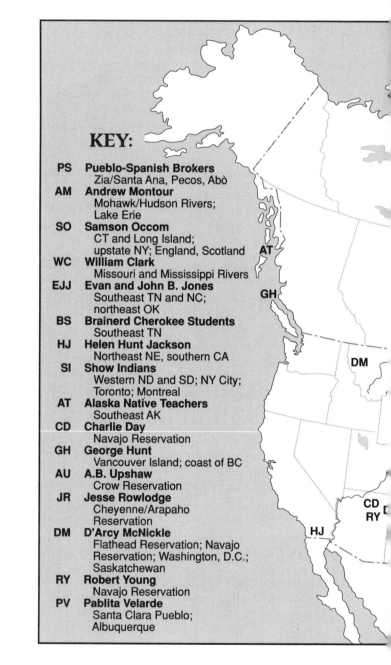

KEY:

PS   **Pueblo-Spanish Brokers**
Zia/Santa Ana, Pecos, Abò

AM   **Andrew Montour**
Mohawk/Hudson Rivers;
Lake Erie

SO   **Samson Occom**
CT and Long Island;
upstate NY; England, Scotland

WC   **William Clark**
Missouri and Mississippi Rivers

EJJ   **Evan and John B. Jones**
Southeast TN and NC;
northeast OK

BS   **Brainerd Cherokee Students**
Southeast TN

HJ   **Helen Hunt Jackson**
Northeast NE, southern CA

SI   **Show Indians**
Western ND and SD; NY City;
Toronto; Montreal

AT   **Alaska Native Teachers**
Southeast AK

CD   **Charlie Day**
Navajo Reservation

GH   **George Hunt**
Vancouver Island; coast of BC

AU   **A.B. Upshaw**
Crow Reservation

JR   **Jesse Rowlodge**
Cheyenne/Arapaho
Reservation

DM   **D'Arcy McNickle**
Flathead Reservation; Navajo
Reservation; Washington, D.C.;
Saskatchewan

RY   **Robert Young**
Navajo Reservation

PV   **Pablita Velarde**
Santa Clara Pueblo;
Albuquerque

Cultural brokers: areas of influence.

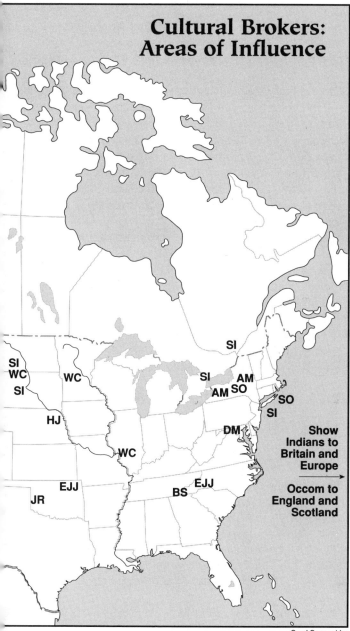

Cultural Brokers:
Areas of Influence

SI

SI
WC   WC
SI

HJ

SI   AM
AM SO

SO
SI

WC

DM

**Show
Indians to
Britain and
Europe**

→

**Occom to
England and
Scotland**

EJJ   EJJ
JR   BS

Carol Cooperrider

Drawn by Carol Cooperrider.

of a powwow struck a ready response. Since they knew the ways of several cultures, they could transpose characteristics of "Indian country" to the border South. Like actors, they retained several identities.

During the five centuries of contact between native and non-native people of the Americas, thousands of these intermediaries have moved across the cultural frontiers of the continent. Some were interpreters, others mediated spiritual understanding. Many served as traders; others, as diplomats. Some bridged native worlds marked by separate and distinct identities. Others forged bonds between native and outside cultures. Even those who entered this pathway through circumstances beyond their control gained multicultural perspectives along the way.

Moving across these frontiers demanded extraordinary skill. Intermediaries became repositories of two or more cultures; they changed roles at will, in accordance with circumstances. Of necessity, their lives reflected a complexity unknown to those living within the confines of a single culture. They knew how the "other side" thought and behaved, and they responded accordingly. Their grasp of different perspectives led all sides to value them, although not all may have trusted them. Often they walked through a network of interconnections where they alone brought some understanding among disparate peoples. These mediators, therefore, have held a distinctive position in our past and into the present. This introduction will evaluate how their role has come to be recognized since World War II.

Contemporary interest in cultural intermediaries has coincided with growing concern for cultural pluralism. In recent decades, as the United States and Canada have been struggling to redefine themselves as multicultural populations, so, too, has the academic world been focusing on the intermediaries who have linked the cultures of these complex societies. This concern began shortly after the Second World War, when historians and cultural anthropologists crafted the interdisciplinary approach of ethnohistory, which has eventually led to further understanding of North America's cultures.

Ethnohistory combines aspects of ethnology and history to form what anthropologist William S. Simmons has described as "a form of cultural biography that draws upon as many kinds of testimony as possible—material culture, archaeology, visual sources, historical documents, native texts, folklore, even earlier ethnographies—over as long a time as the sources allow." Writing from a historian's perspective, James Axtell has defined ethnohistory as "essentially the use of historical and ethnological methods and materials to gain knowledge of the nature and causes of change in a culture defined by ethnological concepts and categories." When the hybrid approach was born, it faced a challenge that anthropologist Marshall Sahlins noted was "to explode the concept of history by the anthropological experience of culture."[2]

The roots of ethnohistory lay at least partly in the Indian Claims Commission, created in 1946 as a means by which tribes and bands could sue the federal government over loss of lands. Prior to this time, ethnologists had been largely ahistorical. Trained "to be participant-observers in real-life situations," they had interpreted the cultures they studied "strictly in terms of the present."[3] Research for Indian Claims Commission cases changed this attitude. When ethnologists began to explore the historical record to substantiate tribal claims, they were forced to reconsider their previous views.

By the 1950s anthropologists had traveled a considerable distance from the turn-of-the-century views of Franz Boas, who perceived precontact native cultures as largely static. Anthropologist Bruce G. Trigger has written of his predecessors that "they were also convinced that native cultures were disintegrating as a result of European contact; hence the primary aim of ethnologists was to record these cultures as thoroughly as possible before they disappeared completely."[4]

As anthropologists began to alter their perspectives, so, too, did historians of native/non-native relations. Contrasting the former approaches of these two disciplines, historian Robert F. Berkhofer, Jr., has written, "Anthropologists studied the aboriginal past and reservation present, while historians devoted themselves to the period in between." Despite changing attitudes, many historians clung to ethnocentrism. "We assumed," historian Francis Jennings observed in 1972, "that we were civilized and that the inferior people of other countries were barbarous or savage. . . Our assumptions were founded in ethnocentrism, and still are to a degree."[5]

Jennings's predecessors had spun their narratives through the eyes of European immigrant cultures. Their sources, largely preserved as archival documents, reflected the perceptions of literate people. Oral records were thought to be peripheral. Those who relied on written sources were often locked into the cultural views of the record keepers. Historian Neal Salisbury has concluded, "Historians and others [who] have described the English conquest of Indian New England . . . have presupposed that the outcome was inevitable because of the incompatibility of Indian and English cultures and the inherent moral superiority of the latter."[6]

During the postwar decades, when cultural anthropology and history reached across the chasm that had separated them, Jennings aptly described the breakthrough as the "bringing together [of] the humanist tradition of history and the scientific tradition of anthropology."[7] In November 1953, a group of anthropologists and historians met to form the Ohio Valley Historic Indian Conference; a decade later this organization became the American Society for Ethnohistory. The "hybrid discipline," as James Axtell dubbed it, had germinated.

William Simmons later reasoned that the breadth of the chasm between historians and anthropologists had affected their understanding of the "encounter between Europeans and indigenous people." As the distance has narrowed and the lines of division have blurred, understanding has enlarged.[8] For two decades, however, the narrowing was scarcely discernible. With the exception of a few historians (including Berkhofer, Dwight L. Smith, William T. Hagan, Donald C. Berthrong, and Helen Hornbeck Tanner), anthropologists (including Trigger, Anthony F. C. Wallace, Nancy O. Lurie, Harold Hickerson, William N. Fenton, Edward O. Spicer, John C. Ewers, and Ermine Wheeler-Vogelin) dominated the forum. Most historians, therefore, were not keeping pace with the growing multiculturalism. Their reliance on the Euramerican perspectives found in written sources closed their eyes to the heterogeneous experiences of this continent. Moreover, their focus on one side of the cultural equation discouraged curiosity about the role of cultural brokers.

From the late nineteenth century forward, ethnologists had been researching directly among the people whose cultures they were recording, and consequently they had often encountered intermediaries, some of whom had become anthropologists themselves. Turn-of-the-century Omaha anthropologist Francis La Flesche, for example, collaborated with anthropologist Alice Fletcher in an effort that culminated in *The Omaha Tribe* (1911). In her biography of Fletcher, anthropologist Joan Mark suggested a dual cultural brokerage for both authors, concluding that the redoubtable Victorian woman "worked all her life not just for some vague understanding between the two societies but for appreciation by each of the highest and best that the other was capable of." The publications of these two ethnologists illustrate their different views of the world. Fletcher's goal was to publish for anthropologists and the public. La Flesche's goal was to educate the internal world of native people, resulting in his study, *The Osage Tribe* (1921, 1925, 1928, 1930).[9]

Well before World War II, anthropologists began editing as-told-to autobiographies of American Indians, many of whom were cultural intermediaries as well as "great literary figures."[10] H. David Brumble, a critic of this genre, has questioned whether it is germaine to depict these as-told-to narratives as "literary biography." Placing them in this category, he has suggested, ignores the editor's cultural refurbishing, the adaptation of oral autobiography to suit Western sensibilities. Brumble has labeled such autobiographies "bicultural documents" because they contain "the assumptions of Indian autobiographers *and* Anglo editors."[11] One of the most enduring of these "bicultural documents," *Papago Woman* (1936), reflects the cultural world of anthropologist Ruth Underhill and the culturally filtered world of Maria Chona, a Tohono O'odham. An even more familiar account, *The Autobiography of a Hopi Indian* (1942), relates the life of Don C. Talayesva as narrated to sociologist Leo W. Simmons. The Winnebago autobiographies *Crashing Thunder, the Autobiography of An American Indian* (1926), edited by Paul Radin, and *Mountain Wolf Woman, Sister of Crashing Thunder, the Autobiography of a Winnebago Indian* (1961), edited by Nancy Oestreich Lurie, and the Mescalero-Chiricahua autobiography *Apache Odyssey, a Journey Between Two Worlds* (1969), edited by Morris E. Opler, have also become classics of this genre.

Although the ethnologists and other scholars who edited these autobiographies gathered considerable primary materials dealing with the border world of cultural intermediaries, they were limited by their singular focus. Since each portrait recreated only a single life, by the 1950s a composite view had not emerged.

Early in the 1960s, anthropologist Irving A. Hallowell began to probe the impact of native culture on non-natives who became Indianized. In retrospect, Hallowell's focus was less directly on the cultural intermediary than on those non-natives who transposed their allegiance to a tribal culture. Nonetheless, he opened the debate by looking at the phenomenon of role reversal. Earlier ethnologists had studied natives who incorporated non-native ways into their lives; Hallowell argued that academics had ignored non-natives who crossed over to the "other side," thereby introducing a theme that would later attract the attention of Axtell.

Reflecting on his graduate student research in the 1920s, when he was "very green in cultural anthropology," Hallowell recalled his surprise when he learned about the eighteenth-century Euramerican who had been an Abenaki chief. Later, Hallowell came to realize the persistence of this cultural assimilation. "Indianize," he wrote, "is an Americanism dating back to the late seventeenth century."[12] Hallowell also coined two terms to accompany "Indianize": "transculturalization" and "transculturite." Although Hallowell's awkward terminology did not last, his ideas were sound, and scholars would return to them later.[13]

If Hallowell had opened the debate on intermediaries, other anthropologists were wrestling with the related phenomenon of cross-cultural mixing, which they described variously as biculturalism or "permissive diversity." Theodore Stern's observations of the Klamath of southern Oregon alerted him to seeming incongruities within individuals who had adapted to a mixture of cultures. In his depiction of "one old friend" among the Klamath, he summarized her years as "a life-way that was an indissoluble blend of diverse elements integrated by their personal import." Like others, this Klamath Elder demonstrated "the ability to shift from one language to another, or from one behavioral modality to another." Stern noted that "the English she spoke, like that of her boarding-school contemporaries, was likewise syncretic; for it bore the impress of Klamath sound pattern and grammatical categorization."[14]

Hallowell's transculturites were not necessarily cultural intermediaries; nor were the Klamaths who participated in "two orders." Transculturites who remained in another society permanently probably did not become cultural translaters; those who were only temporarily detached from their own culture *may* have become intermediaries. Nonetheless, the Klamaths who remained within their native environment after temporary dislocation practiced those skills that intermediaries have relied on as basic survival techniques. In Stern's words, they "fused life-ways out of historically disparate elements." To this degree, they bore similarities to intermediaries.[15]

Stern's colleague, Malcolm McFee, explored further ramifications of acculturation by native people among the Blackfeet of northern Montana. McFee found these "highly bicultural people" to be divided into two groups, "White-oriented" and "Indian-oriented" Blackfeet. Dubbing the "Indian-oriented" group interpreters or intermediaries, McFee suggested that they attempted to combine the "best of the Indian way and the best of the White way." But this choice restricted their behavior; in order to be viewed as Indian-oriented, they displayed lavish generosity; wealth would have cost them their status.[16]

Like Stern, McFee saw cultural syncretism as "supplementing and enlarging" rather than restricting or detracting. The Indian-oriented Blackfeet were gifted in their ability to move from one world to the other. Without this skill, they could not have behaved correctly in diverse social situations. Since they had gained rather than lost, McFee saw them as "150% men," who chose to retain certain Indian characteristics only if they deemed them useful in their own lives. Their choices, therefore, were pragmatic.[17]

Shortly after McFee's research on the Blackfeet appeared, Robert Paine, a Canadian anthropologist, tested his hypothesis on cultural intermediaries through an edited study of contemporary intrusion into Canadian Arctic communities. Paine constructed an equation that incorporated all who engage in culture brokering. His "patron-broker-client" theory envisioned four types of intermediaries: the "go-between." who is exclusively a purveyor between parties without expecting any remuneration or alteration; the "broker," who also purveys values but deliberately changes emphasis or content; the "patron," who dispenses assets to gain access or control over resources by promoting the dependence of the fourth type of intermediary—the "client," who accepts the values chosen by the patron and is rewarded and protected for this loyalty and dependence.[18]

Paine's hypothetical categories represent the poles of the intermediary spectrum, ranging from the nonmanipulative go-between to the patron and client, who engage in directed reciprocity. But Paine's intermediaries are not limited to one role: a broker can become a patron, and a patron can assume a broker's role. Nonetheless, the equation suggests that everyone engaged in cross-cultural negotiation can be classified as one of four types.

If Paine's methodology were applied to this volume, I would have formulated a scientifically phrased hypothesis to be tested by each chapter. The contributors to the present volume, however, view societies through the humanistic lenses of history, English, American studies, and art history. As humanists, they would question this social science approach by citing the many exceptions to theories such as Paine's. Although humanists in this field have often been restricted by their ethnocentric views, they have approached their subjects with the expectation that their research will reveal the unique historical conditions molding the people and communities under study. In this manner, they anticipate that the hypothesis will emerge largely from the research itself. Therefore, even though the increasing acceptance of ethnohistory has merged humanist approaches with those of anthropology and other social sciences, specific aspects of methodology remain distinct.

During the 1960s and 1970s, however, it was primarily anthropologists who explored the role of cultural intermediaries. By the early 1970s, they had laid the groundwork: Hallowell had provided some temporary nomenclature; Opler had explored the mosaic of bicultural or multicultural lives on an individual level; Stern and McFee had looked at the impact of biculturalism within native communities and between them and outside societies. McFee had also designated bicultural Blackfeet as interpreters or intermediaries, and Paine had formulated specific categories for intermediaries.

The academic world may have entered the 1960s with a certain sense of detachment; by the end of the decade, it, too, had been drawn into the maelstrom of ethnic unrest. In 1969, when Vine Deloria, Jr., a Standing Rock Sioux, published a slim volume entitled *Custer Died for Your Sins*, he recorded the bitterness of centuries that had fueled the young Indian activists of this era. In a specific critique reserved for anthropologists, he disputed their underlying premise: "that people are objects for observation . . . for manipulation," and argued that they had used Indians, employing them as tools for climbing the "university totem pole."[19]

Anthropologist Margot Liberty later recalled the "stormy session" of the American Anthropological Association in 1970 that addressed Deloria's charges. In her edited work *American Indian Intellectuals* (1978), Liberty maintained that the 1970 session was "a kind of self-scourging ritual which has continued in one form or another at most meetings of the Association since." Liberty also reviewed the impact of the American Indian on the American anthropology profession, concluding that most of the subjects described in her book had not been exploited by anthropologists.[20] William N. Fenton's account of Jesse Cornplanter, Seneca, demonstrated how an American Indian had used an anthropologist. Recalling their relationship, Fenton commented, "Indeed I wondered who was being exploited."[21]

Deloria's denunciation of anthropologists generally spared the historians. Deloria made it quite clear who had participated in the dialogue between Indian and academic communities. From the nineteenth century forward, anthropologists had been studying North America's native people through research on native communities. With few exceptions, historians did not participate in contemporary native affairs, nor did they adopt an ethnohistorical approach until the 1970s, and even then many of them relied exclusively on the written word. In a review of *Northeast*, volume 15 of the *Handbook of North American Indians* (1978; Bruce G. Trigger, ed.), Francis Jennings queried why Trigger had not included more historians. Suggesting that colleagues such as William T. Hagan had been available, he concluded, "Alas, the answer must be that when this volume was planned, back in 1972, there were not that many professional historians doing ethnohistory."[22]

Jennings tempered his concern by acknowledging that historically trained ethnohistorians had been multiplying since 1972, a conclusion that Axtell reiterated in 1981 when he described his colleagues as "invaluable partners in [ethnohistory's] definition and practice."[23] In the intervening years events had drawn historians into the issues raised by the Red Power movement. If historians were to comprehend these turbulent events, they would need to step out of the archives.

In the 1970s academic interest in native peoples exploded. Universities created departments and programs in Native American studies; history faculty offered popular courses in the field; and the first tribal colleges opened in the United States and Canada. By the mid-1970s this interest had peaked; in the 1980s, it declined precipitously. Course enrollments shrank and Native American studies programs were slashed. In the interim years, however, the numbers of tribal colleges increased and state universities such as New Mexico, North Dakota, Oregon, Oklahoma, and Oklahoma State trained growing numbers of graduate students in the field. Many of these students enriched their historical training by studying anthropology, archaeology, and linguistics. (Today they add native art, music, literature, languages, law, political science, and sociology.) They relied on bibliographies compiled by the historians Francis Paul Prucha and Dwight L. Smith; they engaged in oral history; and they researched at the D'Arcy McNickle Center for the Study of the American Indian, located at the Newberry Library in Chicago.[24]

In short, in the 1970s historians created an infrastructure for younger colleagues moving into ethnohistory who secured academic positions largely in the Midwest/Great Lakes region and the trans-Mississippi West. While most of those attracted to twentieth-century history remained in the West, their eastern colonialist counterparts established history as a major component of ethnohistory. Axtell, Jennings, Salisbury, James P. Ronda, Gary B. Nash, and others merged disciplines so effectively that their cumulative scholarship has revised significant portions of the once standard history of the colonial eastern seaboard.[25]

As ethnohistory infiltrated the peripheries of the historians' domain, so, too, did the idea of cultural intermediaries. One of the first historians to probe the concept, William T. Hagan, was also one of the early leaders in the American Society for Ethnohistory. In 1977, Hagan lectured on Joshua Given, the son of Satank, the famous Kiowa war chief. After he was orphaned, Given chose to attend Carlisle Indian School, traveling east to join the first class in 1879. A decade later, he rejoined the Kiowas as an ordained Presbyterian minister. Like so many other intermediaries, Given stepped into brokering by way of his boarding school experiences; but in Hagan's portrayal Given faced the overwhelming difficulties of the returned student who interpreted between cultures but was accepted by neither.[26]

Given's dilemma was an issue of considerable significance for native people between the 1870s and 1970s, when thousands of native children in the United States and Canada were separated from their homes. Some (like Given) chose to leave, but others were forced. Before the 1970s, anthropologists had edited their stories. Hagan brought the focus of a historian to the issue, thus anticipating his colleagues who began to wrestle with the border worlds of native intermediaries.

Historian R. David Edmonds's edited collection of biographical essays *Studies in Diversity: American Indian Leaders*, which appeared in 1980, was antedated by Alvin Josephy's *The Patriot Chiefs* (1961), but the two books were effectively separated by the dramatic events of the 1960s and 1970s. In *Patriot Chiefs*, which appeared in the context of the 1950s termination era, Josephy selected natives who came down firmly on the side of their own people. Acknowledging that Indian leaders who had cooperated with whites "were, in a way, patriots too," he asserted that "they are not the greatest heroes of the Indian peoples today." Josephy labeled the figures who appeared in his collection, such as the Tewa leader Popé, as the Indian "Nathan Hales, George Washingtons and Benjamin Franklins."[27]

Edmonds's *Studies in Diversity* appeared to use Josephy's volume as a springboard, thereby probing the leadership of Indians whom Josephy had excluded. When he included an essay by historian Peter M. Wright on Washakie, the Wind River Shoshone who cooperated with the whites, Edmonds justified his position by maintaining that Indian leadership manifested itself "in a variety of patterns," including diplomats, mixed-bloods, and even loners, such as Carlos Montezuma, a Yavapai. Edmonds's stance suggested that outsiders cannot determine the criteria by which Indians become heroes to their own people. As Berkhofer has written, an "examination of the whole range of [Indian] political behavior makes individuals, if not heroes, of more Indians than before because it includes men who pursued the politics of the possible as well as those who failed in noble causes."[28]

Neither Josephy nor Edmonds developed the theme of cultural intermediaries, per se. While Edmonds's leaders may have been intermediaries, this concept remained secondary. A third collection of biographical sketches, *Indian Lives: Essays on Nineteenth- and Twentieth-Century Native American Leaders* (1985), edited by historians L. G. Moses and Raymond Wilson, did address issues raised by Hagan's study of Joshua Given.

Moses and Wilson shifted their attention to the varieties of Indian loyalties. Echoing anthropology counterparts, especially Stern and McFee, they maintained that Indians lived "in one world of great complexity that challenged, sustained, and sometimes destroyed them, but never removed their 'Indianness.'" Within this "world of multiple loyalties," the subjects of *Indian Lives* also served as intermediaries. Anthropologist David M. Brugge portrayed Henry Chee Dodge as "an intermediary between Navajos and whites." Historian Lawrence C. Hauptman described Minnie Kellog, the controversial yet powerful Oneida, in a similar fashion: "To white audiences and to her well-educated colleagues in the Society of American Indians, she frequently quoted from Franz Boas, . . . to reservation communities, she spoke in 'ancient tongues,' and with traditional metaphors."[29]

While Edmonds and Moses and Wilson focused on native people of the nineteenth and twentieth centuries, colonialists were assessing earlier intermediaries. In her essay "Many Roads to Red River: Métis Genesis in the Great Lakes Region, 1618–1815," historian Jacqueline Peterson discussed the roots of the métis, who "burst upon the historical stage in 1815." The result of years of contact "at the interstitces of two civilizations or nations," the métis exemplified the process whereby a group began "to serve as a conduit for goods, services, and information and to see its function as a broker." Ultimately, however, its dependency on the "nations or societies [that] it links or separates" meant that "its life would be snuffed out" when its services were no longer needed. The upsurge of interest in métis history promises to provide new insights into our understanding of intermediaries.[30]

In his article "'Middlemen in Peace and War': Virginia's Earliest Indian Interpreters, 1608–1632," historian J. Frederick Fausz added another figure to the intermediary equation, the non-native broker. Fausz explored the hazardous position of English intermediaries in colonial Virginia, but contrary to McFee, Fausz depicted these "culture brokers" as "marginal men," or "weathercocks buffeted by the shifting political winds in one or both cultures." The most "Indian like" of these interpreters usually "survived the longest and enjoyed the greatest success in relations with native populations [but] their colonial countrymen reacted to their acculturation with a confusing mixture of admiration, appreciation, apprehension, and abhorrence."[31]

If these Virginia interpreters achieved their greatest successes "as skillful brokers between the cultures while ultimately remaining loyal to traditional English values," the "mediators" that historian Daniel K. Richter assessed in "Cultural Brokers and Intercultural Politics: New York–Iroquois Relations, 1664–1701" wove an even more complex web of relations. Richter saw these brokers as participants in a "world systems approach," serving as "links between local political structures and regional and international sources of power." Within their own cultural worlds, however, they were also "members of two or more interacting networks (kin groups, political factions, communities, or other formal or informal coalitions)." On both sides of the cultural divide they drew connections within the "bundle of localized communities," stretching those connections to link with regional structures, both Iroquois and Euramerican. Richter moved beyond Fausz, arguing that while these individuals were important to internal harmony, they were also crucial to the formation of the late seventeenth-century alliance between New York and the Five Nations, known in native diplomacy as the "Covenant Chain."[32]

Richter's article challenged ethnohistorians looking at the cultural intermediary because his perspective was not culturally exclusive: these mediators emerged from both native and non-native worlds. The article also caught the attention of a broader spectrum of historians by appearing in the respected *Journal of American History* and incorporating "cultural broker" in its title. Thus it alerted American and Canadian historians to the importance of the intermediary and, incidentally, provided a convenient term, "cultural broker."

In the final years of the 1980s cultural brokering became fertile ground for research.[33] Close on the heels of Richter's piece, a second article incorporating brokers in its title appeared in 1988. Historian Nancy L. Hagedorn's essay "'A Friend To Go Between Them': The Interpreter as Cultural Broker during Anglo-Iroquois Councils, 1740–1770" further attested to the rigor of scholarship on eastern colonial America and its influence on ethnohistory. In Hagedorn's article, which provides an apt background for her chapter on Andrew Montour in this volume, she argued that colonial interpreters were vital conduits not only of language but of "culturally different methods of doing business." Paralleling the brokers studied by Richter, these interpreters were cultural mediators within and among the many colonial worlds.[34]

A year after these colonialists had dangled the idea of cultural brokering before their colleagues, anthropologist James A. Clifton drew attention to the theme with his edited work *Being and Becoming Indian: Biographical Studies of North American Frontiers* (1989). Paralleling his historian counterparts, Clifton approached his theme through biographical sketches of individuals who, in this case, were linked by a common search for identity. Like the subjects of the Moses and Wilson essays, these individuals were characterized by shades of "cultural, ethnic, and personal identity." Like Edmonds, Clifton included individuals from a wide range of American history—from historian Colin G. Calloway's study of colonial mediator Simon Girty to anthropologist Ann McElroy's sketch of Oopeleeka and Mina, contemporary Inuit women of Baffin Island. Those subjects who were not native or métis by birth had been, in Hallowell's words, "Indianized."

The underlying issue of Clifton's collection, the question of identity, spurred his introductory assessment of being and becoming Indian in the late twentieth century. Like Liberty, Edmonds, and Moses and Wilson, Clifton reflected the milieu of his time. The mid- to late 1980s saw a backlash against native people. This was particularly evident in Clifton's state of Wisconsin, where white anger exploded in a campaign designed to destroy Ojibwa spearfishing rights. Some of this mood spilled over into Clifton's introduction. Attacking the idea of the "Indian" as a piece of fiction invented by Euramericans, Clifton reasoned that contemporary natives were acting as merely one more "interest group" playing "interest group politics." He praised the cultural brokers of his edited collection because they had learned "to assume, accommodate, and coordinate different roles"; simultaneously, he censured contemporary native leaders for attempting to "manipulate . . . guilt feelings" in Canada and the United States in order to secure "a larger share of the resources available." Those who lived in the "cultural middle ground" merited higher praise than those who perceived themselves in what Clifton labeled "racial terms."[35]

In his general discussion of cultural intermediaries, Clifton added insights that complemented those of Richter. While Richter encompassed both internal and external mediation, Clifton focused primarily on the border region among cultures. Clifton's brokers lived on this frontier, "a culturally defined place where peoples with different culturally expressed identities meet and deal with each other." Reiterating McFee, Clifton maintained that these so-called marginal people, whose lives cross cultural boundaries, become "culturally enlarged."[36] Richter and Clifton and other ethnohistorians of the 1980s had created a framework for the study of these intermediaries that relied on an interdisciplinary approach.

By the end of the decade, the term cultural broker had gained broad acceptance. Studies that did not focus exclusively on brokerage began to rely on the term. In 1989, when Margaret B. Blackman's biography *Sadie Brower, Naekok: An Inupiaq Woman* appeared, Blackman described Brower as a "cultural broker." In 1991, when Joan Weibel-Orlando published her study of Native Americans in Los Angeles, *Indian Country, L. A.: Maintaining Ethnic Community in a Complex Society*, Weibel-Orlando referred to specific urban Indians as being engaged in "cultural brokerage" or as "cultural interpreters." By the 1990s, it appeared as though the term had come to stay.[37]

If the lives of cultural intermediaries have spanned the breadth of this continent and the five centuries since contact, then it is time to bring some coherence to their experiences. Despite the infinite variety of intermediaries, most of their lives have followed certain patterns. They have been interpreters, or linguistic brokers; they have been traders, or economic brokers. Some have been spiritual intermediaries; others, educational intermediaries. Some have brokered between governments; others have brokered through music, the humanities, and the arts; still others have moved between western science and medicine, and native healing and understanding of the land. Finally, a notable group, such as Vincent Craig, Navajo

(Diné) creator of the cartoon character "Mutton Man," have brokered through humor.

Regardless of the directions they have followed, all of these intermediaries have been molded by their own personal circumstances and the cultures that have nurtured them. All of them have also been shaped by the historical conditions that affected societies and individuals during their lifetimes. In the following introductions to each section, I have sought to explain how the cultural brokers in this volume were formed by these circumstances, both cultural and historical. In the conclusion, I have drawn upon their motivations to explain the unique qualities of brokerage that set them apart as a group from those who chose to remain within a single culture.

Cultural brokers have often moved in the "middle ground" explored by Richard White in his recent book *The Middle Ground: Indians, Empires and Republics in the Great Lakes Region, 1650–1815* (1992), but they have also moved between cultures when no "middle ground" was readily apparent. Through their mediating influence, they have earned a prominent place in North America's past. Over the centuries their successes and failures have served as a barometer of the health of cultural pluralism in American and Canadian societies. Despite their significance, popular histories have largely ignored them. As ethnohistorians reinterpret this multicultural past, and native voices influence the media through focus on issues raised by the quincentenary, perhaps cultural intermediaries will finally be acknowledged. It is time to address their contributions.

PART ONE

BROKERS OF THE COLONIAL WORLD

Cultural intermediaries have contributed to the history of North America in significant, albeit largely unheralded, ways. Moving among the diverse peoples of this continent, they have breached language barriers, clarified diplomatic misunderstandings, softened potential conflict, and awakened that commonality of spirit shared by the human race. Across the centuries, from the colonial era to the present, they have endured hostility as well as danger, but their persistent curiosity about the "other side" has given them the incentive to thrive on that supersensory awareness necessary for moving between and among different worlds. They have stepped outside, while others have remained within.

In colonial North America, the contribution of the cultural intermediary was crucial. The sixteenth, seventeenth, and eighteenth centuries witnessed the innumerable initial contacts between the peoples of this continent and the peoples of Europe, Africa, and Asia. The impact of these encounters lies beyond human comprehension, even though the quincentenary led many authors and film producers to attempt to reduce it to a comprehensible story. In these first centuries after Christopher Columbus's voyage, the need for brokers was evident in all of the clashing worlds, whether in the Gulf of Alaska, between Alaska native and Russian; through the Tidewater of Virginia, between Powhatan Algonquian and Jamestown English; along the coast of California, between California native and Spanish Franciscan; or along the Great Lakes, between Huron and French.

The borders that divided native from outsider shifted through the colonial era. Some were breached by trade and warfare; some were penetrated by spiritual and educational colonialism; others, by disputes over land and natural resources. A few were resolved by diplomatic negotiation. Brokers entered these shifting regions, and, relying on their multicultural experience, they eased differences and brought about some understanding.

The colonial brokers depicted here came to the forefront when the shifting borders of their regions demanded skillful intermediaries who were knowledgeable about the cultural patterns and nuances of both natives and outsiders. As John Kessell suggests in chapter 1, the conflict generated by ancient Pueblo cultures encountering their seventeenth-century Spanish counterparts created conditions ripe for the emergence of native intermediaries. Nancy Hagedorn, in chapter 2, re-creates the explosive environment of the eastern Great Lakes region in the eighteenth century, where diplomatic and military maneuvering among the Six Nations, as well as other tribes, the French, and the English, opened an entrée for the skilled mixed-blood interpreter, Andrew Montour. In chapter 3, Margaret Connell Szasz describes another clash of cultures in eighteenth-century southern New England, where increased English pressure against the Algonquian-speaking groups led to the rise of Samson Occom, a timely intermediary who counseled selective adaptation by his people.

The brokers discussed in these chapters were molded, therefore, by the cross-cultural tensions that surrounded them. But the singular role they were to play within these turbulent conditions emerged from the shaping forces of their own lives as well. Each of them chose to move into an intermediary position after personal experiences within cross-cultural environments: Occom, through the overlay of Eleazar Wheelock's tutoring and his life among the Montauk; Bartolomé de Ojeda as a prisoner of Diego de Vargas; and Montour in his own métis childhood. They also drew strength from their internal tribal networks, often relying on kinship links to achieve their goals. They were also strongly motivated. For the Pueblo brokers—Ojeda, Juan de Ye, and Don Felipe Chistoe—a taste for potential power propelled some of their actions. They used their alliances with Vargas to gain control within their own pueblo or to strengthen their own faction among their people. For Montour, financial re-

muneration and acknowledgment of personal prestige by all sides of the cultural equation prodded his actions. For Occom, the enthusiasm of the Great Awakening provided the initial motivation, but to this he later added a growing sense of nationalism and the urgent need to find an escape for his people.

The colonial intermediaries, like their contemporary counterparts, also struggled with what Hagedorn has labeled an "identity crisis." This sense of confusion affected Ojeda, who fought in 1680 with his fellow Pueblos to drive out the hated Spanish and then reversed this position in 1689 during his imprisonment with the Spaniards at El Paso. Personal uncertainty also dominated the life and career of Montour, whose identity changed both in his self-perception and in the perception of others: for negotiators, he was like a chameleon, assuming the identity of the group for which he was translating. The sense of indecision also affected Occom, who suffered such severe trauma over this issue that he could not determine the direction of his brokerage until he resolved his relationship with Wheelock and confirmed his loyalties to his own people.

The colonial brokers set the pattern for those who were to follow. Their skills were crucial for both natives and outsiders in these first centuries of post–Columbian North America. Those who followed them would meet different conditions, but the challenges of moving between worlds would remain.

CHAPTER 1

THE WAYS AND WORDS OF THE OTHER: DIEGO DE VARGAS AND CULTURAL BROKERS IN LATE SEVENTEENTH-CENTURY NEW MEXICO

JOHN L. KESSELL

THE people of Zia have not forgotten. They still know the story. Their ancestors were ready to fight. They would have attacked the returning Spaniards had it not been for the presence on the other side of one of their own. As the Spanish column approached, the Zias recognized their former war captain, Bartolomé de Ojeda, who led the way, carrying a cross. That day, battle was averted.[1]

By the Spaniards' reckoning, it was Friday, October 24, 1692. Gov. Diego de Vargas (1691–97, 1703–04) had the occasion recorded in his campaign journal. The Zia Pueblo Indians, occupying at the time a defensive site on the mesa of the Cerro Colorado, had welcomed him with arches of evergreen branches and crosses. "With the people of the pueblo on the plaza, I told them through the Indian Bartolo, who acted as interpreter, about my coming and took possession for his majesty, as in the other pueblos."[2]

Vargas was not the first governor of Spanish New Mexico; he was the thirtieth. Late in the summer of 1692, he had left the refuge camps of El Paso, where the colony had endured in miserable exile since the Pueblo Revolt of 1680, and led some two hundred Spaniards and Indian auxiliaries north on what proved to be a four-month armed reconnaissance and ritual reconquest.

This chapter takes a look at several individuals culturally Native American or Hispanic, racially mixed or not, who, when pushed or pulled, participated to a notable degree in the other's culture. Whether that made them cultural brokers, I am not prepared to say. When such intermediaries worked to disrupt intercultural relations, did they cease to be brokers? Ideally, I assume, brokers could live comfortably in either culture and move back and forth with ease. They formed, or burned, bridges between. But because cultural exchange was so dynamic, rarely, it seems, did anyone maintain that balance for long.

The contest for superiority in colonial New Mexico, pitting the more rigid and exclusive Hispanic culture against an adaptive yet equally resilient Pueblo Indian culture, made neutrality almost impossible. Brokers went too far and became part of the other, drew back disillusioned into their own culture, or found themselves ostracized by both.

Always the Spanish aristocrat, Vargas routinely gave Pueblo Indian leaders his hand and embraced them. He parleyed and negotiated with them, demanding their ceremonial submission to the crown of Spain and, as swiftly as his meager resources permitted, punishing their resistance. While affirming his perceived superiority, even in the words he chose to address them,[3] Vargas served Indians chocolate, dispensed gifts and favors, and stood as godfather to the children of their leaders. In response, some Pueblo factions swore obedience, accepting Spanish honors, protection, spoils, and trade, while others, proclaiming that Spaniards were too different or demanded too much, fought or fled.

For Vargas, this intercourse with Indians was learned behavior. Born of a proud but indebted noble family in Madrid, capital of the Spanish empire, he had arrived in New Spain in 1673 and found employment in the royal service. His firm resolve was to enhance, by the grace of God, the wealth and honor of the house of Vargas. At first, he found the Spanish Indies strange and discouraging. Writing from a mining town in the mountains of Oaxaca, south of Mexico City, he admitted to a brother-in-law "missing my homeland and toiling continually over alien lands and roads, whose ruggedness it is not easy to convey to you, and living among Indians, which is the same thing as being in a wilderness."[4] Over the years, however, as he administered mining districts, dealt effectively with people of other races, and maintained a residence in cosmopolitan Mexico City, Vargas adapted.

Accepting of others who knew their places in the Hispanic scheme of empire, skilled in personal diplomacy, inured to military campaign, physical ills, and service in distant places, Diego de Vargas assumed the governorship of New Mexico at a crucial time. The colony was convulsed by a violent, three-phase readjustment of cultural relations—the Pueblo–Spanish War, which occurred between 1680 and 1696.

The two peoples had first come together as early as 1540, when Francisco Vázquez de Coronado and his medieval outfit, with glint and clatter, had broken in on the interlocking world of sixty thousand or more Pueblo Indians and just as suddenly vanished. Then, between 1598 and 1609, proprietor Juan de Oñate planted a tenuous Spanish colony but failed to make it pay. Convinced that the Pueblo, or town-dwelling, Indians were New Mexico's only worthwhile resource, the Spanish crown converted the remote outpost into a government-subsidized Franciscan ministry to the Pueblo people. For three generations, thus empowered, Spanish missionary friars competed fiercely with Spanish governors and other colonists for the Pueblos' loyalty and their land and labor, suppressing Pueblo religious practice as best they could.

Throughout most of the century, Spaniards had dealt with Pueblo Indians on a case-by-case or pueblo-by-pueblo basis. They knew the Pueblos by the names of their individual communities (the Pecos, Taos, or Santa Ana) or by language groupings (Tiwas, Tewas, Tanos, or Keres). In August 1680, that assumption of disunity was swept away. All but united in their grievances, the Pueblos now taught their outnumbered exploiters how they had come to know Spaniards, with few exceptions—as foreign oppressors. Urged on by a charismatic leader the Spaniards called Popé, dozens of Pueblo communities erupted as one, killing some four hundred colonists, about 15 percent of the total, and causing the survivors to flee down the Rio Grande to refuge in the El Paso area or beyond. Plainly, the Pueblos had won the first round.

In the next decade, 1681 to 1691, Pueblos and Spaniards lived mostly apart, each group suffering adversity and dissension. The Pueblo coalition fell apart, and Popé was deposed. Despite a threat

Portrait of Diego de Vargas by an unknown artist, Capilla de San Isidro, Madrid, Spain. Courtesy of the Museum of New Mexico; neg. 11409.

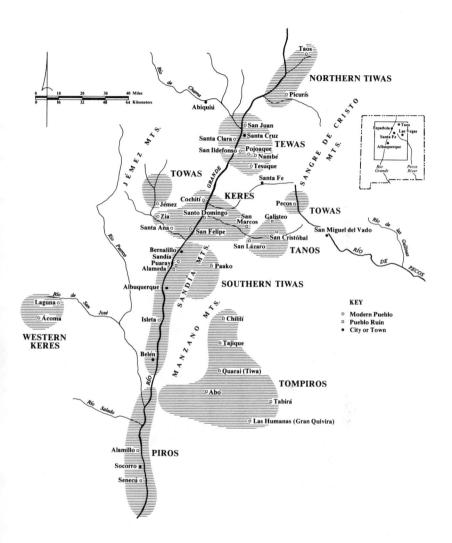

*Pueblo language groups. The western pueblos of the Zunis (Zunian)
and Hopis (Shoshonean) are not shown. After Albert H. Schroeder.
From* Kiva, Cross, and Crown: The Pecos Indians and New Mexico,
1540–1840, *by John L. Kessell (Washington, D.C.: National Park Service,
1979).*

of the death penalty for desertion, a good many former New Mexican colonists scattered from El Paso to the south in search of security. In the final phase of the Pueblo-Spanish War, 1692 to 1696, Spaniards under Vargas, several hundred of them new recruits, moved back upriver and reestablished the Spanish kingdom and provinces of New Mexico.[5]

Vargas was not a cultural broker. His intent was to reimpose Spanish dominion. In the classic mold of Hernán Cortés, he used native leaders to divide and conquer, taking full advantage of factionalism among the Pueblos. At the same time, he created a climate conducive to cultural exchange. He relied on *indios ladinos*, Spanish-speaking Pueblo Indians like Bartolomé de Ojeda, Juan de Ye, and Felipe Chistoe, and on Pueblo-speaking Spanish colonists, such veteran New Mexicans as Pedro Hidalgo, Juan Ruiz de Cáceres, and Francisco Lucero de Godoy. Regardless of their racial makeup, these individuals, before the Pueblo Revolt of 1680, had learned the words and ways of the other.

Although Spaniards dominated the Pueblos for most of the seventeenth century, certain members of both cultural collectives had served as intermediaries. Spanish missionaries and civil officials, often at odds, demanded that the Pueblos convert to Spanish Catholicism, pay their due tribute in maize and cloth or skins, and respect Spanish law. In so doing, a few of the friars and local colonists gained enough knowledge of one or more of the half-dozen Pueblo languages to deal more intimately with the Indians.[6]

The Pueblos, for their part, designated certain of their own to treat with outsiders, as they were accustomed to do even before the Spanish occupation.[7] Whether or not they truly were more racially tolerant than the Spaniards, Pueblos more readily adopted the offspring of interracial couples into their lineages, seemingly without social penalty. Still, neither Indians nor Spaniards, it would appear, looked favorably on members who renounced their cultural heritage and adopted too fully that of the other.

The case of Diego Romero illustrates how orthodox Spanish society perceived Spaniards who fraternized with Indians. A rough-and-ready second-generation New Mexican, Romero wanted the Plains Apaches to invest him ritually as their head war chief. Claiming that his father, Flemish armorer Gaspar Pérez, had been so honored, the determined Romero led a trading party that included a "half-mestizo" blacksmith, a Mexican Indian, a mulatto, and a delegation of Pecos Pueblo Indians far out on the plains east of New Mexico in the summer of 1660. At a populous Apache encampment Romero called the ranchería of don Pedro, the Indians feted the Spaniard in an elaborate ceremonial that culminated in what his accusers later interpreted as a heathen marriage rite. To seal his inauguration as "chief captain of the entire Apache nation," he had sexual intercourse with an Apache woman in the hope of leaving, as his father had, a son among the Apaches.

Just as the Spaniards bestowed canes, dress, weapons, and other symbols of authority on Indians, the Apaches presented Romero with a symbolic white feather. Had he not stuck it on his hat and swaggered and had the Franciscans of New Mexico not been gathering at that time testimony against the Spanish governor and his associates, Romero's adventure might have gone unnoticed. Instead, he was arrested in the name of the Holy Office of the Inquisition, tried in Mexico City, and sentenced to ten years banishment from New Mexico. That was bad enough, but when Romero stood again before the Inquisition, the second time found guilty of bigamy, his punishment rang like a death sentence: six years labor on the Atlantic galleys. He did in fact die soon after, in a dank cell in Veracruz in 1678. Deeply depressed by his lot in Spanish society, Romero had at one point confessed his thoughts of fleeing back to the heathens "and living with them in their manner."[8]

Other Inquisition cases tell of New Mexicans allegedly using Indian concoctions or spells as love potions or curses—recipes they got from their domestic servants[9]—but there is little documentation of Spaniards who chose to live as Pueblo Indians. Although we may think that cultural brokers were naturally drawn from the occupied or subordinate society toward the dominant, occupying society, there may have been more who went the other way than we know.[10] Like the so-called crypto-Jews of colonial New Mexico, individuals raised as Spaniards who later disappeared among the Pueblos left no paper trail.

There is, however, an engaging story, recorded by W. W. H. Davis in the 1850s and Frank Hamilton Cushing in the 1880s, about a well-liked Franciscan missionary spared by the Zunis during the Pueblo Revolt. In return for his life, he agreed to be adopted into the tribe and wear Zuni attire. He hid, so the story goes, when Vargas appeared in 1692 and, by choice, lived out his days incognito with the Indians who had delivered him from martyrdom.[11]

Babies born of mixed unions and out of wedlock were probably more numerous than either Spaniards or Pueblos have cared to admit. The offspring of culturally Spanish males and Pueblo women, raised among the Pueblos, explain the racial mixtures of some of the leaders of the Pueblo Revolt in 1680, men like the elusive mulatto Naranjo or the mestizo Alonso Catití. The latter was said to be the natural son of Capt. Diego Márquez, one of eight Spaniards beheaded in Santa Fe in 1643 as accomplices in the murder of Gov. Luis de Rosas.[12]

It would be interesting to know how the Franciscans, the only Roman Catholic priests in seventeenth-century New Mexico, looked on these natural children. Often, one suspects, they did not know that a baby presented for baptism was illegitimate. Unfortunately, none of the mission registers of baptisms, marriages, or burials survived 1680. Later, in more than a few cases, the friar simply noted that a child was born to a specific mother and an unknown father. Some of the male mixed-bloods grew up in the missions along with Pueblo boys, serving the friars and learning to read and write Spanish. Forced to decide their allegiance in 1680, several Pueblos or part Pueblos who had adopted Spanish ways and served the friars or colonists tried to warn their Spanish masters or died alongside them.

One notable product of the Franciscans' training was Esteban Clemente, raised in the pueblo of Abó, who went on to become the most Hispanicized, honored, and trusted Pueblo Indian east of the Rio Grande. Spaniards addressed him by the honorific "don." "Very conversant in Spanish, intelligent, and a good Christian," don Esteban served as "native governor of the pueblos of Las Salinas and Tanos, and very capable interpreter of six languages of this kingdom." Like Romero, his contemporary, the resourceful Clemente traded with Plains Indians, at times carrying goods on consignment for the Spanish governor.

In 1660, at the urging of the friars, Clemente wrote in his own hand a denunciation of Pueblo kachina ceremonials, some of which, he testified, were performed in "ugly painted masks." Don Esteban may have been leading two lives all along, or perhaps he experienced a sudden change of heart. Whatever the process that brought him to decide, late in the 1660s or early in the 1670s, when drought and famine hung over the land, Clemente sought to purge the colony of Spaniards.

According to them, he planned a general uprising in which the mission Indians everywhere would secretly drive the Spaniards' horses into the mountains and fall on their unsuspecting owners gathered for services on Maundy Thursday night, "sparing not a single friar or Spaniard." But the Spaniards found out and hanged Clemente. Seizing his property, they discovered in his house "a great quantity of idols and whole pots of idolatrous powdered herbs, feathers, and other disgusting things."[13]

Clemente's example—indicative of the stress experienced by some cultural brokers—stands in sharp contrast to that of Popé, acknowledged leader of the successful revolt in 1680. The Spaniards did not even know Popé by a Christian name. Evidently a highly respected Pueblo spiritual leader, he stayed undercover and formed his confederacy through a network of religious and war chiefs that cut across Pueblo language barriers.[14]

When Diego de Vargas took command of the New Mexico colony-in-exile at El Paso on February 22, 1691, the most prominent cultural intermediary among the several hundred Pueblo Indians relocated nearby was the Spanish-speaking, literate Bartolomé de Ojeda. His story began the same way Clemente's had but ended in reverse. Educated by the Franciscans at the Keres pueblo of Zia or Santa Ana, Ojeda became a respected war captain. In 1680, without hesitation, he joined the revolt. Nine years later, after fighting ferociously to repel a Spanish assault, he changed his mind.

Gov. Domingo Jironza Petrís de Cruzate (1683–86, 1689–91), Vargas's predecessor, had led a force of two hundred Spaniards and Indian allies upriver from El Paso in August 1689. At Zia, where hundreds of the Keres had fortified themselves, the invaders launched a bloody, daylong attack, finally overrunning, sacking, and burning the pueblo. Reportedly, six hundred of the defenders died that day, and seventy were taken captive. The valiant Ojeda, wounded by a musket shot and an arrow, thought he was dying. As a last act, he called for the Spanish chaplain to hear his confession and absolve him.

But Ojeda survived. Carried back to El Paso, he recuperated and gave valuable testimony before Governor Jironza about Pueblo Indian disunity. He also recounted in grisly detail what he had heard about the deaths of seven of the twenty-one Franciscans killed in 1680. In so doing, he admitted that he, too, had at least a trace of Spanish blood. At Acoma, the Keres had stripped naked two friars and a woman named Juana Maroh. They tied the three together, abusing, humiliating, and eventually killing them. Juana, a mestiza who Ojeda described as a good Christian, was his grandmother.[15]

Vargas judged the Keres leader a trustworthy ally; Bartolo or "Bartolillo" (Little Bart), as patronizing Spaniards sometimes called him, seemed eager to join in the Spanish reconquest of the Pueblos. But who was using whom? It appears that Ojeda, who had witnessed the Spaniards' devastation of Zia in 1689 and of Santa Ana the year before, had concluded that military resistance was futile. He may have decided that the best service he could render his people was to cooperate with the Spaniards and ease the trauma of their inevitable reentry into the Pueblo world. In the twentieth century, Ojeda has been remembered at Zia as a cultural hero and bringer of peace.[16]

With the aid of Ojeda and other Pueblo Indians, Governor Vargas carried out the reconquest of New Mexico in two stages. During the first, his bold four-month-long expedition in the fall of 1692, Vargas demonstrated his mettle to Ojeda, who made himself indispensable. The Keres leader commanded Indian auxiliaries, interpreted for the Spaniards, and facilitated negotiations that culminated in ceremonial acts of resubmission in pueblo after pueblo.[17]

Yet during the second stage of the reconquest, when Vargas returned the following year with colonists, the Spaniards and their Pueblo allies had to fight and defeat the Tano occupants of Santa Fe. From that base, for the next three years, Vargas engaged in an energetic plan of divide and reconquer, counting all the while on Ojeda to keep the Keres survivors of Zia, Santa Ana, and San Felipe as allies.[18]

Occasionally, cultural brokers betrayed Vargas. An interpreter on his 1692 entrada, mixed-blood Pedro de Tapia, deserted. For vengeance or notoriety, Tapia told Tewa and Tano leaders that he had privileged information about the real and dastardly intent of Governor Vargas and the Spaniards. Although he died before the colonists reappeared in 1693, the rumor Tapia spread lived on. Vargas heard it first from the Pecos headman, don Juan de Ye. The deceitful Tapia, at a council held in the Tewa pueblo of San Juan, had convinced the assembled Indians that despite the pardon the Spanish governor and friars had granted in 1692, their secret plan was to slaughter all the Pueblos, sparing only the children born since 1680. As a result, Ye cautioned through an interpreter, the Tewas and Tanos were urging united Pueblo resistance. When their principal leader, don Luis Tupatú, meeting with Vargas in 1693, corroborated the rumor, the Spanish governor denied it vehemently. If only Tapia had not died, swore Vargas, he would have had him shot and quartered.[19]

According to the Spaniards, Ye's devotion knew no bounds. Obviously, such cultural brokers emerging from the Pueblo side had personal and factional motives. Association with Spaniards helped them to achieve ends within their own culture. As for don Juan de Ye of Pecos, the important Indian town east of Santa Fe at the gateway between pueblos and plains, alliance with Vargas strengthened the position of his faction within a deeply divided community. Inside the close-built, multistoried walls of Pecos, tension had apparently existed since pre-Spanish times between a more conservative, agriculturally oriented summer people, who looked back toward the Rio Grande Valley for inspiration, and a less community bound, trading, and warring winter people, who looked toward the plains. The Spaniards' entry tipped the balance.

Back in September 1692, after the initial capitulation of the Tanos at Santa Fe, Vargas had been warned of likely resistance by the Pecos people and their Apache allies. So he had charged that pueblo, only to find it deserted. For four days he waited at Pecos, while his soldiers and Indian allies brought a succession of stray Pecos captives before him for interrogation. Pedro Hidalgo, a New Mexican in his mid-forties who had witnessed the killing of the missionary at Tesuque in 1680, interpreted.[20] The people of the pueblo were split. If Hidalgo got it straight, the Pecos elders had wanted to welcome the Spanish governor, but the young men who opposed the Spaniards had caused everyone to evacuate.

When the peace emissaries he sent out with rosaries brought no quick response, Vargas determined to move on, leaving the pueblo and its stores intact. He released the Pecos captives with the admonition that everyone be present when he returned. Of the eight non-Pecos women and children the Spaniards took with them, one youth claimed he was a son of Cristóbal de Anaya Almazán, a Spanish colonist killed in 1680. The boy had grown up as a captive of the Pueblos. Unfortunately, he wrote no captivity narrative of his experiences between 1680 and 1692. The Pueblos, it would seem, based their treatment of captured Spanish women and children not on vengeance but on utility. One wonders what happened, on ransom, to young Anaya and dozens of others like him, Spanish and Indian, female and male, who had spent twelve years in Pueblo homes. How were they accepted by the other colonists? How many of them became cultural brokers in the more tolerant postwar colony?

Another of these captives, redeemed by Vargas at the pueblo of San Juan, was Juana de Apodaca, a mestiza. Even though her two children seem to have been fathered by a Pueblo man, they, according to Pueblo social practice, went with her, escorted to El Paso by a relative. In 1697 at Santa Fe, Apodaca married an African black, the prominent drummer and herald Sebastián Rodríguez, and later was accused of witchcraft.[21]

When Vargas doubled back to Pecos on his first expedition in 1692, the people were there, old and young alike. Jubilantly, he led them through the rite of repossession in the name of Carlos II, "king of the Spains, of all this new world, and of the kingdom and provinces of New Mexico, and of these subjects newly won and conquered." Two blue-robed Franciscans absolved the Pecos of their apostasy, urging them to bring forward for baptism all their children born since 1680. They presented 248, and don Diego de Vargas, as was his custom, became godfather to a son of don Juan de Ye, "the captain they obey," and many other children. Then, at the request of the principal men, Vargas installed as pueblo governor Ye, his new compadre.[22]

It was easy enough for Governor Vargas to serve as godfather at the baptism of the children of Pueblo Indian leaders. That linked him by *compadrazgo*, in Roman Catholic terms, not only to the children but also to the parents. They all became compadres. Although ceremonial parents were also a feature of the Pueblo world, it would be interesting to know what Ye really thought about his pseudofamilial relationship with Vargas. It was no more reciprocal in terms of equality than most cases of compadrazgo among Spaniards, which bound patron and client. The Spaniard, a leader of the dominant culture, may have thought he was offering encouragement to a leader of the subordinate culture to move a step closer to Hispanicization.[23] At the same time, Vargas was a pragmatist. "I took advantage," he boasted in a memorial to the King, "in all the pueblos of the ruse of being the compadre not only of the headmen and leaders, but also of the other Indians."[24]

In 1693, Ye did what he could to alert the Spaniards to alleged treachery on the part of the Tewas and Tanos, traditional enemies of the Pecos. He had access to Vargas's tent and through interpreters revealed the plot to ambush the shivering and vulnerable colonists. The Franciscans, to underscore Ye's credibility, pointed out that it was he in 1680 who had warned the Pecos missionary and other Spaniards of the impending revolt. When negotiations at Santa Fe finally broke down, and it became clear to the Spanish governor that the Tano occupants were not going to move out peaceably into the howling winter, he resorted to ejecting them by force. The fierce room-by-room assault lasted the better part of two days, December 29 and 30, 1693. Without the aid of Juan de Ye and 140 Pecos fighting men, the Spaniards might not have won.

From then on, Ye kept Vargas in his debt. A frequent visitor to Santa Fe, the Pecos governor provided auxiliary troops for the Spaniard's campaigns against recalcitrant Pueblos. He escorted Plains Apaches to the villa and won from Vargas approval for a traditional autumn trade fair at Pecos. In late August 1694, Sebastián Rodríguez would proclaim the fair in both plazas of Santa Fe. Spanish items for trade, Ye knew, were good for business. Sad for him, he would not be present.

When on campaign with Spaniards, the Pecos leader dressed the part. At the head of his company, armed and uniformed more as a European than a Pueblo, Ye joined Vargas's foray north from Santa Fe earlier that summer of 1694. Another contingent of more than two hundred colonists had reached Santa Fe, and the Spanish governor was hard pressed to feed them. As Vargas's column approached Taos, the inhabitants abandoned the pueblo. A party of Apaches, acquaintances of Ye, arranged a parley with the pueblo

Taos Pueblo, *by Henry R. Poore.*

governor, Francisco Pacheco, at the mouth of the deep mountain canyon where the people had taken refuge.

Ye, who told Vargas that Pacheco was his friend, tried to convince the Taos leader to come down to the pueblo and accept a pardon from the Spanish governor. But it was getting late; the sun had already set. Impulsively, Ye volunteered to go and stay the night with Pacheco and continue the dialogue. Several Spaniards reminded him of the danger, and Vargas reiterated the warning. But Ye insisted, and the Spanish governor recorded the scene in his campaign journal.

He removed his spurs and the powder pouches from his belt, handing them over with the mule and his cloak to the sergeant along with the arquebus and his shield, telling him to look after them for him. He said goodbye to me, giving me an embrace and his hand. He did the same to the others. The Taos looked on attentively with their governor, Pacheco, to whom I repeated, "God be with you," and said that I would be waiting for him, and for don Juan de Ye, early at my tent to serve him chocolate.[25]

That was the last Vargas ever saw of Ye. The Taos refused to come down out of the mountains, so the Spaniards and Pueblo auxiliaries broke into the pueblo and carried off great quantities of maize to succor the colonists in Santa Fe. A few days later, Vargas learned from Taos captives that Ye was still alive but a prisoner. Hope faded. Back in Santa Fe, the Spanish governor presented to don Lorenzo de Ye his father's weapons and cloak. He tried through an interpreter to express his sympathy. He would never forget don Juan de Ye. No Spaniard, Vargas confessed, was more deserving of the title "reconqueror."[26]

Other Pecos leaders, especially don Felipe Chistoe, assumed Ye's mantle as cultural brokers to Governor Vargas and in so doing finally tore the divided pueblo apart. At times, the desire of Pueblo Indians to settle grudges against other Pueblos influenced their decisions to oppose or support the Spaniards.[27] Availing himself of the brutal uprising of Tewas, Tanos, and Jemez in the summer of 1696, Chistoe moved to get rid of several leading members of his own pueblo who did not agree with him.

Although the words of the Pecos leader were culturally filtered through the Spanish language, Vargas recorded what happened. Chistoe came to him in confidence, identifying Diego Umbiro, "old and principal personage of this nation," and other leaders of the Pecos faction that favored the uprising. He feared they might contaminate the entire community. He had a plan and wanted the Spanish governor's blessing. He would invite these opposition leaders to a parley, really a trap, and hang them. Vargas gave his consent.

Chistoe arranged the talks in a Pecos kiva, a sacred ceremonial chamber of the Pueblos. When he asked Umbiro and four others how they felt about the uprising, they responded that it was good to kill the Spaniards: they were, all things considered, "of different

Summons from Diego de Vargas for one hundred Pecos fighting men to come to Santa Fe, written on the day of the second Pueblo revolt (June 4, 1696). Spanish Archives of New Mexico, II:60a.

flesh." At that, Chistoe rose menacingly and announced, "Here we are the king's men." His followers then seized the others, bound them, and executed them by hanging. One, a younger man called Caripicado (Pock Face), got away. Later, when he sneaked back into the pueblo, Chistoe killed him with a musket shot through the temple. To prove it, he and some of his men called on Vargas in Santa Fe: "So that it might be of record with me, he presented me the head, hand, and foot. All the citizens of the villa saw them, marveling at the loyalty of this Indian. I thanked him and gave him a gift, as well as the others."[28]

The relatives of the slain leaders did not forget. They tried to incite the people to assassinate Chistoe. At least five times, the community verged on armed conflict. Don Felipe, with the Spaniards' backing, prevailed on each occasion, until at last the rival leaders and their families left the pueblo.[29] After that, the gateway pueblo declined steadily. Finally, in the late 1830s, a sorry Pecos remnant of some twenty souls abandoned the place altogether.[30]

Although he never applied it to Chistoe, Ye, or Ojeda, Diego de Vargas introduced a cultural term in 1692 which later in New Mexico took on wider meaning. He referred to "a *genízaro* Zuni, nicknamed Agustín, El Cabezón" (Big Head), a Spanish-speaking Pueblo leader who may have looked to him like a mixed-blood.[31] In Spain at the time, the word *genízaro* was applied to the child of parents of different nationalities, and in New Spain, it was used also for mixed-bloods of various sorts.

Later, in eighteenth-century New Mexico, there evolved a rugged servant class whose members were called genízaros. Descended primarily from ransomed non–Pueblo Indian women and children who were baptized, given Spanish names, and raised in their masters' households, these genízaros acted, in a sense, as a category of cultural brokers. They dealt regularly, as intermediaries, with Plains and other nonsedentary Indians. They scouted, interpreted, hunted, settled on exposed frontiers, and served in the militia. Their numbers after midcentury seemed to keep pace with the growing Hispanic population's demand for servants.[32]

After Vargas, things were different in New Mexico. Building on the precedents of his forceful administration and whatever lessons they had learned in the Pueblo-Spanish War, the people of both cultures

Wahu Toya, an aged Pecos Indian, 1880. Photo by John K. Hillers, Courtesy of the Museum of New Mexico; neg. 2604.

achieved a fitful, live-and-let-live accord. Pueblos and Spaniards, faced by heightened threats from Comanches or Frenchmen, found themselves campaigning together and sharing the hardships and the spoils. At home, the great majority of both groups, integrated in the local economy, bartered sheep and beans, lived in close proximity, shared words and cultural traits, and became compadres.[33]

Motives are difficult enough to discern among historical people of a single culture. What made certain Pueblo Indians and certain Spaniards embrace the ways of the other, to whatever degree, is a question doubly difficult but eminently worth asking. Such individuals functioned before and after the Pueblo-Spanish War, but at no time did they play more active roles than during the momentous cultural readjustment that took place between 1680 and 1696. By learning more about the manners and motives of these cultural intermediaries, we may come to better understand not only the human dynamics of colonial New Mexico but also the cultural diversity so much discussed today.

CHAPTER 2

"FAITHFUL, KNOWING, AND PRUDENT": ANDREW MONTOUR AS INTERPRETER AND CULTURAL BROKER, 1740–1772

NANCY L. HAGEDORN

ANDREW Montour, the métis son of Indian interpreter Madame Montour and an Oneida war chief named Carondawana, rose to prominence as an Indian interpreter and cultural broker in New York and Pennsylvania during the mid-eighteenth century. As a contemporary and companion of both Pennsylvania agent and interpreter Conrad Weiser and English Superintendent of Indian Affairs Sir William Johnson, he was frequently involved in Indian affairs during the 1750s and 1760s. Although most visible as a broker in the public arena of Anglo-Indian conferences, Montour also mediated complex cultural contacts and exchanges in other, less well documented settings as interpreter, Indian officer, husband, father, and friend. His knowledge of European and Indian cultures and his skill in translating not only languages but also culturally prescribed world views, ideas, and expectations made him invaluable during the daily contacts between Europeans and Indians.

Montour received his early training and exposure to interpreting at his mother's knee. Although Madame Montour achieved fame as an interpreter during the early eighteenth century, she has never been positively identified. By her own account, she was the daughter of a Frenchman, captured by the Iroquois in the mid-1690s at the age of ten, and adopted by the Oneida, who raised her. She was probably Catherine Couc, born in 1684 to Louis Couc (Montour) and a Sokakis Indian at St. François du Lac. Her father was active as a trader among the "Far Indians" of the Great Lakes region. For several years before his death in 1709, he sought to bring those

Indians into Albany's trade orbit, winning favor for himself (and possibly his daughter) among the Albany trading establishment.[1]

Madame Montour began to serve as interpreter at Anglo-Iroquois conferences in New York at about the time of her father's death. By the time of her son's birth in the mid- to late 1710s, she exercised considerable influence in New York's Indian affairs, having made herself indispensable to the colony's lieutenant-governor, Robert Hunter (1710–19). Cadwallader Colden, Surveyor-General of New York, remarked that at public conferences with the Indians, Hunter "had allwise a French woman [Madame Montour] standing by him, who had married one of our Indians, to inform him whether the interpreters had done their part truely between him and the Indians."[2] Throughout the 1710s and 1720s, Madame Montour and her Oneida husband, Carondawana, their young children presumably nearby, attended many Indian conferences in New York. Following her husband's death in 1729, Madame Montour moved the family to Pennsylvania, where she remained active in Indian affairs until about 1744. She died there in the early 1750s.

At about the time that his mother left the diplomatic arena, Andrew Montour entered it. Little is known of his life before he stepped onto the intercultural stage and into the colonial records in the early 1740s. As a child, Montour presumably lived with his parents, his brother, Lewis, and several sisters in New York. Life in a multiethnic household exposed the Montour children to a variety of Indian cultures and languages as the family resided first among the Oneida in New York and then among the Delaware and Shawnee of Pennsylvania. In addition, their mother was obviously familiar with several European languages and spoke at least French fluently. Montour and his siblings seemed natural candidates for the position of cultural broker and interpreter, but only Andrew became a prominent and trusted interpreter.[3]

Montour's oral command of languages, both European and Indian, was impressive. He was fluent in a variety of Indian languages and proficient in English and French. Although he began his public service in 1742 interpreting primarily for the Delaware at Shamokin, he quickly demonstrated his abilities and usefulness in other areas and languages. In that same year, Conrad Weiser employed him to escort Count Nicolaus Ludwig von Zinzendorf and a party of Moravian brethren to the Six Nations of New York.

By the late 1740s, he often translated between Mohawk and Delaware for Weiser and frequently traveled to Philadelphia in the east and Logstown in the Ohio Valley to the west to interpret the words of Delawares, Miamis, Shawnees, Wyandots, and Six Nations Indians for Pennsylvania agents and officials.

Linguistic proficiency, while a vital skill for an interpreter, was not the only knowledge needed. The elaborate protocol and ritual associated with public treaty conferences required an intimate familiarity with the cultures of all groups involved. During councils, interpreters performed many functions and fulfilled a variety of roles both behind the scenes and before the council fire. Since the English and the Indians brought different cultural perceptions and expectations to the elaborate rituals and specialized oratory of Anglo–Iroquois councils, interpreters like Montour mediated the exchange of cultures as well as the exchange of words and promises as they translated and explained "disparate languages and rituals infused with culturally based meanings and values."[4] Montour probably gained much of his specialized, nonlinguistic training in diplomatic and political protocol and interpretation from his mother. His youth undoubtedly also provided ample opportunities to observe Anglo–Indian diplomacy in action. Once he began interpreting, he received additional training from Weiser and his Indian colleagues.

Montour acted as interpreter, speaker, and adviser on numerous occasions. The complexity of roles that he could be called on to fulfill was illustrated during the Logstown treaty conference of 1752. Andrew served as interpreter for the Ohio Company (a group of Virginia land speculators interested in the Ohio Valley) and the Virginia colonial government, while simultaneously representing the Ohio Iroquois, primarily Senecas, as their newly recognized councillor.[5] As a result, he was active in the private and public sessions of the conference on both sides of the council fire. Ultimately, he used the Indians' trust and esteem to convince them, in private sessions, to accept the settlement desired by the Ohio Company. His presence during the public sessions was equally vital since Christopher Gist, the company's official representative, had difficulty with Iroquois languages and James Patton, the commissioner for Virginia, was ignorant of Indian protocol. (Patton threw the validity of the treaty into question by failing to accompany the original invitations to the Indians with appropriate belts of wampum.) Without Montour's presence and expertise, it is doubtful that the Virginians would have achieved even limited success.[6]

Possession of the requisite skills, however, did not guarantee Montour's employment and prominence as an interpreter. He entered the diplomatic arena on his mother's coattails. For the first few years of his employment by Weiser, he seemed, in fact, to have no identity other than "Madame Montour's son Andrew." Yet even then, in the early 1740s, his mother's health was failing, and she became increasingly unable to perform effectively as an interpreter. Conveniently, Montour was ready to step into the position she vacated. With his mother's departure from the diplomatic arena after 1744, Montour came into his own.[7]

In the 1740s, Montour also achieved independence in his personal life. He married a granddaughter of Olumapies, a hereditary chief of the Delaware. Their first son, John, was born in 1744 or 1745. The Montours had at least one more child, a daughter named Kayodaghscroony, or Madelina, before the marriage ended several years later.[8] Whether the marriage succumbed to the pressures of Andrew's frequent, extended absences from home or resulted from the death of his wife is unknown.

Circumstances that may have placed strains on Montour's family life aided his career. Anglo–French rivalry for the Ohio Valley trade focused attention on hitherto obscure Indian groups of that region and created a pressing need for Montour's linguistic talents. Most of the prominent English interpreters and agents of the 1730s and 1740s focused their skills and attention on the Iroquois and their allies and therefore lacked sufficient command of the non-Iroquoian Far Indians' languages. Only the Ohio Indian traders, active in the Ohio Valley since the 1710s, had the required language skills, but the English colonial governments and the Indians viewed them with considerable distrust and suspicion. Of the trusted Pennsylvania and New York agents, neither Weiser nor Johnson could operate effectively in any language other than Mohawk. Montour's proficiency in Delaware, Miami, and Shawnee, in addition to several Iroquois languages, put him in demand and enhanced his value with the Pennsylvania, New York, and Virginia colonial governments.

By 1750, the Pennsylvania authorities recognized the necessity of having "some discreet Person" among the unpredictable Ohio Indians, "who by his Influence may be able to regulate their Conduct and keep them firmly attached to the British interest." Weiser, already convinced of Montour's abilities and having found him to be "faithful, knowing, and prudent" in his activities in the Ohio Valley, began committing "Matters of Consequence" to him. George Croghan, deputy agent of Indian affairs, held much the same opinion, asserting that Montour took "a great deal of Pains to promote the English Interest amongst those Indians, and has a great sway amongst all those Nations." From that time on, nearly every conference and expedition employed his talents, and agents were clearly instructed to obtain his assistance in presenting and interpreting their messages to the Indians. Montour, already living on the borders of Lake Erie, became Pennsylvania's "Interpreter at Ohio," promoting English interests among the Ohio Indians and sending intelligence reports on French activities to Weiser, Croghan, and the Pennsylvania government. As tensions built between the French and English and their various Indian allies, he found himself increasingly in demand, gathering intelligence, adapting government speeches to "Indian Forms," and delivering messages and presents.[9]

Montour's expanded activities accompanied significant changes in his personal life. By the early 1750s, before he took up residence on the banks of Lake Erie, Andrew had entered into his second marriage. His new wife, Sarah Ainse, was an Oneida.[10] This marriage would also end prematurely in the mid-1750s—apparently because of Montour's increasing public duties, drinking problems, and debt—leaving three young children in the care of the Pennsylvania government and a fourth with Sarah among the Oneida in New York.

The beginning of formal hostilities in the summer of 1754 wrought additional, far-reaching changes in Montour's life as his career entered a predominantly military phase that lasted throughout the Seven Years War and Pontiac's uprising. Following the Winchester conference with the Ohio Indians in 1753, Gov. Robert Dinwiddie of Virginia commissioned Montour to raise and lead a company of Indian scouts for George Washington and to assist him as his interpreter during the campaign to retake Fort Duquesne from the French. Washington had requested Montour's services, convinced that he would be "of Singular use . . . here at this moment, in conversing with the Indians," since he had no one else he could "put an[y] dependence in." "For want of a better acquaintance with their customs," Washington often found himself "at a loss how to behave, and should be relieved from many anxious fears of offend'g them" if Montour was there to assist him.[11] Montour raised a company of eighteen white traders and joined Washington on the Monongahela, but his efforts to obtain Shawnee and Delaware assistance against the French were unsuccessful, largely due to Washington's obstinate refusal to heed the Indians' advice. The campaign ended with Washington's surrender to a superior French force at Great Meadows on July 3. Despite Montour's failure to accomplish the desired military ends, Gov. Horatio Sharpe of Maryland wrote Governor Dinwiddie that Montour's behavior had "prejudiced me in his favor & as I esteem him a very useful Person I will endeavor by all means to keep him firm in our Interests." Sharpe concluded that Montour was "a well-meaning well-disposed Man & of all the Traders Interpreters or Woodsmen without Comparison the most promising & honest."[12] Pennsylvania and the Crown apparently agreed, for they continued to employ him as an Indian officer during the next decade.

The duties of an Indian officer and those of an interpreter required similar skills. Both demanded intimate knowledge of English and Indian languages and customs. Both required Montour to "keep up a good Understanding" between the Indians and the English.[13] Most important, to perform efficiently and effectively, interpreters and Indian officers needed the confidence and trust of both the English and Indians. Montour inspired this confidence—a feat achieved by only a handful of Indian interpreters and agents. His apparent trustworthiness, combined with his linguistic proficiency, multicultural expertise, and an increasingly volatile climate of Anglo–Indian affairs, explains Montour's meteoric rise to prominence on the intercultural frontier of Anglo–Indian relations during the 1740s and 1750s.

Montour's personality and familial ties to the Pennsylvania and New York Indians, coupled with his demonstrated knowledge and skill as an interpreter, fostered his influence with the Indians and gained him the trust of the English. First, his personality combined a necessary aggressiveness and ambition with a sincerity, likability, and honesty that allowed him to get along with all types of people on both sides of the cultural divide. Second, by the early 1750s, his familial and marital ties with the Oneida and Delaware enhanced his stature and influence with them. His first marriage to a prominent Delaware woman was perhaps predictable, since he and his mother had been living among those Indians for at least fifteen years by the mid-1740s. The marriage cemented his ties to the Delaware and probably deepened his understanding of their language and culture. His second marriage to an Oneida confirmed, perhaps, older familial ties to that tribe and helps to explain his influence with the Iroquois. His leadership of several Oneida war parties and his close friendship with Scarouady, or "Half King," the Oneida chief and spokesman for the English-allied Ohio Indians, also indicated the nature and significance of his close links with the Oneida. These family, friendship, and tribal networks increased his influence among the Indian groups of Pennsylvania, New York, and Ohio and laid a solid foundation for his role as cultural broker between the English and the Indians of the region.

Neither Montour's personality nor his connections would have been sufficient, however, to gain trust as an interpreter and cultural broker without his acknowledged linguistic skill and expertise in intercultural protocol and diplomacy. The best judges of Montour's abilities were men like Weiser and Croghan who were in constant contact with him, saw him in action, and had similar experiences on which to base their opinions. By the early 1750s, Montour had convinced both agents of his abilities and trustworthiness. They readily acknowledged that he seemed "very capable of doing business" and, more important, that the Indians regarded him "as one of their chiefs."[14]

The esteem Montour commanded among the Indians was demonstrated in a variety of ways but perhaps most clearly by their frequent employment of him as a speaker. On numerous occasions, beginning in the late 1740s, Montour temporarily stepped out of the theoretically neutral role of interpreter and acted as Indian speaker. The first recorded instance of his service in this role occurred at Lancaster in 1748 when he spoke first for the Shawnee and Miami on July 19 and then for the Six Nations of Ohio on July 20. In addition to the normal complexities and subtleties of translation, public oration as an Indian speaker required Montour to speak persuasively in the Indian group's own language and to "observe and perform all the ceremonies expected by and in use among Indians, from persons when the[y] spake on publick matters."[15] Few Indians ever attained the requisite mastery of their language to serve as speakers; their selection of Montour indicated their high regard for his oratorical skills and integrity. Indeed, Montour spoke for a variety of Indian groups whose disparate languages represented at least two distinct language families (Iroquoian and Algonquian) and several cultural frameworks.

In 1752, the Ohio Indians made their regard for Montour more tangible. At Logstown on June 10, Scarouady addressed the Indian Eghnisara (Montour) and reminded him that he was "one of our own People." Montour was "not Interpreter only" but also one of the Ohio Iroquois councillors. He had an equal right to all their lands and was empowered to "transact any publick Business in behalf of us the six Nations." The Oneida chief confirmed Montour's councillorship before the Pennsylvania officials at Carlisle in October 1753. The Six Nations "set a Horn on Andrew Montour's Head" so that the English could "believe what he says to be true between the Six Nations" and them. He was now "a great Man" among the Indians, and they "love him dearly."[16]

Montour's elevation to the Six Nations council in Ohio strengthened his position with the colonial authorities. After 1753, the Pennsylvania government accepted Weiser's and Croghan's confidence in Montour's abilities and appointed Montour and Croghan "to do the Publick Business of this Government" among the western Indians. The French, too, were impressed with his influence among the Ohio Indians—enough to put a price on his head. As Anglo–French–Indian tensions escalated, Montour's "great sway" among the Ohio Indians became crucial to the British.[17] Even a skeptical Richard Peters, Pennsylvania's provincial secretary, grudgingly reported to his master, Thomas Penn, that Montour, "a dull stupid creature," had "managd mighty well & has really a great Influence on the Ohio Indians & is the only person fit to be trusted with Business in those parts."[18]

By early 1756, Pennsylvania officials began to suspect Montour's loyalties and to fear his desertion to the enemy Delaware and French. While Montour and Scarouady managed to prove their loy-

alty to the English and remove these "bad impressions and prejudices," the Pennsylvanians' fears that he might leave the colony
were well founded. Montour's performance and abilities during the
early years of the Seven Years War won him the respect and attention of the new Superintendent of Indian Affairs, Sir William Johnson. Through reports from Croghan, and possibly through personal
meetings with Montour at Onondaga and Albany in 1753, 1755, and
early 1756, Johnson discovered Andrew's remarkable abilities.[19]
Montour, in turn, learned of the Superintendent's plans for his new
Department of Indian Affairs and became enamored of the opportunities it offered.

In the spring of 1756, Scarouady, Montour, and a group of Indians resolved to leave Pennsylvania and live among the Six Nations, since times were so troublesome in the Ohio Valley. To
forestall their defection to New York and "secure their Return" to
Pennsylvania, the Pennsylvania government promised Montour
and Scarouady the rank and pay of captain. In fact, the governor
hoped that they would bring some Indians back with them who
could be "taken into Soldiers Pay and formed into Indian Companies" for Pennsylvania's defense.[20] The Pennsylvania governor also
agreed on April 20, 1756, at the Indians' request, to place Montour's
children under his care. Whether this arrangement was designed to
please Montour or was merely a ploy on the part of the Pennsylvania Indians and the government to ensure his return by keeping his
children in Pennsylvania, the bid failed, and neither Montour nor
Scarouady returned to the colony's service. On July 25, Johnson
appointed Montour captain of a party of Iroquois.[21] From that time
until the end of Pontiac's war in 1765, Montour remained in the
service of Johnson and the Northern Department of Indian Affairs.

Between 1756 and 1765, Montour became one of Johnson's most
prominent, trusted Indian officers and interpreters. He repeatedly
demonstrated his influence, skill, and trustworthiness, both as a
leader of Indian scouts and warriors in the English cause and as an
interpreter and speaker during frequent conferences at Johnson
Hall and throughout Indian country. At times, he seemed indispensable. Thomas Butler, another of Johnson's Indian captains,
wrote from Onondaga in April 1757 that he and Montour had been
waiting since February for the Six Nations council to convene and
that Montour was growing impatient. Butler feared Montour's im-

minent departure for home, as he did not see how he alone could "do any great Service after he [Montour] is away especially at the Grand Council."[22]

Montour's fortunes and prestige waned, however, as hostilities with the Indians abated and his services, particularly among the western Indians, were less in demand. By March 1766, Johnson no longer required Montour's constant presence and dispatched him to Fort Pitt for Croghan "to dispose of him . . . as you shall judge best." Montour remained assigned to the western post as a salaried interpreter until January 1772, though little is recorded of his activities. On January 22, 1772, Maj. Isaac Hamilton reported from Fort Pitt that "Captain Montour the Indian interpreter was killed at his own House the Day before Yesterday by a Seneca Indian who had been intertained by him at his House for some Days; he was buried this Day near the Fort."[23]

Andrew Montour's career illustrated both the benefits and the problems and complexities of cultural brokerage. Born into the culturally mixed family of a prominent métis interpreter, he seemed destined to fulfill the role of cultural mediator. Straddling the cultural divide was not easy, however. His brother and sisters never rose to the same prominence that he did, though they occasionally served as interpreters. One sister, a Moravian convert at New Salem, Ohio, was described in 1791 as "a living polyglot of the tongues of the West, speaking English, French & six Indian languages." Her absence from the ranks of official interpreters may perhaps be explained by her gender; as a woman, she might never have learned the diplomatic and political protocol required of a council interpreter. Lewis, Andrew's brother, presented a different case altogether. Although occasionally employed as a messenger and interpreter, colonial officials never fully trusted Lewis and suspected that he was "a Frenchman in his Heart." Circumstances that fostered Andrew Montour's career as cultural broker seem to have combined with other factors to work against his brother and sister.[24]

In addition to personality, circumstance, and skill, Montour's personal motives and ambitions gave impetus to his career. On the most basic level, interpreting offered him a measure of financial security in the form of both material and monetary rewards for his

During the late 1750s and early 1760s, Montour frequently interpreted during Indian conferences at Johnson Hall. Indian Council at Johnson Hall, oil painting by E. L. Henry, 1903. On loan from the Knox family to the Albany Institute of History and Art.

service. During the 1740s, Pennsylvania rewarded Montour "for his trouble" on a mission-by-mission basis, relying on Weiser's reports of his conduct to determine the nature and extent of remuneration. Most of these "rewards" consisted of a combination of cash, clothing, and supplies. Montour also reaped considerable benefit from lands granted him by both his English employers and his Indian sponsors.[25] By 1748, however, Montour became dissatisfied with the sporadic, uncertain nature of these payments, apparently believing them incommensurate with his importance to the interests of the government. As a result, he upped the ante, and in return for his services at Lancaster, he "pitched upon a place in the Proprietor's manor, at Canataqueany." He expected the government to build him a house and furnish his family with supplies. His demands alarmed even Weiser, who was "at a lost what to say of him. . . . He seams to be very hard to please."[26] The Pennsylvania government agreed with Weiser's concerns but bowed to the inevitable as escalating tensions with the Indians and French put Montour's special talents ever more in demand.

By 1750, Montour's rewards from the Pennsylvania government assumed a more standard monetary form, but he apparently remained dissatisfied and accepted a salaried position as Virginia's interpreter in 1753. His continuing dissatisfaction may also have encouraged his defection to Sir William Johnson and New York in 1756. Initially, Andrew's move to the Northern Department of Indian Affairs paid handsomely: he drew a substantial yearly salary of £100 sterling as an interpreter and Indian officer. When hostilities with the French drew to a close and his duties as an Indian officer declined during the early 1760s, however, circumstances changed. At the end of 1762, his salary was reduced from £182.10.0 to a mere £50. Pontiac's uprising offered a short reprieve, as Montour's services as an Indian officer were again in demand, but his primary income between 1763 and 1771 remained his interpreter's salary of £50 sterling per year.[27]

Cultural brokerage also offered other, less tangible rewards. Most significant was the importance that attached to Montour as a representative of the English colonial government and as a speaker and councillor for the Indians. Such prestige, however, also had its drawbacks. Indian culture required hosts and public figures to provide travelers and guests with hospitality, victuals, and entertainment. As a private citizen, Montour must have found these demands a strain on his financial resources. Governor Hamilton reported to the Assembly in 1750 that Weiser's appointment of Montour to handle business in Ohio gave him "a sort of publick Character which has put him to some Trouble and Expence." Four years later during a sojourn at Montour's plantation, Weiser recorded the exact nature of the trouble. Weiser found "about fifteen Indians, Men, Women, and Children, and more had been there but were now gone." Almost every day Indians came from Ohio "with some Errand or another, witch always wanted some Victuals in the Bargain." Weiser gave him £10 of the government's money. At about the same time, Governor Sharpe of Maryland noted that Montour's service during Washington's campaign against Fort Duquesne had resulted in "no small Detriment" to his "private affairs & credit," which induced Sharpe to advance him £45. The financial burdens associated with interpreting undoubtedly contributed to Montour's debts during the early 1750s.[28]

Despite the financial hardships, however, Montour seems to have found satisfaction in his public role. Maybe it answered an internal longing for a sense of identity and belonging. Whereas separate métis societies emerged in the Great Lakes region and Middle West, friction between the French and the English and their potential allies discouraged such a development in the East. This lack of a separate métis society may have forced children of mixed unions to identify with either the Europeans or the Indians. Montour's behavior indicates that he may have been troubled by the necessity of making such a choice. In fact, it may have been his inability or reluctance to choose that prompted Montour to seek a role and an identity in the middle. Montour's position as interpreter, Indian officer, and Six Nations councillor provided him, perhaps, with clearly defined roles in the confusing morass of intercultural relationships in his life. Interpreting offered a measure of prestige and influence in both worlds as long as he maintained the fine balance between the two and performed satisfactorily. In the European world, Montour gained respect, financial rewards, and a measure of influence based on his sway among the Indians and his demonstrated skill and integrity. The Indians esteemed and accepted him as speaker, councillor, and friend—as long as he remained trustworthy.

In a sense, Montour's frequent forays back and forth between European and Indian cultures trapped him permanently in the no-man's-land in the middle, regardless of his personal inclinations. In the records, perhaps even in his own mind, Montour's identity fluc-tuated with his role from "Mr. Montour" the (white) interpreter to "Sattelihu" or "Eghnisara" the Indian speaker and councillor.[29] Part-ly the result of his métis heritage, this identity crisis must have been aggravated by the need to constantly rove back and forth between the disparate cultures that produced him, assuming vastly different roles as diplomacy, politics, and even self-interest demanded.

Montour's English employers mirrored this confusion. From the beginning of his career, Montour occupied an ambiguous ethnic position in the minds of his European employers, as Count Zinzen-dorf clearly revealed in his description of his first meeting with Montour at Shamokin in 1742. Montour's "cast of countenance is decidedly European and had not his face been encircled with a broad band of paint, applied with bear's fat, I would certainly have taken him for one." His elaborately European dress, combined with distinctly Indian facial paint and ear ornaments, reflected his eclec-tic mixing of the material cultures of his heritage.[30] His selective adoption of specific aspects of Indian and European material cul-ture did not necessarily indicate personal confusion about his cul-tural identity, however, as such mixing was typical among both Indians and European traders and Indian agents. Regardless of his own perceptions, however, the ambiguity and confusion surround-ing Montour's varied cultural identities and roles remained unre-solved for many colonial officials throughout the 1740s and early 1750s. Pennsylvania officials continued to have difficulty deciding whether to classify him as an Indian or a European at treaty coun-cils, listing him at times with the Indian attendees and at others with the Europeans as "Mr. Montour." They usually settled for the sim-plest solution and equated his identity with his role. He was "white" when acting as an English agent or fulfilling the role of interpreter and Indian when serving as the Indians' speaker or councillor.

Whether Montour suffered similar confusion about himself is un-clear, but he exhibited the strains of his intercultural position in several ways. First, his successive marriages indicated the difficul-ties of maintaining a stable home and family life while constantly on the move between treaty sites and cultures. While the reasons for the breakup of his first marriage are unclear, the second, to Sarah Ainse, was apparently dissolved by mutual consent after the family relocated to New York. Part of the stress on his second marriage probably resulted from his indebtedness and drinking, much in evidence during that period.[31]

Andrew Montour's newfound prestige as a cultural broker after 1750 neatly coincided with his debt and drinking problems. In 1753, Montour nearly went to jail for a £50 debt. Peters, who bailed him out because Pennsylvania required his services at Onondaga, indicated that the problem lay with Sarah, his wife. While her extravagances may have contributed to the family's financial difficulties, however, she cannot be held solely accountable. In addition to the burden placed on the family by the necessity of providing food and hospitality to visiting Indians, Montour's drinking also played a role. In 1760, long after his marriage to Sarah ended, Montour again found himself threatened with imprisonment—this time because of a tavern debt.[32]

More serious than his indebtedness and perhaps also more indicative of inner turmoil and insecurity were Montour's drinking bouts. The first recorded instance of drunkenness occurred during a conference at Aughwick in September 1754. Weiser described Montour's shocking, drunken behavior in a letter to Peters.

He abused me very much Corsed & Swore and asked pardon when he got Sober. did the Same again when he was drunk again. damned me more then hundred times so he did the governor & Mr. peters for not paying him for his trouble & Expences, he is vexed at the new purchase told me I Cheated the Indians, he Says he will now Kill any white men theat will pretent to Setle on his Creek, . . . Saying *he* was *a Warrior*. . . . I left him drunk at Achwick.[33]

The resentments and hostilities Montour voiced while his inhibitions were diminished by the effects of alcohol indicate his psychological confusion. He was dissatisfied with the Pennsylvania government's payments for his interpreting and clearly resented Weiser. When combined with the concern he expressed about

Weiser's allegedly unfair treatment of the Indians during a recent land deal and his emphatic reference to himself as "a Warrior," these sentiments reveal his strong subconscious identification with the Indians. However, as soon as he was sober, he courted Weiser's forgiveness and "Asked pardon for offences given" in a conscious effort to maintain his coveted though somewhat precarious position as Pennsylvania's interpreter.[34]

By the late 1750s and early 1760s, Montour found a measure of security and peace under Johnson's tutelage and employ, though his drinking apparently continued to be a sporadic problem. Once he left Johnson's immediate service for his post at Fort Pitt, however, he again succumbed to boredom and perhaps melancholy for his lost prestige, returning to "his drunken frolicks." Ultimately, his weakness for alcohol led to his death and ended an impressive career.[35]

Unfortunately, since Montour never recorded his thoughts and feelings, all musings about his motives and desires must remain largely speculative. His behavior, however, strongly suggests that he probably identified himself primarily as Indian in his values and beliefs but found it necessary to adopt many English ways to maintain his position as interpreter. His successive marriages, indebtedness, and drinking also suggest that he found this in between ethnic role difficult to maintain. The need to suppress or ignore personal inclinations that at times conflicted with the behavior required by his position as an English agent and interpreter must have caused Montour considerable stress. Ironically, while his position as cultural broker in one sense offered him a clearly defined intercultural role, its mediating nature made a clear choice of ethnic identity nearly impossible; by definition, he had to be able to identify with both sides. Maintaining a life balanced on the razor edge of the dividing line was not easy.

During his thirty years as an interpreter and Indian officer for Pennsylvania, Virginia, and Sir William Johnson's Department of Indian Affairs, Montour's linguistic talents, extensive knowledge of Anglo–Indian affairs and cultures, and apparent integrity gained him the respect and esteem of both English colonial officials and the Six Nations and their allies. He performed a vital service for both the Indians and the English as they confronted each other across the council fires of New York and Pennsylvania. In addition to translating words and promises, Montour mediated the exchange of disparate cultures and ideas on the northeastern frontier. His knowledge and guidance in affairs of diplomacy and protocol increased understanding on both sides and helped to fashion a hybrid system of forest diplomacy. Ultimately, however, Montour's life reveals the hardships and pitfalls of an existence that straddled the cultural divide and chronicles one man's attempt to carve a niche and claim an identity in the no-man's-land between Indian and European cultures in the eighteenth-century Northeast.

CHAPTER 3

SAMSON OCCOM: MOHEGAN AS SPIRITUAL INTERMEDIARY

MARGARET CONNELL SZASZ

THE traveler bound along the turnpike road to New London, Connecticut, in 1764 might have noticed the construction of a large, two-story house just east of the town of Norwich. But the home would have attracted little attention unless a local resident had explained that it belonged to Samson Occom, a Mohegan Indian.

By the 1760s, when the Occom family home was being built, Samson Occom had traveled a considerable distance from his traditional childhood. His move from native wigwam into an English-style home marked the passage from Mohegan upbringing to prominence as a cultural broker moving between Indian and non–Indian worlds. From the era of the American Revolution to the early years of the republic, Occom achieved a singular fame as minister and missionary, fund raiser and author, tribal leader and schoolmaster. Known throughout New England, New York, and nearby colonies and admired in England and Scotland, Occom shattered so many stereotypes, it is virtually impossible to force him into any mold. His contemporary influence and his legacy emerge from his position somewhere between the native and non–native cultural worlds of colonial America.

This chapter looks at Occom as cultural intermediary. During his life he donned many robes, but in the long run all of the parts that he played served to further his preeminent gift as cultural broker. Over the course of his life, Occom hammered out the role of an intercultural eighteenth-century American.[1]

The Reverend Samson Occom (1723–1792), painted by Nathaniel Smibert. Occom was a familiar figure to both Indians and settlers in colonial New England and New York. Courtesy of Bowdoin College Museum of Art, Brunswick, Maine. Bequest of James Bowdoin III.

The path that led Occom to construction of a frame home in the 1760s was an extraordinary one. Born in 1723 in his native lands along the Mohegan/Thames River in southern Connecticut, in his childhood, Occom remained firmly rooted in the old ways. "My parents Lived a wandering Life," he recalled. "They Chiefly Depended upon Hunting, Fishing & Fowling for their Living and had no Connection with the English, excepting to traffic with them in their small Trifles." These Algonquian-speaking people, like their Niantic and Pequot neighbors, had tended small garden plots, raising corn, beans, and squash. Like other Mohegan children, Occom lived in a wigwam, spoke his native language, and successfully avoided the occasional visit of a minister from nearby New London.[2] The Great Awakening changed this cultural pattern and altered the direction of his life. At the impressionable age of sixteen or seventeen, Occom was converted. "From this Time the Distress and Burden of my mind was removed, and I found Serenity and Pleasure of Soul, in serving God."

The conversion catapulted Occom into new paths. It led directly to his becoming literate—"I just began to Read in the New Testament without Spelling"—and to his studies with the Rev. Eleazar Wheelock, a Congregational New Light minister of Lebanon, Connecticut.[3] Within a decade after his conversion, Occom had completed a formal education roughly equivalent to that of frontier ministers of his day, and he had earned the position of schoolmaster and minister among the Montauk Indians of Long Island, where he remained until his late thirties.[4]

When Occom arrived at Montauk, he had been a student for six years, having survived by boarding with Wheelock and other Connecticut ministers, who supported him with funds supplemented by the Boston Board of Commissioners of the New England Company, a Congregational missionary organization. Even as a student, he had begun to mediate. At the same time that he was grappling with the Scriptures, Latin, Hebrew, and music, he became counselor to the Mohegan tribe and also went among his people as a novice itinerant preacher. From the beginning, therefore, he was both internal leader and spiritual intermediary.

Occom's years at Montauk were hard ones. Although the Presbyterians ordained him as a minister and he also taught school for the Montauk children, he never received adequate compensation for his position, a condition he would later reflect on with considerable bitterness. His income from the Boston Board of Commissioners, which averaged £15 a year, scarcely supported Occom, his

Montauk wife, Mary Fowler, and their six children. The stringency of the Boston board forced Occom to find other means of support. He planted corn, potatoes, and beans ("I used to be out hoeing my Corn Some times before Sun Rise and after my School is Dismist, and by this means I was able to raise my own Pork"); he caught fish and hunted fowl ("I Could more than pay for my Powder and Shot with Feathers"); and he became a craftsman ("At other Times I Bound old Books for Easthampton People, made wooden Spoons and Ladles, Stocked Guns, & worked on Cedar to make Pails, Piggins, and Churns, &c."). Despite the struggle for survival, Occom continued to shoulder responsibility for his people. He maintained his position as adviser to the Mohegan, and he often sat as judge for the Montauk and other tribes. In this capacity, he traveled to different Indian groups, "to See into their Affairs Both Religious, Temporal."[5]

In 1761, at the invitation of the New York Correspondents of the Society in Scotland for Propagating Christian Knowledge, a Presbyterian missionary organization, Occom traveled to Iroquois country in response to news that the Oneida had requested a missionary. During the journey Occom was accompanied by his Montauk brother-in-law, David Fowler. Fowler, who was in his twenties, was studying with Wheelock at Moor's Indian Charity School, the institution that Wheelock had founded on the basis of Occom's educational achievements. Travel expenses came from two sources: funds hastily collected by the New York correspondents, and a small donation secured by Wheelock from the Boston Board of Commissioners. Wheelock sent Fowler along to recruit Iroquois students for Moor's school.

Success for the Occom–Fowler mission hinged on the reaction of the Iroquois themselves and the response of Sir William Johnson, Irish friend and neighbor to the Iroquois and British Indian superintendent for the northern district. Johnson's support enabled Fowler to obtain three Iroquois students, one of whom was Johnson's Mohawk brother-in-law, the famous Thayendanegea, or Joseph Brant. The Oneida were also receptive. They spoke of a missionary and possibly a school, and as symbol of their trust, they sent a belt of wampum, which, they said, "shall bind us fast together in perpetual Love and Friendship."[6] But full success was marred by the Oneidas' deep poverty. Fowler described them as "exceeding poor," a condition that raised the question of their ability to help support a missionary, let alone a schoolmaster.[7] Moreover, Occom's overtures appeared aggressive to them. Another minister familiar with the Iroquois reported that the Oneida resented Occom's zealous instructions. Occom ordered them to grow their hair long, "as the English do," and told them "they must not wear the Indian ornaments, as wampum and the like: but put them off and burn them in the fire."[8]

Occom made two additional trips in 1762 and 1763, but the conditions he encountered proved overwhelming. The Oneida, faced with starvation, were preoccupied with the "Pigeon hunt," "going-a-fishing," and hunting deer, which prevented them from attending his meetings. Occom himself suffered a recurrence of his rheumatism when he slept "upon the wet." In 1763, he did not even travel beyond the Mohawks because of the fear engendered by Pontiac's rebellion, which became the coup de grace for his Iroquois mission.[9] By December of that year, he had gone to Mohegan to choose a site for the house he was planning to build.

The following spring of 1764 appeared to promise Occom a permanent homecoming when he and Mary moved their family to his inherited lands at Mohegan. The construction of the house implied that Occom's long-held dream of serving as missionary to his own people had come to fruition. Acting as catalyst for the dream, the Boston commissioners had offered him a new position as missionary to the Niantic, Mohegan, and nearby groups, at a salary of £30 per annum. As soon as Wheelock heard of the proposal, however, he intervened. Seeking a means to incorporate Moor's school, Wheelock had persuaded the society in Scotland to establish the Connecticut Board of Correspondents, which promptly fell under his thumb, enabling him to convince the Boston commissioners that they should release Occom to the Connecticut correspondents. Unlike the Boston board, Wheelock's correspondents had no funds to pay the missionary. Moreover, Occom's move to Mohegan threatened a conflict between the Indian minister and the Rev. David Jewett, the English minister there.[10]

At this juncture, Wheelock turned to the Rev. George Whitefield, the renowned English evangelist. Whitefield, then in New York, had already met Occom and Wheelock and had recently collected

£120 for Moor's school. Consequently, Wheelock assumed White-field would fund yet another Occom-Fowler mission to the Iroquois. For Wheelock, the trip was urgent. He expected it to fend off a clash between Occom and Jewett, to add students to Moor's school, and to provide Occom with both salary and missionary work. Even if Whitefield funded the journey, however, Wheelock still faced another dilemma: who would finance and supervise the construction of Occom's house in his absence?

When Occom agreed to this trip, he had serious reservations. En route to New York late that summer, he wrote to Wheelock, promising, "Sir I shall end *eavour* to follow your Directions in all things." But Occom remained concerned about the funding. He wrote, "I'm sorry you couldn't get at least Some Money for David." And leavening the message with his occasionally wry humor, he cautioned, "[It] looks like Presumption for us to go on Long Journey thro' Christians, without Money, if it was altogether among Indian Heathen we might do well enough." Finally, he resolved the question of family support. "But I have determined to go, tho' no white missionary would go in such Circumstances—I leave my House and other Business to be done upon your credit. . . . I leave my Poor Wife and Children at your feet, and if they hunger Starve and die let them die there."[11]

Mary Occom and the children were not left alone for long. No sooner did Occom and Fowler arrive in New York than they were forced to turn around and come back to Connecticut. Wheelock had misjudged Whitefield. After the English evangelist had met Occom in Connecticut, he had anticipated becoming Occom's patron, but when the Boston commissioners and the Connecticut correspondents assumed arbitrary decision making over Occom's career, Whitefield opted out. Wheelock later apologized. "It was my compassion to him [Occom] not knowing what else to do with him that moved me to act at all in the Affair."[12]

This turn of events reminded Occom of the humbleness of his position. Eventually he would understand that Wheelock and his colleagues saw him as a convenient tool for their goals. His twelve years at Montauk should have been justly rewarded, because he combined in one person the talents of several Englishmen. In another instance, the Boston commissioners had paid a young, non–Indian missionary (without any family) £50 for one year, plus

£50 for an interpreter and an additional £30 for an "introducer." Some years later Occom recalled, "In my Service . . . I was my own Interpreter I was both a School master and Minister to the Indians, yea I was their Ear, Eye & Hand, as Well as Mouth." For this he was paid £180 total for twelve years. In retrospect, Occom said, "I leave it with the World, as wicked as it is, to Judge, whether I ought not to have had half as much . . . but I *must Say*, 'I believe it is, because I am a poor Indian.'"[13] Although the Boston commissioners had finally increased his salary on his removal to Connecticut, the Connecticut correspondents had moved quickly to cut off these funds and sent him on another fruitless mission to Iroquoia. In the negotiations with these two missionary groups, all he had gained was the house at Mohegan. By 1764, therefore, Occom was a step closer to assessing the nature of his role as intermediary. Another lesson on brokerage awaited him on his return from New York that fall.

When Occom settled on his lands at Mohegan, the clash between the Indian missionary and the English minister forecast by Wheelock soon dominated the local scene. As Wheelock noted, "Mr. Occom returned . . . into a Fire which had been for some time enkindling." The animosity between the two men was not restricted to a battle over territory. It fed into a larger struggle over the Mohegan land claims, known as the "Mason Case" or the "Mason controversy."[14]

This case had been in dispute since 1640 when the seventeenth-century Mohegan leader, Sachem Ben Uncas, had deeded between 700 and 800 square miles of Mohegan lands to Maj. John Mason, who later conveyed all but 5,000 acres of "sequestered" lands to the colony of Connecticut. When Occom returned in 1764, final resolution of the controversy was imminent.[15] As a counselor for the Mohegan, Occom felt a strong commitment to their defense, but even the Mohegans were divided on the matter. One group supported Sachem Ben Uncas, who leaned toward the colony's position; the other group, led by Occom, supported the Mohegan claim. When Occom began to preach at the Mohegan schoolhouse, his supporters, both Mohegan and English, came to hear him, and in a short time he had acquired a number of enemies, including Jewett. Rumors spread. Occom was portrayed "as a very bad, mischevious, and designing man." Jewett wrote to the Boston board about Occom's activities, which so alarmed the commissioners that they withdrew the pension that Whitefield had secured for Occom.[16] Eventually, the Connecticut correspondents persuaded Jewett and Occom to come to terms, although several months elapsed before Wheelock's sharp prodding led Jewett to write a retraction to the Boston board.

The final decision on the case, which granted all of the disputed lands to Connecticut except the 5,000 acres of sequestered lands, jolted Occom. The case had split the tribe, thereby rendering it almost defenseless. It had also demonstrated the value of maintaining legal records, which Occom would heed in the future. Above all, it had revealed the power of English acquisitiveness. Occom concluded, "I am afraid the poor Indian will never stand a chance against the English in their land controversies because they are very poor, they have no money. Money is almighty now-a-days, & the Indians have no learning, no wit, no cunning, the English have it all."[17]

While Occom was engrossed in these momentous issues, Wheelock and his colleagues were planning further use of his talents. Plagued with debts and "want of money" in New England and eager to expand Moor's school into Iroquoia, Wheelock was devising a scheme that would draw on the mother country's proven sympathy for the Indian cause. After months of intensive correspondence, Wheelock revealed plans for a fund-raising tour in the British Isles to be led by the Rev. Nathaniel Whitaker of Norwich and the Rev. Samson Occom of Mohegan.

Many of those involved in the tour believed that sending Occom was a stroke of genius. But the Boston commissioners, who saw Wheelock as an interloper in their domain, opposed Occom's role. Representatives of the oldest nonconformist missionary society in the colonies, the commissioners resented Wheelock's failure to include them in the planning of the tour. When they learned of Occom's position, they launched a campaign that questioned the degree of Wheelock's influence on the Mohegan, suggesting that Occom was already schooled and Christianized when he went to Lebanon. When Occom arrived in Boston, he and Whitaker tried in vain to placate the commissioners.[18] Their failure meant that the distrust engendered by the commissioners' criticism plagued Occom throughout the tour, leading him eventually to write an account of his own childhood, wherein he refuted all of their assertions. His narrative began, "Having seen and heard Several Representatives in England and Scotland, by some Gentlemen in America, Concerning me, and finding many gross mistakes in their Accounts, I thought it my Duty to give a Short, Plain, and Honest Account of my Self."[19]

The English tour has been well covered in Leon Burr Richardson's *An Indian Preacher in England* (1933). For Occom, the tour was both exhilarating and exhausting. The grueling ocean voyage, the stint of the smallpox inoculation, and months of preaching to vast crowds in England and Scotland and of meeting prominent ministers and royalty kept Occom away from his family and his people for two and a half years. But those who had faith in Occom saw that faith reconfirmed in the financial success of the trip. In England alone, the two ministers raised £9,497; their brief stay in Scotland garnered £2,529. This was the largest amount collected through direct solicitation by any American institution in the colonial era.[20]

A number of conditions led to this achievement. These included the guidance of Whitefield, who provided entrée into powerful, wealthy, and sympathetic circles. Occom wrote, "[He] takes *unwearied Pains* to Introduce us to the *religious Nobility* and others, and to the best men in the City of London—yea he is a *tender father* to us."[21] The ultimate secret of the tour's success, however, was Occom himself. The first American Indian minister to visit the British Isles, he found himself in the spotlight. Whether he was in London or the West Country, in Whitefield's Tabernacle or a humble church, as an American Indian, he proved to be the embodiment of his preaching. His previous experiences at Montauk, in Connecticut, and among the Iroquois served him well, as did his maturity; on his arrival he was forty-three years old. When he spoke of "the miserable & wreched situation of the poor Indians, who are perishing for lack of spiritual knowledge," he often convinced his listeners through a combination of his Mohegan birth and his own conviction.[22] The Rev. Peter Jilliard wrote of Occom, "As far as I hear he pleases in every Town & city—So much Simplicity appears in the man: So honest, guiles a Temper, with Seriousness in his public Service."[23] Occom's popularity reached its apogee in the summer of 1766. On returning to London that June, he wrote, "This Evening I heard, the *Stage Players*, had been *Mim-*

The Reverend Samson Occom. Mezzotint by J. Spilsbury from an oil painting by Mason Chamberlin. The original painting is lost. This portrait was completed during Occom's fund-raising tour of England and Scotland in the 1760s. Courtesy of Dartmouth College Library.

icking of me in their Plays, lately," adding, "I never thought I Shou'd ever come to *that Honor*,—O God wou'd give the greater courage—."[24]

In New England, however, Wheelock persisted in his belief that Occom needed fatherly counsel and guidance. While his counterparts in England treated the Mohegan with admiration and respect, Wheelock chided him about his pride. During the first months of the tour, he wrote to Occom, "I hope God has made you more humble than you have commonly been." Some twenty months later, he wrote to Whitaker, "Give my love to Mr. Occom; I want to see him; does he keep clear of that Indian distemper, *Pride.*"[25]

Wheelock never seemed able to separate his emotional relationship with Occom from his recognition of Occom's accomplishments. On many occasions he indicated that he had not broken loose from a relationship that was both that of parent to child and of superior (civilized and English) to inferior (partly civilized but still Indian). During the tour, Occom not only distanced himself from this psychological strain, he also found himself being treated as an equal. The adulation of the crowds combined with the respect of his contemporaries provided Occom with a long delayed sense of self-worth.

Occom's biographers have portrayed the years between 1768, when he returned, and 1772–73, when his salary was restored and he began to plan for the emigration of his people, as the low point in his life. It is difficult to judge this period, partly because there is no diary for this time. It is known, however, that Occom apologized to the Connecticut correspondents for drinking; that he and his family struggled to survive without any regular source of income; and that both Occom and his wife were in poor health. Finally, during this time Occom split with Wheelock because of the latter's decision to spend most of the British funds for English rather than Indian students at his newly founded Dartmouth College. One of Wheelock's former English students relayed Occom's position on Dartmouth: "The Indian was converted into an English School & . . . the English had crowded out the Indian youth."[26] This reversal embittered Occom, and although he and Wheelock exchanged further letters, he never visited the campus that was indebted to him.

Occom's disillusionment may also have been rooted in the contrast between the respect he received in England and the patronizing attitude of Wheelock. His feelings toward Wheelock also mirrored the declining fortunes of the Mohegans. With the death of Uncas, the final resolution of their land claim, and a dwindling population, Occom's people needed his leadership.[27] As he gained in stature within his tribe, he grew increasingly suspicious of those who pretended to have Mohegan interests at heart.

One of these was his rival, Jewett. In the spring of 1768, Occom wrote to Wheelock, "Br. Jewett is picking up his charges to shoot at me, but I hope that he will overload, that his old musket may break."[28] Two months later, when Jewett was presiding over funeral services for Uncas, Occom and his followers got up and walked out before the services were concluded. Although Occom had been loyal to Uncas, he was also convinced that the colony's agents had used the sachem for their own purposes. By leaving early, he could indicate his displeasure both with Jewett and with the agents of the colony. Stressing the departure in a description of the funeral, the agent reporting to Connecticut authorities warned, "The tempers of a Number of ye Indians is Worked up, to the highest pitch of Jealousy, & Distrust of ye Govemnt, and also of any Dependence of them, Either for advice, protection, Regulation, Friendship, or even as much as to be Treated with as Friend."[29]

The agent may have exaggerated for effect, but the Mohegan attitudes were perceptibly hardening. These years, then, were a time of retrenchment for Samson Occom. Although he and his people suffered during this interim period, Occom emerged in 1773 as a stronger person. His decades of preaching and counseling, his experiences in Britain, the break with Wheelock, and the legal blows against his people—all had molded his will and determination.

Prior to this time his urge to serve his people, as itinerant preacher, counselor, and mediator, was constantly usurped by Wheelock and the leaders of the missionary organizations. From his earliest studies with Wheelock through the British tour, his cultural mediation had been commandeered by the English. Even the tour itself had been an exercise in deception.

By 1773, therefore, Occom was ready to alter the direction of his brokerage, and from this point forward, he centered his energies on his own people. The resolution of their untenable position in southern New England emerged as his ultimate goal, and he devoted much of the remainder of his life to its fulfillment.

Before the emigration movement was fully under way, however, Occom plunged into a creative work designed to appeal to these natives. Both Algonquian and Iroquoian people of the Northeast had always enjoyed music, and many colonial intermediaries, including Fowler and Occom, had tapped into this dimension of native cultures. Occom's English visit coincided with a rigorous hymn-writing period in Britain, and while there he met many people who knew the famous hymn writers Isaac Watts and Samuel Wesley. On his return, he brought a number of hymnals to his Mohegan home, increasing the size of its already well-known library.

The immediate inspiration for his own hymnal, however, may have come in 1772, when his sermon on temperance, delivered before the execution of Moses Paul, an Indian who committed a murder while drunk, was published in New Haven. Since this was probably the first colonial publication of a sermon preached by a native minister, the initial printing sold out quickly, and it was subsequently reprinted many times in America and Britain. Only a year and a half later, Occom's hymnal appeared. The title page read, *A Choice Collection of Hymns and Spiritual Songs Intended for the Edification of Sincere Christians, of all Denominations*, by Samson Occom, Minister of the Gospel.[30] Reprinted twice, the second time in 1792, the year of Occom's death, the collection gathered a number of Occom's favorite hymns. One of his biographers has suggested that Occom probably wrote many of the hymns. Perhaps the most famous of them, which began with the line, "Awaked by Sinai's awful sound," was reprinted elsewhere, thereby becoming part of nineteenth-century hymnody in America.[31]

In this manner, Occom left a legacy that was carried into American society. But those who cherished his hymns were the native people whose lives he had touched. When the southern New England Algonquians were gathered, especially after moving to Oneida country, they often concluded their meetings with singing. On a trip to the young settlement in 1785, Occom wrote, "And then we arrived at Davids [Fowler's] house as we approached I heard a Melodious Singing, a number were together Singing Psalms hyms and Spiritual songs we went in amongst them and they all took hold of my hand one by one with Joy and Gladness from the Greatest to the least and we Sot down awhile, and then they began to Sing again."[32] By the following year, the singing group had gained in stature. That fall, Occom noted, "I went home with our People, we got there just before Sun Set; and our Singers got together and they Sung some Time, We had some new Comers, at the Singing meeting." Occom added that the singers often sang for up to two hours in a single evening.[33]

Occom's *Choice Collection of Hymns* appeared in the midst of emigration preparations. In July 1774, when Occom and Fowler left for Iroquoia to negotiate the boundaries of the land that the Oneida had promised to them, only three months had elapsed since the hymnal was published. Since emigration preparations had been under way for almost a year, Occom may have considered the hymnal as a singular contribution to the new and distant home for his people. If this was the case, then the postponement of emigration must have been a harsh disappointment.

The proposed settlement in Oneida country suffered innumerable setbacks before it finally began to take shape. The initial proposal for the venture had come from Wheelock, but his offers to Occom (and Fowler), made in 1769, were ill-timed. At this stage of his life, Occom was not only unable to go because of poverty and lameness but was also unwilling because of the recent severing of relations between the Oneida and Wheelock (the Oneida had removed all of their children from Moor's School); finally, he rejected the offer because he was moving toward greater independence from Wheelock's paternalism.

The proposed move was stymied, therefore, until new Indian leadership emerged. In 1769, Occom had written to Wheelock from Mohegan concerning the status of religion. He observed, "Religion Decays, and the Devil Reigns."[34] Two years later, however, the mood began to change, and in the Indian town near Farmington, Connecticut, Occom led a revival that affected a number of natives, including Joseph Johnson, a young Mohegan who had recently returned from two years at sea. A former student at Moor's School and then a schoolmaster among the Oneida, Johnson had left his post because of drunkenness. After his conversion, however, he became a schoolmaster and a minister; and he married Occom's daughter, Tabitha. It was Johnson who provided the impetus for the move to Oneida country.

Twice in Occom's life, therefore, a religious awakening had become the catalyst for change. The first Great Awakening led him to his schooling and career; the second local revival, three decades later, led him to the climax of his role as a spiritual intermediary. After negotiations in 1773–74, both with the Oneida and among themselves, leaders of seven Indian communities of southern New England—Mohegan, Farmington, Montauk, Groton, Charlestown, Niantic, and Stonington—concluded their plans to form a community among the Oneida on a tract of land that Occom took care to register legally in 1774. But the March 1775 departure date for the first group of emigrants, which included Fowler and Johnson, coincided with the onset of the American struggle for independence, and as a result, Occom's people were stymied for almost a decade.

One year after the Peace of Paris, in 1784, Occom led the first group of postwar emigrants, who established their new Indian community of Brothertown. Occom's relatives and longtime friends formed the nucleus of the young settlement. These included Mary Occom's brothers, David and Jacob Fowler, who were among the earliest to arrive. Gradually other members from the seven Indian communities added their strength to Brothertown, although the exodus was not a universal one. Nearby, Indians who had removed from Stockbridge, in the Housatonic Valley of western Massachusetts, formed their own community in exile. Of the pioneer leaders of the Brothertown movement, only Johnson, a casualty of the Revolutionary War, was missing.[35]

When Occom and David Fowler began the land negotiations with the Oneida in 1774, Occom had written, "Spent the week with an aggreable view of the Situation and helpful Prospect of the Indians future happiness."[36] At this juncture in his life, he was looking both into the future and back to the past. He had not been to Oneida since 1762, and the visit made him nostalgic. Of the Oneida themselves, he noted, "Great alteration has been made . . . since I was here 12 years ago."[37] Perhaps he was also describing himself. He, too, had undergone "great alteration" in the intervening years.

In certain respects, however, Occom had not changed. As itinerant preacher, he served as spiritual mediator from his student days with Eleazar Wheelock through the emigration to Brothertown.

Whether his base was Lebanon, Montauk, or Mohegan, between the 1740s and 1770s, Occom had been a familiar visitor to wigwams located in the Algonquian towns outside many Connecticut communities. So, too, had he become an integral figure in the non-native communities of southern New England. In the early 1760s, during his first journeys to Iroquois country, he added the Dutch residents of the Hudson River Valley to his widening audience. On the British tour, he included the English and Scots among his supporters. The post-Britain years saw a strengthening of his reputation in southern New England and along the routes that he followed to Iroquoia—up the Hudson via New York City or across northwestern Connecticut and along the Housatonic.

Occom appealed to the wide variety of people who gathered to hear him during his travels. Seldom described as a sophisticated theologian, Occom held his audiences through an evangelistic style, possibly intensified from observing Whitefield, and through the use of allusion and illustration. The few sermon notes that remain suggest his feel for the rhythm of the language and convey a sense of the persistent kinship network of his native culture. "Be perfect / —i.e., be united, compact together everyone in proper place as every Limb & joint of a Human Body must be otherwise it will be deformed, imperfect & weak . . . Be of good comfort. . . . Be of one Mind . . . all going Heart & Hand in ye Easy-Difficult Road to Zion." He also spoke to the condition of his largely rural audience. For example, "Live in peace. . . . Cultivate peace, i.e.— / take care to plant manure & cherish it as ye vintner his Vine, or ye Husbandman his corn."[38] The Brothertown years saw the culmination of Occom's itinerant preaching. Since Mary Occom did not move to the new community until 1789, during the preceding five years he was constantly on the move, in Brothertown, en route to Brothertown or Mohegan, or traveling to communities within a day's ride from Mohegan. During these journeys he reached out to his rural listeners through his increasingly extemporaneous preaching, through his willingness to listen and to offer counsel, both to natives and non-natives, and through evenings of singing and/or "exercising" with his "Christian cards," a set of playing cards with biblical verses printed on them which served as both entertainment and instruction. Occom carried these cards on all of his travels and used them frequently. In the summer of 1787, en route to Oneida, he noted in his journal,

> Took Dinner here in the after Noon the People collected . . . there was
> very good attention; . . . and after I sat a while in the House, I had Exercise
> with my Christian Cards with some young Women that came late for the
> Sermon, and Some were somewhat Startled, but Some began they were all
> delighted, and behaved very decent, and Some Old People Chose Texts
> also, and it was agreable exercise. I Lodged at the Same House and was
> Extreamly well treated by the Whole Family.[39]

Although Occom's itinerant preaching appealed to both native
and non-native, his heart and affections lay with the natives, whom
he often described as "my people." He addressed not only his immediate family but other native people, as well as "Brother" or
"Sister." For the English or Dutch, however, he reserved the more
formal titles of "Mr.," "Mrs.," "Capt.," "Elder," "Esqr.," or "Deacon."
The joy that he expressed when he was united with his people at
Brothertown was unequaled by any experience with non-natives.
One summer in the late 1780s, he recorded in his journal, "I and my
sons went to the Lake, which was about·half a mile off & it was just
Night, and we Fishd, and we Catchd a fine parsel of fish presently,
& made up a Fire by the Creek and had fine supper of F and
afterwards Prayd, & then we went to Sleep by our fire quietly."[40]
Wheelock once described his former student as "Mr. Occom the
Indian minister." A stranger whom Occom met en route to Oneida
spoke of him as "the strange mister." But the family name of Occom, which translates as "the other side," was perhaps the most apt
name for this Mohegan intermediary. From the 1740s through the
1760s, Samson Occom had moved between native and non-native
cultures, and in so doing, he had learned much from "the other
side" of the cultural divide. From the early 1770s forward, however,
he recast that knowledge in the form of a tool that native groups
might use to maintain a degree of autonomy.

If Occom chose to lead these native·people toward a form of
spiritual syncretism, by the 1770s, he had lost any illusions about
English willingness to eradicate the natives' cultural heritage. The
actions of Wheelock, his colleagues in the missionary societies, and
the Connecticut authorities had delivered a clear message. Few
choices remained for these natives. They had seen their communi-

ties become as islands in the ocean of Euramerican settlement. If they chose to remain, their future was uncertain; if they chose to flee, there was hope. Flight offered them a respite and an opportunity to regain a sense of control over their lives. It appeared to promise an avenue for selective adaptation by enabling them to merge nonconformist Protestantism into their native world view without losing their sense of community and the unique heritage that set them apart from the English. For this reason, Occom, David Fowler, and others determined to lead the emigrants in their northwestern migration. Several decades later, their grandchildren would make a similar decision, when they emigrated from New York to lands near Green Bay, Wisconsin, where their descendants live today.

The decision to move to Oneida was a deliberate one that had required considerable thought. The fact that Mary Occom did not make the long trek until five years after her husband had led the first settlers suggests the complexity of the choice and explains why some Mohegans remained in Connecticut and others returned later, thereby splitting the tribe. In 1789, when the Occoms moved to Brothertown, they thrust a familiar land behind them. It was a third move for Mary Occom, a second for her husband; for both it meant turning their backs on the Mohegan house that had been their home for twenty-five years. When the home was under construction, Occom's trust in the English was still intact; twenty-five years later, it had not recovered from the events of the early 1770s. Like the move to Mohegan, the move to Brothertown symbolized Occom's stance as intermediary between cultures. For twenty years he had cooperated with the English, but when they had betrayed his trust, he had moved away from the other side and toward his own people.

PART TWO

BROKERS OF AN EXPANDING REPUBLIC

These intermediaries of the early to mid-nineteenth century were drawn together by their era, which bound them by the common anxieties of removal, warfare, and cultural colonialism. All of them dealt with issues thrust to center stage by American expansion and tribal resistance. But to suggest that they shared a common experience, amenable to a formula analysis, is to remove them from the daily reality of their unique conditions. Despite the centrifugal force of their era, their own experiences belied the commonality of that force by pulling it in diverse directions. None was quite like the other.

Although two of the following chapters look at brokers among the Cherokees, even this bond was limited. The experiences of the Brainerd School pupils, as described by Michael C. Coleman, reflected only one segment of the changing Cherokee society that Evan Jones and John B. Jones, the Baptist ministers depicted by William G. McLoughlin, encountered during their lengthy commitment to a multifaceted brokerage.

Yet when one compares the milieu of brokering within the Cherokee world with the flavor of William Clark's brokerage, as portrayed by James P. Ronda, the striking differences enable the Brainerd pupils and the Joneses to gain a degree of commonality. Clark moved in a western landscape, centered largely in the Missouri Basin, western prairies, and Great Plains, and focused on the tribal-outsider relations unique to this vast region. Even though the U.S. military response to the Black Hawk War echoed among southern tribes like the Cherokee who were facing the possibility of forced removal, thereby forging a tenuous link between the two regions, the environment that William Clark moved in and the environment of the Cherokee were singular.

The subjects of the three chapters that follow were reflections of their unique worlds as well as of the larger milieu of the era in which they lived. Thus Coleman has demonstrated how the Brainerd pupils were a microcosm of one segment of Cherokee society. A nation bent on retaining its independent status within a larger and more powerful nation determined to exclude it as a persistent subculture, the Cherokee homeland that nurtured the Brainerd pupils also lent them its tensions and anxieties, which were mirrored in the attitudes of these daughters of Cherokee progressives. While they were drawn toward the outside culture represented by their teachers, they remained fervent nationalists. While they saw themselves as brokers to traditional Cherokees, they also acted as intermediaries to non-Cherokees.

In a similar fashion, John Jones and Evan B. Jones perceived inherent values in both cultures. Consequently, they took a forceful stance on selective positions within the spectrum of Cherokee society, and, with equal force, they rejected others. Their honest respect for Cherokee culture earned them stature among both mixedbloods and fullbloods, but their independence also guaranteed enemies among Cherokees and outsiders.

The biculturalism of these intermediaries set them apart from William Clark. Clark's record as an intermediary does not lend itself to facile analysis. As Ronda points out, Clark's brokerage retained some resilience for over two decades. As long as white pressure remained moderate, Clark promoted mediation between cultures and even celebrated native life through his Indian museum. His true position, which was rooted in his "belief in the inevitability of American expansion," intruded only when mediation succumbed to the persistence of Black Hawk, his fellow loser in the brokerage game.

CHAPTER 4

RED-HEAD'S DOMAIN: WILLIAM CLARK'S INDIAN BROKERAGE

JAMES P. RONDA

AT first glance William Clark seems an unlikely candidate for the office of cultural broker. As soldier, explorer, bureaucrat, and entrepreneur, he represented all those forces determined to dispossess native people of land and culture. But neither Clark nor his contemporaries saw him quite that way. Writing to Thomas Jefferson in 1825, Clark portrayed himself as an official of "Small Means" ready to defend Indians against the forces hurrying their "rapid decline."[1] Many Indians agreed, seeing the "Red-Head Chief" as a sympathetic listener. Delegation after delegation filled his St. Louis council room with stories of fraud and violence. White Americans, many of whom would have turned a deaf ear to such complaints, praised Clark for his diplomatic skill. One group of Illinois residents believed that Indians held Clark in "reverential awe."[2] Not everyone agreed. Thomas Forsyth, Clark's ablest, best-informed Indian agent, doubted the superintendent's knowledge, skill, and motives. After being removed from his agency for political reasons, Forsyth blasted Clark as "a perfect ignoramus" in Indian affairs.[3] Whatever the validity of Forsyth's charges, many saw Clark as a successful go-between, someone bridging the cultural divide.

Plainly, that was the way he saw himself. Clark imagined himself as an explainer, someone who stood between rowdy white settlers, avaricious land speculators, opportunistic politicians, and vengeful Indians. In a world of mounting violence, Clark played the patrician broker. He sought to hold back the twin tides of white land hunger and violent Indian resistance. But as an explainer, Clark never transcended his own cultural and national loyalties. There was no question in his mind about the legitimate power and ultimate triumph of the American empire. Some Indians seemingly accepted this and came to terms with the federal leviathan. But Clark insisted that whites also needed to be reasonable. Committed to the Enlightenment vision of Reason and Civilization, Clark was certain that the universals of law, education, and agriculture could overcome greed and misunderstanding. As territorial governor and federal Indian superintendent, Clark trusted that goodwill, rational dialogue, and "civilization" would somehow temper conflict between the two peoples. The cost of assimilation for native people was the loss of land and sovereignty. Clark thought it a cheap price to pay for survival. Clark's brokerage was more than a paper chain of treaty promises. It amounted to a substantial set of institutions and personal relationships. Seeing them in action before 1832, we may better understand what the Black Hawk War destroyed.

In many ways, William Clark's Indian brokerage was like a complex theatrical production, acted out on several stages with large casts delivering sometimes contradictory lines. The first of these was the arena of public policy. Through the years Clark's script called for him to fill the roles of federal Indian agent (1807–13), territorial governor of Missouri (1813–20), and superintendent of Indian affairs (1822–38). As administrator, Clark created and managed a substantial network of agents, subagents, interpreters, and clerks. His behind-the-scenes administrative duties included planning treaty councils and the launching of delegations bound for Washington. But in all this Clark did more than follow a script imposed by others. In many instances he made policy. As he once wrote to Superintendent of Indian Affairs Thomas McKenney, "I therefore have taken upon myself a great deal, in acting as I thought best."[4] By the end of the War of 1812, Clark was the single most influential American officer in the West. Surveying his domain in 1815, he estimated that he had policymaking responsibilities for some sixty-four thousand native people in twenty-two tribes and bands. Clark surmised that another one hundred thousand Indians lived on the margins of his brokerage. To oversee this empire, Clark relied on six resident agents, three subagents, and six interpreters. From St. Louis, Clark could chart a territory that stretched from Council Bluffs on the Missouri to the Falls of St. Anthony on the Mississippi and south to Rock Island.[5]

The first act of Clark's brokerage drama spanned the years between 1807 and 1815. American sovereignty had to be proclaimed and validated, native alliances required constant attention, and, above all, the British-Indian threats of the War of 1812 demanded a strong response. On the frontier of the Northeast woodlands, earlier brokers like Sir William Johnson had met similar challenges by playing one native alliance against another. Although Clark had made intertribal peace a key point in his diplomacy during the travels of the Lewis and Clark Expedition (1804–06), mounting British influence caused him to abandon that tactic. Instead, he pursued a policy designed to encourage Indians who might be favorably inclined toward the United States to attack pro-British neighbors. Writing to Secretary of War William H. Crawford, Clark offered a blunt description of his role as frontier power broker. "I adopted the only expedient in my power calculated to check the British Influence and the extension of British warfare, which was to set some of the large Tribes of the Missouri, nearest our southern Frontiers, at War against the Tribes of the Mississippi who were our most destructive Enemies."[6] Clark did more than just declare a willingness to set Indian against Indian. At his directive, Auguste P. Chouteau took a store of gifts to convince the Osages to launch raids against various pro-British bands, and Manuel Lisa pursued a similar enterprise on the northern plains. Clark claimed that such missions "succeeded to my expectations and has produced valuable changes in the dispositions of those Tribes."[7]

Whatever the validity of his claims, the conclusion of the War of 1812 offered Clark his first real opportunities to act on an enlarged western stage. Two themes now came to dominate his official dealings: mending fences with native people, and defending the factory trading system. In each case, whether negotiating a treaty or fending off an attack on the factory system, Clark relied on appeals to reason, order, and authority.

Clark saw treaties as the contracts for such a society. At the end of the War of 1812, he led a series of delegations to negotiate treaties of peace and friendship with western tribes, many of which had openly supported the British cause. Between 1815 and 1818, Clark met with twenty-one bands and tribes at Portage des Sioux and St. Louis. Clark's standard peace-and-friendship treaty contained three articles. Each treaty began with a ritualized formula proclaiming that both sides desired "reestablishing peace and friendship . . . and of being placed in all things, and in every respect, on the same footing upon which they stood before the late war." Recalling those woodland rituals that erased blood and bad feeling, Clark sought to "cover" the past with a blanket of friendship and goodwill. "Every injury, or act of hostility, by one or either of the contracting parties against the other," said the treaty formula, "shall be mutually forgiven and forgot." Believing that fine words and noble intentions could repeal the past, Clark's treaties went on to reaffirm earlier agreements and proclaim "perpetual peace and friendship."[8] In retrospect, these treaties seem naive, even hypocritical. But in Clark's vision of the future, treaties could restore damaged relationships and lay the groundwork for an orderly world.

As he saw it, economic regulation lay at the heart of this new order. Despite extensive frontier business experience, Clark harbored a deep-seated distrust of competition, especially within the fur trade. He lamented the continuing presence of British traders and used every diplomatic means at his disposal to curb their influence among the Indians. Even after the War of 1812, he remained convinced that Canadian agents were the source of much native suspicion and hostility. Equally distressing to him was the behavior of rival American traders. Their cutthroat business practices and fraudulent dealings were alienating potential Indian allies, driving them into the arms of the British. Like Jefferson, Clark believed that the orderly management of the fur trade was the key to peace and security on the frontier.

This view led Clark to champion the federal factory trading system as an essential part of his brokerage empire. Established during the Washington administration, the factory system sought to rationalize the fur business. The trading posts were to be buffers standing between native peoples and the global fur market. When the policy came under increasing fire from John Jacob Astor and the American Fur Company after 1814, Clark was one of the system's staunchest defenders. He argued that trade was "the great lever by which to direct the policy and conduct of the Indian tribes towards the United States." Working from this assumption, Clark openly

This Andrew Jackson peace medal, dated 1829, carries a powerful set of images that symbolized William Clark's conception of his broker role. The words Peace *and* Friendship *were common in treaties Clark negotiated with the tribes. The crossed tomahawk and peace pipe may have represented the resolution of conflict. Surely the most compelling symbol, one that crossed cultural boundaries, was the clasped hands. Many nations and fur companies presented medals to native leaders as signs of diplomatic alliance. Indians did not view them as badges of political subordination. Chiefs and headmen wore the medals as emblems of influence or conduits of spirit power. Courtesy of the Gilcrease Museum, Tulsa, Oklahoma.*

confronted Astor and the private interests. "Our own traders," he insisted, "acting in violent opposition to each other (as they very commonly do) create nearly as much confusion and dissatisfaction among the Indians as foreign traders."[9]

Clark believed that the factory system might ameliorate some of the worst abuses in the fur business while keeping native people firmly attached to American interests. Dependency without resentment was Clark's goal. But he also realized that Astor and the private traders were formidable opponents. He proposed a remarkable scheme, one that sought to blend private profit and the public good. What Clark suggested was a grand plan for a large joint-stock trading monopoly with close ties to the federal establishment.[10]

Clark's passion for order and his patrician view of the world reached to every corner of his domain. As his policy empire grew in size and complexity, he was drawn inevitably into the debate between those who dreamed of native assimilation and those who promoted Indian removal. For Clark, the argument was never that simple. As a broker, he saw native destiny as part of a continuum. Assimilation and removal were not two diametrically opposed options but aspects of a larger native survival policy.

Clark's views became clearer in the mid-1820s. With the demise of the factory system in 1822, he put increased emphasis on assimilation. In 1825, he negotiated land cession treaties with the Osage and Kansa Indians. Like Jefferson, Clark was convinced that the goal could be reached through the use of powerful cultural institutions. The Osage and Kansa treaties make it plain that he put enormous faith in European-style agriculture, formal education, and the Christian mission. Osages, for example, were promised substantial numbers of cattle, hogs, and fowl as well as farm implements. Agricultural agents and a blacksmith were part of the program. Equally important, proceeds from the sale of certain parcels of land were to be earmarked for the education of Indian children. Farming and schools were bound together by the force of Protestant Christianity.[11]

The language in these treaties echoed Jefferson's rhetoric. But Clark's assimilationist vision was not of a homogeneous nation where racial and cultural differences between native and newcomer would disappear eventually. Boundaries, both geographic and racial, would be necessary. Indian and white communities would be similar but separate. This separated-homelands approach led Clark to embrace removal as the best way to ensure order and stability. Just a year after the Osage and Kansa treaties, he put his thoughts on removal in a long report to Secretary of War James Barbour. Reflecting on the consequences of the Indian wars east of the Mississippi, Clark found those native people "weak and harmless, and most of their lands fallen into our hands." Rational values—"Justice and humanity"—now demanded that the American republic reconstruct shattered native peoples along Euramerican lines.

At the heart of Clark's vision was an unshakable belief in the transforming power of private property. "It is property which has raised the character of the southern tribes," he asserted. Noting that many of them had already voluntarily submitted to removals, he insisted that it was roads, fields, private homes, and slaves that had "enabled them to live independently, and to cultivate their minds and keep up their pride." In this scheme of cultural evolution, Clark believed that the federal government had a decisive role to play. He imagined himself the midwife in the process as native people moved from a hunting to an agricultural economy.[12] Certain the move was best for all, Clark became as ardent a removal advocate as any Jackson man.

In September 1832, as the aftershocks of the Black Hawk War rumbled through the western frontier, Clark wrote acting Secretary of War John Robb a letter urging him to be skeptical of reports by whites "who are unacquainted with their [Indian] manners."[13] The remark reveals another aspect of Clark's broker domain: his fervent wish to explain native ways to whites. For him, the explainer's task went beyond federal policy and reached into the world of science, museums, and patronage for artists and explorers.

Clark's Indian Museum was perhaps the most public demonstration of his role as cultural intermediary. His Indian collections began as a direct result of his role as a western explorer. The Lewis and Clark Expedition returned from the Pacific in 1806 carrying a virtual encyclopedia of western North America. Like other eighteenth-century Virginia Tidewater gentlemen, Clark had a taste for the curious and the exotic. As Indian superintendent and territorial governor, he was in a uniquely favorable position to acquire gifts from visiting tribal delegations, foreign travelers, and fur traders. By 1816, his collection had grown so large it required an entire room in the new Clark home on North Main Street. That year Clark decided to add a wing to his recently built brick house. One hundred feet long and thirty feet wide, the addition functioned as museum and official Indian council chamber. Soon after its completion, William C. Preston, a visitor from Virginia, paid a call on Clark and recorded what is probably the earliest account of the museum. Preston found the room "adorned with a profuse and almost gorgeous display of ornamented and painted buffalo robes, numerous strings of wampum, every variety of work of porcupine quills, skins, horns, claws, and bird skins, numerous and large Calumets, arms of all sorts, saddles, bridles, spears, powder horns, plumes, red blankets, and flags."[14] Visiting scientists agreed. The noted ethnologist Henry Rowe Schoolcraft paid a call in summer 1818 and found the museum "arranged with great taste and effect."[15] Capt. John R. Bell, a member of Stephen H. Long's western expedition, was similarly impressed, pronouncing it "tastefully arranged."[16] The museum attracted most of the foreign travelers and scientists who flocked to the West in the 1820s and 1830s, including Prince Paul Wilheim of Württemberg (1826), Bernard, Duke of Saxe-Weimar-Eisenach (1826), Captain William Drummond Stewart (1832–33), and Prince Maximilian of Wied-Neuwied (1833).

But Clark's Indian Museum was meant to be more than a quiet archive for scholarly visitors. Like Charles Willson Peale's Philadelphia museum, it was designed to entertain and inform a wider public. By 1821, the Indian Museum had become a well-known St. Louis attraction. Paxton's St. Louis city directory gave it a glowing review: "The Council Chamber of Governor William Clark, where he gives audiences to the Chiefs of the various tribes of Indians who visit St. Louis, contains probably the most complete Museum of Indian curiosities to be met with anywhere in the United States; and the governor is so polite as to permit its being visited by any person of respectability at any time."[17]

Shortly before his death in 1838, Clark began to prepare an extensive catalog of the museum collection. The list contains 201 items and reveals both the variety of Clark's holdings and his collecting method. The Indian Museum held mercifully few of the freakish curiosities that dominated so many amateur collections. There was a two-headed calf but evidently no hoop snakes or rune stones. Instead, the museum was filled with pipes, moccasins, clothing, domestic utensils, and many kinds of weapons. The largest object was a Sioux tepee given to Clark by Maj. Lawrence Tallaferro. Visitors to the museum saw a bewildering assortment of objects, arranged with little regard to provenance or tribal identification. A sample of Cherokee textile work might be displayed next to a Cheyenne bow or a Teton Sioux pipe.[18] Clark's museum was an important effort to explain native material culture to white Americans. What proved elusive were the "manners" that gave meaning to those silent objects.

Clark once described himself as a man of few resources struggling to defend native peoples against greed and violence.[19] Like so many other white brokers, Clark had to face the test of war. What could a well-intentioned intermediary do when the forces of anger and revenge occupied the field? Would treaties and museums hold back the tide of battle and dispossession? To some extent, Clark's brokering abilities had already been tested in the War of 1812 and in the removal controversies. In those crises, he proved both adept and lucky. Clark's final challenge—the Black Hawk War of 1832—demanded much greater skill and a far larger share of good fortune.

The Black Hawk War is a familiar tale of greed, misunderstanding, and revenge.[20] On the eve of the war, the Sac and Fox tribes—sometimes called the confederated tribes—numbered approximately five thousand persons. Perhaps two-thirds of them were Sacs. The largest tribal village was Saukenuk, located at the mouth of the Rock River in present-day Illinois. As the white population grew, the Sac and Fox people found it increasingly difficult to protect ancestral lands. At the heart of their problem was the Treaty of 1804. A tribal delegation had sold lands on the west side of the Mississippi for a paltry sum. The treaty was unpopular, but there was little protest since the document allowed Sac and Fox families to remain on the land until federal authorities opened it for white settlement. Lenient only for the moment, the treaty decreed that native days on the land were numbered.[21]

Intense band factionalism also weakened the Sac and Fox people. After siding with the British in the War of 1812, factional tensions increased. Keokuk, a Sac headman, urged accommodation with the United States, thereby winning favor with Clark and Indian agent Thomas Forsyth. Keokuk's most formidable political opponent was Black Hawk, an older and more prominent warrior. Leader of what came to be known as the British Band, Black Hawk clung tenaciously to a vision of past glory and armed resistance.[22]

On the eve of the Black Hawk War, William Clark's Indian brokerage was showing signs of age and decay. Having lost his bid to become Missouri's first state governor in 1820, Clark saw his political power wane. His personal influence began to decline among Indians as well as whites. Changes in federal Indian policy further weakened his position, as the new Jackson administration imposed sharp restrictions on his official jurisdiction. Illinois statehood in 1818 curtailed his dealings within state boundaries. And the loss of Forsyth, Clark's ablest agent, diminished his effectiveness among the Sac and Fox. All these problems were compounded by Clark's own frailties of body and mind. By the late 1820s, he was distinctly unwell. Worst of all, ill health was joined by a growing sense of personal failure. Political rejection was matched by a feeling that his Indian brokerage was on the edge of collapse. Treaties and good intentions had failed to stem the tide of violence.

By 1827, it must have been plain to Clark that the future of the Sac and Fox people was troubled. After the so-called Winnebago War, Illinois Gov. Ninian Edwards began to press for removal of all Indians from lands within the state. Rumors of removal sparked intense controversy between Keokuk and Black Hawk, controversy that a worried Forsyth reported to Clark.[23] By the spring of 1828, Edwards and other Illinois politicians had convinced Washington to invoke the removal clause in the 1804 treaty. Edwards also began to press Clark for action against the Sac and Fox. Twice during late May 1828 the Illinois governor wrote to Clark demanding prompt Indian removal. The most ominous was his letter of May 29. Edwards described the presence of Sac and Fox families in Illinois as "an invasion of the rights of a sovereign and independent State" and threatened to use the state militia to force removal if Clark did not press for it himself.[24]

Forsyth agreed that removal was inevitable and probably in the best interests of the Sac and Fox people.[25] Thinly veiled threats from Edwards and advice from Forsyth might have moved Clark to urge immediate removal. But Clark the broker sought time and a peaceful solution. Sometime during spring 1828 Clark met quietly with a Sac and Fox delegation led by Whishcobaugh and Nawtwaig. Representing the Keokuk faction, the delegation reported that two prominent warriors, Bad Thunder and Ihowai, were urging armed resistance. Clark was also told that many Indians were now listening to Canadian "bad birds." The delegation wanted Clark to know that removal would proceed peacefully so long as sufficient time was granted.[26] Some weeks later another delegation, this one led by the Fox chief Wapello, met with Clark. Again Clark was assured that removal would take place if Illinois officials were patient. Caution and goodwill seemed to be working, and federal officials instructed Governor Edwards to move slowly and not press too hard.[27]

Clark's diplomacy appeared successful. When Black Hawk and the British Band returned from winter hunts west of the Mississippi, Forsyth held a series of meetings with them at Fort Armstrong. While most Indians seemed ready to accept removal to Iowa, those in the British Band were utterly opposed.

And there was more potentially unsettling news. The British Band claimed an alliance with some Chippewas, Ottawas, Potawatomies, Kickapoos, and Menominees. Such an alliance was sure to weaken Keokuk's standing. Forsyth also reported that white families were beginning to settle on Sac land. A frustrated Forsyth insisted that he had "done everything in [his] power to get the Indians to remove their own Lands, but the Black Hawk with a few others are the Indians who are making all this fuss."[28]

Forsyth's gloomy report made it clear that any mediating Clark might do would meet with strong opposition. In an atmosphere of mounting fear and threats of violence, Clark began a slow retreat from his role as broker. Writing to Forsyth in early July 1829, he ordered the agent to mince no words with the British Band. "You must say to them that they cannot remain East of the Mississippi, that they must remove to their own Lands West of the River."[29] And it appeared for a moment as if this tough talk had carried the day. After negotiation sessions at Fort Armstrong with Forsyth, most

Indians, including the British Band, appeared ready to accept the Iowa resettlement alternative. Keokuk put a sharp point on the whole proceeding, telling Forsyth that "if any Indian did attempt to return to reside at Rocky River next spring they must take their chance."[30]

Black Hawk and his followers evidently weighed the chances and decided that returning to lands around Rock River was worth the risk. Urged on by Canadian officials and encouraged by talks with the Winnebago Prophet, the British Band was back in the spring of 1830. Forsyth was now convinced that only a massive show of force could defeat Black Hawk's growing influence. Forsyth urged Clark to call for the mobilization of the Illinois militia.[31] While brokering seemed less and less possible, Clark was not quite ready to abandon the role that had been so much a part of his public life. Once again he turned to treaty negotiations as a way out of potential confrontation.

Early in the spring of 1830, Clark prepared for what would prove to be the last large-scale, multitribe treaty conference of his career. The Sac and Fox troubles were of central concern, but tensions with several Sioux bands were also matters that required attention. Clark began his planning for the Prairie du Chien gathering by holding a series of three important meetings in St. Louis with Sac and Fox delegations. The first came in March, when Keokuk and his large party filled the superintendent's council room. Keokuk recited a litany of troubles and complaints, most dealing with land claims and controversies with various Sioux bands. Unspoken but ever-present was tribal anger over the 1804 treaty. Clark acknowledged that resentment but reminded Keokuk that Sac and Fox headmen had reaffirmed the treaty on at least two occasions. When Keokuk lamented the consequences of tribal factionalism, Clark quickly shifted the discussion to the removal issue and the sale of valuable mineral lands. What divided the tribes, so he claimed, was the Mississippi. Would it not be better to reunite all bands and factions somewhere west of the river? This notion did not sit well with many in Keokuk's delegation. However, their request for an immediate audience with President Jackson collided with the federal decision to have a grand council at Prairie du Chien in midsummer. The March meeting ended inconclusively, leaving both

Clark and Keokuk wondering about an increasingly uncertain fu-ture.[32]

Clark's second meeting with Keokuk came in late May. Frontier tensions were running high. In a bloody encounter known as the Warner Incident, some one hundred Menominee and Sioux war-riors had ambushed an unarmed party of Fox. It took all of For-syth's persuasive skill to keep the massacre from sparking a wider war. Clark heard all this and more when Keokuk and a large Sac and Fox delegation descended on St. Louis. Many Indians blamed the massacre on the ineptitude of Capt. Wynkoop Warner, govern-ment representative to the Foxes at Dubuque's mines. They in-sisted that Clark provide substantial gifts to "cover" the dead. And there was a further demand. The delegation refused to go to Prairie du Chien, calling for the meeting to be held instead at Rock Island. Clark was able to promise a ritual cover payment, but all other issues remained unresolved.[33]

A third gathering in early June carried the same message. The confederated tribes refused to go to Prairie du Chien, insisting that their enemies come to them. Clark saw the demand as irrational obstructionism. In his mind, another treaty, followed by prompt removal, was the tribes' only hope for peace and survival. Clark had grudging respect for what he called the "national character of the Sac and Fox tribes." Yet he was determined not to let native nationalism stand in the way of the larger American nationalism.[34]

At the end of the third meeting with Keokuk, Clark concluded that a "firm and decisive course" was now required. That meant pressing ahead with the Prairie du Chien conference no matter how much the Sac and Fox headmen protested. By early July, Clark had succeeded in cajoling some seventy Sac and Fox Indians, in-cluding Keokuk, to gather at Prairie du Chien. In talks lasting nine days, Clark laid out federal demands. The government sought land cessions, purchase of important mineral lands, and prompt remov-al. On July 15, 1830, negotiations were complete. Bearing the marks of prominent Sac and Sioux headmen and warriors, the treaty promised peace in return for land cessions and cash pay-ments.[35]

Perhaps Clark thought that the Treaty of Prairie du Chien had finally settled the entire Sac and Fox dilemma. When the Indians left Saukenuk in September, Keokuk told Forsyth they would not be coming back. Keokuk knew that lands around Saukenuk were opening for white settlement; plainly, it was time to leave. Black Hawk and his supporters were charting a far different course. Felix St. Vrain, Forsyth's replacement as agent, reported this troubling news in an early October message to Clark. The British Band would surely attempt to return in the spring, he wrote. Black Hawk had told him he hoped to speak with Clark directly, but the superintendent decided not to pursue the invitation.[36]

During the winter of 1830–31, talk of Black Hawk's return was everywhere. Illinois's new governor, John Reynolds, was determined to see all Indians removed from the state permanently. Urged on by Reynolds, the Illinois General Assembly began to debate various means to force removal. In the swirl of threats, rumors, and confusion, Clark found it increasingly difficult to play his traditional broker role. At first he hoped that a larger annuity payment might change some native minds. If that failed, he admitted, force would be the only recourse. With that admission, Clark moved another step away from brokering and much closer to advocating military action.

Clark's conversion from broker to advocate was guaranteed by the events of spring and summer 1831. On May 15, a deeply worried St. Vrain wrote him with the unsurprising news: Black Hawk and the British Band were back at their old village, busily planting corn. St. Vrain cautioned against the use of force, hoping that yet another treaty might resolve the affair.[37] Governor Reynolds was not about to be so patient. Using highly charged language, the governor wrote Clark a scathing letter, claiming that his state was being invaded by hostile forces. Reynolds had called out the Illinois militia and had ordered the troops to remove the British Band by force if necessary. Still, Reynolds hoped that Clark might be able to convince Black Hawk to leave voluntarily.[38]

With the prospect of a military confrontation involving the British Band, the Illinois militia, and regular forces under Gen. Edmund Gaines looming, Clark could do little to hold back the tide of violence. Writing to Secretary of War John H. Eaton at the end of May, he finally endorsed the use of troops. Armed force "cannot fail producing good effects, even should the Indians be disposed to remove peaceably to their own Lands; and if not, their opposition should in my opinion be put down at once."[39] Whether Clark approved it or not, force was being used against the British Band. After Gaines's troops occupied Saukenuk, Black Hawk's followers fled to the west side of the Mississippi. Keokuk now played the intermediary role, carrying messages between Black Hawk and Gaines. When negotiations at Fort Armstrong were complete, Black Hawk and others agreed to abandon all claims east of the Mississippi. Equally important from Clark's point of view was the British Band's promise to "shut their ears" to the words of Canadian "bad birds."[40]

Despite the promises made at Fort Armstrong, rumors persisted that the British Band still dreamed of returning to Saukenuk. Throughout the winter of 1831–32, Clark worried about Black Hawk as a potential Tecumseh. Mediation no longer entered his mind; strength, vigilance, and retaliation were the superintendent's new watchwords. In April, the storm came. Invited by the Winnebago Prophet, Black Hawk and his followers crossed the Mississippi and headed up the Rock River to the Prophet's home village. Governor Reynolds's response was immediate. The state militia was mobilized, and regular troops were alerted. Reynolds told Secretary of War Lewis Cass that Illinois was being invaded by "insolent and restless Indians."[41] Preparing his own assessment of the situation for Cass, Clark fully supported Reynolds's strong stand. The superintendent recommended that force be employed "to drive those hostile Bands from the Lands they have invaded." For Clark, the course seemed clear. "I am inclined to the belief that those Indians have well merited a severe chastisement."[42]

The weeks that followed brought a nightmare of violence and confusion. Events swept past Clark, and he became little more than a helpless observer. He knew that the Jackson administration was determined to crush Black Hawk, no matter what the price. In an early June 1832 report to Cass, Clark revealed just how far he had strayed from the broker role. Reading the order drafted for Gen. Henry Atkinson and his regulars, Clark found it "highly gratifying, inasmuch as it develops the determination of Government in relation to the war in which we are now involved with bloodthirsty and ferocious savages." What was happening in the Rock River country seemed to spark memories of the terrible violence in the Ohio country at the end of the eighteenth century. Reaching back to the racial rhetoric of that time, Clark unleashed a torrent of angry words.

> The faithless and treacherous character of those at the head of our Indian enemies appears now to be so well known and understood, as to permit the expression of the hope, that their wanton cruelties will eventually result in their own destruction; and as they have afforded sufficient evidence not only of their entire disregard of Treaties, but also of their deep-rooted hostility in shedding the blood of our women and children, a War of *Extermination* should be waged against them. The honor and respectability of the Government requires this: —the peace and quiet of the frontier, the lives and safety of its inhabitants *demand it*.[43]

William Clark had changed much since those days when he preached peace and counseled caution. The Black Hawk War was over by the fall of 1832. After the decisive Battle of Bad Axe, Joseph M. Street wrote to Clark reporting that "Horses and Men fell like grass before the scythe."[44] Clark's son Meriwether, aide-de-camp to General Atkinson, declared his willingness to fight with an enthusiasm that might have dismayed his father just a few years before. The young Clark hoped to lift a scalp from any "Red Rascal" and bring it home as a "trophy."[45] The war that had eroded his own son's moral values also took its toll on Clark's reputation and brokering domain. William Campbell, an influential merchant and militia officer, offered a tactful but negative evaluation of Clark in a letter to Pres. Andrew Jackson. "Perhaps the Head of the Indian Department in the West may lack a head—he has too many men at the Head—the hart may be good while the head may not."[46] Forsyth shared Campbell's views but saw no reason to be tactful. In April 1830, he had urged Clark to recommend massive force against Black Hawk, a course Clark was reluctant to pursue. A year later, Forsyth launched a bitter series of letters denouncing Clark's administrative abilities. "Great men," he scoffed, "always wish to do great things, so that it may sound well at Washington, for the more anything may cost the better it ought to be."[47] Forsyth issued a virtual bill of indictment against Clark in late May 1832. Illinois militia forces had just been soundly defeated at the Battle of Stillman's Run, and many were predicting a long and bloody Indian war. Forsyth pointed the finger of blame directly at Clark. Mocking his Indian name, Forsyth called Clark "Old Red Thunder" and dismissed his reports as "all stuff and nonsense."[48]

For all the venom in his words, Forsyth was right on one score. The events of the Black Hawk War tested Clark's brokerage and found it wanting. Good intentions, kind words, treaties, and the Indian Museum had not kept native and non-native from misunderstanding each other and ultimately resorting to violence. Clark's shortcomings were both personal and national, clear failures of age and determination. He had often been an absentee, part-time federal official, and by the late 1820s, he was deeply involved in family business affairs. Political setbacks, squabbles with subordinates, and constant ill health made matters worse. But the demise of Red-Head's domain had its origins in tensions and contradictions beyond illness and preoccupation. Clark's brokerage was based on paternalism and a profound belief in the inevitability of American geographic expansion. He expected native people to see by the light of his logic and reason the good road he had charted for them. His brokering was built not on equality but on the presumption of dependency. If native people did not accept his good fatherly advice, it was because they lived in darkness and deserved their fate. Clark's Indian Museum embodied these paternalistic attitudes. The "curiosities"—moccasins, arrows, and pipes—were reminders of what he thought was a useless, dying past. When Native Americans refused to play by his rules, Clark could speak only of punishment and extermination. In the spiral of violence, the center had not held; and in the chaos that followed, Clark and Black Hawk shared a common fate. Beaten and captured, Black Hawk was put in chains. Clark was shunted aside by the policymakers, his views largely ignored. The Red-Head Chief had become a stranger in the country he had helped to fashion.

CHAPTER 5

AN ALTERNATIVE MISSIONARY STYLE: EVAN JONES AND JOHN B. JONES AMONG THE CHEROKEES

WILLIAM G. McLOUGHLIN

> *Anything you may wish that I can do, make no hesitation in commanding my feeble efforts.*
>
> —Evan Jones to Chief John Ross offering assistance in resisting removal in 1838

> *I suppose you know that the fullbloods are at least three-quarters of this Nation. To prevent them from being crushed, I would make any sacrifice.*
>
> —John Butrick Jones to his mission board

NINETEENTH-century missionaries to Native American tribes faced a dilemma. To commit themselves and their families to lives of hardship and service among alien peoples, they had first to be certain that they preached a superior spiritual and social ideal, and second, to treat the Indians fairly, they had to free themselves from their own cultural and political biases. These prerequisites were contradictory. The "failure of the missionary enterprise," Robert F. Berkhofer argues, was "inevitable given the participants' cultural assumptions."[1] Or as Reinhold Niebuhr would put it, the missionaries "absolutized the relative." They believed that the values of Protestant American culture were the absolute and universal truths of revelation. They assumed that white Americans were God's chosen people with a manifest destiny to mold the world over in their own image. Blind to their own cultural captivity, they often appeared smug, paternalistic, and patronizing to the Indians, who, in turn, absolutized their own cultural values. Many twentieth-century historians have criticized the missionaries for their ethnocentrism and portrayed their soul saving as an effort to stamp out Indian pride, dignity, and culture. As Berkhofer has said, most missionaries believed that "the only good indian was a carbon copy of a *good* whiteman."[2]

Moreover, the claim most missionaries made, that they had not come "to meddle in politics," seemed hollow when they insisted on transforming Indian laws, traditions, customs, and behavior to fit white American mores. Like the politicians in Washington who set Indian policy, they were convinced that they knew what was best for the Indians and that they need not consult them or seek their cooperation.

It is easy to condemn missionaries for lacking the relativistic twentieth-century perspective on politics and cultural pluralism. To be fair to the missionary movement, however, historians must show that alternative approaches were practiced at the time and that these practices were not only viable but more consistent with fundamental Christian and American values. The two missionaries described in this chapter were not typical, but they did provide such an alternative. Throughout their careers, they questioned whether God was the patron of white expansionism; they sought the views and cooperation of the people they came to serve; they tolerated a syncretic adaptation of Christian faith and practice to the perspectives of Native Americans. Moreover, they frankly and openly meddled in politics when they thought morality and justice were on the side of the Indians and not of federal policy or frontier intrusion. What makes these missionaries (and the board that supported them for over half a century) important for the current reassessment of Indian missions is that by using this alternative approach, these two men became the most successful Protestant missionaries of their day. They are still remembered with honor and respect, even by Cherokees who did not become Christians.

The careers of Evan Jones and his son, John B. Jones, from 1821 to 1876 are significant because, unlike most of their fellow missionaries, their sincere dedication to Christianizing the Cherokees did not weaken their ability to transcend the trammels of ethnocentrism. For them, Christianity became a source for sustaining and revitalizing Cherokee culture against the juggernaut (or, as Charles Royce called it, "the giant anaconda") of white civilization. The Joneses saw no contradiction between preserving and evangelizing the Cherokee Nation. God was not white. Nor was he red. In becoming the most successful missionaries of their day, the Joneses found the key to good relations with the Cherokees in establishing close personal ties with the full-blood majority and with those leaders, like Chief John Ross, who supported the majority in defense of national unity and autonomy (Ross called it "Cherokee sovereignty"). They identified their goals with those of the Cherokees; they had come to help the Cherokees, not to transmogrify them. To do so, they convinced the Cherokees that the God of Christians was a source of power, hope, consolation, and justice to all who believed in him regardless of race or nationality. While they might differ with traditionalists regarding the true way to define, worship, and commune with the Great Spirit, the Giver of Breath, this in no way hindered or lessened their respect for the Cherokee people and their concern for Cherokee treaty rights and tribal structure. If God wanted peace, harmony, and love on earth, he did not want it at the expense of the Indians. The Joneses taught that the best of the traditionalist world view could be combined with the best of Christianity to restructure and strengthen their fragmented culture. Cherokee revitalization and not assimilation was their goal, as it was of those they came to assist.

For these reasons, they supported bilingual education for all Cherokees; they established a native ministry to lead Cherokee converts and trained those they ordained to be supporters of their people in politics as well as in religion. Between Cherokee national survival and the prosperity of the United States, they saw no necessary contradiction. Emerson, Whitman, and Thoreau saw this as "a nation of nations," and the Joneses agreed. The Joneses believed the Cherokees would find more strength, unity, vision, and spiritual assistance from the God of Christianity than from their traditional worship, but that did not mean they had the right to deride or disdain those Cherokees who clung to the old ways. To divide the nation between a Christian party and a Pagan party would be self-defeating. Over time, Christianity would prove itself more helpful; they labored to make it a live option.

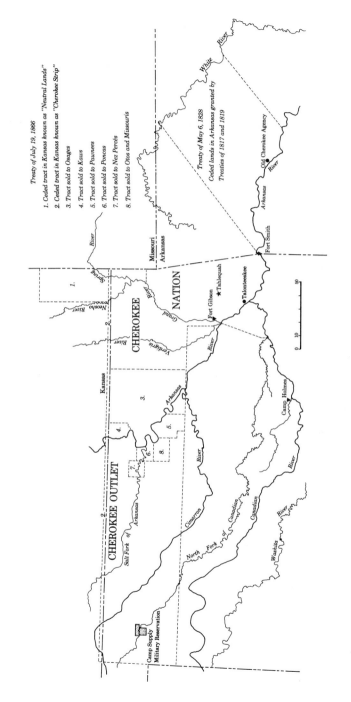

Cherokee lands in the West. From Historical Atlas of Oklahoma, 3rd ed., by John W. Morris, Charles R. Goins, and Edwin C. McReynolds. Copyright © 1965, 1976, 1986 by the University of Oklahoma Press.

Treaty of July 19, 1866

1. Ceded tract in Kansas known as "Neutral Lands"
2. Ceded tract in Kansas known as "Cherokee Strip"
3. Tract sold to Osages
4. Tract sold to Kaws
5. Tract sold to Pawnees
6. Tract sold to Poncas
7. Tract sold to Nez Percés
8. Tract sold to Otos and Missouris

Treaty of May 6, 1828
Ceded lands in Arkansas granted by
Treaties of 1817 and 1819

At bottom, the great weakness in evangelical theology from the Native Americans' point of view was its insistence on helping individuals while neglecting the well-being of the community. The Joneses realized that a religious system that placed private salvation above community solidarity threatened destruction to the Cherokees. They resisted the constant pressure of their mission board to measure success in terms of conversion statistics. Instead, they worked to build a new sense of Cherokee community in terms of the evangelical concept of brotherhood and sisterhood rather than to exalt the Protestant ethic of self-reliance. Similarly, they defended the traditional belief in the communal ownership of the land and opposed the views of contemporary reformers who insisted that only the division of Indian land into privately owned tracts could save the Indians from "disappearing."

To demonstrate their confidence in the justice and mercy of God, the Joneses spoke out against federal policies that they considered contrary to the best interests of the Cherokees. In so doing, they were rebuked by their mission board, the federal authorities, and their fellow missionaries for "meddling in politics" instead of simply saving souls. But the Joneses and their converts emphasized those biblical texts that said that God was on the side of the oppressed; he was no respecter of persons or nations but only of righteousness. Too many other missionaries placed worship of the flag on the same par as worship of the Cross or else shrugged off injustice as "God's will."

When Evan Jones, at the age of thirty-three, entered the Cherokee Nation with his wife and four children (under the aegis of the Baptist Board of Foreign Missions in Philadelphia), the Cherokees were already badly divided.[3] Almost 25 percent of the tribe of twenty thousand were of mixed ancestry, chiefly white men who had married Cherokee women and raised their children by white standards. Many of these whites came to live among the Cherokees as Tories who, after 1776, had expected that the Cherokees (loyal allies of King George III) would help defeat the Revolutionists. After 1783, these whites and their Cherokee families did not feel comfortable about returning to white society, and, having been adopted into the nation through their marriages, they stayed on to wage guerrilla warfare on white American frontiersmen until 1794. Thereafter,

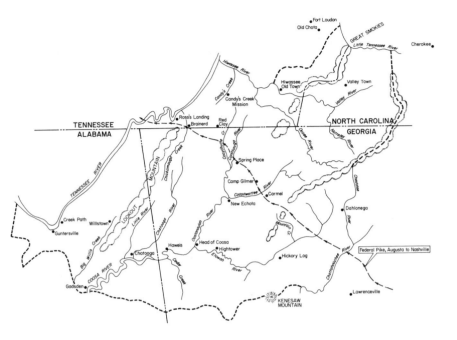

The Cherokee Nation, 1819–1838. From Fire and the Spirits: Cherokee Law from Clan to Court, *by Rennard Strickland. Copyright © 1975 by the University of Oklahoma Press.*

they played important roles in making peace with the United States and in the economic transformation of the tribe from a self-subsistent communal farming and hunting society to a market economy with intensive farming, cotton growing, cattle grazing, and trading. Many of these mixed-bloods and intermarried whites brought black slaves into the nation to do their hard labor. Because those of mixed ancestry spoke English, they proved very useful to their adopted nation by jealously guarding the treaty rights and tribal sovereignty that protected them and their enterprises. Most considered themselves nominally Christian.

Three-fourths of the Cherokees remained traditionalists. Evan Jones came to live among this Cherokee-speaking portion of the nation, which was chiefly located in the Great Smoky Mountains in the region of western North Carolina and northwestern Georgia. This group took much longer to adapt to a system of horse-and-plow farming. The chiefs, recognizing that the tribe must adapt to a new way of life now that they were surrounded by whites, sold off the hunting grounds and used the invested income to encourage nuclear families to move out of their communal villages, build log cabins, and start tilling the soil to grow their own food. At the same time, they organized a more centralized form of government and encouraged road building, trade with whites, and the admission of missionaries to start schools. However, as acculturation proceeded more rapidly among the mixed-bloods and a new national police force began to enforce laws promoting a market economy and patrilineal inheritance (and laws prohibiting polygamy, witchcraft, infanticide, Sabbath breaking, and gambling—at the insistence of missionaries), a cultural gap developed between the mixed-bloods and fullbloods. By the mid-1820s, the fullbloods, believing that acculturation was moving too fast and too far, tried to overthrow the elected government in what historians describe as "White Path's Rebellion."[4] Many of them advocated total rejection of the white man's ways and expulsion of the meddling missionaries. Most of the missionaries had shown more deference to the mixed-blood, English-speaking faction than to the fullbloods. As one missionary put it in 1816, "Those who will be the first educated will be the children of the halfbreeds and the leading men of the nation. . . . On their education and influence the character of the nation will very much depend."[5] Evan Jones rejected this elitist view of acculturation from the top down, preferring to work from the bottom up.

The most critical intratribal division developed after 1832 over the question of Indian removal. When it became clear that Andrew Jackson and the Democrats would support any state's right to expropriate Indian land, the Cherokees, like many other tribes, split over whether to move at once across the Mississippi or to remain on their ancestral land and insist on their treaty rights. In 1835, a handful of mixed-blood leaders signed a fraudulent treaty at New Echota yielding their homeland and agreeing to remove. About 3,000 Cherokees (mostly mixed-bloods) soon left for new land in what is now northeastern Oklahoma. They were known as "the

Removal party" or "the Ridge-Boudinot party." However, the over-whelming majority, 15,000 Cherokees, called "the Patriot party," led by Chief John Ross, refused to acknowledge the validity of the treaty and stood fast.

At the same time that the division grew between mixed-bloods and fullbloods (and parallel to it), there arose a division of rich and poor. Although all land was tribally owned, wealth and status accrued more rapidly to those who owned slaves. Between 1810 and 1860, the number of black slaves in the Cherokee Nation grew from 583 to over 3,000. The same pattern of social and class distinctions developed among the Cherokees as had developed between the slaveholding plantation holders in the surrounding white slave states and the poor white nonslaveholders. This division was exacerbated by the tendency of missionaries to show preference toward the "progressive" mixed-bloods and disdain toward the "backward" fullbloods. It was increased by the fact that missionaries from the slaveholding states preached that black slavery was perfectly compatible with Christianity, while missionaries from the North (especially after 1831) preached that slaveholding was a sin.

All of these internal divisions (fullblood vs. mixed-blood, slave-holding vs. nonslaveholding, Cherokee-speaking vs. English-speaking, rich vs. poor, Christian vs. traditionalist, proremoval vs. antiremoval) greatly influenced the behavior of the missionaries. Mission agencies received regular financial support from the federal government for their work and until 1832, had supported the United States' Indian policy. The War Department, which controlled Indian Affairs until 1849, considered missionaries to be the paid agents of the government and thus bound to support all official policies. The four mission agencies active among the Cherokees (Moravian, Congregational, Baptist, and Methodist) either supported removal or accepted it as an unfortunate necessity.

From the Cherokee point of view, there could be no neutrality on the issue. The Patriot party believed the missionaries should support resistance because removal was unconstitutional and unjust. The Removal party believed that the missionaries should support them because removal was unavoidable. The Reverend Samuel A. Worcester of the American Board of Commissioners for Foreign Missions agreed that the policy was unjust but, having suffered eighteen months in the Georgia Penitentiary in an unsuccessful effort to force Jackson to uphold Cherokee treaty rights, accepted removal as inevitable in 1832. With his interpreter, Elias Boudinot (a leader of the Removal party), Worcester moved west in 1835. For this he was severely criticized by the Ross party, especially the fullbloods. He never again enjoyed the popularity that was his prior to 1832. All of the Methodist missionaries opposed removal, but for this they were censured by their mission board in Tennessee. The Moravians, though opposed to removal in principle, gave up their mission stations in 1832 rather than oppose the government.

The Baptist Board (which had moved from Philadelphia to Boston in 1825) at first favored removal but modified its stance in 1832 largely because Evan Jones persuaded them that their mission would lose support if they did not take the side of the Cherokees in their struggle. The fullbloods, among whom Jones worked, were among the staunchest supporters of the Patriot party. Sympathizing with them, Jones supported their cause, but because his board preferred not to oppose removal openly (due to the large proportion of southern and frontier people in the Baptist denomination), he gave his support secretly. He did not tell his board how actively he worked with Chief John Ross and Ross's fullblood supporters in sustaining Cherokee resistance to removal. Yet this work included writing (anonymously) several antiremoval petitions to Congress signed by the Cherokees in his part of the nation, writing a tract opposing the arguments of the Removal party (which was signed by the Patriot chiefs), and openly speaking to the fullbloods in their own language at councils called to oppose removal.

While this won the admiration of the fullbloods and Ross party mixed-bloods and helped to show that not all Christian missionaries were against them, it ultimately led to Jones's being driven out of the Cherokee Nation by U.S. officials. This occurred in the summer of 1836 when the War Department sent Gen. John Wool to the Cherokee Nation to seize all guns and ammunition, fearing an armed rebellion by the Patriot party. Wool insisted that Jones assist him in his work. When Jones refused, Wool ordered him out of the nation. Jones established his family in eastern Tennessee near the Cherokee border. From there, he continued to itinerate, preach, and arouse resistance along with his Cherokee preachers. When this was discovered, federal officials threatened him with arrest, but even this did not stop him, although three Cherokees appointed to assist in removal wrote to the Commissioner of Indian Affairs on March 16, 1838, "Preacher Jones is a violent and notorious enemy of the treaty and has gone to all lengths to defeat it. He uses the sacred desk to denounce the treaty and the government, and being a proficient in the Cherokee language, he has in this way exerted an immense and dangerous influence."[6]

In June 1838, the federal government ordered General Winfield Scott to invade the Cherokee Nation, forcibly round up all Cherokees, and ship them to the west on riverboats or overland on foot, in wagons, or on horseback. When Chief Ross persuaded the general to let the Cherokees manage the removal process themselves, Ross chose Evan Jones to lead one of thirteen contingents of Cherokee emigrants along the eight-hundred-mile journey through the winter of 1838–39. Jones reported that he made more converts during the removal crisis than he had in the preceding fifteen years. Following removal, the Baptists had the largest number of Christian preachers and converts of any missionary agency. Although most traditionalists did not become Christians, they came to respect Jones for his stand; over the next thirty years, more and more traditionalists eventually became Baptists.

After Jones brought his contingent of 1,200 Cherokees safely to their new home over the Trail of Tears, he so annoyed the federal government and the Removal party by aiding the Ross party to gain dominance in their new home that complaints were lodged against him by Ross's Cherokee opponents. The War Department agreed that Jones should not be allowed to remain in the nation, but his mission board refused to appoint another missionary and protested to the secretary of war on his behalf. So did Chief Ross and the council. But not until the Jacksonians were thrown out of office and a new secretary of war was appointed in March 1841 did the federal government allow him to return to missionary work.

John B. Jones was born in the North Carolina area of the Cherokee Nation in 1824. His mother taught at the mission school, while his father, having been ordained that same year, itinerated through the nation. John grew up with Cherokee as his native language, as did several of his brothers and sisters. By the age of twenty, he had determined to become a missionary to the Cherokees. He underwent a crisis conversion at a revival meeting conducted by a Cherokee Baptist preacher whom his father had converted and ordained. His first great contribution to the Cherokees was to help his father translate the Bible into Cherokee.

Evan Jones had begun translating parts of the Bible into Cherokee as early as 1822. "It would be a great improvement in our system," he wrote to his board in 1826, "if those who don't understand English were taught to read first in Cherokee. To condemn them to the hard fate of acquiring every idea of God and his salvation, as well as the art of civilization, through the medium of an unknown tongue . . . appears to be at variance with reason."[7] By 1830, Jones had learned to write the Cherokee language in the syllabary that Sequoyah had designed in 1821. Nothing gave the fullbloods more pride than the fact that one of their own people (who himself neither read nor spoke English) had discovered a way to write their language and had made them a literate people. It also pleased them that Jones admired their language and wanted to print the Bible ("the Great Book" of the white man) in it. Jones started teaching the Sequoyan syllabary in mission schools in 1830, even though his mission board insisted that its schools be taught in English. Most mission boards believed that Indian languages were too primitive and crude to convey the complex concepts of a civilized, Christian society. As one Moravian put it, the Cherokee "language cannot be attained by Adults and when attained is incapable of conveying any Idea beyond the sphere of the sense; there seems to be no other way left by which the Spiritual or Temporal Good of these people can be promoted than by teaching them in our language."[8] Jones disagreed: "The Cherokee language possesses a great facility of combinations by which new ideas can readily be expressed." It has a "native fertility" and "we have met with several instances in which the Cherokee language expresses passages of scripture with peculiar force and beauty."[9] When the Baptist board finally provided a printing press for his mission in 1841, Jones began in earnest to translate the whole Bible. His son, John, who was more familiar with Cherokee colloquialisms, assisted him. Later John was sent East to college and divinity school where he learned Hebrew and Greek so that he could translate directly from original sources into Cherokee. Book by book, the two men produced a Bible that the Cherokees considered the best translation available to them. It was their practice to publish each book separately in their bimonthly magazine, the *Cherokee Messenger* (published wholly in Cherokee), and then to seek reactions from their readers. Passages that were unclear or did not seem to convey the true sense of the text to the average Cherokee were then revised and reprinted. The Cherokees, not the missionaries, were the judges of the translation. Other missionaries found this outrageous and believed that their translations were more accurate, but as one Cherokee who was bilingual put it (and Jones reported to his board), "Our translation is admitted to be the most correct," and "it is better Cherokee, more readily understood, and more gladly received by the full Cherokees" than any other.[10]

Although the Joneses were committed to bilingual education, the Cherokee council ruled that its public school system (adopted in 1841), supported by Cherokee funds and taught by Cherokee teachers (all mixed-bloods), must be taught in English. Not until after John Ross's death in 1866 were the Joneses able to persuade the council to try their plan. In 1866, the council adopted a series of bilingual textbooks in arithmetic, geography, and history that were to be written by John Jones and published on the Baptist printing press. These books contained the text in English on one page and the same text in Cherokee on the opposite page so that fullblood and mixed-blood children could learn all of their subjects in both languages at the same time. Unfortunately, the Cherokee Nation lacked the funds to implement this plan fully. It was strongly opposed by the wealthier English-speaking parents who wanted nothing to do with the old language.

The most difficult problem faced by the missionaries among the Cherokees in the antebellum years was the existence of black slavery.[11] In the years 1794 to 1831, they largely ignored the question, but the emergence of Garrisonian abolition in 1831 and its claim that slaveholding was a sin that must not be countenanced by Christians gradually produced a crisis in mission work. Evan Jones always disliked slavery and in 1832–33 had persuaded some slaveholding Cherokees to free their slaves. But he was no Garrisonian. Most of his converts were too poor to own slaves, and the mountain area in which he worked was not suitable for plantations. When his board asked him in 1844 to report how many of his 1,100 church members owned slaves, he replied that only four owned any, and these owned no more than two or three. He admitted that some of the Baptist missionaries had occasionally hired slave labor. He also told his board that neither he nor any other Baptist had ever preached against slavery because the Cherokee constitution and legal system accepted the institution. On this point Jones was not eager to meddle in politics.

Once the Baptist denomination in the United States split into Southern and Northern branches in 1845, the matter became more complicated. The Cherokee missionaries stayed with the Northern Baptists (ultimately competing with Southern Baptist missionaries for converts). Some Northern Baptists adopted Garrisonian principles and produced a rival board to that which supported Jones. Fearing loss of support, Jones's board urged Jones to persuade his four slaveholding members to free their slaves or leave the mission churches. At this time there were seven Cherokee Baptist churches and ten branch churches. Jones was slow to carry out this request, for he knew it would arouse a storm of protest from the Cherokee slaveholders and that the federal agent (himself a southerner who had brought his own slaves into the nation) might force his expulsion for meddling in Cherokee politics. Not until 1852 did Jones report that he had accomplished the goal and that the Baptist mission among the Cherokees was free from all collusion with slavery. Thereafter, Evan and John Jones became more ardent opponents of the institution.

The growing opposition to slavery by the Joneses did not hurt their position with the fullbloods, for they had little stake in the system and little sympathy for the wealthy mixed-blood elite who profited from it. Jones's friend, Chief Ross (himself a slaveholder of mixed ancestry), told him to restrain himself on this divisive issue. Ross knew the surrounding slaveholding states feared that the Cherokee Nation might be a haven for runaway slaves and a station on the Underground Railroad if abolitionist missionaries got a foothold there. After 1850, the tension over "Bleeding Kansas" on the northern border of the Cherokee Nation further exacerbated the situation. In addition, the other northern-based mission agency, the American Board (also located in Boston), was putting the same pressure on its missionaries that Jones had been under. However, Samuel Worcester, superintendent of the American Board's Cherokee mission, strongly disagreed with the Joneses and adamantly refused to persuade his slaveholding converts to free their slaves or leave their mission churches.

As tension mounted after 1850, the mixed-bloods who dominated the Cherokee council passed several laws restricting the work of missionaries among blacks and demanding the expulsion of any missionary tainted with abolitionism. When Ross vetoed these laws, the slaveholders founded a secret, proslavery society called first the Blue Lodge and later the Knights of the Golden Circle. Membership was limited to slaveholders who agreed to vote only for office seekers who were slaveholders (a fact that caused great concern to the nonslaveholding fullbloods when they discovered it). In addition, members were committed to take the law into their own hands against any abolitionists; that is, to raise a mob and drive such persons out of the nation. Some members of these societies broke up Baptist religious meetings and threatened bodily harm to the Joneses. This, in turn, solidified the fullbloods who feared that the proslavery faction would force the nation into an alliance with the Southern states (now threatening secession) and bring their country into a war that was not theirs.

In 1855 or 1856, the fullbloods formed their own secret society called the Keetoowah Society, partly as a counter to the Knights of the Golden Circle and partly to gain control of the Cherokee council. In effect, the Keetoowah Society was a political party created to wrest control of the government from the mixed-blood minority. But unlike White Path's Rebellion in 1824–27, this movement was much more carefully organized and politically sophisticated. It may well have drawn some of its ideas from the new Republican party in the United States. It certainly drew its chief support from the well-organized Cherokee Baptist churches and their Cherokee ministers. There seems little doubt that Evan Jones and John Jones were involved in the formation of the society and in supporting its goals. Significantly, however, the Keetoowah Society was not limited to Christians. Its constitution defined membership in terms of Cherokee-speaking persons committed to voting into office nonslaveholders and supporting a policy of neutrality in the growing animosity between the Northern and Southern states of the country. While Keetoowah meetings opened and closed with Christian prayers, the society accepted as equals any traditionalists committed to their goals. Their meetings were held secretly, usually at night in the woods. They were conducted around a council fire, and the deliberations followed the traditional ceremonial and consensual procedures of ancient Cherokee councils. Ancient dances were performed; tobacco was smoked for its spiritual powers. The syncretic nature of this organization indicated the commitment of the Joneses to tribal unity and their unwillingness to draw a sharp distinction between Christian and pagan Cherokees. Members of the Keetoowah Society guarded the religious meetings of the Baptist missionaries against proslavery agitators. Once, when the federal agent sent a sheriff to arrest the Joneses for alleged abolitionist activities, Keetoowah members gathered in front of their homes and prevented the sheriff from carrying out his orders. When proslavery leaders circulated petitions to have the Joneses expelled from the Cherokee Nation, the Keetoowahs refused to sign them. The Rev. Samuel Worcester said the Joneses could easily have obtained three times as many signatures in their defense as the totals found on proslavery petitions. The Department of Interior tried in vain to break up the Keetoowah Society.

In the end, however, the federal government proved stronger than the Cherokee majority. John B. Jones had written to his board in Boston in 1859 that proslavery mobs were threatening their work but that he was confident antislavery feeling was growing. The board published his letter in its missionary magazine. When proslavery Cherokees showed the letter to the federal agent, a Georgian named Robert Cowart, in September 1860, Cowart ordered John Jones to leave the nation within two weeks for "propagating abolition or anti-slavery sentiments among the Cherokees."[12] To avoid a possibly violent confrontation between the authorities and the Keetoowahs, Jones left. Nine months later (two months after the Civil War began), Evan Jones was forced to flee for his life to Kansas.

The story of the Cherokee Nation during the Civil War is too complex to describe in detail. However, John Ross appears to have favored support for the Union and would have welcomed military assistance in resisting the efforts of the Confederacy to force him into a treaty. Abraham Lincoln failed to send troops to protect the Indian nations in Oklahoma, and Ross felt compelled to make a treaty with the Confederacy lest it assist in a coup d'etat against him by his proslavery opponents. Evan Jones carried word from Ross to the federal officials in Kansas when he fled in June 1861, to the effect that the Cherokees were loyal but needed military aid. Jones worked desperately to have troops sent to rescue the Cherokee Nation, feeling confident that Ross would abrogate his treaty with the Confederacy as soon as federal forces arrived. In June 1862, Jones accompanied a Union regiment into the Cherokee Nation, which defeated the Confederate forces there.

Unfortunately, a mutiny prevented the permanent occupation of the nation. However, Ross agreed to return to Kansas with the retreating regiment. Two regiments of Cherokee volunteers (most of them Keetoowah members) were then formed to defend the nation. Ross went to Washington, D.C., to negotiate with Lincoln. Though Lincoln seemed favorably disposed, a decision was postponed until the end of the war. From 1862 to 1865, the Cherokee Nation was engaged in its own devastating civil war, as the Cherokee Union soldiers fought bitterly against the Confederate Cherokees. John B. Jones returned to serve as chaplain to one of the Union Cherokee regiments, and for a short time, Evan Jones served with the other. However, the latter spent most of his time in Washington with Ross trying to obtain a favorable treaty and raising funds to send food and clothing to the beleaguered pro-Union Cherokees.

In October 1865, the Cherokee council met and voted that the Joneses (and their families) should be adopted as full citizens of the nation; this act also provided grants of land for themselves and their heirs. No other missionary obtained this mark of gratitude from the Cherokees. But the services of the Joneses did not end there. John, a Cherokee by adoption, joined a delegation sent by the council to Washington where he took his father's place next to Chief Ross to negotiate, at last, a treaty that preserved the land and autonomy of the Cherokee people (despite strong government opposition on the grounds of Ross's initial betrayal in signing a treaty with the Confederacy).

The Cherokees loyal to Ross had voted to end slavery in January 1863, but this had little effect while the slaveholders retained their power under the Confederacy. During the treaty negotiations in 1866, John Jones quarreled with Chief Ross over a clause that granted Cherokee citizenship and equal rights to former Cherokee slaves. Ross shared the view of most slaveholding Indians that former slaves should be given their own tract of land in the West and not be included as members of any tribe. The federal negotiators sided with Jones, and Ross was forced to accept former slaves as full and equal black Cherokees. In the ensuing years, Jones worked hard to see that these freedmen received fair and equal treatment.[13] As missionaries, Evan Jones and John Jones felt obligated to help the Cherokees overcome the racial prejudices they had learned from the white man.

The Joneses returned to their missionary work among the Cherokees in 1866. They and the remaining native Baptist ministers reconstituted the scattered churches, rebuilt meetinghouses, and continued to evangelize among the unconverted. At the same time, they tried to help solve the new problems created by the building of railroads through the nation, by illegal squatters who settled on Cherokee land or stole their timber and coal, and by the continual effort of Congress to denationalize them by creating a federal territory in Oklahoma prior to statehood—a program that included forcing the Cherokees to adopt private ownership of land and the sale to whites of any land not occupied by Cherokees. Evan Jones lost his health after 1868 and died in 1872, but John carried on his work.

John's hand was strengthened by the continued power of the Keetoowah Society (now no longer secret) and by Pres. Ulysses S. Grant's new Indian policy. In 1869, Grant decided to appoint missionaries to be federal agents as a way of reforming corruption in the system. In 1870, he appointed John Jones as federal agent of the Cherokee Nation. John was the first Cherokee citizen to obtain this post and the first missionary to hold it. As federal agent, he used all of his skills and influence to protect Cherokee interests and to encourage the rebuilding of the wartorn nation. In 1872, he persuaded the federal government to give him sufficient cavalry troops to drive 1,500 white intruders out of the Cherokee Nation, burning the log cabins they had built as squatters, tearing down their fences and barns, and burning their fields of corn and wheat. He wanted to show the white frontiersmen that the Indians had rights that the U.S. government was bound to protect. Few whites in the West shared that view. Jones meted out the same treatment to cattlemen from Texas who drove their large herds through the Cherokee Nation before there were railroads to carry them to Kansas and ultimately to St. Louis and Chicago. The government had acknowledged the right of the Cherokees to tax such herds at a given amount per head. When the cattlemen refused to pay and threatened to shoot any Cherokee sheriff who tried to collect the tax, Jones used his authority to back up the Cherokees. He did the same with railroad companies that by the Treaty of 1866, were allowed to build one railroad from north to south and one from east to west through the Cherokee Nation. These railroads took thousands of acres of Cherokee land for their tracks and stations, paying far less than its true value; they took Cherokee timber for their ties and bridges without paying for it; they killed thousands of Cherokee cattle as food for construction gangs (or when locomotives accidentally ran into them on the tracks) and refused to pay for them. Jones used his powers as federal agent to force the railroads to make good on all the claims for redress brought by Cherokees.

While he gave up his salary as a missionary on becoming agent, he did not give up his missionary work. He continued to itinerate around the nation, strengthening the eight mission churches; he also conducted regular meetings at the Baptist mission headquarters in Tahlequah (the Cherokee Nation's capital). The Cherokee council had donated the use of 640 acres for the mission, and Jones hired experienced agronomists, nurserymen, and breeders to develop an experimental farm where they planted fruit trees and hybrid grains; they also bred horses, mules, hogs, and sheep so that Cherokee farmers could profit from the latest advances in scientific farming. He encouraged Cherokees to form agricultural societies and granges to hold annual county and national fairs to display their own successful crops, livestock breeding, and the household work of their wives and daughters. A white Baptist, married to a Cherokee, was effusive in his praise of John Jones's performance of his double responsibilities.

Brother Jones has exhibited unwearied industry since his appointment. While faithfully discharging his duties as U.S. Agent he has not left unperformed his missionary duties. Keeping up his appointments with his weekly Thursday evening prayer meeting at this place, and then mounting his horse, he has traveled to the most distant meetings at this place, and then mounting his horse, he has traveled to the most distant meetings in the various districts of the Nation, preaching in Cherokee. His labors seem almost superhuman. For the first time has the U.S. Agency truly exemplified in his social and business intercourse with this semi-civilized aboriginal people, the virtues of a Christian government. I have lived here fifteen years and can speak from personal observation.[14]

While Jones was preeminently concerned to protect the Cherokees from injustice, he was also ready to point out failings within their own social order. He protested discrimination against Cherokee freedmen when they were denied equal access to tribal land and equal participation in the Cherokee orphan fund. He criticized the tendency of the fullbloods to exclude all white men from entering the nation, even those who could be beneficial through their skills and trade. He criticized the effort of the mixed-blood elite to alter the public school system. The elite wanted to place the fullbloods in "industrial training schools" where they would be taught useful mechanical skills and thus be limited to the roles of laborers or farmhands, leaving the public schools (with their broader, more comprehensive curriculum) to the more acculturated. Jones believed this plan would promote a caste system and reduce the fullbloods to second-class citizenship.

In his annual reports to the commissioner of Indian affairs, Jones spelled out a series of long-range programs that the government should promote to assist the progress of the Cherokees. "I would therefore recommend that the Government come to the aid of the Cherokees in their noble efforts to educate their children" by providing money for two high schools where "farming, gardening, and the mechanic arts should be taught." He stressed "the importance of having all the boundary lines of the Cherokees located and marked" so that whites could not claim ignorance when they trespassed or settled inside the nation. He asked for mounted troops to patrol the borders against timber thieves, outlaws, and illegal whiskey dealers. The railroads brought in many lawless whites who were weakening the Cherokee efforts to live orderly lives. "The great majority of the [Cherokee] people," Jones wrote, "regret these [rail]roads as introductions of calamities rather than a blessing." He particularly implored Congress to resist efforts by the railroads and other special interests to detribalize the Indian nations and make Oklahoma a federal territory open to white settlement. "At each session of Congress bills are introduced and pressed for the establishment of a territorial government over the Indians and looking to the opening up of this country to settlement by the whites." These continued actions produced "among the Cherokees a deep feeling of insecurity." They felt such legislation would bring "still more crushing injuries." Thus, he said, "a feeling akin to despair is very generally prevalent." And, "the common people will be the victims" if "these evil prognostications are realized." "If the government would give them assurance that white settlers will not be permitted to force themselves into their country—that the treaty guarantees [of tribal autonomy] will be maintained," then the Cherokees would "work on the farms and in the shops, in school and church" far more "joyfully and therefore more efficiently." While Indian reformers in the East were arguing for detribalization and private ownership of land by Indians, Jones was telling his superiors,

The masses of the people . . . are utterly opposed to it . . . . I feel it my solemn duty to protest against all the bills that will rob them of their nationality [tribal identity], that will open the floodgates of immigration and pour in upon them a population that will rob them of their lands and overwhelm them with their votes, drive them to the wall, finally sweep them out of existence. I protest against it in the name of the pledged faith of the United States, in the name of honor, justice, humanity and religion.[15]

Perhaps the most important aspect of the Joneses' work after 1866 was their effort to overcome the deep animosities between the pro-Union and pro-Confederate factions. The latter, called "the Southern party," petitioned the government after the war to divide the nation into two self-governing geographic areas. The Joneses supported the majority of the Cherokees in opposing this. They regretted that Chief William Potter Ross (who succeeded his uncle, John, as chief in 1866) was so bitter toward the Southern party that he would appoint none of them to offices of any kind. Believing that this lingering division was detrimental to rebuilding the nation, the Joneses persuaded one of their ministers, Col. Lewis Downing, to run against W. P. Ross in 1867. Downing had been a leader of the Keetoowahs, a colonel of one of the Cherokee Union regiments, and was a fullblood who spoke only Cherokee. But as a Christian, he shared the Joneses' belief that charity must be shown toward former enemies, that a live-and-let-live policy was the only way to heal the factional scars. The Joneses encouraged Downing to make overtures to the Southern party and to promise them that he would treat them fairly and appoint them to high offices. This aroused the bitter animosity of Ross and even of some fullbloods loyal to the Ross party, but in the end, the Downing party triumphed. Downing's victory meant the fulfillment of the Keetoowah Society's goal of full-blood domination of the council. It also fulfilled the Joneses' goal of promoting tribal unity, peace, and harmony after years of bitter factionalism.

From the point of view of the missionary movement, the Joneses' chief accomplishment lay in their creation of a genuine Cherokee Baptist organization with its own native ministry, its own Cherokee-built and Cherokee-sustained churches, Sunday schools, and temperance societies. This had been a major goal of theirs, but it was difficult to achieve among a people so poor and so unfamiliar with Protestantism and the separation of church and state. From early in his career, Evan Jones had established places along his preaching circuits where he held revival meetings, established prayer and Bible study groups, and selected pious, conscientious converts to lead a local branch of the mission church. Following the congregational autonomy of the Baptist persuasion, he allowed branch churches to license their own exhorters, evangelists, and preachers, and when he thought they were ready, he ordained them.

Since the days of Roger Williams, the Baptists had eschewed the idea of a learned, hireling ministry. They believed that the ability to preach was a gift of God and that the gospel should be preached without pay. They saw no need for learning, for the Holy Spirit carried the word of God to sinners through the grace of God. While this view was changing in the urban areas of the United States, it remained strong on the frontier. Evan Jones himself had never attended college or divinity school. He had, however, attended a secondary school where he learned Latin, Greek, and a little Hebrew. He recognized that it would be difficult for a Cherokee not raised in a Christian community to understand the more complex aspects of the Bible. Consequently, he began in the 1830s to provide regular "meetings for instruction in theology and pastoral care" for all those who were exhorters, deacons, evangelists, preachers, and ordained pastors. Once a month, they gathered at the mission headquarters, each carrying his well-thumbed books of the Bible printed in Cherokee. They asked Evan Jones (and later his son, John) to explain those texts that they did not understand or could not explain to their congregations. Jones had collected his own library of theological books and did his best to resolve their difficulties. He also explained how to carry out their duties of church order, discipline, baptism, marriage, and counseling. Because the Baptists practiced an egalitarian, democratic church order, they shared a common tradition with Cherokee egalitarianism. They tolerated each other's weaknesses and worked in cooperation as Christian brothers and sisters. Together they built their own meetinghouses, contributing to buy nails, hinges, and window panes. They supplied out of their own larders the food needed for revival meetings. They built a sense of community and fellowship that replaced the old communal villages and local councils and clans. In these respects, Christianity—and the sense of hope, self-respect, self-discipline, and spiritual power that Christianity provided—served as a crucial revitalization movement in each of their crises.

The Joneses were successful missionaries also because they had less rigid and doctrinaire attitudes toward conversion and church membership. For this, they were severely criticized by the Moravian, Presbyterian, and Congregational missionaries. They were said to be too quick to baptize, too tolerant of loose behavior, too unconcerned with a thorough knowledge of doctrine, too negligent about church discipline. One critic said of them, "Persons can scarcely be convinced of sin or begin to think seriously on eternal things before they are dragged into the bosom of some church." The danger of this, he went on, was that "having joined a church the work is done in their estimation. Their means of receiving members is directly calculated to lead souls to hell." He continued, "No more than one out of twenty of their members is a real Christian."[16] But the Joneses' concept of evangelization was to treat conversion as the beginning of the effort, the commitment to try to become a good Christian, not the summation of or the perfect attainment of sainthood. Church membership was to provide encouragement and assistance to those struggling with the difficulties of a new set of beliefs, values, and morals. Setting membership standards too high discouraged even the most sincere efforts and often produced a sense of spiritual pride among the few who successfully met the standards.

They felt the same way about the Cherokees they licensed as preachers and ordained as pastors. They did not expect perfection, and they bore with weaknesses. This did not mean that the Joneses did not discipline and expel members who persisted in un-Christian conduct and dismiss pastors who failed to be examples to their congregations. But compared with the American Board mission churches, which excommunicated 20 to 50 percent of their members despite their high standards of admission, the Baptists were lenient and forgiving. If statistics were a measure of success (as most mission boards believed), they proved the superiority of the Baptists' practices. The American Board churches among the Cherokees reached a peak of 249 members in 1846 and declined to 136 in 1859 when the mission declared itself a success and discontinued its work in the Cherokee Nation. The Baptist mission churches had a total of 244 members in 1835 and over 1,500 by 1860. The same figures apply to the creation of a native ministry. The American Board ordained three native ministers prior to 1835 and not a single one thereafter. By 1835, Evan Jones had licensed or ordained 7; by 1860, a total of 14. John Jones ordained another 6 between 1866 and 1874. Only the Methodists rivaled the Baptists, but their convert totals included white members, and it is difficult to know exactly how many Cherokees were converts; the best estimate is that in 1860 there were 1,100.[17]

The Joneses did not convert all, or even a majority, of the full-bloods, but they did make Christianity a live option for them. Cherokees came to see that they could find strengths in Christianity that the traditional way no longer offered. And through native ministers and exhorters who preached the Bible in their own idiom and in terms of Cherokee cultural experience, the Cherokees were able to make Christianity their own and not the white man's religion. Above all, the Joneses helped the Cherokees see that Christianity had more than simply an individualistic approach to communion with the Great Spirit. They showed by their own commitment to the tribal welfare, as well as by the tribal loyalty they instilled in their members, that Christianity had a powerful binding, healing, and inspiriting power for the Cherokee Nation. By enabling the Cherokees to find in Christianity the same sense of community loyalty, family loyalty, and national loyalty that had sustained them in the past, the Joneses helped them to bridge the gap between the best of the old and the best of the new. The Joneses did this not by altering the Cherokees' identity as a people but by enhancing it: they demonstrated that one could be a good Christian and still be a good Cherokee, not a carbon copy of a white man.

CHAPTER 6

AMERICAN INDIAN SCHOOL PUPILS AS CULTURAL BROKERS: CHEROKEE GIRLS AT BRAINERD MISSION, 1828–1829

MICHAEL C. COLEMAN

We ought to strive to learn very fast, so we can teach our brothers and sisters and other heathn children.

—Susan Taylor (nine years old)

INDIAN men and women who developed special knowledge of white American society often played crucial mediatory roles as interpreters, as leaders and defenders of tribal interests, as teachers of Christianity and "civilization" to their own peoples, or as educators of whites to the realities of Indian life. Historians are aware of the influence of formal schooling on those Indians who would as adults become such cultural brokers, and Margaret Connell Szasz reminds us that "the greatest inroads upon native culture were made through their youth."[1] Yet the mediatory role of Indian children while still at school has not been given due prominence.[2]

In this chapter, I examine the ways in which a group of Cherokee girls saw themselves as cultural brokers. Pupils at the Brainerd school of the American Board of Commissioners for Foreign Missions (ABCFM) in the year 1828–29, these eleven girls, aged nine to fifteen, did not in their surviving correspondence use such a term to describe themselves. But they identified with both their Cherokee Nation and with the "Christian civilization" of their teachers. I demonstrate the specific ways in which the girls believed they were acting as mediators and suggest motivations for their behavior. Finally, I broach the complex issue of manipulation among teachers, pupils, and Cherokee adults. By providing a composite picture of one group of pupils, I intend to alert scholars to the existence of such young cultural brokers at other missionary and government schools in the United States and beyond.

When Spanish explorers first made contact with them in 1540, the Iroquoian-speaking Cherokees claimed a vast area stretching into the present states of Tennessee, Kentucky, Georgia, Alabama, Virginia, and the Carolinas. Individual Cherokees focused their loyalties on the matrilineal clan and on their village or town. There was no accepted tribal chief or government center until increasing European pressures and their own adaptive resourcefulness produced gradual centralization of political authority. During the eighteenth century, the subsistence hunting-gathering-farming economy of the tribe also began to change. Trade with and dependence on Europeans increased. Some Cherokees began to forsake communal farming, in which women played the major role, for the more individualistic, male-centered European agriculture.[3]

Although missionaries of the ABCFM claimed that the Cherokees had no real religion, they of course possessed their own rich religious beliefs, mythology, and ritual. Like many Indian peoples, they highly valued the concepts of harmony, balance, order, and sharing. "The essence of good conduct," writes William G. McLoughlin, "lay in the careful ordering of human life in relation to the natural and spiritual world." Social and moral order thus prevailed "when man was in proper harmony with his fellowmen and with all other aspects of nature."[4]

The Cherokees had long traded and—despite their ideals of harmony—fought with other Indian peoples. By the time of the American Revolution, however, they found themselves "entangled in a web of intrigue and rivalry spun in far off England, France, and Spain." Though sometimes divided among themselves, Cherokees generally sided with the British and fought against the rebellious American colonists, thus earning the enmity of many in the new nation. After two decades of continuous guerrilla warfare, most devastating to themselves, the Cherokees appeared by the 1790s to be "a ruined people."[5]

But a "Cherokee renascence" had already begun. A part-white minority enthusiastically accepted American political and legal forms, Western economic values and technology, black slavery, and the formal schooling provided by the ABCFM, Moravian, Baptist, and Methodist missions in cooperation with the U.S. government. This process culminated in the tribal constitution of 1827, which established an executive, a bicameral legislature, and a judiciary. The white-oriented elite believed they were on the way to creating a "civilized" Cherokee nation, or at least state, within the Union. The ABCFM declared with satisfaction that year, "A very considerable advance has been made recently in the organization of a regular civil government."[6]

Such developments, along with the invention by Sequoyah of a method of writing their language, caused whites to rank the Cherokees among "the five civilized tribes." But many of these "advances" provoked bitter divisions among the people. By 1827, the majority of the fifteen thousand Cherokees looked with varying degrees of suspicion on the efforts of a minority to force the pace of change and to remake the tribe according to white models. Yet most traditional (generally "full-blood") tribal members accepted the need for some change. They realized that the "half-blood" elite had become increasingly sophisticated in the ways of American politics and law and were an important buffer against the tide of white settlement rising around the much-diminished Cherokee lands. Even members of the elite had come to appreciate the precariousness and irony of their achievement. "It is true we Govern ourselves," wrote John Ridge, a tribal leader, in 1826. "Yet we live in fear."[7]

And justifiably so. For by 1838, the state of Georgia, assisted by the U.S. government, had forcibly removed most of the Cherokees from their southeastern lands and sent them on the infamous Trail of Tears to the Indian Territory in the present state of Oklahoma.

Founded in 1810 by Northern "Presbygationals" (Presbyterians and Congregationalists in union), the ABCFM was the first of many American foreign missionary societies inspired by the vibrant optimism of the Second Great Awakening. In the characteristically ethnocentric rhetoric of nineteenth-century evangelical Protestantism, the 1823 *Annual Report* of the ABCFM declared its faith in the gospel to change "heathen" Indians into "civilized" Americans, for "Christian principles only" could "transform an idle, dissolute, ignorant wanderer of the forest into a laborious, prudent and exemplary citizen."[8]

Brainerd boarding school and farm in southern Tennessee, the first Indian enterprise of the ABCFM, began operation in 1817. In the next two decades, it wielded a major influence, especially on the white-oriented Cherokees, in part fulfilling the hopes of the Boston-based society that Brainerd should be "a Primary Institution, to serve as a center of operations for evangelizing and civilizing the Cherokee nation." The ABCFM clearly intended a mediatory role for the school: soon pupils would "be mingling with their countrymen, and imparting their acquired character to others, and they to others still, in a wider and still wider range."[9] Acculturating Cherokee families were also willing to utilize Indian children as bearers of the new knowledge, which they hoped to adapt to personal and tribal needs.[10]

By the late 1820s, the ABCFM Cherokee mission had become "an international showpiece"; it had grown to eight schools, with an enrollment of about two hundred boys and girls, overseen by thirty-five missionaries, wives, teachers, and other staff. The regimented school day began at 5:30 A.M. and ended at 9:00 P.M. and was divided into periods for learning and for productive recreation. The curriculum at Brainerd, the major school, included English, arithmetic, history, geography, and constant religious instruction. The board also demanded physical labor appropriate to "correct" gender roles: "domestic" work such as dressmaking and cooking from the girls, "men's" work such as farming from the boys. In 1827, there were about fifty pupils at the school, almost half of them girls—the sexes were schooled in separate buildings—and the *Annual Report* proudly claimed that Brainerd "continue[d] to flourish." A recent examination had been "peculiarly gratifying." Two of the senior girls, Nancy Reece and Susan Taylor, "answered sixty two questions in geography; (many of the answers being very long and complicated) without any mistake except in regard to the southern boundary of one of the United States."[11]

The same Nancy Reece, fifteen-year-old daughter of a Brainerd church elder and interpreter of mixed ancestry, wrote one-third of the fifty or so letters on which this study is based. Sent to white benefactors, fellow Cherokees, and Choctaws, these letters appear to be copies in the same hand. Yet with their varied voices, differing language sophistication, and moving blend of anxiety and optimism, they are undoubtedly verbatim copies. Lucy Ames, who arrived from New England as the girls' teacher in 1827, probably copied out the impressive and often touching efforts of her pupils before sending the letters on to potential contributors. She thus provided the historian with a small but rich source for analyzing how one group of young Indians felt about their own roles in an adult scheme of things.[12]

Because of the influences of their acculturating families, who began the process of alienating them from traditional culture, and then of their teachers, these girls strongly identified with the new order. They thus delivered a powerful message of Cherokee potential and missionary achievement. "First I will tell you about the Cherokees," wrote twelve-year-old Sally Reece, Nancy's sister. "I think they improve. They have a printing press and print a paper which is called the Cherokee Phoenix. They come to meetings on Sabbath days." Inseparable from this pride was sense of humiliation that some of the tribe should cling to the ways of the past. There were "yet a great many bad customs but I hope all these things will soon be done away. They have thought more about the savior lately. I hope this nation will soon become civilized and enlightened."[13]

Elizabeth Taylor, daughter of a prominent member of the elite, wrote the most sophisticated English of these Cherokee pupils. Implying that even to discuss the old ways was to risk contamination—a vestigial sense of taboo, perhaps—she acceded to the teacher's request that she do so but only for the worthiest, most mediatory end. "I am willing," she wrote, "because I think when Christians know how much we need the means of knowledge; They will feel the importance of sending missionaries." Obviously, she had learned the attitudes as well as the language of "civilization."

The unenlighted parts of this nation assemble for dances around a fire. . . . And keep up their amusements all night. . . . When they wish it to rain; they will send for a conjuror who will throw a black cat into the water, hang up a serpent, etc.

Likewise when they are sick they get one to blow and throw cold water on them and mutter over talk that cannot be understood—Every year when the green corn, beans, etc. are large enough to eat—they dance one night and torture themselves by scratching their bodies with snakes teeth before they will eat any.[14]

By using "they," Taylor distanced herself from the "unenlighted." And, like many of the girls, she expressed anxious gratitude to her teachers. "I hope I feel thankful for the good that the missionaries are doing in bringing the word of God to this people."[15]

These Brainerd pupils had deeply internalized a guilt-provoking Calvinism, stripped of predestination but not of a severely judgmental God. "Among others the girls of this school have thought more about the Savior and that they were sinners," declared Nancy Reece. "I have thought more than I did and some times I think that my heart is changed and at other times I am doubtful." Pupils could express their sense of spiritual humiliation far more starkly. Noting that some girls had been "serious about there wicked hearts" and had "retired to there Chambers to pray," ten-year-old Lucy McPherson contemplated her own state. "I think you wish to know about my feelings I feel as though I am a great sinner and very wicked sinner. . . . When I sing I always felt very bad it seems that I was mocking God." No doubt teachers influenced such thinking. Yet the varied voices and language levels lend credibility to the words, and individuals could write with great enthusiasm for the new religion. Nancy Reece, for example, ended her anxious passage, "I love to think about the Savior and love to pray to Him, and pray that there may be a survival [sic] of religion here."[16]

Identification with their teachers' message did not lead to total cultural transformation. The girls could have become so fascinated by the ways of white society that they sought escape from the Cherokee Nation and its "unenlighted" majority. Although they expressed strong curiosity about the outside world and often begged benefactors to visit the school, none indicated that they intended to live beyond the nation. What enabled these children to be brokers, then, was an equally strong identification with all of their own people, the majority as well as the elite.

This identification, as McLoughlin notes, could also provoke deep anxiety. Convinced of the inferiority of traditional Cherokee values, they sometimes wondered if their people might be racially inferior to "civilized" folk. Nancy Reece caught both the fears and the hopes when she wrote of two white pupils in the school. "We often say that they can do well because they are white girls." But then she added her teacher's and her own corrective. Miss Ames said "people in the North think that the Cherokees have as good a genius to learn if it was only cultivated. And I think they have. I feel more encouraged to learn every day." And Elizabeth Taylor ended her contemptuous account of the old ways with the optimistic comment, "Many about this station are more civilized. Some come to meeting and appear as well as white people. . . . I have learned that the white people were once as degraded as this people; and that encourages me to think that this nation will soon become enlighted."[17]

In words clearly intended to win support for both the mission and the Cherokees, these girls declared the potential of *all* the nation; they did not trace the achievements of the elite to their part-white "blood." The girls' desire for "civilization," combined with a contempt for traditional ways, coexisted with a proud, if sometimes shaky, Cherokee identity. This new form of tribal patriotism received support from the missionaries. They had, in other words, a many-sided effect on their pupils. They generated within them a sense of spiritual and cultural self-loathing; yet they also worked to convince the girls that they could be as good as whites. "My teacher says that I can write as well as the scholars in the North if I try," Lucy McPherson told a correspondent. "When Miss Ames first came into school she said that 'can't' was a phrase which must not be allowed in school. In a short time I felt that I did not wish to use the word."[18]

These girls did more than identify with both the mission and the Cherokee people. In letter after letter, they described their own and their classmates' mediatory roles.

The use of older pupils to tutor younger ones was an important element in the Lancastrian system of pedagogy espoused by the ABCFM at Brainerd. "I am writing fine hand," claimed Lucy McPherson. "I begun about three months ago. First I began long marks. Betsy Taylor wrote it for me and begun it for me." Fortunately for the mission, some acculturated children still spoke Cherokee. Nancy Reece, for example, noted that she acted as interpreter for Miss Ames. The young Cherokee taught a Sunday School class, probably to "full-blood" pupils. "I ask those children who do not talk English if they understood the sermon that was read. . . . I try to tell them how to spend the Sabbath day and tell them where they will go when they die if they are not good. When they first enter school if they are asked these questions they often say that they don't know." Reece was clearly aware of her brokering role, as she eased "heathen" children into the new way.[19] Enlightened pupils could also make their influence felt beyond Brainerd. Lucy A. Campbell, a twelve-year-old, wrote that she intended to "take care of [her] mother's house, and to teach poor children who can not come to missionaries school." Nancy Reece hinted at the impact of schooling on traditional Cherokee respect for age, when she suggested that pupils could "take care of their houses and their brothers and sisters and perhaps can learn their parents something that they do not understand." Children also directly advised parents and other relatives. "Mother and Father you must talk to my Brothers about God, who lives in heaven," admonished Lucy McPherson, "[and] tell George that he must pray to God."[20] Despite the challenge to adult authority, the very act of writing home in English must have impressed acculturating families. The attempt to influence kin is especially evident in the letter written by twelve-year-old Polly Wilson to her brother John, apparently a pupil in another school.

Dear Brother,

I cannot say much but I will speak a few words to you. Love your God and pray to him and you must not play on the sabbath; think about God, and you must mind your teachers and love your school mates. You must not quarrel with them. John I think it is about five years since I saw you last. Mothers [sic] is well and Brothers and sisters are well. . . . I wish to know how you are learning. You must not be idle in school. I hope that you are learning fast. You must study diligently, speak up plain and loud when you read. I am still living with my Grandmother she is very kind to me. . . . Aunt Peggy McCoy's little boy is bu[r]nt to death by catching fire to his clothes. This is another call for us to repent of our sins. I hope you will think of this. From your affectionate

sister Polly Wilson[21]

The juxtaposition of family news with religious and scholarly exhortation indicates pupil authorship of at least the final draft of this letter. Whatever the degree of teacher influence, Wilson and her classmates clearly saw themselves as responsible for the education of those outside Brainerd. "We ought to strive to learn very fast," wrote Susan Taylor, Elizabeth's younger sister, "so we can teach our brothers and sisters and other heathn children."[22]

A preachy yet deferential letter addressed to young Choctaws indicates how the mediatory ambitions of the Brainerd girls extended beyond the Cherokee Nation. It also suggests how missionary teachings could promote cross-tribal influences and even stimulate Pan-Indianism. "We heard that the Choctaws were improving further than they formerly did in their learning," wrote twelve-year-old Lucy A. C. Reece, "that they left off drinking ardent spirits and I hope they will still continue to do so. I think our Nation ought to follow the good example of the Choctaws." Recounting that Miss Ames had encouraged the girls to form their own missionary organization, Nancy Reece hoped they could thus help the unevangelized outside America. "We have a Society," she wrote. "We are trying to make something as the Northern ladies do in their Societies to get some money for the Board so that they can send out more missionaries to the heathen." The extent of her identification with the mission is clear, as she continued, "I have been thinking that perhaps we shall have enough to support a heathen child." She was very interested in the society, which met "in the hours that were given to us to play." Without one, she said, "we should be wasting our time." Her account conveys the skillful means by which Miss Ames evoked youthful gratitude, guilt, enthusiasm, and racial ambition to elicit cooperation.[23]

Pupils could also become personal brokers for their own teachers. When Nancy Reece noted that her time had "been occupied in writing to Miss Ames friends," she intended no complaint. Though often requested to write these letters, the pupils generally saw the task as a privilege. Reece said, "[I] love to write to our teacher's friends and love to hear from them." She was especially "glad of the opportunity" to correspond with the Ames family. She expressed concern when Miss Ames failed to receive letters from home, thereby mediating between her teacher and distant relatives and friends. The Cherokee pupil even preached the Protestant work ethic and offered Indian children as examples to Miss Ames's young sister. "Some of the little girls [at Brainerd] rather have their books to read than to play. I hope you keep to your books and try to learn all you can."[24]

Much of the girls' writing was for the purpose of thanking benefactors for gifts of clothes or religious tracts or for letters written to the school. Missionaries realized the unique impact of letters penned by Indian children to potential supporters of the cause. While concerned about their "unworthiness," pupils too could sense their own exotic value. "I think that you would be as well pleased to receive a letter from a Cherokee girl," wrote Lucy A. Campbell, "as you would from a child that had been educated better." Many would have found it difficult to resist such an introduction, or a similar plea from Nancy Reece: "I know you are a kind friend of the Cherokees."[25]

"Civilized" manners demanded gifts in return; sending small samples of their handicrafts to supporters probably also appealed to what remained of the girls' Cherokee sense of reciprocity. Lucy A. C. Reece was clearly aware of the effect of such gifts. "We have sent many Specimens of our work to different parts of the United States," she wrote, "and we are very happy to hear that people are pleased with them and that they are convinced that Indians can learn."[26] If there is a hint of anxiety in her words, there is also satisfaction that she has played a role in persuading "civilized" men and women to think well of the Cherokees. Despite the humility, another girl carried off her gift-giving task remarkably well.

To the President of the United States

Brainerd Cherokee Nation

Sir,

We heard that the Cherokees were going to send you a mink skin and a pipe. We thought that it would make you laugh; and the Scholars asked our teacher if they might make you a present and she told us that she did not know as there was anything suitable in the whole establishment. Then she looked among the articles of the girls society and told me that I might make you a pocket book. Will you please accept it from a little Cherokee girl aged nine years.

Christiana McPherson[27]

Perhaps McPherson and her classmates hoped that such gifts would soften President Jackson's heart, because by 1829, the Cherokees were entering on their greatest battle against removal. In this struggle, some Brainerd girls demonstrated an awareness of their own roles as defenders of tribal interests. "We heard you was at Washington," wrote twelve-year-old Ann Bush to the ABCFM secretary, Jeremiah Everts, "and I think you are pleading for the Cherokees that they may stay in their own country." The older Nancy Reece skillfully worked on the feelings of a potential ally. "I do not think that all the people are friends to the Cherokees," she wrote to a correspondent on Christmas Day 1828. "Perhaps he [the president] does not like the laws of the Indian tribe for he says 'This state of things requires that a remedy should be provided.'" Although Miss Ames had encouraged the girls to accept whatever happened as the will of God and to get enough education to teach the people in the new land, some of the younger pupils were far from resigned to removal. Their words, quoted by Reece, strike the only resentful tone in these letters. Perhaps by including the complaints, Reece gave vent to her own feelings without openly offending her teacher. "'If the white people want more land let them go back to the country where they came from,'" said one pupil; "'they have more land than they can use, what do they want to get ours for?'" complained another. Then, in an abrupt change of tone, Reece continued, "I will tell you something of our happy school, so you may know how we shall feel if we should be separated from each other, and from our teachers and other missionaries." It was an inspired attempt, no doubt partly missionary inspired, to convince a benefactor of the true awfulness of removal, which would not only cost the Cherokees their homelands but would also destroy decades of Christian endeavor in the Cherokee Nation.[28]

If much of the mediation of these girls was a one-way promotion of the Christian civilization among their own people, they also sought to convince non-native Americans of the rights and racial potential of the Cherokees. Although generally supporting the missionary contempt for traditional ways, they also conveyed something of Cherokee values to the whites. By seeking northeastern support against removal, for example, they implied that even the new, "civilized" Cherokee identity was grounded in older concepts of the sacredness of a homeland. And in a defense of tribal concepts of responsibility, Nancy Reece wrote, "Orphans among the Cherokees have generally some kind friends, who do not think it right if they do not take them and give them victuals and clothes and often they do as well by them as they do by their own children."[29]

Thus, there were many dimensions to the Brainerd girls' brokering, ranging from admonishing Cherokee kin to pleading for their people's rights to interceding for a teacher. By writing to distant benefactors, irrespective of how freely they did so, the pupils became morale-sustaining and fund-raising accomplices of the mission. They mediated between Americans and Cherokees, then, and among groups of Americans, missionaries in the field and supporters on the home front. And, when Ann Bush asked a distant clergyman to "pray for the Cherokees," she enlisted him as co-mediator between her people and their new God.[30] Such responsibilities would have demanded much of adults. Why were young girls willing to accept them?

The tribal constitution of 1827 stated that "schools and the means of education shall forever be encouraged in this Nation." Although she may have been unaware of these words, Lucy McPherson knew that the "more civilized" parents felt "more anxious that their families should have an education." Charles Reece sent nine children to Brainerd, supporting Sally Reece's contention that he believed it was "a great privilege to learn to read." Cherokee girls may have been unusually sensitive to such parental pressures, because members of the elite were particularly anxious that their daughters become submissive "ladies"—in deliberate contrast to the socially, economically, and politically influential women of traditional matrilineal society. Perhaps Elizabeth Taylor's words best express the pupils' respect for such parents: "Father is very well satisfied with my improvement this last season."[31]

The girls' surrogate parents provided an almost equally powerful incentive. "We out [sic] to be thankful to the Missionaries for what they have done for us," wrote Lucy A. Campbell in a typical passage. "If they had not come out to teach us we should not have known any thing about the Bible or any other reading." Then she concluded, "They teach us for nothing [and] this ought to teach us to be grateful and to do good to others as [they] have done good to us." Missionaries probably emphasized their own sacrifices to provoke student indebtedness, but, as we have seen, they could also inspire affection and loyalty. Nancy Reece called Miss Ames her "dear teacher" and worried to the woman's parents about her being so far from home. "I sometimes think that I should be willing that she should leave the school to visit you," she wrote, "though I should be sorry to part with her." At Brainerd, as elsewhere, the teacher was crucial to motivation, especially for gifted but shy students such as Reece.[32]

The fear of damnation prompted students to both greater examination of their own souls and greater efforts on behalf of their unconverted people. The hope of small rewards, such as books or tracts, may have encouraged cooperation. Peer dynamics also played a part in motivation: one pupil reported that she was writing a letter because others did so. Further, the Lancastrian monitorial system and the need for interpreters allowed older pupils to wield a degree of influence or even power over younger children. Along with burdens, then, the brokering could provide privileges that were sometimes unevenly distributed.[33]

Yet none of these factors fully explain Nancy Reece's enthusiasm. "The girls are learning fast," she wrote. "I love my school very much. I love it better every year." The joy of hearing about the strange world outside the Cherokee Nation ("I can see such things when Miss Ames is telling me about them"), the thrill of encountering her first piano, of succeeding as well as whites at academic challenges—such pleasure suffuses her letters. "Mary Ann Vail [daughter of white missionaries] and I are just beginning to study grammar," she informed one correspondent. "We understand it better than I expected. . . . I think I will try hard and I shall continue it better after a while." By asking the correspondent to write to her individually, the young Cherokee sought to continue both her exploration of the great world outside and her work on behalf of the mission and her people. James A. Clifton has argued against the facile stereotyping of cultural brokers as being inevitably diminished psychologically by their supposed "marginality" between cultures. Pupils like Nancy Reece give weight to Clifton's claim that the brokering experience could also produce "enlarg[ed] cognitive worlds" and great personal satisfaction.[34]

Certainly, a sense of doing important work for both the people and the mission emanates from accounts of tutoring younger pupils, admonishing kin and whites, forming the missionary society, appealing to benefactors on the issue of removal, and presenting gifts to white men and women. The girls were convinced that they were in a privileged position as scholars: to be allowed to write to "ladies" and "gentlemen," to the secretary of the ABCFM, to the president of the United States, and above all, to feel they were potentially equal to white Americans—this was heady stuff to children of families struggling to become "civilized."

Yet it could be argued that these girls were above all victims, exploited or at least manipulated by both their own families and the missionaries. More than pupils at most white schools and more than Indian children within tribal patterns of education, the girls of Brainerd had to bear heavy responsibilities. But there were strong inducements for them to cooperate in this work of brokering between the often differing needs of parents, teachers, and those outside the nation. If few complied as enthusiastically as Nancy Reece, the fact that all accepted their mediatory role should warn us against too easily perceiving them exclusively as victims. Further, the manipulation emanated from both cultures. Nancy Reece described how a pupil once promised to give Miss Ames "a Cherokee cotton frock" if she would sing with the girls.[35] More significant, the pupils saw themselves as helping their families to build a new kind of nation, one that could resist white demands for removal. Many Cherokees believed that "civilized" education was a prerequisite to achieving this end. So despite apparently selfless devotion to teachers, the Brainerd girls—and their parents—were in fact making use of the mission for their own purposes and for the good of the Cherokee Nation.

I make no claims for the representativeness of one group of girls. Even within the ABCFM Cherokee mission, there were pupils who responded less positively or prematurely left the schools.[36] The words of Nancy Reece and her classmates have survived because they appealed so strongly to missionary sensibilities; uncooperative pupils, or those who wrote weaker English, would hardly have been encouraged to write to benefactors. Yet these young Cherokee mediators were not unique. Pupils at missionary and U.S. government schools during the nineteenth century and into the twentieth century also accepted mediatory tasks—or had mediatory tasks thrust on them.[37] In performing such demanding yet sometimes personally satisfying duties, the Brainerd girls, like many other young Indian pupils, played an important part in the complex cultural confrontations between their own peoples and white Americans.

PART THREE

BROKERS FOR THE WILD WEST

The tensions borne by cultural brokers of the removal era may have been daunting, but in retrospect, they may have been no more challenging than those borne by brokers of the late nineteenth century and early twentieth century. In this era, brokers confronted an American nation that was closing in on the West.

The decades between 1875 and 1915 saw the completion of the transcontinental rail lines, the destruction of the buffalo herds, the last of the wars between natives and outsiders, and the enforced migration of remaining Indians onto reservations. These events all pointed to a pincer movement surrounding the West and its native people, thereby encouraging eastern reformers and land-hungry Euramerican westerners to seize the initiative in the passage of the General Allotment Act by the U.S. Congress and the establishment of federal Indian boarding schools in the United States and Canada. These actions were met by considerable resistance. In these transitional decades, native people employed numerous strategies designed to preserve their tribal structures, ceremonies, and heritage as well as their shrinking land base. Conflict between the powers of change and the powers of continuity meant that the stakes were high on both sides of the cultural divide.

Those brokers who dealt within this highly charged atmosphere contended with intensive pressures. On one side, they encountered the acquisitive Gilded Age mentality, along with the ethnocentric reformers and fledgling anthropologists; on the other, they encountered tribal peoples who were often of several minds about the pas-

sage of the old ways. The brokers of this era frequently relied on their own cultural values for guidelines, but they also practiced the art of compromise, which meant knowing when to yield for the benefit of future generations (a tactic that might have benefited both Black Hawk and William Clark).

Consequently, as they moved toward their goals, a number of these intermediaries followed a rather circuitous route. The three female Tlingit teachers described by Victoria Wyatt in chapter 9 found themselves torn between the older cultural patterns and those that were imported. Although they chose to adopt the Protestant, Western world views of their teachers, they did not forego all of their own heritage. By translating the Bible into Tlingit and celebrating mythology through their writing, they blended the familiar with the new. Perhaps they saw the merits of a syncretic pattern attained by sifting the outside beliefs through a Tlingit screen.

In a similar fashion, the three intermediaries who served as liaisons for Edward Curtis were torn between two ambivalent commitments. They valued Curtis's ethnological enterprise but recoiled from the prospect of violating the laws or customs of the Navajo, Kwakiutl, Crow, or other tribes. In some instances they were successful in fulfilling demands from both directions. Despite Curtis's bullying behavior, the keepers of the ceremonies were, on occasion, able to satisfy him without revealing the secrets he sought. This does not suggest that these intermediaries were not without scruples. Their unethical trading of certain items was clearly a violation of tribal culture codes, as Mick Gidley reiterates in chapter 10. But it does suggest that their brokering was a two-edged sword: their determination to educate outsiders demanded compromise within.

By contrast, the portrait of Helen Hunt Jackson drawn by Valerie Sherer Mathes in chapter 7 suggests that Jackson's unusual brokering stance was at variance with that of the others. Jackson could afford to be more straightforward because she was not defending her own heritage. Consequently, she made few compromises. When she stepped on the toes of Secretary of the Interior Carl Schurz, it was a measure calculated to gain public support and congressional action. With little hesitation and with an intensity of purpose, she gained land and specific rights for the tribes she supported and left a heritage of concern among other reformers—all in the space of six years.

Like Jackson, the Indians of the Wild West shows compromised less than the Tlingit teachers or the brokers for Curtis. To the contemporary reformers and some historians, it appeared as though the show Indians were being manipulated by the show organizers, such as William F. Cody. In chapter 8, L. G. Moses argues, however, that they traveled through their own volition, that they were paid well, and that they enjoyed both performing and seeing the outside world. Hence, they achieved Cody's goal as interpreters in dual directions: they depicted the "real" West to outsiders, and they portrayed the strange world east of the Great Plains to their own people. But the show Indians also explored the ways of the outsiders, and to the degree that they incorporated these cultural patterns into their own communities, they, like the Tlingit teachers, were instructing their people in lessons of adaptation.

CHAPTER 7

HELEN HUNT JACKSON AS POWER BROKER

VALERIE SHERER MATHES

"FROM my death bed I send you message of heart-felt thanks for what you have already done for the Indians," wrote fifty-five-year-old Helen Hunt Jackson to President Grover Cleveland on August 8, 1885. She hoped it would be his hand that was "destined to . . . [right] the wrongs of the Indian race."[1] Writing of her passing four days later, friend and mentor Thomas Wentworth Higginson remarked that she met death fearlessly "in the hope of immortality" because she saw "positive evidence that she had done good by her work."[2]

Jackson was a prominent nineteenth-century literary figure who for seven years relentlessly exposed the dismal condition of America's Indians through her articles and books, *A Century of Dishonor* and *Ramona*. Her writings were so persuasive that after her death, philanthropists and reformers within the Women's National Indian Association (WNIA), the Indian Rights Association (IRA), and the Lake Mohonk Conference carried on her unfinished work.[3] But her impact was not limited to the public and reformers. She also worked tirelessly with and sometimes against government officials in the hope of protecting the Indian land base. In this brief interlude, she became a cultural broker by serving and protecting Indian rights.

Her role as cultural broker can be divided into three stages. The first began with her introduction to the Ponca chief, Standing Bear, and was followed by her highly visible campaign on behalf of the tribe. The second phase was her attempt in *A Century of Dishonor* to awaken both Congress and the public to the plight of all Indians. The third was her work among the Mission Indians and the subsequent writing of her protest novel, *Ramona*.

What is remarkable about her work is that it was condensed into the short period between 1879 and her death in 1885. Unlike many nineteenth-century Indian reformers, Jackson did not participate in other humanitarian movements, but once she was exposed to the Indian cause, she became quite possessed. "I shall be found with 'Indians' engraved on my brain when I am dead . . . . A fire has been kindled within me which will never go out,"[4] she wrote to Charles Dudley Warner, editor of the *Hartford Courant*, in December 1879. To Higginson she confided, "I cannot think of anything else from morning to night."[5]

Born in Amherst, Massachusetts, on October 14, 1830, Jackson was the daughter of an Amherst College professor of languages. As a highly inquisitive youngster, she fit well into the academic circle and would later be comfortable mingling in the literary circles of Newport, Boston, and New York. Following the deaths of her first husband, Edward Bissell Hunt, and the couple's two sons, Jackson turned to a career in writing. In 1875, she married William Sharpless Jackson, a Colorado Springs banker and railroad promoter, whose position enabled her to commute on free railroad passes between the East and Colorado Springs.

In fall 1879, she traveled to Boston to visit her eastern literary friends. Her chance attendance at Standing Bear's lecture profoundly changed her life. She listened to the dignified sixty-year-old Indian relate his people's anguish over the loss of their South Dakota homeland, which had inadvertently been included in the Great Sioux Reservation. When the Sioux had demanded Ponca removal, Secretary of the Interior Schurz, fearful of the fate of the small Ponca tribe, had ordered them moved to Indian Territory in 1877. Within two years almost two hundred Ponca had perished, including Standing Bear's son, whose dying wish was to be buried in their ancestral land. With the body of his son, the old chief and a small band of followers headed north on January 2, 1879. Ten weeks later they arrived at the Omaha reservation in Nebraska.

Brig. Gen. George Crook, commander of the Department of the Platte, ordered the Poncas arrested for leaving without permission. During the Indians' detainment at Fort Omaha, Crook, accompa-

Helen Hunt Jackson. Special Collections, The Jones Library, Inc., Amherst, Massachusetts.

nied by newspaper editor Thomas Henry Tibbles, interviewed them. Tibbles, deeply moved by their story, hired lawyers and publicized their condition. A former evangelical circuit preacher, he organized fellow ministers and Christian laymen into the Omaha Committee, a group interested in reuniting all Poncas on their former Dakota lands.

In the case of *Standing Bear v. Crook*, Nebraska District Court Judge Elmer S. Dundy determined that Indians were "legal persons" entitled to sue for a writ of habeas corpus. With this victory in hand, Tibbles organized a six-month tour of eastern cities to generate support. Among those drawn to the plight of the Ponca were Gov. John D. Long, Boston Mayor Frederick O. Prince, Massachusetts Sen. Henry L. Dawes, poet Henry Wadsworth Longfellow, Delano Goddard (editor of the *Boston Daily Advertiser*), and Helen Hunt Jackson. They organized the Boston Indian Citizenship Committee to fight for the rights of the Poncas and other Indians.[6]

Thus began the first phase of Jackson's role as cultural broker. Ironically, as a publicist for the Poncas, she also became what she believed to be the "most odious thing in life"—"a woman with a hobby."[7] Inspired by the Poncas, she began to spend five to six hours a day researching in the Astor Library in New York City. She also made strong demands on friends, admonishing Warner of the *Hartford Courant* to reprint an article about the Poncas and not to be "funny" about the Indians. If he was "agin" them, he was not to mention it when they next met.[8]

Others who received her verbal blows included the Reverend Moncure D. Conway, former Unitarian minister and abolitionist. To elicit some interest from him, she described the Indians as "higher nobler creatures" living under conditions far worse than those of slaves. They were prisoners "left to starve—and forced into poisonous climates to die."[9] She failed, however, to gain him as an ally. Whitelaw Reid, managing editor and owner of the *New York Daily Tribune*, also displeased Jackson. "I can't make Reid print my things," she wrote to Warner, "and I am chafing under the misery of not saying half I want to."[10] Later she apologized to Reid for attacking his paper, which recently not only covered the Poncas' New York City visit but had also published Jackson's letter of December 11 to the editor and an editorial drawing readers' attention to it.

In this letter, Jackson offered ten questions for the public to ponder. She asked, for example, if they were aware of the condition of the Poncas and of the White River Utes. The latter were dying because their annual supplies were deliberately withheld by government officials. She wondered if the government intended to "keep the Indians as National paupers."[11]

Schurz's reaction was immediate. After telegraphing the *Tribune* for an interview, he wrote a lengthy rebuttal, addressing each one of the questions. Delighted by his response, Jackson described the secretary as a "blockhead" to William Hayes Ward, editor of the *New York Independent*.[12] At various times she referred to Schurz as stupid, a liar, and an arch hypocrite. Observing him during governmental hearings in Washington, D.C., in early 1881, she wrote to Warner that she would never forget "the malignity & craft of [his] face—never.—It was a study. I could *paint* it, if I knew how to paint."[13]

As she engaged in a one-woman campaign to save the Ponca homeland, she intensified her criticisms of Schurz. After reading in the Indian Bureau's 1880 *Annual Report* that the Poncas in Indian Territory were prospering and preferred not to return to their Dakota homeland, Jackson wrote to a friend that she was pleased he could see through that "audacious" report. "For pure cheek and lying I never saw its equal," she concluded.[14] She was well aware that many Poncas from Indian Territory had already joined Standing Bear's band in the north.

Despair sometimes overwhelmed her. At one point, she wrote that it looked "as if Carl Schurz and Satan were a match for God."[15] Yet other letters reflected a strong spirit. Writing to Warner about Schurz's Indian educational plan, she exclaimed, "His plan!—I declare I think I shall burst a blood vessel some day in my indignation at the cheek of that man."[16]

Close friends were not the only recipients of her barrage of letters. Turning to the literary community to enlist support, in March 1881, she wrote to Oliver Wendell Holmes and Longfellow enclosing one of her articles and an editorial. Schurz, she noted, had developed "such malignity towards innocent people, and such astounding and wholesale lying"[17] that the true friends of the Indians should denounce both him and his methods.

The plight of the Poncas reached the White House, and Pres. Rutherford B. Hayes appointed a special commission to confer with Poncas living in Indian Territory and the Dakotas. Jackson, strongly reacting to its composition, implored Sen. Henry L. Dawes in December 1880 to intervene. She was absolutely certain that only General Crook could be trusted not "to be either hoodwinked or influenced."[18] But her fears did not materialize. Congress appropriated $165,000 to pay for losses incurred during removal and offered the Indians the choice of living in either location.

Although Tibbles had organized Standing Bear's schedule, the exposure was limited to the cities on the tour. It was Jackson's writings, therefore, that had brought the Ponca controversy to the entire nation and hence to a successful conclusion. Her appetite whetted, she began to expand her focus. She defended the White River Utes after learning that agent Nathan Meeker's arbitrary policies had been a contributing factor in the fall 1879 attack on their agency. Sometimes she focused on the individual, such as Henry Harris, a Winnebago who was murdered in 1880 by a white man who was arrested, tried, and freed because "it was only an Indian that was killed."[19] A similar situation occurred on her California mission tour. Juan Diego, an unarmed Cahuilla Indian, was brutally murdered by Sam Temple. Again the murderer was acquitted, prompting Jackson to remark that it was "easy to see that killing of Indians is not a very dangerous thing to do in San Diego County."[20] In *Ramona*, she reconstructed the incident to explain the murder of Alessandro.

As the public outcry against the Utes increased, she recounted the activities of Col. John M. Chivington and his Third Colorado Volunteers against Cheyenne Chief Black Kettle's peaceful band of Cheyenne and Arapaho in 1864. In a letter to the *New York Daily Tribune*, she described the atrocities committed against the Indians. Nevertheless, she believed that Chivington's methods were more humane than the current government policy of withholding rations from those involved in the uprising. "To be shot dead is a mercy," she wrote, "and a grace for which we would all sue if to be starved to death were our only other alternative."[21] The condition of the Utes was not due to natural disasters such as inclement weather, blight, or pestilence; it was the result of the arbitrary actions of Secretary Schurz, who deprived them of one-half of their food.

Jackson's stance on the Chivington massacre embroiled her in a controversial exchange of heated letters with William N. Byers, former editor of the *Rocky Mountain News*. Byers accused Jackson of ignoring the causes for the Sand Creek Massacre as so to dramatize the condition of the Utes. He claimed that the Cheyennes had been engaged in plunder along the Platte River Road and were not under government protection as she had argued. Furthermore, he felt that Schurz was justified in withholding supplies from the entire Ute tribe as punishment for the agency massacre.

In a letter of rebuttal, Jackson provided evidence gleaned from the Senate investigation of Sand Creek that the Indians had been under government protection.[22] Again she called on editorial friends to publish her letters; and each time Byers answered, Jackson refuted him with information from government documents or congressional investigations. When he ceased writing altogether, Jackson turned her attention to other tribes. Her March 1880 article, "The Wards of the United States Government," in *Scribner's Monthly*, included not only the Poncas but the Nez Perces and their unsuccessful flight to Canada as well.

The extensive information she had gathered at the Astor Library prompted her to write a longer manuscript condemning the treatment of the Indians. Calling it *A Century of Dishonor*, she informed Ward that she had put her heart and soul into it.[23] To Warner, she confessed, "I never so much as dreamed what we had been guilty of."[24]

Published in 1881 by Harper & Brothers, *A Century of Dishonor* opened with a legal brief on Indian land rights, followed by seven tribal histories and a chapter on massacres of Indians by whites. At her own personal expense, she gave every congressman a copy. Embossed in red on the cover were the words of Benjamin Franklin: "Look upon your hands! They are stained with the blood of your relations." Although neither Congress nor the public responded with enthusiasm, her condemnation of the country's Indian policy laid solid groundwork for her next Indian crusade, that of the Mission Indians of southern California—the final and most successful phase of her career as cultural broker. Jackson had first visited California in 1872 while under commission to write travel accounts for the *New York Independent*. Thoroughly enchanted with the state, she was disappointed when she was forced for personal reasons to turn down an assignment by *Harper's* in spring 1881 to write four articles on California. However, months later when *Century Magazine* offered her a similar assignment, she accepted and set out for Los Angeles, arriving on December 20, 1881.

To her dismay, she found most of the Mission Indians of southern California landless and living in poverty. Their condition was even more serious than the Poncas', who had finally been given a new reservation. By contrast, the Mission Indians had received virtually no protection of their land base. Following the secularization decree of 1833, the Franciscan missions had been converted to parish churches, and lands had been distributed to wealthy individuals instead of to the neophyte Indians. Some Indian lands were protected by clauses in original Mexican land grants, but in most cases, the Indians were scattered in inaccessible valleys and mountains, where they ran livestock and engaged in limited agriculture. Moreover, they were constantly in danger of being run off their lands by more aggressive whites.

In spring 1882, Jackson arrived in San Diego. Accompanied by Father Anthony D. Ubach, a local parish priest, she visited a number of small villages inhabited by former neophytes of Mission San Luis Rey de Francia, founded in 1798. The mission's agricultural lands had expanded, spreading to neighboring Pala Valley where a granary and later a chapel (or *asistencia*) had been built in 1816. By the time of Jackson's visit, the chapel and other buildings lay in ruins, and few Indians remained.

In neighboring regions, a similar pattern emerged. San Pasqual Valley had been set aside as a reservation in 1870, but settlers had recently preempted Indian lands. Temecula Valley, originally protected by a clause in the Mexican land grant, had also been reclaimed in the 1870s following a successful legal suit in a San Francisco court. These Indians, forced from their home, had moved three short miles to Pachanga Canyon, which Jackson described as a "dreary, hot little valley, bare, with low, rocky buttes; . . . [and] . . . not a drop of water in it." There she found what she perceived as sad faces "stamped . . . by generations of suffering, [and] immovable distrust."[25]

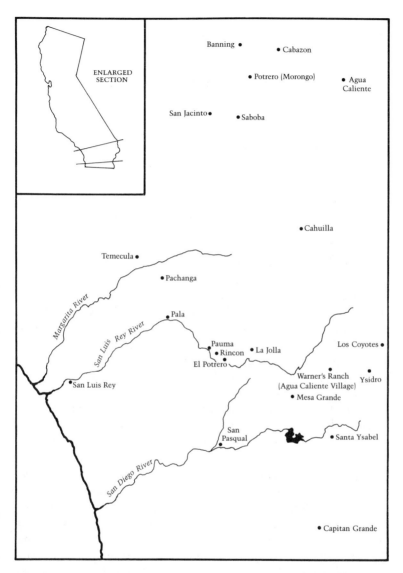

The Southern California Mission Indian villages during the 1880s. Re-produced from Helen Hunt Jackson and Her Indian Reform Legacy *by Valerie Sherer Mathes. Copyright © 1990 by the University of Texas Press. Courtesy of the publisher.*

Jackson believed that the condition of the California natives resulted from cruelty and greed at the hands of American settlers and ignorance, indifference, and neglect at the hands of government officials. Her indignation at their treatment prompted her to write to Warner, "There is not in all the Century of Dishonor, so black a chapter as the history of these Mission Indians." They were "Peacable farmers for a hundred years—driven off their lands like foxes & wolves—[and] driven *out* of good adobe homes."[26]

Her favorite village was Saboba, located in the valley that lay at the foot of the San Jacinto Mountains. It was home to 157 Indian farmers who lived in substantial adobe houses and tended wheat fields and peach and apricot orchards. The original Mexican land grant of 1842 still protected their rights, but over the years, various surveys had encroached on these lands, and part of the original grant had been sold to a San Bernardino merchant who wanted them removed. Jackson feared Saboba would meet the same fate as Temecula and San Pasqual.

After visiting San Pasqual, Temecula, and Saboba, Jackson returned to many of the same villages later that month with Henry Sandham, the artist illustrating her articles. The weary travelers were back in Los Angeles by month's end. Settling in comfortably at the Kimball Mansion boardinghouse, Jackson met a young man who would play an important role in her work with the Mission Indians.

Abbot Kinney was a well-read, wealthy world traveler, fluent in Spanish, acquainted with California land laws, and interested in the Indians. He readily accepted Jackson's invitation to join her on another tour. In early May, Kinney, Jackson, and her husband set out for a twenty-day journey to Monterey. By July, the Jacksons were in San Francisco. There Helen learned from Indian Commissioner Hiram Price that she had been appointed to head a government commission to visit the Mission Indians. This appointment originated with her concern for Saboba, which had prompted her to write fellow Coloradoan Henry Teller, Secretary of the Interior, about these Indians' tenuous hold on their lands. The appointment authorized her to visit the Mission Indians of southern California, to examine their land titles, and to locate suitable lands within the public domain to be set aside as permanent reservations.[27]

Mission Indians at home, Saboba. Seaver Center for Western History Research, Los Angeles County Museum of Natural History.

Jackson spent fall 1882 writing her *Century Magazine* articles. In November, she boarded a train for New York and Boston and in February 1883, set out for southern California. Her initial task was to visit the government land office to learn what lands had been patented to homesteaders and what lands remained available for Indian use. She then turned her attention to the Saboba village, gaining background material from Mary Sheriff, the young schoolteacher whom she had first met in April 1882. After much reflection, Jackson recommended that the government hire the Los Angeles firm of Brunson and Wells to protect not only the land rights of Saboba but those of other villagers. The firm immediately went to work.

In early spring, Jackson, Kinney, Sandham, and a driver set out for a tour of eighteen Indian villages. On returning, she wrote a friend that her opinion of human nature had decreased by 100 percent. "Such heart sickening fraud, violence, [and] cruelty as we have unearthed here—I did not believe could exist in civilized communities."[28]

Jackson did, however, find some things that pleased her. Since her last visit to Pachanga Canyon, the area had been set aside as a reservation, and numerous improvements had been made. The party also journeyed high into the San Jacinto Mountains to the Cahuilla village and conferred with the widowed schoolteacher. They continued their visit to the various villages on Warner's Ranch, then headed for San Ysidro, Santa Ysabel, Mesa Grande, and Capitan Grande. During the tour, Kinney served as interpreter or intimidated squatters (when necessary) while Jackson took notes and recorded names for use in future publications.

Along with visits to the villages, Jackson also conferred with Mission Agent S. S. Lawson. Believing him inadequate for the position, she became embroiled in an exchange of letters similar to that with Schurz and Byers. Soon both Lawson and Jackson were looking to Commissioner Price for support. Ultimately, the agent resigned, possibly as a result of Jackson's campaign against him.[29]

In early July 1883, Jackson completed the fifty-six-page Jackson/Kinney report. It recommended that existing reservations be resurveyed and properly marked, intruders be removed, more government schools be constructed, proper inspections be made annually for each village or settlement, several tracts of land be purchased, a law firm be hired to serve as special attorneys in all cases relative to the Mission Indians, and finally, that a fund be established to buy food and clothing for the aged and infirm.

On January 10, 1884, Commissioner Price submitted a bill to Congress implementing many of the recommendations. Although the bill passed the Senate on July 3, 1884, it failed in the House of Representatives. Undaunted, the Indian Office annually submitted the bill until on January 12, 1891, "the Act for the Relief of the Mission Indians in the State of California" passed both houses and was signed by the president. Although this was six years after Jackson's death, her legacy had encouraged reformers to continue her work.

As her Mission bill was floundering in Congress, Jackson was contemplating another writing project. Her various tours of the Indian villages had resulted in the gathering of enough background material for a novel set in pastoral California. As early as May 1883, she had wistfully commented to a friend that she wished she "could write a story that would do for the Indian a thousandth part that Uncle Tom's Cabin did for the negro."[30] A year later, when the novel was published, Jackson, still preoccupied with following Harriet Beecher Stowe's path, wrote to the WNIA's president, Amelia Stone Quinton, "I do not dare to think I have written a second Uncle Tom's Cabin—but I do think I have written a story which will be a good stroke for the Indian cause."[31]

Although she did not write the first page of *Ramona* until December 1, 1883, the plot had occurred to her the previous October. Struck with the power of the story, she had rushed into her husband's room to share it with him. Once at her writing table in her hotel room in New York City, she seemed engaged in a struggle with an outside power, writing two thousand to three thousand words a morning. She felt that keeping away from her work was "like keeping away from a lover, whose hand . . . [she could] reach."[32] At eleven P.M. on March 9, 1884, with the manuscript completed, she put her head on her desk and lamented, "My life-blood went into it—all I had thought, felt, and suffered for *five* years on the Indian Question."[33]

Initially serialized in the *Christian Union* in May 1884, *Ramona* was published in book form by Roberts Brothers in November. A historical novel, it combined fact and fiction. Kinney commented later that while touring the villages, he and Jackson had met with many of the "characters whose pictures were afterwards drawn with fidelity."[34] Less than a year after its publication, Jackson died of cancer. Shortly before her death, she informed her husband she was ready to die; her only regret was that she had not done more for the Indians. Perhaps *Ramona* and *A Century of Dishonor* would have some impact. "They will tell in the long run," she said. "The thought of this is my only consolation as I look back over the last ten years."[35] She informed Higginson that these books were the only ones that pleased her and hoped that "they will live, and . . . bear fruit."[36]

Both books have had a long publication life. At the time of her death, *Ramona* had already sold fifteen thousand copies and since then has gone through more than three hundred reprintings and inspired numerous stage and screen versions as well as scores of other books. *Ramona* has endured because it is perceived as a love story rather than an Indian protest novel, and as such, it has created a myth about the southern California experience. Although less popular, *A Century of Dishonor*, because of its timeliness, probably had a greater immediate impact. The disruptions of the Civil War, the appointment of incompetent Indian agents, graft, fraud, and the relentless westward-moving settler had brought grief to the Indians. Although some contemporary writers described *A Century of Dishonor* as "sentimentalism," it exposed the perfidy of the government's Indian policy. Current major studies of Indian policy all note the importance of her books. As William T. Hagan wrote, Jackson "publicized the Indian cause as it had never been publicized before."[37]

If Jackson's writings did not immediately sway the public or the government, they did have a profound influence on other reformers. In spring 1884, less than a year after the Jackson/Kinney report appeared, Albert K. Smiley and Gen. E. Whittlesey of the Board of Indian Commissioners visited various agencies in the Southwest. Their California leg of the tour was in direct response to the report, and while there they conferred not only with Brunson and Wells but with Kinney and the current Mission Indian agent. Like Jackson, they believed the Mission Indians had been wronged and their lands should be defended.[38]

Smiley, the influential founder of the Lake Mohonk Conference, returned to California in 1889 and again in 1890. Following the passage of the 1891 Mission Indian bill, he was appointed to the California Mission Indian Commission authorized by the Department of Interior to satisfactorily settle the Indians on reservations. In this capacity, he worked closely with Charles C. Painter, the full-time lobbyist of the Indian Rights Association.

Jackson's influence on Painter was more personal. When they met shortly before Jackson's death, Painter believed that the ailing woman was comforted knowing that the IRA would undertake the investigation of the Indians whom she portrayed in "*Ramona* with such moving pathos, and whose wretched and hopeless condition weighed so heavily upon her heart."[39] Inspired by Jackson's deathbed plea, he set out on a second tour of Mission Indian villages that summer. When he returned from his October 1886 and June 1887 visits, he claimed to have visited "Ramona" at her little

The widow of Juan Diego, Ramona Lubo, assumed by many to be the Ramona of Jackson's novel. Seaver Center for Western History Research, Los Angeles County Museum of Natural History.

hut in the Cahuilla village. He described her as "full-blooded and homely,"[40] unlike the portrayal in Jackson's novel. Like many readers, Painter failed to understand that Jackson's Ramona was a composite of several people.

Painter's most important contribution in Jackson's behalf was his service on the California Mission Indian Commission. After spending eleven months surveying and setting aside reservations, he wrote the secretary of the IRA that he felt he had fully redeemed the promises he had made to Helen Hunt Jackson.

In addition to funding Painter's trips to California, the IRA worked closely with G. Wiley Wells, formerly of Brunson and Wells. After Brunson's election as judge of the Los Angeles Superior Court, Wells acted alone as special assistant to the United States Attorney in all cases affecting the Mission Indians. His primary interest was to save Saboba. The case of *Byrnes v. the San Jacinto Indians* (the Saboba village) came to trial during summer 1886 in the superior court in San Diego County. The court found in favor of the plaintiff, but Ward, supported by the IRA, appealed. On January 31, 1888, the California Supreme Court found in favor of the Indians on the basis that the original Mexican land grant had included their right of occupancy.[41]

Jackson's work also influenced Mrs. Osia Joslyn Hiles of the Wisconsin Indian Association, a branch of the WNIA. Although Hiles never met Jackson, she had found *Ramona* to be "one of the tenderest pleas that has ever been made for an oppressed race."[42] Hiles headed west in 1886 to investigate the condition of the Mission Indians and reported her findings before the Lake Mohonk Conference. The following summer, she conferred with the secretary of the Interior and the Indian commissioner, served as chair of the WNIA's Mission Indian Committee, and revisited California in January 1888. Her activities led to the establishment of the Lake Mohonk Mission Indian Committee, which supported a field agent authorized to gather background information for court cases. Hiles remained active until poor health restricted her travel.[43]

The last reformer influenced by Jackson's work was Amelia Stone Quinton, longtime president of the WNIA, an organization devoted to improving the condition of Indian women and children through education and Christianization. In their Ramona mission, the WNIA sponsored teachers and ministers to Cahuilla, Saboba, the Potrero, and other Mission Indian villages so dear to Jackson's heart.

Quinton, personally drawn to California by Jackson's writings, claimed to have purchased a basket made by "Ramona" during her summer 1891 visit to Cahuilla. Like Painter, she was disappointed, describing the home as a mere cabin and "the life in it . . . evidently not that of the heroine of the story whose character was of course purposely idealized."[44]

While arranging with the Moravian Rev. William H. Weinland to undertake missionary work among the Cahuilla, Quinton suggested that he inform the Indians that "Mrs. Jackson who was their friend . . . begged that we would send a friend & missionary to them."[45] During summer 1889, Weinland and his wife chose to concentrate initially on the smaller area of Saboba and the Banning reservation, instead of working among all the villages. Like Jackson, Weinland came to depend on Mary Sheriff. And when Weinland moved on to other missionary fields, Sheriff was supported by WNIA as their missionary at Saboba until 1891, when a Catholic church was completed.

WNIA missionary policy required that once a missionary field was properly established, it would be turned over to a Protestant missionary society willing to accept it on a full-time basis. The Potrero mission near Banning was given to the Missionary Board of the Moravian Church in 1890; and in 1896, the Cahuilla mission was transferred from the WNIA Missionary Committee to the Southern California Auxiliary headquartered at Redlands. And finally in January 1899, the New York City Auxiliary closed its Agua Caliente mission, transferring it to the Moravian church.[46] In this manner, Jackson's followers maintained her efforts among the Mission Indians of California.

Jackson's chance attendance at Standing Bear's lecture, her obsession with the Ponca defense, and her championing of the Mission Indians had a profound effect on the protection of the Indian's land base and on Indian reform in general. Even after death, her poignant writings prompted members of the Indian Rights Association, the Women's National Indian Association, and Lake Mohonk Conference members to carry on her work. Their combined efforts resulted in the 1891 passage of the Mission Indian Bill, based on the Jackson/Kinney report. Jackson's obsession with the condition of America's Indians had truly been contagious.

Ideas advanced by other late nineteenth century reformers led to federal Indian policies Jackson probably would have opposed, such as the breaking up of reservation lands. Nonetheless, her prophetic statement to Higginson that she hoped her works would live and bear fruit was borne out. The Ponca and Mission Indians remain in her debt, and her own writings have endured. A Century of Dishonor retains its position in the literature of the reform era, and Ramona has recently been reissued in a new annotated edition, over a century after it first appeared.

CHAPTER 8

INTERPRETING THE WILD WEST, 1883-1914

L. G. MOSES

WILD West shows offer unique examples of cultural brokerage. William Frederick ("Buffalo Bill") Cody, who best represents the Wild West show entrepreneur of the late nineteenth and early twentieth centuries, and the show Indians who performed with him, may be regarded as cultural interpreters. As brokers, they spoke to one another and to their audiences across a chasm of cultural diversity. As performers, they presented vignettes from "The Winning of the West" and "Scenes of Other Days" to the nation and the world.[1] Re-creating portions of the violent struggle over the American West, however, was only the most obvious aspect of cultural exchange. The victory tableau that Buffalo Bill and the Indians in his employ offered to a paying public ostensibly depicted the replacement of one civilization by another. In reality, Cody and company, a multiethnic community that traveled between 1883 and the start of World War I, intended other lessons. Unfortunately, these were largely overlooked at the time. Most got lost in the war of words between show entrepreneurs and the reformers and their allies in the Indian service over what image of the Indians was suitable for public presentation. Neither side ever consulted the Indians themselves.

Since their heyday, even the most objective historians and critics have disapproved of the imagery created by the Wild West shows, thus taking up where the reformers left off. In the polite company of academic historians, Buffalo Bill Cody has been dismissed not only for being the crass self-promoter he admittedly was but also for hindering "the serious study of the real region,"[2] the American West. The show Indians who accompanied him also presumably hindered the study of real Indians.

Cody intended to make cultural brokers of the show Indians— not mere propagandists for Euramerican culture and values. He expected them to serve as interpreters who would speak to non-Indian listeners about their cultures and to their own people about their experiences in the white world. The show Indians, according to Cody, would contribute to what he called the great mission of "harmonizing the races," one of the goals of his Wild West show.[3]

By the mid-1880s, remnant bands of Apaches from Arizona and New Mexico territories, last of the supposedly "hostile" western tribes, had been restrained by the army. It appeared to many non-Indian Americans, especially in the East, that the West and its first inhabitants were quickly passing from existence.

With the beginning of Wild West shows, Americans who knew nothing about the West except what they read in newspaper accounts and dime novels now could attend performances and partake vicariously in a few of the adventures. Capitalizing on the signal event of Custer's defeat at the Little Bighorn as well as countless skirmishes between Indians and "settlers" in the West, Wild West shows fostered the image of Plains Indians as the quintessential American Indian. These Indians provided the Wild West shows with their enduring imagery. In the twentieth century, motion pictures and television picked up only the most vulgar aspects of the imagery.[4] From film and television far more than the Wild West shows, the public came to regard "real" Indians as those who lived in tribes, slept in tepees, wore feather bonnets, rode painted ponies, hunted the buffalo, fought the U.S. Cavalry, and spoke in words, hand signs, and smoke signals.[5]

These "Pretend Indians" could be many things.[6] In the late nineteenth century, American Indians were often perceived as treacherous. Cody himself is often cited as the principal author of this derogatory image that persisted into the twentieth century. This is unfair. He claimed that Indians were never treacherous. Cody's compassionate view of Indians led him to argue that it was the treatment of Indians by Euramericans that was treacherous.[7] One had to look no farther than the government's failure to meet its treaty obligations, Cody insisted, to understand this. Cody never

Group portrait of Buffalo Bill's Wild West Show troupe, Chicago, 1893. Courtesy of the Buffalo Bill Historical Center, Cody, Wyoming.

suggested that the Plains Sioux were the only American Indians; but he did claim that those who performed with his company were "real." Moreover, they had more to tell other Americans about their cultures than mere attacks on Cody's Deadwood Stagecoach might suggest.

Cody's program for 1883, the first season of the Wild West show, included a grand introductory march; a bareback pony race; a re-creation of the Pony Express; an Indian attack on the Deadwood mail coach; races between Indians on foot and Indians on horseback; two series of trick shooting by the principals of the show; a horse race by "cowboys," thereby coining the term; a demonstration of riding and roping by cowboys; riding wild Texas steers; roping and riding wild bison; and a "Grand Hunt" topped off by a "sham battle" with Indians.[8] Including the opening parade, Indians participated in six of the events, four of which had nothing to do with warfare. Later, when Cody added a feature called "The Drama of Civilization," he included Indian dances and ceremonials.[9] Although not necessarily ethnographically "correct" in every instance, given the show's stage managing, these were nevertheless similar to demonstrations of skill and artistry that would later be found in modern powwows.

The original show Indians may be regarded as members of a transitional generation. They grew up before the reservations closed in; yet they encountered the governmental programs designed to eradicate native life. That they re-created portions of that earlier life for public consumption caused great distress among Indian bureau personnel and members of protectionist groups such as the Indian Rights Association. Yet neither reformers nor leaders of the Indian service could compel the Indians to remain at home and lead "more productive" lives. The Indian bureau possessed no statutory authority to force Indians to stay on their reservations, but it could regulate their employment in the shows. If the shows failed to abide by the terms of the contracts, they would forfeit their bonds and the right to employ Indians in the future. The show Indians would be unemployed. They would be forced to return to the reservations. Then perhaps they could be persuaded to apply themselves to the government's "civilization" programs. Regulation of show Indian employment, however, did not mollify Indian policy reformers.

Almost from the beginning of Indian participation in Wild West shows, Indian policy reformers denounced the performances as contrary to the best interests of the Indians. Arguing that the shows encouraged unsettled habits and brought Indians into contact with disreputable characters, they encouraged the bureau to ban Indian participation in the shows, but the government could not legally interfere. Following the Standing Bear decision, peaceable Indians were free to come and go as they pleased.[10] John Noble, secretary of the interior during the Harrison administration (1889–93), recognized this fact. He reminded Thomas Jefferson Morgan, Indian commissioner during his tenure, that an Indian could obtain a writ of habeas corpus against anyone endeavoring to confine him or her. Thus, forcing Indians to remain on reservations violated both the letter and the spirit of the law. A rarity among bureaucrats involved in Indian affairs, Noble foresaw favorable results emerging from Indian participation in the shows. He declared, "I suppose, on the one hand, it is a matter for public instruction to have the Indian exhibited where he is fairly treated and is enabled to make some money by this . . . important industry." Besides, he told Morgan, show Indians would probably have little effect on the tribes "as the numbers of the exhibited are at best but very small." He reminded the commissioner on this occasion that no particular law existed that would punish either the Wild West show entrepreneurs or the show Indians for exhibitions by the Indians' own consent.[11]

Yet if Indian participation in the shows could not be banned legally, it could be banned for practical considerations. Starting in winter 1886, the Office of Indian Affairs began to regulate Indian employment in the shows. The bureau required the owners to place their Indian employees under contract. They had to provide the Indians with adequate food, shelter, and medical care; pay "fair and reasonable" salaries; hire chaplains and interpreters to accompany the performers; and return the show Indians to their reservations at the close of their contracts. Violation of the contract carried the penalty of forfeiture of surety bond (usually $10,000–$20,000) and the inability again to employ Indians. No Wild West show ever forfeited its bond. But it is in the challenges brought by reformers and Indian bureau personnel against the shows that the role of cultural brokerage is most evident.

Almost from the beginning of Indian employment in Wild West

shows, allegations of mistreatment and exploitation reached the Department of Interior and the Office of Indian Affairs. Such statements caused the various secretaries and commissioners down to the First World War to be concerned about the shows' effects on assimilationist programs, on the image of the Indian in the public mind, and on the bureaucrats' careers should the reformers decide that they were also part of the problem. Granting formal permission to such enterprises as Cody's Wild West show for the employment of Indians seemed inconsistent with the larger aim of assimilation then being advocated by the Indian bureau. While having pledged itself to advance productive citizenship through education, Christianity, and agriculture after the fashion of Euramericans, the bureau had also allowed Indians to work for shows that glorified Indians' "heathenish ways." Regulation of show contracts did not go far enough to suit reformers. They preferred that Indians remain on their reservations, forbidden by the government to run off and join the circus. Comm. John H. Oberly, Morgan's immediate predecessor, stung by criticism in his last months at the bureau for his failure to protect his charges, had to remind reformers that docile Indians had every right to come and go as they wished, especially if they had subscribed to allotment under the Dawes Severalty Act and could, therefore, be justly regarded as citizens. In a letter to Sen. Henry L. Dawes of Massachusetts, sponsor of the legislation on which bureau programs were then based, Oberly remarked that, as commissioner, he could not "restrain the liberty of the law abiding person or citizen because in [his] opinion or the opinion of someone else that person or citizen will make an injudicious use of his liberty."[12] Although mistreatment and exploitation never approached the extremes claimed by Indian policy reformers, their view of Wild West shows has prevailed.

While the Indians' physical welfare remained a paramount concern of these humanitarians, the major issue revolved around the question of the image of the Indian. The reformers claimed that the shows played up the Indians' savagery by celebrating their martial spirit. The days of free-roving bands of Indians had ended. The natives had been sufficiently disciplined by the military so that they no longer posed a general threat to lives and property. Reformers believed that Indians would soon embrace "civilization." Thus, the image they envisioned was that of an assimilated Indian who came into being through allotment of reservation lands, education, and industry.

Although Indian policy reformers and their allies in the Indian service have themselves often been the targets of historical criticism, their views have prevailed among historians in their general perception of Indians in the Wild West shows. The public may yet cherish the tepee and war bonnet image of show Indians; but among many historians who write about the subject, the buckskin-clad showmen are generally reviled and their faithful Indian adversaries condescendingly dismissed as if they did not have the good sense to grasp their exploitation. Had the show Indians remained on their reservations and, one assumes, become ethnologists' informants, telling stories about how life used to be before the arrival of Europeans (if not their horses), then they may have fared better in the record. Instead, show Indians' lives have been discounted. Their words, except for Black Elk's, have remained unheard.[13]

The approach of Cody's Wild West organization, ironically, was not unlike that of the reformers: both favored assimilation of the first Americans. Indeed, Buffalo Bill continually emphasized that Indians should adapt to a modern world. So also did the show Indians themselves. Cody claimed that the innate virtues of Indians would make them as honorable in their citizenship as they had been in their struggles to preserve their cultures.

Wild West shows created popular images of Indians—such as the ambushes on wagon trains or settlers' cabins—that persist to this day; but it was never Cody's intention to offer the public only this lesson. Cody consciously stressed the educational value of his show for both the public and the Indian performers. Part of his reasoning was doubtless due to his desire to deflect criticism by reformers. As Cody's manager, "Arizona John" Burke, once explained to the commissioner of Indian affairs, it was Buffalo Bill's "honorable ambition to instruct and educate the Eastern public to respect the denizens of the West by giving them a true, untinselled representation of a page of Frontier history that is fast passing away."[14] The Indians whom they employed were to be admired and understood. And if they were to be pitied, it was for the fact that they had been cowed into submission by the government. Let the people, Cody and company insisted, be concerned instead for Indians who were forced to farm marginal land on reservations with only meager government largesse to sustain them. Cody argued that traveling would enable the show Indians to appreciate the inevitability of progress as represented in the numbers, achievements, and technology of "the white race." Further, when they returned to the reservations, they would serve their people as advocates for change. Cody never denounced the right of Indians to retain their cultural and ethnic identities, and those unique characteristics would become apparent to audiences once they observed Indians' skills, if only in the arena.

Cody once explained to a Scottish journalist that he refrained from employing the same Indians for successive tours. Otherwise he would have been staging "authentic" re-creations with trained actors rather than with Indians "in puris naturalibus." When the show Indians returned home, they would tell their people about all they had seen and thus "bring the white and red races closer together." If Americans and Europeans needed any proof of the ability of different groups to live and work together harmoniously—and yet retain their individual and group identities—they could tour the encampment.[15] That was one of the ethical lessons of Cody's Wild West show and Congress of Rough Riders of the World.

Cody's Wild West played at Madison Square Garden, New York, during the winter of 1886–87. Steele Mackaye, the noted theatrical director, staged what he called "The Drama of Civilization" in five acts. It was to be a pageant of American "pioneer life."[16] On hearing about it, New York Congressman Darwin Rush James assailed the production for what he termed "The Drama of Savagery" from the floor of the House. Charging that Cody's show Indians appeared drunk in public and frequented saloons and whorehouses, James urged Congress to ban government licensing of the shows. In reply, George H. Bates, who served Cody's show as chaperone to the Indians, challenged James's comments in a letter to the commissioner. After denying the charges of public drunkenness and pandering, Bates outlined company policy toward the Indians. Because his words contain the essence of Cody's frequently repeated apologia, they are quoted at length. He told the commissioner,

Our object has been, is now and will continue to be, to guard our "Wild

West" Indians from all evil influences, and to promote their moral, physical and intellectual interests in every way possible.

I have taken the liberty to send you evidence of this on several occasions and for further evidence, I refer you to the Rev. C. H. Maul, pastor of the Baptist church, Mariners Harbor, Staten Island, whose church they attended twice each Sabbath for three months; to the Rev. Henry Ward Beecher, Plymouth Church, Brooklyn; to the Rev. J. DeWitt Talmage, Brooklyn Tabernacle, where our Indians attended divine service and where they are to attend again next Sunday; to the Rev. Hughes, Trinity Baptist Church 55th St., New York, where they attend service every Sunday evening; to the officials of the city hall where the Indians were taken, introduced, and instructed in the working of the city government; to Postmaster Person of the city Post Office where they were taken and instructed in the working and objects of the office; to *The World* office where they were taken and instructed in newspaper making; to the authorities of central Park where they were taken and taught the object of the same and the character of the animals therein confined; to officials of Bellevue Hospital and Blackwells Island where they visited and were instructed as to the object and working of all the institutions therein; to the Principal of Public School 23, New York, where we have arranged to take all our Indians tomorrow and instruct them as to the object and working of the white man's school. I refer you in fact to all the principal places of legitimate public entertainment in New York, most of which they have attended with the above objects in view.

I know from personal knowledge that these Indians are acquiring benefits in their Eastern Life. . . . I am making this statement not in the interests of wild west management, but in behalf of the Indians and as indisputable evidence that you did not err in permitting them to leave their reservations to engage in this present occupation.[17]

According to Cody's official company policy, his organization did as much as any governmental program to foster acculturation. He encouraged the Indians in his employ to participate in the amusements and cultural events of the larger society. To bring this about, Sergeant Bates and other interpreters took the show Indians on what in retrospect seems to be a relentless tour of Euramerican culture. Conversely, Cody also encouraged his audiences to come early to the performances, so that they could visit the encampment and talk to the performers before taking their seats in the stands.

What evidence is there to support Cody's claim that he was making cultural brokers of the show Indians? Statements by the Indian performers indicate that Buffalo Bill was doing more than diverting criticism from his show by making lavish claims of social responsibility. Like the Indian leaders who were taken to Washington, D.C., to meet with the Great Father and to tour the sights in the East, the show Indians were dutifully impressed with all they had seen and experienced. The hundreds of show Indian ambassadors who traveled every year (something that John Noble had never anticipated) dwarfed the numbers of Indian leaders calling on the Great Father. These performers spoke to anyone from the Euramerican community who cared to listen, explaining that they understood why Indians needed to adapt to new realities on and off the reservation. What was often lost in translation, however, was the right of Indians, regardless of their adaptations, to retain their cultures. Few Euramericans during the heyday of Wild West shows were willing to acknowledge Indians' right to be and to remain Indians.

Sitting Bull, the renowned Hunkpapa leader and holy man, toured with Buffalo Bill briefly in summer 1885. Popularly identified as the killer of Custer, by all newspaper reporters' accounts he bore the jeers of the arena crowds "impassively" or "stoically"—or rather, perhaps, with more dignity than the other Americans who rudely accosted him. When he returned to his home near Standing Rock Agency, Dakota Territory, he had much to tell. The sheer numbers of Euramericans and the size of their cities had impressed him. According to Annie Oakley, perhaps his closest friend within the troupe, he had given much of the money he had earned to the ragged children he encountered in the cities. Their presence had corroborated what he already suspected. Euramericans would not do much for Indians when they let their own people go hungry. Indians must rely on themselves. "The white man knows how to make everything," Stanley Vestal quotes him as saying, "but he does not know how to distribute it."[18] When taken to Washington, D.C., Sitting Bull studied the impressive buildings and marveled at the crowds in the streets. "I wish I had known this when I was a boy," he reputedly remarked. "The white people are so many that if every Indian in the West killed one every step they took the dead would not be missed among you."[19] It is little wonder, then, that he appeared phlegmatic to those who saw him enter the arena to the jeers of the crowds. The East had impressed him. He did not, however, determine to become anything but what he was. After the final performance of the 1885 tour, newspaper reporters asked Sitting Bull through an interpreter what he thought about his travels and whether he would travel with the show the following year. He told them that his lodge was a better place to live. He had grown weary of the houses and the noise and bustle of cities in which other Americans lived.[20]

Cody did try to contract Sitting Bull for the 1886 season, but Agent James McLaughlin at Standing Rock Agency refused to support the offer. McLaughlin complained to Cody's manager (and also to the commissioner) that Sitting Bull had spent the money he earned with Buffalo Bill trying to secure his position in the tribe. McLaughlin, ever hostile to Sitting Bull, described scenes of profligacy. McLaughlin wrote that Sitting Bull

is such a consummate liar and too vain and obstinate to be benefitted by what he sees, and makes no good use of the money he thus earns, but on the contrary spends it extravagantly among the Indians in trying to perpetuate baneful influences which the ignorant and non-progressive element are too ready to listen to and follow. Of the money and property that he brought home last fall, he did not have a dollar, or anything else (except the gray horse) left, after being three weeks at home & it was all used in feasting the Indians and trying to impress upon the Indians his own great importance, and I had a great deal of trouble with him and through him with other Indians caused by his own bad behavior and arrogance.[21]

A more discerning observer might have understood that Sitting Bull's gift giving was nothing more than the altruism expected of a Lakota leader by his people.

Sitting Bull was the first of the great show Indians to tour with Cody's Wild West show. He was himself a headliner, attracting as much attention as Buffalo Bill. In newspaper advertisements for the 1885 season, Sitting Bull's name appears only slightly smaller than the caption "Buffalo Bill's Wild West." Although he toured just one season, his employment established a pattern for all subsequent shows. Nonetheless, few of the show Indians possessed Sitting Bull's stature or notoriety; his association with the Sioux victory over Custer at the Little Bighorn secured his exemplary status. His tour, along with that of eight others from his band, represented the shift of show Indian employment to the northern plains. Sitting Bull is described as "the renowned Sioux Chief."[22] After his season with

Two Oglala members of Cody's World's Fair troupe, ca. 1893: left, *Has No Horses;* right, *High Heron. Courtesy of the Buffalo Bill Historical Center, Cody, Wyoming.*

Cody, the Sioux became the most prized show Indians. Their presence provided the necessary aura of authenticity for the shows in re-creating scenes from "the Wild West." Their reputations as warriors confirmed the image of Indians in the minds of Americans and, beginning in 1887, those Europeans who saw their performances.

When Sitting Bull returned to his reservation, he let it be known that he had been impressed by all that he had seen, but even so, he had not been sufficiently cowed to suit his agent. He did not advocate a return to the old days before his imprisonment; nor did he advocate slavish devotion to governmental programs that would have stripped him and his people of their cultural identity. Many of the show Indians who followed Sitting Bull also proclaimed the necessity for Indians to adapt to a changing world. None, however, ever suggested that they would simultaneously cease to be Indians. On a few occasions, when returnees remarked on the overwhelming nature of Euramerican civilization, they recalled that they had longed to return to their homes and people, far from the tumult of the eastern United States.

A reporter once asked American Horse the younger, who had replaced Sitting Bull as the Indian headliner in Cody's show for the 1886 season, what he thought of the East. American Horse replied, "I see so much that is wonderful and strange that I feel a wish sometimes to go out in the forest and cover my head with a blanket, so that I can see no more and have a chance to think over what I have seen."[23] Two other showmen commented to John Burke, Cody's manager, that the travel often frightened them. They found the pandemonium of cities and going rapidly from place to place disorienting. They felt bewitched or wondered if they were dead. They had to tie handkerchiefs around their eyes so that they could no longer see the disorder around them. Only then could they restore calm and order to their lives.[24]

In 1887, Cody took his successful show to England to participate in Queen Victoria's Golden Jubilee. Buffalo Bill recalled the pride he felt when sailing for England: pride in himself, his show, his country, and his civilization. He described the Indians who accompanied him as "that savage foe that had been compelled to submit to a conquering civilization and were now accompanying me in friendship, loyalty, and peace, five thousand miles from their homes, braving the dangers of the . . . great unknown sea, now no longer a tradition, but a reality." Mackaye incorporated much of "The Drama of Civilization" into the show, which performed in the west end of London at Earl's Court where Indians and other rough riders combined in an exhibition "intended to prove to the center of the old world civilization that the vast region of the United States was finally and effectively settled by the English-speaking race."[25] Cody's triumphant tour of England with the Wild West show has been viewed by historians in a number of ways. Some have seen it as a symbolic coming of age for the republic torn from the mother country by revolution a century before. Buffalo Bill himself sounded this theme. Instead of a prodigal son returning home and thereby admitting failure in the larger world beyond his sire's domain, it was a proud and profane son announcing to a parent that he had conquered new worlds and had come home only to display his trophies. For the show Indians, their esteem in England raised their status from caricatures to persons of character.

Red Shirt (Ogilasa), the most prominent Sioux leader among the troupe, became the spokesman for the show Indians in London. His handsome features and stately bearing caused reporters to hang on his every word. He became the most quoted show Indian, not only of Cody's tour but also in the history of Wild West shows. Red Shirt explained to a reporter from Sheffield,

> I started from my lodge two moons ago knowing nothing, and had I remained on the Indian Reservations, I should have been as a blind man. Now I can see a new dawn. The great houses which cross the mighty waters, the great villages which have no end where the [whites] swarm like insects in the summer sun. . . . Our people will wonder at these things when we return to the Indian Reservation and tell them what we have seen.[26]

In the same interview, Red Shirt also commented on the treatment of Indians in the United States.

> The red man is changing every season. [Indians] of the next generation will not be the Indian[s] of the last. Our buffaloes are nearly all gone, the deer have entirely vanished, and the white man takes more and more of our land. But the United States government is good. True, it has taken away our land, and the white men have eaten up our deer and our buffalo, but the government now gives us food that we may not starve. They are educating our children and teaching them . . . to use farming implements.

Our children will learn the white man's civilization and to live like him.[27]

Readers in either the United States or England who were confident in the inexorability of progress could applaud such a sentiment. Cody confidently reported the inestimable educational value for "blanket Indians" performing in his show. It is easy to understand how, at first glance, Red Shirt's testimony could be read as endorsement; but he never said that Indians would cease to be Indians if they learned to live as whites did. American Indians, just as people from other cultures, changed from one generation to another, but they still retained their Indian identity. Recognition of that fact eluded other Americans for generations. Thus, it was not that Red Shirt and his companions had failed as cultural brokers. It was simply that Euramericans and Europeans did not listen; or if they did, they heard a different message—one that confirmed in their own minds the superiority of their civilization.

Indians joined the shows for money, travel, and adventure. They received each in abundance. Black Elk (who appears on the contract under the name "Choice") remembered that during the dangerous ocean crossing in spring 1887, he had to remind himself that he was "there for adventure." The Oglala visionary composed himself. He dressed for death and began to sing.[28] One writer, using John Neihardt's book, suggests that Black Elk enjoyed performing his part in the show; but he disliked the roles played by the whites. She quotes Black Elk with added emphasis. "I liked the part of the show we made, but *not* the part the Wasichu [whites] made."[29] Black Elk very well may have disliked the whites playing warriors triumphant. How then could he revel in "playing" Indian if that part called for him constantly to be defeated? Raymond DeMallie, using his own translation of Neihardt's recordings of Black Elk, quotes the holy man differently in this regard. Black Elk comments about the show in New York the winter before the trip to England: "I enjoyed the Indian part of the shows that we put on here at Madison Square Garden, but I did not care much about the white people's parts."[30] Black Elk could just as easily have disliked all the riding, roping, wrestling, and trick shooting of the principals in the show.[31] Perhaps his enjoyment came (as he alluded to it even in times of great danger) in the adventure of it all, in performing re-creations of brave deeds, and in getting paid for it. In

*The autographed photo that Buffalo Bill presented to Red Shirt. Ogilasa
proudly carried it with him through many seasons in the United States
and abroad. Courtesy of the American Heritage Center, University of
Wyoming.*

addition, by traveling in the East and abroad, he and the other
show Indians enjoyed something they had never experienced
before.

When Black Elk became separated from Cody's troupe while in
England, he joined another show and traveled through western
Europe. Later, when he rejoined Cody, the showman acceded to
Black Elk's wishes and sent the weary Oglala home. Black Elk
arrived back in the Dakotas in time to become involved in the
Ghost Dance, while others in the main contingent were returned
by Cody to their reservations just before the disasters of December
1890. Most of these did not adopt the religion; rather, they counseled patience and avoiding confrontations with the government.
Even Commissioner Morgan, who despised the show Indians, was
forced to concede that they had learned much in their travels. He
praised them for remaining loyal to the government and for not
succumbing to the delusion that an Indian messiah was then walking the earth.[32] Actually, some of the show Indians had had spiritual experiences in Europe and were not averse to imagining an
Indian deliverer. They simply did not believe that the deliverer was
the author of the Ghost Dance. In this instance, therefore, the show
Indians served as mediators.

Although commissioners of Indian affairs in these decades never
abandoned their advocacy of forced assimilation, most came to
believe that the Wild West show Indians, despite their evidence of
self-sufficiency (a hallmark of acculturation), were incapable of
"civilization." After the Wounded Knee tragedy, for example, Commissioner Morgan authorized the ringleaders of the Sioux Ghost
Dance to join Cody's latest European tour. The recalcitrant spirits,
according to Morgan, belonged in a Wild West show—along with
the other show Indians.[33]

At the close of an era that still largely celebrated laissez-faire
capitalism and the entrepreneurial spirit, why were the show Indians despised by the reformers and the Indian office? The Sioux
performers alone had earned in excess of $75,000 from 1886 to the
spring 1891.[34] Part of the reason surely was that the show Indians
did not behave after the fashion of other "good" Indians according
to government perception. They did not stay at home, send their
children off to boarding schools, and farm their marginal lands. As
Rocky Bear once told the commissioner,

If [my employment in the Wild West show] did not suit me, I would not remain any longer . . . . [I] eat everything; that is reason I am getting so fat. When I came back to the reservation I am getting poor.

If the Great Father wants me to stop, I would do it. That is the way I get money. If a man goes to work in some other place and goes back with money, he has some for his children. [Rocky Bear had sent money to his children and had on his person $300 in gold.][35]

Black Heart, an Oglala compatriot of Rocky Bear, was even more specific in his desire to stay with Cody's Wild West. He told the commissioner that "these men [Cody and Salsbury] have got us in hand. We were raised on horseback; that is the way we had to work. These men furnished us the same work we were raised to; that is the reason we want to work for these kind of men . . . . If Indian wants to work at any place and earn money, he wants to do so; white man got privilege to do the same—any kind of work that he wants."[36] Performers such as Red Shirt, Rocky Bear, Black Elk, and Black Heart spoke about how they wished to live their lives.

Although the argument between reformers and showmen is well known, what is not as well known is that the particular *form* of the show—that of a nomadic circus—only confirmed for the reformers and their allies in the Indian service what they saw as the worst tendencies of the Plains tribes. Where Indians had once in freedom seasonally crisscrossed the prairies and plains in search of bison herds, now they traveled oceans and continents in search of audiences. Out from under the thumb of the bureau, Indians were again free to do as they pleased. Polite, middle-class reformers already harbored deep anxiety toward the unsettled gypsy life of traveling entertainers. Such people were free from constraints that bound others to civilized society's conventions. Show Indians were lost to assimilation, the reformers reasoned. They could not be tamed and then tethered by Euramerican customs. Because show Indians belonged in show business, the reformers maintained, they had nothing to say that merited listening. The ambivalence of the show Indians' status in the debate reflects their difficult position. Reformers supported everyone's interest except theirs. Looking at the records, one is struck by how often their opinions were asked and given and then ignored. Despite the ethnocentrism of the

period, it is still difficult to understand why nobody listened. Perhaps it is an anachronism to suggest that there were many roads to acculturation. Even though the show Indians were among the most eloquent speakers to attest to the necessity of Indians adapting to a modern world, the Indian bureau and reformers disregarded the message. Like later historians, they did not take the show Indians seriously.

For three decades, Indians traveled throughout the Western world (with at least one show appearing in Australia), offering audiences glimpses into the recent American past and providing the Wild West show with its most distinctive features. Indians did more than play supportive roles in the victory tableau of "pioneer" virtue triumphing over "savagery." They were spokespersons for the right of Indians to be themselves. They survived the contest. Although they were defeated in the preliminary struggle to maintain sovereignty over their lands, they were never destroyed.

Cody and his imitators portrayed Indians in their shows as worthy adversaries, for how else could the showmen-entrepreneurs validate their own prowess in battle or their heroism? Cody, however, trumpeted the fact that where Indians and Euramericans had once been adversaries, now they were friends; where there had once been hostility, now there was peace; and where for centuries there had been misapprehension, now there was the possibility of understanding. Thus, he offered more to his audiences than celebrations of the triumph of Western civilization. He counseled Americans to respect and understand the first Ameri-

---

A strange confederacy: Navajos and Hopis, the men wearing plains-style war bonnets, are photographed at the Indian Village, the Pacific Southwest Exposition, Long Beach, California, in 1928. The sign adorning the entrance to the "authentic Indian Pueblo" told visitors that these Indians "are Wards of the U.S. Government," although Indians had been symbolically granted citizenship by Congress four years before. By the 1920s, the popular image of Indians created by Wild West shows, sustained by world's fairs, and reinforced by motion pictures beginning with Edison's first reels of Buffalo Bill's shows required that all American Indians—whether Paiutes from Nevada, Cherokees from Oklahoma, or Hopis and Navajos from Arizona— wear feather headdresses. Courtesy of the National Archives.

cans. He also celebrated the ethical lesson of human harmony that thrived each day in his encampment. That few people listened to the message is not necessarily the fault of the messengers, red or white.

The frontier never really passed away; what disappeared was the way some Anglo-Americans viewed their historical and geographic experiences. Indians survived "the Winning of the West," and whether on or off the reservations, they drew strength from their cultures to sustain them. It is testimony to their remarkable resilience that, given the hostile environment created by governments and Euramericans, Indians and their cultures endured.

Wild West shows never offered an alternative to forced assimilation because they were, after all, only entertainment. Still, in a sense, both Cody and the commissioners regarded the Indian performers as cultural brokers: the one as a positive influence; the others, as a negative one. Commissioners feared that the show Indians would lead lives twisted by debauchery. There is little evidence to sustain this opinion. The commissioners also feared that the show Indians would persuade others to join the show. Here, the commissioners were correct. Wild West shows provided one of the few sources of decent income for Indians. Each year between 1883 and 1914, the ranks of show Indians grew. The shows offered greater prosperity than all the enticements of the reservation imagined by the Indian office. Moreover, when they performed, the Indians had only to be themselves. It is difficult to judge the effect of the show Indians on their people back at the reservations. Except for the Ghost Dance, the records reveal little about show Indians' direct influence. Although the reformers and Indian bureau personnel maintained that the shows had deleterious effects, there is no question that show Indians earned a good living, a singular feat in the difficult era between the Dawes Act and the First World War. Unlike the wooden Indians that adorned shop entrances or the Indians who appeared as silent, supportive characters in the histories of the era, the show Indians left behind extensive records of their experiences, expressed frequently in their own words, telling about their lives and their joy and pride in being Indians.

CHAPTER 9

FEMALE NATIVE TEACHERS IN SOUTHEAST ALASKA: SARAH DICKINSON, TILLIE PAUL, AND FRANCES WILLARD

VICTORIA WYATT

IN the late nineteenth and early twentieth centuries, Tlingit and Haida Indians in Southeast Alaska faced tremendous challenges as non-native settlers moved into their region. Even more than the Russians who had previously occupied native lands in Alaska, the American settlers appropriated traditional fishing and hunting areas and imposed new economic, religious, legal, and political systems.

Native people had to develop strategies quickly to respond to these changes and to the political and cultural oppression they brought. U.S. naval gunboats discouraged native peoples in coastal Alaska from using force to oppose the foreign invasion. Almost certainly, too, native leaders there got news of the very violent federal policies toward Indians in other areas of the United States in the 1860s and 1870s and wanted to avoid similar experiences in Alaska. Thus, leaders sought ways to help their people survive and cope with the new developments.

As elsewhere in the United States, different individuals chose different methods of achieving this end, and opinion was divided—then and now—about the desirability of each strategy. Many of the choices involved a considerable amount of accommodation and either the appearance or the reality of adopting the value system of the foreign culture.

This was certainly true of the many native women and men who worked among their own people as Christian lay workers and educators. They accepted a new form of spirituality and a new type of educational system and sought to use it as a vehicle to help their peers. Their mission was to educate their people about the non-native society that was growing around them and to prepare the coming generation to function and compete successfully in the new system.

Like all Indians in Southeast Alaska at the time, they faced hard choices. Often white prejudice, cultural oppression, and harsh economic realities forced them to relinquish time-honored customs to maximize chances for survival. Given these grim circumstances, they did not necessarily reject their ethnic identity when they chose to counsel change. They turned from their past so as to turn toward their people.

Native women, as well as men, chose to be Christian lay workers and educators. Women traditionally were both influential and respected in Tlingit and Haida society, both of which are organized by matrilineal descent. The churches established by missionaries generally did not give women the same opportunities as men to hold church offices or to be ordained, either in Alaska or elsewhere. However, there were opportunities for native women to work actively as educators, and many did. Trained and employed by missionaries, they taught about Christianity as well as about secular matters, and the distinction between educator and lay worker is a fine one indeed. Their activities went far beyond classroom teaching: missionaries expected them to devote enormous energies to their role, to be available at all times, and to model and encourage a very specific way of life.

This chapter explores the activities of three women who chose to be Christian educators so as to help their people face the challenges visited on them. Sarah Dickinson assumed that role as an adult. Tillie Paul developed the wish to do so as a girl in an Alaskan mission school. Frances Willard was sent to a seminary in New Jersey and returned eager to teach. The decision they each made to embrace this work was only one of many difficult options various native leaders explored to try to help their people. It is not my intent to suggest their decision was any more or less laudable than those of their peers who chose other routes. I do suggest that no matter what methods native people chose, their determination to ensure that their people survived is a testimony to cultural strength under adversity. Whatever they were forced to relinquish then, they helped lay the foundation for the cultural revival occurring in many places in Southeast Alaska today.

Unfortunately, very little information is available in written sources about the lives of native lay workers, whether female or male. Oral history would certainly reveal more information about some of the women discussed below and would be an essential component of any comprehensive study. The discussion here must be restricted to written sources—most left by non-native missionaries. These records are usually episodic: I have recounted some seemingly mundane incidents below to convey the range of activities the women's work entailed. However, the sources provide little insight about the thoughts and feelings of the individuals discussed. Indeed, even the descriptions of their activities contain large chronological gaps; and often the women abruptly drop altogether from the record. Also, it is important to remember that missionaries had a vested interest in portraying their work as successful and may have deliberately or unknowingly misrepresented the native educators.

However, as Western historians have recently pointed out, we cannot omit peoples or genders from the historical record because the sources about them are incomplete. Even scanty written records may provide a basis for some understanding of their lives and work and give a good foundation with which to approach the oral history that could reflect native voices more directly. The discussion below must be restricted to those ends.

Often native lay workers and educators started their careers as interpreters for missionaries. Women who had married non-native men were prime candidates for such work, for they already knew both languages and both cultures. Sarah Dickinson was one such woman. As in most such cases, there is little written information on her life, but enough exists to piece together some biographical information and gain some insight into her experiences.

Sources disagree about Dickinson's exact ethnic background. One white commentator described her as "a woman of great personality and devotion who was of mingled Thlingit, Tsimpshean and white blood."[1] However, the Presbyterian missionary S. Hall Young, for whom she worked as interpreter and who knew her more closely, referred to her as "a full-blood Tongass native," explaining that "her tribe was the most southern of the Thlingits, living just across Dixon's Entrance from the Tsimpsheans of Port Simpson and Metlakatla." Young added that she had "early acquired the Tsimpshean language as well as her own."[2]

In any event, Dickinson had been educated by the missionary William Duncan at his first "model village" of Old Metlakatla in British Columbia and reportedly was converted to Christianity there.[3] Undoubtedly, she learned some English at the time, and she also spoke Tsimshian and Stikine, the dialect of the Tlingits living near Wrangell.[4] She married George Dickinson, an American fur trader. They may have met in Wrangell; at any rate, she was living there, where he worked, by 1877. When Young arrived in 1878, she had two children—a son, Billy, who was then fifteen, and a daughter, Sarah. The children had learned to read and write English, which the family spoke at home. Young's impression was that they "held themselves rather aloof from other natives, speaking of them as 'they' and of the whites as 'we.'"[5]

Sarah Dickinson was already helping in a native-run school in Wrangell at that time.[6] Tlingit Indians in Wrangell became interested in a mission when Christian Tsimshian Indians began worshiping there in 1876, and in the absence of an ordained minister, a Tsimshian man known as Clah began giving instruction. This indication of interest eventually led the Presbyterian Board of Home Missions to send a white lay worker, Mrs. Amanda R. McFarland, to Wrangell to start a school in 1877.[7] The Rev. Sheldon Jackson, who brought Mrs. McFarland there, described his meeting with Dickinson as follows. "When we reached Wrangel this woman was a hundred miles up the Stickeen River gathering the winter supply of berries. Learning from a passing steamer that the missionaries had come, she placed her children, bedding, and provisions in her canoe, and paddled home, against heavy head winds, to give us a welcome."[8]

Leaving Mrs. McFarland in Wrangell, Jackson asked Dickinson to become her interpreter. McFarland opened a school and reported that the native people were "very much interested in it" and that the class averaged thirty students. Sarah Dickinson was one of them; McFarland made a special note that she and Clah were in a class together. "They study reading, spelling, geography, and writing." McFarland taught in the morning, and Clah took over a "short session" in the afternoon. McFarland explained, "Since Mrs. Dickinson came home, Clah preaches in Tsimpsean, and Mrs. D. interprets his sermon into Stickeen."[9]

When the Presbyterian minister Rev. S. Hall Young arrived in Wrangell in 1878, he immediately made Dickinson his "official translator." Her son Billy also served as an interpreter, and Young trained him "for prayer-meetings and conferences."[10] Dickinson's influence in prayer meetings extended beyond translating. Young wrote, "Mrs. Dickinson must be given credit for checking the practice of entering complaints against and berating one another in these prayer-meetings and confessions."[11]

Dickinson also played influential roles outside formal gatherings. She was the voice through which McFarland and Young spoke in a wide range of situations in which they represented mission interests to the native community. Thus, in a sense, she acted as an advocate for the mission. On at least one occasion and possibly more, she helped McFarland and Young persuade reluctant parents to allow their daughter to be placed in the mission's residence for girls.[12]

Dickinson's responsibilities led her into extremely tense situations, sometimes reluctantly. Young determined to stop certain Tlingit practices that he and other missionaries felt were incompatible with Christianity, and he relied on Dickinson to act as translator when he intervened in native affairs. Much more than Young, Dickinson was in a position to understand the anger his actions would generate and to appreciate the potential consequences.

Particularly trying for Dickinson were the times when Young opposed shamans, or spiritual healers (known in Tlingit as *ixts*). Young and other missionaries in Southeast Alaska were particularly offended by ixts, who derived their power through communication with spirit helpers. Shamanism represented a competing belief system that threatened missionaries' success, and missionaries claimed ixts accused people of witchcraft and promoted their torture. Young waged an ongoing battle with them and on several occasions called on Dickinson to translate. He reported that she was very fearful of his actions, in part because of the power of the ixts and in part because she thought people were so angry at Young that they might use violence. During one incident, he threatened to fire her as interpreter if she refused to accompany him, and he implied it was only that threat that made her cooperate.[13] He claimed his success in that incident increased her confidence, and she was more willing to cooperate later.[14] However, it may be that this statement was merely an attempt to vindicate his actions and perhaps should not be accepted at face value.

In being asked to help fight shamanism, Dickinson faced a dilemma she shared with many native people in Alaska and elsewhere who worked with non-native authorities. Young, who liked his writing to be dramatic, may have exaggerated her reactions, but without question she was in a situation that many other native people also found tense. In the early 1880s, L. Beardslee, the naval commander, established a native police force in Sitka and reported that the only instance in which these policemen failed to cooperate with him was a case involving shamanism.[15] Similarly, Indian agents on reservations in the contiguous United States also found that the native police forces there were often reluctant to become involved in cases concerning accusations of witchcraft.[16]

Dickinson's own work with Clah and her diverse services as interpreter in Wrangell made her well suited to assume primary teaching responsibilities elsewhere on her own. The Presbyterian Board of Home Missions was quick to take advantage of her skills and her willingness to teach. When her husband was transferred to the Chilkat region in 1880 to run a store that was opening there, the board commissioned her to start a school for Chilkat Tlingits. She helped lay a foundation for the Presbyterian missionaries Rev. and Mrs. E. S. Willard, who arrived a year later to open Haines Mission. They employed her as a teacher and an interpreter. Mrs. Willard's first impression of Dickinson was tinged with the condescension characteristic of the period. She wrote, "She is a very good woman, I think, and has done well under the circumstances. We shall soon need a teacher of larger scope."[17]

Besides helping locally, Dickinson sometimes accompanied Reverend Willard when he traveled to more distant villages in the Chilkat country. She went with him and his wife on the first of these trips, shortly after the Willards arrived in the Chilkat region. As Mrs. Willard described it, the trip was not without dangers, including crossing rapids in a canoe. She explained, "I sat with my back to the head of the canoe, and saw the dangers only to be thankful that we had escaped them, while Mrs. Dickinson, turned the other way and seeing always the rock we were to split upon, kept uttering little cries of alarm."[18]

Dickinson was generous with her time, and she also used her ties with the trading post store to help the Willards. During their first Christmas in the Chilkat country, Mrs. Willard held out the promise of Christmas presents as an incentive to encourage children to attend school. Thus, she had to "grade every child and every present," a task involving some sixty-nine children. She reported that Dickinson "knit several little collars of yarn and two small scarfs, and gave me about a dozen tiny dolls out of the store, which helped a good deal."[19]

At times, Dickinson and her husband were the only other people near the mission who spoke English, and thus her company was important to the Willards psychologically as well as practically.[20] She was also their source of information when they were absent. In the summer of 1882, the Willards both suffered dangerously poor health and made an emergency trip to Sitka.[21] Dickinson sent them news before leaving for a two-month vacation in Oregon.[22]

If Sarah Dickinson had initially been reluctant to participate in Young's campaign against ixts, her actions were different in the Chilkat country. During the Willards' absence in Sitka, she heard of an elderly Tlingit woman who had been accused of killing a small boy through witchcraft. Indian leaders from the mission freed her with the help of Dickinson's husband. When the Willards returned to the mission in spring 1883, they found that Sarah Dickinson was sheltering the woman in her home. The woman had admitted using witchcraft but was still given protection.[23]

Caroline Willard's published letters conclude in November 1883, and information about Dickinson after that time becomes more scarce. In 1886, she was still teaching in the school at Haines and had an average of seventy students.[24] By June 1887, she had resigned that position.[25] Oral history or other written sources unavailable for this study might give more information about her life and her activities after that year.

Sarah Dickinson devoted at least a decade of her life to missionary and educational work among her own people. Despite Young's impression that she held herself aloof from native people, she clearly cared deeply about them and acted in ways she felt would help them. As noted above, her work involved episodes of considerable tension, exacerbated by the fact that she did not choose when to intervene in native affairs but was expected to cooperate nonetheless. Her services were tremendously important to Young and the Willards, who could not have functioned without an interpreter with a clear understanding of their teachings and a willingness to help promote their goals. Considering her importance to them, she appears very much in the background in their writings, primarily mentioned only in passing. It is impossible to know whether this reflects the way she was treated by them or simply the particular focus of their accounts.

Sarah Dickinson must have been at least in her thirties when she became a teacher. Some other native women and men in Southeast Alaska were encouraged from the days of their mission schooling to become teachers among their own people. This was an explicit goal of the missionaries. They felt converted Indians could be good role models for other Indians; they hoped that converts who taught themselves would develop a stronger commitment to Christianity; and they also faced a shortage of non-native workers. Caroline Willard expressed her views in an article written in 1888 entitled "Native Sabbath School Teachers." By that time, she and her husband were working in Juneau and had established a weekly class for the training of teachers. She wrote,

> When we started the Sunday School of the Juneau Thlingget Presbyterian Church it was with the determination of making it a Christian Training School,—that is of bringing into activity our whole Christian force among the natives . . . . Realizing that inactivity was full of danger for these young Christians, and that the best means of growth was labor for the bringing-in of others, we made them teachers in the school.[26]

This same philosophy undoubtedly informed missionary goals for some years before Caroline Willard described it; and students in mission schools had shown an interest in becoming teachers before such formal classes were formed. Tillie Kinnon Paul is one such student. She was born around 1864. Her mother was a Tlingit woman from the Wrangell area, and her father, a Scotsman, was a factor for the Hudson's Bay Company in Victoria.[27] She spent her early years among her mother's people. When she was about twelve, she was briefly in the Methodist mission in Port Simpson and then returned to Wrangell and entered Mrs. McFarland's Home for Girls.[28]

The girls at the school were expected to help with chores and to take classes in domestic work. Mary Lee Davis, a white writer who knew Paul later, suggested that this took a real adjustment, for she was from a high-ranking Tlingit family. Davis observed, "It often seems to me that even the best of our missionaries have not quite realized or given all the credit that they should to the stout-hearted perseverance shown by many a high-caste Thlingit girl, in going through with courses that meant manual labor." She added that most of the first girls at the McFarland home were of lower rank and that it would be difficult for someone of higher rank to work side by side with them.[29]

Whether or not this is true, Kinnon seems to have become committed quickly to her life at the home. In November 1879, she was the oldest girl there and was a leader among the other students. A teacher there wrote that she had become a Christian, that she "expresses a great desire to be trained for a teacher. She is already quite a help in teaching the younger children. She is a girl of much promise and decision of character."[30]

When Sarah Dickinson left Wrangell, Tillie Kinnon started working with S. Hall Young as interpreter. Davis suggests that this was a complicated responsibility for a young girl, for she had to adapt the images in the Bible to make them meaningful to her own people. Davis explained,

You may catch a notion of all the latent lurking difficulty, when you recall how very many choicest sections of our scripture deal with the symbolism of the shepherd, the lore and feeling of a long-time pastoral people, and of men as sheep that wander from the fold—sheep that are timid, frightened, lost. But Thlingit word for sheep refers to mountainy wild creatures . . . skilful in defence with their sharp horns and hoofs against even the most powerful prey-beats. All the rich color and the connotation of Bible story are quite lost, if this word sheep should be translated literally.

Davis concluded, "You will guess the struggles this young girl must make, using an art so alien to her nature, to turn such themes into intelligible Thlingit."[31]

Tillie Kinnon married Louis Francis Paul, a man of Tlingit and white ancestry. In 1882, the couple was commissioned by the Presbyterian Board of Home Missions to open a school in Klukwan, some thirty miles from the Willards' mission.[32] They arrived in Klukwan in late May, stopping first at the Willards' mission, where they were given slates and other supplies.[33] Davis points out that the fact that they were both from high-ranking families may have helped open doors for them among the Chilkat people.[34] Louis Paul reported that the Indians said they were sorry a teacher had not come sooner, "that by this time they would know more about God." Thirty-seven men and twenty-seven women attended the school with just twelve primers among them. The Pauls made regular circuits of the village, visiting each house three times weekly.[35]

Like Sarah Dickinson, the Pauls tried to decrease the practice of shamanism. Without providing details, Davis implies that this proved difficult and dangerous work for them, too. She suggested that their ties to both the Wrangell and the Tongass tribes helped protect them, as any harm done to them would have offended these powerful groups.[36]

The Pauls also opposed the manufacture of alcohol, a technique Indians had learned from whites. Tillie Paul suggested that drinking caused fights to break out between Indians. She sent an appeal that was quoted later, unedited, by Julia McNair Wright. "I would like if there were law to restraint those Indians from making liquor, for there is plenty of it in this place, for it is the root of all evil amongst them. If the liquor was taken from them, the [sic] would be peaceable Indians."[37]

Tillie and Louis Paul returned to Wrangell early in the summer of 1883, possibly in part because they were expecting their first child. Caroline Willard was pleased with what they had achieved. She stated, "The experiment has been well tried." Presumably she meant the "experiment" of sending native teachers to a remote location on their own. She added that "good work has been done. . . . The people have learned to want education, and now will be more ready to receive it."[38]

The Pauls' first son, Samuel, was born in Wrangell. They then moved to the Tongass region and opened a school among Louis's people. Their second son, William, was born in 1885.[39] Louis and Samuel Saxman, a white government teacher, drowned in 1886.

Shortly thereafter, Tillie Paul gave birth to her third son, whom she named for his father.[40] She moved to Sitka and started teaching at the town's native school and at the Sitka Industrial Training School (later called the Sheldon Jackson Institute), a Presbyterian residential school for native students. When her oldest son was four, she allowed Sheldon Jackson to take him east to live with Mrs. Saxman, who had moved there.[41] Saxman later went to Ashland, Oregon, and joined the staff of the Sitka Industrial Training School late in 1890.[42]

Tillie Paul played a variety of roles in Sitka. As in Dickinson's case, serving as a teacher meant a commitment of time and energy that extended far beyond the formal classroom. In 1889, a listing of the staff of the school gives her title as "General Worker and Interpreter."[43] The *North Star*, the school's publication, mentions her from time to time, and occasionally she contributed articles to it. The April 1889 edition notes that she was in charge of a "Sabbath School class" of about fifty "untutored natives."[44] Around that time, one of her duties at the Sitka Industrial Training School was to supervise sewing classes.[45]

In October 1889, Paul traveled to Oregon to visit her eldest son and Mrs. Saxman. It was the first time she had traveled outside Alaska. She later published an account of the trip in The *North Star*, noting that she had never before seen "the cars" (presumably streetcars) or ridden in a horse-drawn buggy. "It is wonderful—the works of man!" she wrote. "When you compare the works of God and man how wonderful the world seems!"[46]

Paul returned from Oregon in spring 1890 and was immediately commissioned assistant matron at the Sitka Industrial Training School. The *North Star* reported that she conducted a temperance meeting in the native village; by the beginning of 1891, she was the president of the native temperance society in Sitka.[47] She still served as interpreter when needed for classes in the native village.[48] For a six-month period in 1890 when the matron of the girls' department was absent, Paul acted in that position. Late in 1890, she was placed in charge of the Boys' Hospital and became the attendant nurse there.[49] The physician in charge, Clarence Thwing, wrote that she was "very devoted to her work and untiring in her attention to the sick."[50]

The Sitka Industrial Training School strongly emphasized English; children were not expected to use their native language. In 1891, Jackson reported that for five years, English had been the sole language at the school.[51] However, Paul and other native workers at the school did not reject their heritage; in fact, they found ways to express it and preserve it which were acceptable to school officials. Paul published articles in the *North Star* on native "folklore." One article, recounting a myth, concluded with the comment, "Old customs have bound us like chains of steel, but the missionaries have brought us a light—God's Word—which will yet save the remnant of our race."[52] It is unclear whether these words were written by Paul or by William Kelly, the principal of the school and an editor of the paper, whose name is written in by hand on the by-line as coauthor with Paul. What is clear is that whatever denunciation was added at the end, Paul was interested in publishing detailed accounts of native mythology.

Similarly, Paul helped to preserve the Tlingit language by working with Frances Willard to prepare a Tlingit dictionary and a means to put the language in writing.[53] Further, although students were prohibited from speaking Tlingit, there were special contexts in which the language was celebrated, and Paul took part in that celebration. Thus, on May 13, 1890, when the Sitka Industrial Training School sponsored an evening of "school entertainment," Paul and two other Tlingit women sang a hymn in Tlingit. They were followed by some Tsimshian students who sang in their language.[54]

The written record thus reveals a few ways in which Paul showed a strong interest in helping to preserve her culture. Undoubtedly, there were other occasions that have gone unrecorded. In the work she chose, Paul clearly had to distance herself from her native language and mythology most of the time, but these few glimpses from the written record suggest that she did not reject her heritage.

Davis reports that eventually Paul was promoted to the position of girls' matron; she claims the salary offered was $250 per year, half that paid to white women in the same post. Reportedly Paul decided to move to Wrangell because of the salary injustice and the jealousies her promotion had generated, but Jackson persuaded her to remain and increased her salary to $400 per year.[55] In 1903, the Presbyterian Board of Home Missions asked her to move to Wrangell to help resolve a problem that had caused some of the native Presbyterians to leave the church there. She moved to Wrangell and in 1905 married William Tamaree, who like Paul was of Tlingit and white ancestry. She served as organist in the church, acted as interpreter for ministers, and translated Christian hymns into Tlingit. After the Presbyterian General Assembly held in Cincinnati in 1930 declared women eligible to be elected as church elders, the Native Presbyterian Church of Wrangell made Tillie Paul Tamaree an elder. Thus, she became one of the first women in the United States to hold such a position.[56]

From her early years, Paul was encouraged and perhaps groomed to become a teacher among her own people. She must have been quite conscious of the fact that she and her husband were the first native couple to be sent by the Presbyterian Board of Home Missions to a post alone, and it may well have generated a considerable amount of pressure on people so young to live up to the hopes and expectations of their mentors. Clearly, though, Paul's devotion to her work went far beyond a desire to meet others' expectations. She was sincerely committed to her roles as teacher, interpreter, nurse, administrator, and temperance worker—and these responsibilities made up much more than a full-time job. At the same time, she cared about preserving knowledge of her native language and mythology, and made opportunities help do so. The work she chose in no way implied a lack of pride in her heritage.

Missionaries in Southeast Alaska sent some native children to Eastern institutions for training. Just as they hoped the children in the Alaskan missions would grow up to be teachers and lay workers, they hoped the students they sent East would return with those aspirations. One who did was Frances (Fannie) Willard, a Tlingit woman whom missionaries named for the famous Presbyterian worker active in the Women's Christian Temperance Union. She spent about five years at a young ladies' seminary in Elizabeth, New Jersey.[57] Graduating in June 1890, she took an appointment as an assistant teacher at the Sitka Industrial Training School. The *North Star* commented, "Miss Willard is the first Alaskan with sufficient training and education to be considered competent to take charge of a school."[58] A later edition commented at more length.

> Miss Frances Willard, who has been East for five years, returned and will assist in the work of the school. We are highly pleased with the education and the culture which she has acquired in the short space of five years. A debt of gratitude is owing the ladies who so generously and kindly provided and cared for her; and we trust that they may in a measure be recompensed by her life of usefulness. Miss Willard shows a commendable spirit and a sincere desire to help to elevate her people.[59]

The paper added that it was "most essential" that she learn "the art of housekeeping in all its departments" so that she could be ready for "successful missionary work and for making her life most useful."[60]

Willard's career exemplified the path missionaries hoped their native students would choose, and she was often cited by missionaries and their supporters as a model. One writer commented in The *North Star* in April 1891, "If you doubt the intellectual capacity, capabilities, or possibilities of the native girl, I advise you to become acquainted with Miss Willard."[61] Clearly, this writer defined these qualities in ethnocentric terms, measuring potential by the extent to which a person chose particular missionary-approved goals; Willard was probably surrounded by white contemporaries who did the same. Nevertheless, she did not sever her ties with her own heritage; like Tillie Paul, she wrote about Tlingit mythology for The *North Star*.[62]

Willard maintained contact with missionary supporters outside Alaska, contributing notes about her activities to the *Home Mission Monthly*. The *North Star* reproduced one of her reports in that journal.

> Nine of my little ones have been advanced to the First Reader. It would have done you good to have looked in upon us in our school rooms the morning that I announced the important fact of their raise in the intellectual world—nine pairs of shining black eyes looking so eagerly and delightedly into mine; all so overjoyed to have a book all their own to study. I expect great things from this class.[63]

This suggests that Willard derived much pleasure from her work in Sitka. Nevertheless, she aspired to go outside Alaska for more training, as she felt it would enable her to help her people more. The *Home Mission Monthly*, hearing her plans, wrote, "She will be warmly welcomed by many who have learned to love her for her work's sake."[64]

These aspirations played a major role in her personal life. When she first arrived at Sitka, Fannie Willard may have met Edward Marsden, a Tsimshian man from William Duncan's mission at New Metlakatla who served as the band teacher and the organist at the Sitka Industrial Training School.[65] Marsden's choices were similar to Willard's, but as a male he had more opportunities available to him within the Christian church systems. He attended Marietta College in Ohio and became ordained as a minister in 1897, after which he returned to work in Southeast Alaska. Like Willard, he broke new ground and was held up by his missionary mentors as a model. Since they had such similar experiences and goals, a union between the two probably seemed logical to many people who knew them, and at some point Willard became engaged to Marsden. White missionaries were encouraged to work as couples, and it is possible this proposed marriage may have been one of convenience.

At any rate, Willard found she wanted a different kind of life. In 1898, she broke the engagement and left Alaska temporarily to continue her schooling. Writing to Jackson from Seattle, she explained, "If I had become Edward Marsden's wife, that would have been the end of my ambition." Her ambition was to return to Alaska "not only as a teacher but as a trained nurse." She wanted to enroll in a three-year nursing course in San Francisco. Using self-deprecating humor to emphasize her determination, she implored Jackson to support her plans. "Did you ever hear of a Tlingit who never begged? I am not an exception you see. I *beg* you to help me in this manner."[66]

It is not clear whether Willard pursued more training, but she returned to Alaska and continued to teach at the Sitka Industrial Training School. It was then that she and Tillie Paul wrote a Tlingit dictionary.[67] Unfortunately, like so many of her people, she died early of tuberculosis.[68]

Like Paul, Frances Willard broke new ground in the eyes of her missionary mentors and must have lived most of her life knowing she was considered a model on display for others. Having been educated in the East, she had experiences very different from those of her contemporaries in Alaska; even Paul, with whom she worked and whose goals she shared, traveled outside Alaska for the first time only in 1899. Willard seemed strongly committed to working for her people in Alaska, but she also kept ties with the country outside Alaska, hoped to spend more years in school there, and rejected the life of a minister's wife in a small Alaskan village. Possibly her interest in spending more years outside Alaska reflected a certain restlessness with life in Alaska after her five years in the East, as well as her wish to be better prepared to help her people. While her experiences must have distanced her to some extent from her own people, she was dedicated to them.

Sarah Dickinson, Tillie Paul, and Frances Willard all chose similar routes to help their people. They each felt that an education in English and Christianity would prepare their people to face the changes to which they had to adapt and would help them survive economically and spiritually in the new society growing around them. They must have felt that this education had benefited them personally given the circumstances, for they each tried to make it possible for other native people to have the same sort of training they had received. Studying in non-native schools, adopting a new language, converting to a non-native religion—even, in Willard's case, studying in the East for five years—did not cause these women to lose their commitment to their own people.

From the records cited here, it is impossible to tell whether these women identified primarily with their native communities or with the non-native missionaries whose work they made their own. Often those determinations are difficult for an individual to make about herself or himself; they are certainly inaccessible to historians almost a century later. These women's contributions to The *North Star* were written for (and possibly edited by) a missionary publication and may reflect the genre encouraged or dictated by the editors; at best, they were not intended as personal testimonials and do not reveal much about identity.

In fact, the choices Dickinson, Paul, and Willard made were extremely complex. Converting to Christianity certainly meant giving up (or never accepting) certain beliefs of their people, but their choices were much more complicated than neatly rejecting one cultural package and adopting another. They devoted their energies to their own people and maintained an interest both in native oral traditions and in the Tlingit language. They opposed some indigenous practices such as shamanism, but much of their efforts were spent fighting the negative effects of white presence—effects such as alcoholism and the white exploitation of young women. They certainly did not view all aspects of white culture as desirable, and they certainly did not reject all aspects of native culture. Despite common assumptions today about missionary activities, these women's choices were simply not that clear-cut.

What is clear is that they were eager to help their own people and believed that the work they did would have that effect. They lived in a time of painful choices; theirs were probably often very difficult. However, in embracing Christianity, in adopting English as their language, in teaching in mission schools, they did not reject their own people. Rather, they viewed this route as the best way to help, given the roles open to women at the time, and they devoted enormous energies toward that end.

All three of these individuals appear to have been independent women with strong determination. Obviously, they were greatly influenced by missionaries, but they made their choices freely. And while they were leaders, they were not alone: around the turn of the century, many native people in Southeast Alaska, women and men, took similar options. In addition to Edward Marsden, these include individuals such as Frederick Moore, a Tlingit graduate of the Sitka Industrial Training School who continued his education in the East and later became a schoolteacher and interpreter;[69] Samuel Davis, a lay worker who taught and led a Presbyterian congregation at Howkan;[70] Mr. and Mrs. James Newton, Robert Harris, Charles Gunnock, John Howard, Dick Smith, and Sam Williams, who worked as lay preachers for Friends Church;[71] and William Benson, George Demmert, and George Field, who worked with the Salvation Army.[72] And while men are mentioned much more often than women in the written record, there were undoubtedly many women who also worked in similar ways and who might be more present in oral history.

In retrospect, some people may applaud their work and commitment, while others may question their degree of accommodation. Such judgments are difficult in hindsight and not particularly useful. These native educators worked as they did in a sincere and earnest attempt to help their people survive the changes forced on them. Their choice to work with non-native missionaries does not reflect passivity. Rather—like some different choices that other leaders made—their actions show great will and determination in facing the adversity of the times.

CHAPTER 10

THREE CULTURAL BROKERS IN THE CONTEXT OF EDWARD S. CURTIS'S THE NORTH AMERICAN INDIAN

MICK GIDLEY

EDWARD S. Curtis's *The North American Indian* (1907–30) is a monumental set of twenty volumes of illustrated text and twenty portfolios of large photogravures devoted to more than eighty different Native American peoples living west of the Mississippi and Missouri rivers who, in Curtis's words, "still retained some semblance of their traditional ways of life."[1] The collection of ethnological data—including movie footage, thousands of sound recordings, and, of course, the photographs—was achieved by a (changing) team of ethnologists, Indian assistants and informants, photographic technicians, and others. The production and distribution of the text, which became the responsibility of a specially created business company, The North American Inc., involved prodigious organization, massive funding from the financier J. Pierpont Morgan, and considerable attention to publicity. *The North American Indian* was sold on a subscription basis—mostly to wealthy individuals and major libraries—in a severely limited edition of luxuriously beautiful, leather-bound books. The project, which also led to the production of the very first feature-length narrative documentary film, gave rise to attendant photographic exhibitions, popular magazine articles and books, lectures, and even a "musicale" or "picture opera." It almost certainly constitutes one of the largest anthropological enterprises ever undertaken.[2]

The ideological position exemplified or implied in the visual imagery produced by the project, which has now begun to be analyzed, was that Indians were a "vanishing race," with many of the nuances in the concept that Brian W. Dippie has discerned in representations of Indians in general, especially at the turn of the century. Curtis's Indians were almost always "traditional," rooted in the landscape, caught in stasis, apparently above and beyond the passage of time, outside history. And many particular constituents of this image, as circulated by the project, were considered beautiful at the time and, whatever their relationship to "reality," have proved enduring ever since, especially as replicated in numerous westerns.[3] Features of this same ideological position also permeated the written text of *The North American Indian* and, as will be apparent here, informed other aspects of the project.

This chapter concentrates on three of the most significant figures from Native American communities who assisted in the creation of *The North American Indian*: Charlie Day, a young white trader who had grown up on the Navajo reservation and strongly identified with Navajo traditions; George Hunt, offspring of a Tlingit woman and a Scottish Hudson's Bay Company trader, a member of Kwakiutl society, and also what Ronald P. Rohner has termed an "anthropologist's anthropologist" for such prominent ethnographers of the Northwest Coast as Franz Boas and Samuel M. Barrett, as well as for Curtis; and Alexander B. Upshaw, a Crow resident of the fertile Big Horn valley on the Crow reservation who had been educated at the Carlisle Indian School in Pennsylvania.[4] Insofar as there was a preexisting pattern for the relationships these men came to have with the North American Indian project, it was one that had been established during trade in Native American material artifacts. Even before Curtis and his field party entered their lives, they were each, if to differing degrees, traders. And trading in Indian arts was an inextricable element of the Curtis enterprise from very early on; it certainly predated his dedication to the publication of *The North American Indian*. On July 31, 1899, back in Seattle at the conclusion of the Harriman Alaska Expedition, the leader of the scientists, C. Hart Merriam, wrote in his diary, "I spent much of the day in [the] Curtis studio looking over photographs and Indian baskets, some of which I purchased."[5] Once the project itself was under way, there was a crucial overlap between the collection of material goods and the gathering of ethnological information, and it is this connection—as a context for cultural brokerage—that I examine here.

On October 31, 1905, in Seattle, Curtis wrote to J. S. Candelario, the Santa Fe trader, about a "shipment" of blankets he had ordered. "Send them to me by express at once. Now, don't," he said, "pick out all the poor ones you have, simply because I am not there to see to the selection. You know that I am larger than you are, and if you don't make a good selection there will be trouble when I am in Santa Fe next year." This was but one purchase in a series that Curtis made to maintain a stock of Indian items for exhibition and sale in his Seattle studio. He wanted the studio to be a place for people to experience his Indian pictures in an "Indian" setting—"the home," as he called it, "of the North American Indian."[6] Usually writing from that home, Curtis encouraged some of his prosperous subscribers to use his services as a broker in acquiring Indian artifacts. He was exceptionally assiduous in his efforts on behalf of Miss Charlotte Bowditch of Santa Barbara. On one occasion, in 1913, he was prepared to let her have a Nootka hat from his "personal collection." She was evidently much taken by it and wanted more; Curtis promised to look out for others, saying, "The first time I find a proud lady who can be induced to sell her hat, I will send it on to you."[7]

Perhaps the starkest instance of this kind of trade was the project's dealings, according to Curtis's own testimony, with various Apache shamans in pursuit of a ceremonial artifact and its meanings.

When starting my work among the Apaches, I found that there was not a word in print dealing with their religious beliefs and practices. I quickly learned that all information relative to their religious beliefs was jealously guarded. . . . One of my interpreters told me who the foremost medicine men were . . . at the same time telling me that a certain medicine man had a chart which told the whole story. . . . I talked with the owner of the sacred chart. He first disclaimed any knowledge of anything of the sort, in fact, had never heard that the Apaches possessed anything like that. I then asked him, "If you had such a painted skin and I offered you one hundred dollars to see it, what would you say?" "I would say no, for if I showed it to you, I would be killed by the other medicine men and all the spirits would be angry and misfortune would come to our people." Then I asked him, "If I would give you five hundred dollars, what would you say?" "I would still say no, for if I was dead the money would do me no good." To make certain that he would realize the magnitude of my offer, I spilled out on a blanket several hundred dollars in silver. The silver held his eyes but did not change his "no" to "yes."[8]

But, as Curtis bragged afterward, later it did.

Lest it be thought that Curtis exhibited a uniquely pecuniary spirit in these practices, it is important to realize that trading was a common feature of ethnological activity of the time. These days, as the writings of James Clifford and others attest, there is concern, at least among museum curators and anthropologists, over the bitter legacy that the expropriation of cultural items has created, with resultant calls for their repatriation.[9]

But such misgivings are of recent origin. In summer 1899, for example, the Harriman expedition spent a whole day loading their ship with trophies from a far northern village. These were two gigantic totems, Chilkat blankets, masks, and carvings—all selected by the most eminent natural historians of the day, including the leading conservationist of the era, John Muir.[10]

One of the most prominent traders Curtis dealt with was Lorenzo Hubbell of Ganado, Arizona, on the Navajo reservation. The two probably met in 1904, and by 1906, Curtis was relying on Hubbell to bring him extra photographic plates for use during the Hopi Snake Dance ceremonies of that year. Later in the same year, in pursuit of blankets "more or less old," Curtis asked Hubbell if he had in his possession "one of the so-called old chief blankets." He also used a Hubbell blanket in his famous "Navaho Still Life" (1906), decorated his newly opened New York office-cum-showroom with Hubbell blankets, and secured more for use in his grand exhibition room at Seattle's Alaska-Yukon-Pacific Exposition of 1909.[11] Intriguingly, though, when Curtis wanted help in acquiring information rather than material goods from the Navajo, he sought it not through the biggest trader on the reservation but through the one with the closest family ties, Charlie Day, son of Samuel Edward Day, Sr.

By the early 1900s, Sam Day had homesteaded for twenty years just south of the reservation at St. Michael's. He had learned Navajo well enough to teach it to the Franciscan missionaries there, and Charlie and his brothers Bill and Sam, Jr. (who later married a Navajo woman, Kate Roanhorse, daughter of Manuelito), grew up speaking Navajo as readily as they spoke English. At the opening of the twentieth century, the Days operated trading posts at Fort Defiance and at Chinle, near the mouth of the Cañon de Chelly. Each of them was interested in the preservation of Anasazi Indian relics and ruins. In 1903, Charlie Day was appointed the official guardian of the ancient Cañon de Chelly sites by the Department of the Interior. Both Charlie and Sam, Jr., made amateur records of Navajo stories and ceremonies, and Charlie even purchased early gramophone equipment to record Navajo songs. He also acquired a camera to begin a photographic archive. It was probably this shared interest, as much as the fact that he was single and relatively free of obligations, that brought him within Curtis's orbit. It is likely that had Day's life not been cut short by an automobile accident on the reservation sometime toward the end of the first decade of the twentieth century, Curtis, who kept in touch with him at least through a terrible fever Day endured in November 1908, would have engaged him again when the project returned to the area to gather more data for the Hopi volume of *The North American Indian*, eventually published in 1922.[12]

Each of the Days interceded at various points on behalf of the tribe in opposition to Bureau of Indian Affairs policies or personnel, and they may be regarded not just as traders but also as cultural brokers. In 1905 and on through 1906, relations between Charlie Day and the Bureau of Indian Affairs were at their worst. With Daniel Holmes Mitchell, who traded with the Hopis, Charlie wrote to President Theodore Roosevelt to ask for the removal of bureau officials, including Navajo Agent Reuben Perry, who he believed had grossly infringed on Indians' rights. Indians had been accused of various crimes, tried and punished, even jailed on Alcatraz Island, without the benefit, in the traders' view, of due process. It seems that the intercession was ultimately successful, in that the Indians were released, but Charlie was in the meantime awkwardly placed.[13] Perhaps in retaliation for his activities, he was forbidden to be present at any Indian ceremonies. So when Curtis, having received Day's help in 1904, sought it again in 1905, Charlie wrote,

An Inspector came out here and I think I will be all right. But he told me not to have any thing more to do with dances in any way. His name was Mead. So if you want me to help you out in any way with my masks etc., you had better go to the Commissioner of Ind. Affairs and get a written permit for you to get what you want and for me to help you. Otherwise I would be running to [*sic*] much risk of being put off of the reservation, and I do not want too [*sic*] get out of here for awhile, at least I would like to finish my sandpaintings.[14]

Curtis complied with Day's request, and his letter to Comm. Francis E. Leupp revealed much more about Day's position. "It is as natural for him [Day] to [go to the ceremonies] as it is for a duck to swim," he said. "He was but a year old when he went to the reservation; his playmates were always Navahoe children, and when the Navahoe children went into the ceremonies, so did he. To him, Yobochai [*sic*] ceremonies count more than the fourth of July to the average youngster." And Curtis admitted how much of his own work had been dependent on the younger man, who was only in his early twenties at the time; in particular, Day's rapport with "the medicine men" had led to "the chance of a life time to secure a large number of sand paintings and their stories."[15] Clearly, Day devoted much energy to this task, and it added immeasurably to the store of Navajo lore recounted in the first volume of *The North American Indian*.

While in the preface to that volume Day did not receive the acknowledgment that was probably his due—though he was always remembered by Curtis and his family as a key figure in the Navajo work—the depth of his involvement may be registered by the content and tone of one of Curtis's 1904 messages.

Just a few days more of this Holiday rush and then I am at my Navaho notes and getting ready for my series of exhibitions and talks, and say, Charley, I am terrifically anxious about my sand painting of the Yebichai, as I want to use lantern slides from those sand paintings in my talks or lectures (say, I do hate the word "lecture")—but I do wish you could hear one of my talks; however, you have heard me talk until you were tired, any way.

The people who have seen my motion picture of the Buffalo Dance say that it gives them the creeps; they feel that the whole howling mob of Indians is coming right at them. Now, Charley, strain a point and get me your Yebichai Dance description and the sand paintings, if possible. . . . I am much in hopes that things go more than well with me on this trip [to the East], and if they do, you and I will have some great old trips.[16]

The Day material helped to make the first volume of *The North American Indian* a solid achievement—however we answer the vexed question of what constitutes a "good" ethnography. The visuals, the numerous plates of sand paintings and, especially, masks, some of them looking almost new, might give us pause, however. It seems that the masks were specially and secretly made for the occasion by Curtis and three Navajos who, in exchange for calico and cash, appeared prepared to defy the tribe, despite what a newspaper reporter called a "powwow" held to talk them out of it. The masks contained small "errors" or deviations in representational conventions. This was because Day knew that the seemingly literal taking of the image by the camera would not have been acceptable to his Navajo kinsmen. He was able, as a broker, mostly with Curtis's cognizance, to achieve a visual production satisfactory both to the Navajo and to Curtis.[17]

One of the things that made the arrangement satisfactory to the Navajos was that they were paid. Matilda Coxe Stevenson, a Bureau of American Ethnology worker and a prolific contributor on Indians of the Southwest, was distressed about this issue, though she was a supporter of Curtis in other ways. "I have always maintained," she wrote to Charles D. Walcott of the Smithsonian Institution, "that the native peoples will not sell their religion and the beliefs sacred to them for money." "Mr E. S. Curtis declared to me," she continued, "that to reach the inner life of the Indian one must have his pocket book overflowing until the money runs out in a stream upon the ground. Had Mr Curtis been an anthropologist I would have taken issue with him but I never argue for the mere sake of argument. Mr Curtis' work is beautiful as it is." While we may disregard the back-biting element in this comment—especially as Stevenson herself was well known for extracting information and materials by pressuring her Indian subjects—it is true that such trading became a consistent feature of Curtis's relationships with Indian peoples.[18]

In his old age, Curtis wrote that his very first Indian picture had been of Princess Angeline, Chief Seattle's daughter, a clam digger: "I paid the Princess a dollar for each picture made. This seemed to please her greatly and with hands and [Chinook] jargon she indicated that she preferred to spend her time having pictures made than in digging clams."[19] But perhaps the best-documented case is that of the Kwakiutl of the Northwest Coast. There the figure in the middle was George Hunt, a native Kwakiutl speaker of considerable standing in the tribe who had also long since made himself indispensable to a number of white scholars, especially Franz Boas.

Hunt was born in 1854, met Boas in 1888, and worked closely with him from 1894. Between 1896 and his death in 1933, Hunt supplied Boas with objects of material culture, several series of photographs, and, most important, some six thousand pages of tales, vocabularies, ceremonial description, and the like, covering not only his own immediate people but the Nootka, the Bella Coola, and other Northwest Coast groups. He was granted joint credit with Boas, if not equal scholarly recognition, for a range of collections of myth material, especially *Kwakiutl Texts* (1905). And the title page of Boas's ground-breaking *The Social Organization and Secret Societies of the Kwakiutl Indians*, published by the U.S. National Museum in 1897, reads, "Based on personal observations and notes made by Mr George Hunt." While a number of scholars have acknowledged Hunt's crucial role in salvaging a coherent record of the complexities of Northwest Coast culture—including Irving Goldman, who has pointed out that Hunt was sometimes more precise and more telling than his mentor, Boas, in his literal translations from Kwakiutl dialects—it is unfortunate that his biography remains unwritten.[20]

It is not surprising that when Curtis and his assistants came to work on Vancouver Island, they too sought out Hunt. Curtis and his chief ethnologist from about 1906, William E. Myers, most likely first met Hunt and his family in 1909, and for several seasons thereafter one or both of them journeyed to Fort Rupert and employed him as an informant, photographic assistant, translator, actor, and, perhaps most important, organizer. Curtis—and hence his family—remembered Hunt as prodigiously effective in achieving whatever was desired for the project as a whole. Many of Hunt's family acted in or helped out on Curtis's documentary feature film, *In the Land*

Filming in Kwakiutl country, ca. 1912. George Hunt holds a megaphone, and Curtis operates a camera. Photograph by E. A. Schwinke. Courtesy of the Burke Museum, Seattle.

of the Head-Hunters (1914). At the same time, improbably enough, Curtis recalled that the Hunt family's miscalculation of the tides had caused a group of them to risk drowning on a rocky island during the filming of a sea lion hunt. In a separate story, Curtis let on that Hunt was profoundly changeable in mood, irascible, and subject, he even hinted, to homicidal rages.[21]

That such accounts were most likely dramatic travelers' tales designed to play on the dominant culture's fears of "savage" and libidinous Indians is borne out by the fact that, at the very material level, for the film alone Hunt organized the construction of a whole village of false house fronts; also, massive canoes were built, masks were refurbished, cedar bark clothing was manufactured, and, just as he had for Boas, Hunt traded for and collected an array of traditional ceremonial items, many of which survive in museum collections. And Hunt's account book also survived, complete with a record of the payments made.[22] The full extent of such transactions—and, perhaps, some indication of their meaning—may be gauged by this newspaper item.

In his studio yesterday, Mr. Curtis was found arranging the prizes he brought from the North Coast country, the land of totem poles, of strange and grotesque masks and costumes, and of the strangest of secret dances; a land where in the old days head hunting was a common and popular pastime, and where man even now seems to hark back to the days when the human race was young and where the gloomy forests still retain something reminiscent of the somber ages before the faintest dawn of history.

On the floor was a chest half filled with ghastly human skulls and containing also a mummified leg and foot. Asked of what use were the grewsome relics, Mr. Curtis explained that they were part of the paraphernalia he had to have as a member of one of the many Indian secret orders. Part of this paraphernalia proved to be a necklace with bangles consisting of four human skulls. Were they the domes of wisdom of chiefs or slaves? Of men or of women? The artist-writer seemingly knew not and cared not. They were the requisite skulls. That was all he cared to know.

[Curtis] said that [Volume 10 of *The North American Indian*, on the Kwakiutl] will be of deepest interest, for it deals with the vigorous tribes of British Columbia, and will contain a wealth of material, in pictures and text, the great problem being to find room for even the best of the facts and illustrations. . . . In point of original genius in designing, [the] masks are in a class by themselves. Each separate costume has its own religious, family or historical significance, the stories of which Mr. Curtis naturally keeps to himself at this time.[23]

Needless to say, it is unlikely that Curtis would have needed any of these objects "as part of the paraphernalia he had to have as a member of one of the many Indian secret orders." Over the years, there were often references in the press, especially in Seattle papers, to Curtis's membership of Indian esoteric organizations, so it was clearly a feature of the publicity for the project. The project was written up as "discovering" unknown things, and *The North American Indian* was featured as being written by someone who knew Indian life from "the inside." (Volume 10 has indeed acquired among scholars the reputation of being the subtlest and most comprehensive version of Kwakiutl culture.) In later life, Curtis wrote a very vivid account of stealing skulls from Kwakiutl burial islands—"islands of the dead"—and, even, of securing the help of George Hunt's wife in getting hold of a complete mummified body. It may be that Curtis exaggerated somewhat, but as this contemporary newspaper account testifies, something of the sort must have happened.

The context, however, was not any participation in secret ceremonies preparatory to whaling, as Curtis's memoir has it, but the gathering of props for a film. *In the Land of the Head-Hunters* includes a number of sequences in which skulls appear, and it even has a section on whaling, a feature of traditional Northwest Coast (if not Kwakiutl) life no longer extant when this newspaper item was composed in 1912. If Curtis needed a mummy to go in the prow of a whaling canoe, as he claimed, it was not to hunt whales but to film the hunting of whales. Either way, graves were robbed and the dead disinterred. On one occasion, some grave boxes accidentally fell from trees while Curtis was photographing. "There was a veritable deluge of bones and skulls," he reported. "Like a boy gathering apples, I quickly picked up the skulls, thus adding five more to my collection." He himself called this pursuit an "unholy quest."[24]

Again, it would be mistaken to think Curtis was alone in such practices. In 1888, despite recording in his diary that it was "unpleasant work to steal bones from a grave . . . [even if] someone has to do it," Boas collected eighty-five crania and fourteen complete skeletons from Northwest Coast sites, and later he got Hunt to arrange the shipment of the whole of a Nootka island burial site, complete with skeletons and carved insignia, to the American Museum of Natural History in New York.[25] Both photographers and anthropologists habitually paid Indians. Hunt himself received a monthly allowance from Boas to cover his expenses for the extended periods during which he was collecting information and sending it from the field to New York, and after his death in 1933, Boas offered his widow a stipend, "if necessary." In fact, payments were made as a matter of course by Boas and his students and colleagues, and employees of the Bureau of American Ethnology were given a special allowance for the purpose. It may well have been the case, however, that the North American Indian project, as a strictly private enterprise, was able to distribute sums in excess of those available to other fieldworkers. And I have come across at least one instance of an anthropologist asking a Curtis worker not to pay too much.[26] Keeping costs down in this complex trading of information meant depressing the living standards of the primary subjects, the Indians, in just the same manner as could so easily happen in the trading of baskets, blankets, and beads.

At the same time, money alone—as Stevenson had discerned—truly was *not* always effective in securing the required goods. W. W. Phillips, Curtis's first ethnological assistant, left a record of one of the earliest thorough attempts of the Curtis party to gather data—in eastern Washington in 1905 after the reburial ceremonies for Chief Joseph of the Nez Perces.

The Indians continued their rites and festivities for several days, dancing at night, racing horses and playing games by day. All throughout the period they were assembled, hard endeavor was made to secure "inside" information, to but little avail. . . . Yellow Bull, the old warrior, though carefully approached, effectually evaded all attempts to get him to reveal anything relative to ritualism, legends, gods, or worlds hereafter. The very seriousness of the deference to the gods and spirits gone to the Great Beyond proved a barrier to the securing of details of its underlying causes. Persuade, reward as we would, veterans of the tribe refused point blank to divulge information. . . . After the dispersal of the gathering . . . I scanned the pages of my notebook, and wondered if succeeding efforts were to be as barren of results.

Phillips's notebook did, in fact survive, and, given his assumptions about the purposes of ethnography, it was, as he said, "barren of results." He and Curtis became, as he phrased it, firm in the conviction that "Indians must be employed to conquer Indians."[27]

And this is how they came to seek out A. B. Upshaw, a man Curtis probably first heard about as the Crow interpreter at the Omaha exposition in 1898. Although the Curtis party had high hopes of Upshaw, the white people at the Crow Agency in eastern Montana had a different view. "No one knew his whereabouts," reported Phillips, "but all knew that he would be of no use to us: lazy, dishonest, meddlesome, here today and there tomorrow; 'a regular coyote,' said the livery-stable man where we hired horses. . . . 'Don't leave anything layin' around loose'."[28] Finding, indeed, no trace of him, Curtis and Phillips drove alone to the Crow Fourth of July gathering on a bend of the Little Bighorn. They joined the revelers. "Though not without protest. Oh No!" expostulated Phillips. "But objections were soon overcome by a liberal use of silver, the men in charge pacified, and our own camp made beside a giant cottonwood." "Upshaw, The Terrible?" he continued. "Not there; but the Indians knew where he could be found. Admiration showed in their faces at the mention of his name, and we had no difficulty in securing a messenger to carry word to him at his home some sixty miles away."

After a fruitless week—at least as far as data gathering was concerned—they returned to the agency. In reporting what happened next, Phillips made one of his rare excursions into the realm of opinion.

It was while we were there that Upshaw, the Renegade, joined us. The reasons for his unpopularity among the white people soon became apparent, the chief being that he was both observing and discerning, and that he had a thought and care for the welfare of his copper-skinned brothers. Such characteristics in an Indian capable of conveying his impressions . . . to sympathetic listeners from the "outside," or to Washington . . . prove fatal usually to his reputation among local reservation authorities. . . . No abler character among Indians . . . have we met than Upshaw; educated in English and in his mother tongue, kindly, honest and shrewd; but to little avail. The odds against the advance of the educated Indian—barriers inter-

A. B. Upshaw, 1906. Photograph by E. S. Curtis. Courtesy of the University of Exeter.

posed by the white people who ought to aid them—are too many to be overcome.

Upshaw, son of Crazy Pend D'Oreille, a prominent Crow leader whose name was a byword for fearlessness, was born in 1875 in St. Xavier, Montana, and after graduation from Carlisle in 1897, eventually became a teacher at the Genoa, Nebraska, Indian School. In 1897, in an article in the Carlisle paper, he expressed assimilationist views, and in 1901, he helped to survey the Crow reservation in preparation for allotment. But by the time he came to work for the North American Indian project, as Phillips saw, he was regarded as someone who had indeed almost "returned to the blanket," as the pejorative saying of the time had it. Perhaps because he had largely turned his back on white ways, he was able to get the confidence of the older people so that the Crow volume of *The North American Indian*—as if in fulfillment of Upshaw's ambition (as remembered by Curtis's own son)—proved one of the richest collections of data in the series, frequently cited by other anthropologists of Plains peoples. Much of the actual writing of the early volumes of *The North American Indian* was completed by Curtis, Myers, and others in the Crow country, in a Pryor Valley cabin that Upshaw probably owned. He worked for the North American Indian project throughout the West until his death in 1909. The Curtis family remembered Upshaw as a gentle man, but perhaps not too surprisingly, in that he aroused racist ire by his marriage to a white woman and by his determined defense of the tribal land base, he came to a violent end: he was murdered in a brawl just off the reservation.[29]

At the end of the first season with Upshaw, in 1905, Curtis used a revealing—and impossibly oxymoronic—expression to a newspaper reporter: "In the Crow country I had an Indian interpreter who in some respects was the most remarkable man I ever saw. He was perfectly educated and absolutely uncivilized." "Through him," Curtis continued, "I was able to get some pictures of the July dances of the Black Lodge clan that were very interesting. And also through him I was able to meet the great Five Bears." W. W. Phillips recalled the way Upshaw worked as he took Curtis and himself through Crow territory in the company of two extremely aged informants.

We could have found no better interpreter than Upshaw, and as he translated the words of Bull Chief or Shot-in-the-Hand into almost fluent English, by the light of the flickering campfire, stretched close beside it, flat on my stomach, I jotted notes at a rapid rate. Shifting winds, changing the drift of smoke and sparks mattered not, tradition and ethnology had to be booked on the instant. Since the old story-tellers rested through the days, they lasted well through the nights, and not once did midnight find the camp asleep. On the day following each long night of note making, while the narratives were fresh in mind, I rounded out my notes, filling in gaps where a deadened fire had made it possible to scrawl suggestions only of the context of the reminiscences.

In 1907, Upshaw helped to arrange a thorough investigation of the Custer battlefield, in the company of elderly Crows who had served as scouts under the ambitious general. Over the years he collected ethnological data from members of a number of tribes, including the Sioux, the Arikara, and the Blackfoot. Most of this material, if without specific acknowledgment to him, found its way into the published volumes of *The North American Indian*. By March 1909, his prominence was such that—though he also had to suffer the attentions of the press, which lent him a deliberate touch of the exotic by dwelling on their surprise that such an educated person was "a full-blooded Crow Indian"—he was able to accompany Curtis on a morning visit to President Roosevelt's White House.[30]

While Upshaw's ethnological work was for the most part to his material advantage and to that of his people, there were prices to pay that Upshaw may have regretted. For instance, Curtis himself recorded an anecdote of the time when, under arrangements Upshaw had painstakingly made over a period of months, the two of them were able to participate in a purification ceremony that allowed them to see the Sacred Turtles—effigies made of thick buffalo hide—of the Mandans. Curtis badgered their keeper, Packs Wolf, and his two "confederates in the unethical affair" into letting him make photographic plates of the Sacred Turtles, even getting them to "strip" them of their decorative adornments and move them into better light, all the while anxious that other members of the tribe would discover this transgression of Mandan lore. When in fact more circumspect Mandans appeared, they "found me," Curtis said, "making notes in a little book. . . . I told Upshaw to tell them we were learning about a tribal myth. As we rode away I hoped we had convinced [them] that our own story was not one too."[31] Some prices Upshaw must have regretted. There were periods, for example, when a shortage of funds for the fieldwork meant that he went unpaid or was virtually laid off. Edwin J. Dalby, another of the Curtis field team in the early years of the project, remembered that on one occasion he and Upshaw had to be physically restrained by Henry B. Allen, a Skykomish friend and interpreter, from waylaying Curtis and manhandling him for the money he owed them.[32] Money was also at the root of another divisive encounter, as recorded by Phillips.

When we bade good-bye to the two old fellows who had been such boon companions, their per diem, for we paid all Indians for every assistance they gave us, was handed to them in paper and silver. The amount was noted by the younger Indians with us—a half-brother of our interpreter, and his brother-in-law who had hired for the trip under a different rate,—so when the time came to settle with them at their homes on the following morning, there was trouble in the air. The surly half-brother couldn't understand why old men were worth more than young men, and demanded equal compensation. He was stout and savage; expostulations addressed to him in English were useless, so he got his demands in full. He had been living a lazy life at Upshaw's expense for a long time, but then and there he received orders to leave the Big Horn Valley and return to his own lands on Prior Creek. . . . His wife and Upshaw's sister were bosom friends and when the rupture occurred between the two men, tears streamed their cheeks. To feel that we were even indirectly responsible for the breaking up of the happy home circle there on Upshaw's ranch filled Mr. Curtis and me with deepest regrets. I have often wondered to what extent the bad blood flowed; Indians, though, are quite the same as mankind in general, forgetful in time, forgiving and accepting forgiveness, but for the day and night that we spent on Upshaw's place, exchanging horses and fitting up for another long drive, the men were grumpy and ugly, and the women tearful.

On another occasion, Curtis actually succeeded in purchasing a tract of 120 acres of the Crow reservation by virtue of "the noncompetence" of "Crow allottee no. 2232."[33] The Dawes or Allotment Act of 1887 had done its utmost to extinguish tribal ownership of reservation land. Vast areas had been individually allotted, but often, the allottees, usually untrained in necessary farming methods, were unable to make a go of their individual plots and were forced to sell out. Upshaw fought hard for tribal members caught in this predicament. In 1909—with, ironically, a letter of support from Curtis—he mounted a vigorous campaign to try to prevent Indian land from being leased out from under them for cattle grazing.[34] That a figure as well known as Curtis, Upshaw's own mentor and employer, could buy Indian land would have been at least an embarrassment to him. As a cultural broker, he was betwixt and between—like piggy in the middle unable to catch the ball. Perhaps fortunately for him, by the time this land transaction took place, in 1911, he was dead.

Something similar happened between Curtis and Charlie Day. In Curtis's letter to the commissioner for Indian affairs, in which he sketched Day's upbringing on the reservation and asked for permission to have him allowed on the land to help with fieldwork again, Curtis, unbeknown to Day, said,

> As to the harmful effects of my work there, I am of the opinion that in breaking their old superstitions sufficiently to get the pictures which I did, did more to disintegrate the same superstitions than any other one ever has. The fathers at St. Michael say my work of the one season did more to break down the old superstitions [than] all the years of their missionary work. . . .
> Hoping that I am not overstepping any bounds in communicating with you in this way, and at the same time putting Mr Day in perhaps a more favorable light than he would be otherwise.[35]

One interpretation of this is that Curtis was cynically playing on Commissioner Leupp's known prejudices against native ceremonial life to place his own activities in a better light. Another interpretation—especially considering how easily brokerage shades over into trading, which, in turn, often allows, even encourages, expropriation by the stronger party—is that Curtis did, indeed, recognize the disintegrative nature of getting people to perform, not for a meaningful ceremony, but for money. Such episodes constitute sharply dramatic examples of the enforced substitution, in quasi-Marxist terms, of exchange values for use values.

In any kind of trading, the buyer does not always get what he or she pays for. Curtis himself admitted that on one of his visits to Hopiland he took a picture—what he called "a character pose"—of a "chief" holding a shield that a Smithsonian ethnologist later told him was "wrong." Curtis "wanted that particular Moki chief," the newspaper reporter put it, "to have a shield, as that was one of their ways of dressing years agone, but as the regular Moki shield was missing Mr Injun rung in one from another tribe."[36] And on this occasion, in the dealings with Charlie Day and the Navajo people, it is worth recalling as a kind of coda that the expropriation, if such it was, does not appear to have been definitive: present-day Navajos knowledgeable about the Yebichai when shown the Curtis film footage and still images of the ceremony, have wryly pointed out that their forebears who performed for Curtis did everything backward, presumably in order *not* to contravene tribal restrictions on the recording of such sacred rites.[37] What that "powwow" actually hammered out, presumably without the image maker's awareness, was not the total acquiescence to Curtis's wishes, as the newspaper journalist reported, but an ingenious way of placating him.

At the same time, insofar as Curtis understood at least the potential cultural destruction involved, it is an awesome paradox that the primary thrust of the North American Indian project was the memorialization of Indian cultures as they existed prior to that destruction. In light of this, the cultural brokers in the middle—whether by parentage fully Indian like Upshaw, partly Indian like Hunt, or white like Day—were in a position already essentially undermined. They each responded differently to the pressures of the situation in which they found themselves, and more could be said about the differences between them. But just as I am stressing that Curtis was not unique—or even exceptional—in his position, in that, as he saw, many aspects of the salvage ethnology of the time helped to "break down" Native American cultures, I believe it is more appropriate to emphasize not the special nature of their experience but its characteristic *ordinariness*. Upshaw, Hunt, and Day, wishing—as they each did—both to contribute to a significant study of the Native American culture with which they identified and to honor the laws, customs, and traditions of that culture were—in their very typicality—representative figures. They simply had to wrest the best they could from an always unequal relationship. But it is to their credit as individuals that they did this so well.

PART FOUR

TWENTIETH-CENTURY BROKERS

The intermediaries of the twentieth century have been strongly influenced by the contemporary world; at the same time, their lives have resonated with echoes of their colonial and nineteenth-century counterparts. Like their predecessors, they have honed their skills on cultural conflict and the search for methods of adaptation. Where the late seventeenth-century Pueblo intermediaries met the needs of readjustment between Pueblo and Hispano, so, too, did Jesse Rowlodge guide his twentieth-century Southern Arapahos in their negotiations with Washington, D.C. Where Evan Jones and John B. Jones filtered Christian values through a Cherokee world view torn by removal and, later, the Civil War, so, too, did Robert Young interpret the federal government's bureaucratic bumbling to the Navajos in the post–World War II era. Where the Wild West show Indians moved as two-way ambassadors between the worlds they knew and the worlds they met on their travels, so did D'Arcy McNickle interpret these different worlds through anthropology, writing, and the Indian New Deal. Where the show Indians proffered a performance for the non-Indian world, so, too, has Pablita Velarde offered a visual representation of her Santa Clara culture for the non-Pueblo world. In each of these broker's lives, changing dynamics within the societies they moved between called on their talents to mediate and, on occasion, to guide the cultures involved.

Thus, twentieth-century brokers have furthered a long and honorable tradition of creative response to crises engendered by cultural clashes. Yet they, too, have reflected their own era, one in which natives have been under increasing pressure to redefine their lives as tribal, pan-tribal, and pan-Indian people competing to retain their claim to a distinctive place in urban, technological society. For five centuries native people have fought to survive, but recent decades have seen this struggle take on a new cast. As Indians have moved into urban areas, both on- and off-reservation, and non-natives have moved into native enclaves through the ubiquitous media, the public schools, broader travel experience, and accelerated communication, the gap between native and non-native worlds has narrowed. The isolated and insular cultures retained by some tribal peoples into the twentieth century have largely disappeared. Today, television reaches into virtually every native home, whether urban or rural, and some form of schooling affects virtually every native child.

Consequently, the brokers of this century have faced a dilemma that is perhaps more acute than that met by any of their predecessors. In their own lives and in their roles as intermediaries, they have confronted the question of how native people of the twentieth century can retain distinctive cultures within the daily onslaught by outside cultures.

If schooling has altered the world views of most Indian people in this century, so, too, has it affected most of these brokers. It was their school experience that prompted most of them to move into multicultural worlds. As a powerful molding force, the school years introduced them to the "other side" and encouraged them to reinterpret that knowledge across cultural borders.

Jesse Rowlodge's career among the Cheyennes and Arapahos of Oklahoma was partially shaped by his schooling. Even as a political novice in his tribe, Rowlodge was quickly dubbed as one of the "schoolboys" because of his graduation from Haskell Institute. Rowlodge's off-reservation schooling did not make him a tribal leader. As Donald Berthrong points out, his training began at home, where he absorbed tribal customs and history. But his schooling did set him apart, marking him as one of those returned students whose knowledge was valued when "the way of doing business" was changing. When Rowlodge (and other returned students) began to represent the Cheyennes and Arapahos in Washington, D.C., he was carving out his dual role as tribal leader and intermediary.

D'Arcy McNickle drew on his early schooling years on the Flat-head reservation in his enduring quest for identity. As Dorothy R. Parker suggests, the writing of his novels pulled him back to a childhood dominated by a mixed cultural message—Indian at school, non-Indian at home. The Salish surroundings of his earliest school and the intertribal milieu of Chemawa Indian School often reminded him of his Indianness when he was far removed from his youth.

By contrast, Robert Young's relationship with the Navajos began not as a youth but as a student at the University of New Mexico, where his acquaintance with Navajo students led to an affinity with this people that has lasted over five decades. Following this commitment, Young eventually became a multifaceted educational broker. As Peter Iverson points out, Young has been an instructor to the Navajos, an interpreter of the Navajos for outsiders, and a pioneer in Navajo-English bilingual education.

Schooling also helped to shape the brokerage of Pablita Velarde. As Sally Hyer notes, the location of Velarde's schools was crucial to her identity. The proximity of Santa Fe to Santa Clara Pueblo meant that Velarde, like other Pueblo children, could return home each summer. In this manner, she was able to maintain her enduring links with the Santa Clara roots that reflect in all of her work. Equally crucial was her art training at Santa Fe Indian School, where the timing of her student years, which coincided with the introduction of the 1930s crafts program, was fortuitous. The twin influences of Tonita Peña and Dorothy Dunn aroused her potential and gave her the conviction necessary to become an eminent artist, thereby leading her into a lifelong career as an artistic intermediary.

Schooling, therefore, provided a shaping force that pointed these brokers in the direction of mediation. As multicultural figures themselves, it was appropriate that they consider the question of multiculturalism for Indians. Should Indians retain distinctive identities as tribal people, or should they become more like other members of society? Each of these brokers has addressed this key issue.

Jesse Rowlodge gave a qualified answer. As an Arapaho leader, Rowlodge clung to his tribal loyalty, never questioning what he had learned as a child about the "tribal obligations of a chief." In the political world, however, he foresaw that the changing relationships between tribes and Washington, D.C., demanded an altered structure of tribal government. The "schoolboy," therefore, advocated political adaptation to deal with a changing political environment.

Unlike Rowlodge, McNickle's view of the position of Indians in twentieth-century society was not tribally based. Despite his community development project with the Navajos, McNickle never viewed non-natives from within a tribal framework. This may have been advantageous, because it gave him a broader perspective; but it was also a disadvantage, because he never fully understood what it was like to look out from the center. Nonetheless, the breadth of his intermediary position gave him a certain clarity of vision, which he put to good use in the founding of the National Congress of American Indians and the establishment of the D'Arcy McNickle Center at the Newberry Library in Chicago. These milestones suggest that for McNickle, Indianness epitomized the future direction for native people.

Young has left the Navajo Nation with a singular legacy. His contributions to language and history of the Navajos remain an invaluable asset for them. His message to the Navajo Nation has been: preserve the language, study it, speak it, and teach it to the children. Therein lies hope for cultural persistence.

Velarde's response to the issue of Indians retaining distinctive identities as tribal people is more complex. Her role as intermediary hearkens back to the circuitous routes taken by the brokers of the late nineteenth century. Like the Tlingit teachers, Velarde has adopted some Western values, most notably that of individualism. But, again, like them, she has also sought to preserve the ways of her people, through her painting. As Hyer suggests, however, Velarde is rooted in a culture that places more trust in oral traditions than in the written word and that does not condone any violations of secrecy. Consequently, Velarde's brokerage may have been almost exclusively one way: from Santa Clara to the outside world. However, Hyer also notes that in recent years, some Santa Clara women have come to view Velarde as a role model. Velarde's impact on Santa Clara, therefore, remains unresolved. Since her own multiculturalism has been selective, however, her choices suggest that she, too, represents a voice for Indianness.

Cumulatively, therefore, these twentieth-century intermediaries have attested to the need for change. But the change they have envi-

sioned lies within the context of Indianness: the choices should be made by natives themselves, whether individually, like Velarde; communally, like Rowlodge; or through Pan-Indianism, like McNickle. In their lifetimes, the choices have increased, and the decisions have gained complexity. Despite these changes, however, cultural brokers have retained a central position as vital figures in a continent peopled by many cultures.

CHAPTER 11

JESSE ROWLODGE: SOUTHERN ARAPAHO AS POLITICAL INTERMEDIARY

DONALD J. BERTHRONG

EARLY in life Jesse Rowlodge began accumulating knowledge to become a political intermediary for his people, the Arapaho tribe of Oklahoma. As a youth, Jesse sat by Row-of-Lodges, his stepfather, an Arapaho chief, when chiefs and elders discussed tribal business. From Row-of-Lodges, Jesse learned tribal customs and history so that he possessed a comprehensive understanding of Arapaho social and political organization. When Jesse was about six years old, his stepfather sent him to the Arapaho boarding school at Darlington, and except for four years, he attended government schools until he was twenty-six years old. Row-of-Lodges and other Arapaho chiefs insisted that their children attend reservation and nonreservation schools so they could later assist their people in relations with non-Indians and government officials.[1]

On tribal censuses, Jesse Rowlodge listed his name as Moapie or Magpie in the Arapaho language. This may have been his preference, indicating his tribal identity or that Row-of-Lodges was not his biological father. Rowlodge calculated that he was born on April 7, 1884, to Owl and Bear Man in the Cantonment district of the Cheyenne and Arapaho (C&A) reservation. In interviews conducted for an Oklahoma Indian oral history project, Rowlodge never mentioned Bear Man and always called Row-of-Lodges his father. He knew, however, that he was the son of Bear Man and shared in his estate but not that of Row-of-Lodges. When heirs of Bear Man were being determined in 1906, Owl deposed that she was living with him when Jesse was born. "The boy [Jesse]," Owl stated, "was the issue of our union. We separated after the boy was old enough to crawl around." Owl, a niece of Little Raven, recognized as principal chief of the Southern Arapahos, linked Rowlodge to a large and important family most useful to him when entering upon his career as political intermediary for his tribe.[2] Arapaho chiefs, including Row-of-Lodges, realized that future tribal leaders needed to be familiar with problems arising from federal treaties and agreements. When Arapaho chiefs visited his stepfather's home, Rowlodge was present at their meetings. "Now this boy [Jesse]," Row-of-Lodges told other chiefs, "sits here with me all the time. He listens close and somedays asks me questions what we are talking about. And I explain to him. Someday he is going to be the only man [the Arapahos can rely upon] cause he notice and observe and I hope he had kept in mind what I've told him." In 1903, Jesse became a "boy chief" because he attended to the chiefs' needs when they met in council. Before his death in 1904, Row-of-Lodges taught Jesse to be compassionate to less fortunate people and to be "public hearted and public spirited." Rowlodge became a member of the Arapaho chiefs council in 1910 and for half a century remained active in tribal affairs.[3]

As a youth, Jesse lived in a large, extended family headed by Row-of-Lodges, who in 1891–92 selected a cluster of allotments east of Greenfield for family members. During school vacations, Jesse rode his pony selected and trained by his stepfather over the family's land. When white farmers fenced their land, Row-of-Lodges abandoned raising horses for sale and turned to cattle, hay, corn, cotton, and large vegetable gardens to provide food for the family and hospitality for visitors. With his family, Jesse attended Arapaho Sun Dances in Oklahoma and then on the Wyoming Wind River reservation after they were no longer performed in Oklahoma. Jesse's participation in men's age grade societies ended with his induction into the Star Hawk or Star Lodge, the second among seven and the last not involving sacred knowledge. He did not join other men's societies based on priestly authorization to avoid potential conflicts with tribal elders arising over differences about how best to foster Arapaho welfare.[4]

Row-of-Lodges insisted that children of his family attend Indian service schools. Henry Rowlodge and Arnold Woolworth, Jesse's cousins, with whom he was raised, were sent to Carlisle Indian

Industrial School in Pennsylvania after completing primary grades at the Arapaho reservation boarding school. Jesse Rowlodge attended the same school and in 1904, decided to enroll at Haskell Institute in Kansas. Between completing the first six grades at the Arapaho boarding school and enrolling at Haskell, he clerked in a store and worked as a cowboy in Texas. Disliking Carlisle's military emphasis, he decided at the age of twenty to attend Haskell, "where some of those pretty well educated Indians came from." From the age of fifteen, Jesse began to attend peyote ceremonies. A vision induced by peyote strengthened his decision when a voice instructed him, "Get an education. But keep this way, this peyote way. Believe in God. He'll carry you through." Although he interrupted his Haskell education to assist his mother, by 1910, Rowlodge completed an eighth-grade curriculum and a course of commercial instruction.[5]

His Haskell years broadened Rowlodge's horizons. He played leads in school dramas, worked in the school's bank office, played in the band, and was a member of the football squad. A sturdy young man, endowed with athletic ability, he attracted the attention of Glenn S. ("Pop") Warner, whose Carlisle football teams successfully competed against the strongest collegiate teams. Warner tried to recruit him to play football for Carlisle, but Rowlodge rejected the invitation. "No, I come to go to school. I didn't come to play football." And Rowlodge was respected by Haskell administrators. Superintendent H. B. Peairs used him to recruit students from the C&A Agency for Haskell. Once he wrote a letter to Superintendent C. E. Shell, who thought that it was "rather commanding." Peairs, however, assured Shell that Jesse was an "exceptionally good boy" and that the letter was not intended in that spirit.[6]

Erosion of Rowlodge's trust funds and land began while he was attending Haskell. Although tuition, books, some medical attention, food, and basic clothing were provided, Haskell students still incurred expenses for transportation, additional clothing, and medical expenses not provided at government Indian hospitals. Rowlodge at first defrayed those expenses by using money received from leasing his allotment annually for $200. Young men and women who spent more than a decade attending nonreservation schools acquired tastes for expensive consumer goods. When laws and Bureau of Indian Affairs (BIA) regulations permitted, older students pressed agency officials for their pro rata shares of tribal trust funds and for sale of their trust land. In February 1909, Rowlodge received $366.57, his pro rata share of tribal trust funds, and when that money was exhausted, he quickly sought to sell some of his trust land.[7]

After Bear Man's estate had been probated, Rowlodge received $500 from the sale of his allotment. He used the ploy, as was often done by older students seeking trust funds, that he would use the money to buy farm implements. This coincided with the government's policy that Indians' self-support depended on use of allotments for agricultural production. Rowlodge assured Superintendent Shell that he intended to farm on returning to the agency as he had "considerable training in Agricultural lines." He continued, "I am greatly interested in the same . . . and if I should succeed in getting the money I will not use it until I get home." Soon Rowlodge wanted more money, and within a year, he asked for a fee patent to eighty acres of his allotment and any remainder from Bear Man's estate, explaining that he would farm eighty acres of Owl's unimproved land. His maneuvering to sell his land stalled when Shell accused him of signing a contract to sell his land before a fee patent had been issued, in violation of BIA regulations. Rowlodge's denial that he signed any contract was insufficient to gain Shell's recommendation for the fee patent.[8]

For Rowlodge and most returned students, subsistence farming was a tedious occupation. Some, like Rowlodge, found employment in agency offices or Indian service schools. Jesse was first employed at the C&A Agency, which was followed by a brief period as an office clerk at the Seger Agency boarding school. In 1911, Superintendent W. B. Freer commented on Rowlodge's renewed fee patent application that he was "not very accurate and not very rapid when writing leases" and with "very limited experience as a stenographer and typewriter" he was unsatisfactory as a clerk. Although Freer described Rowlodge as farming "very well," he was not self-supporting. For perhaps four years, he farmed his mother's land, and one year he claimed he had planted fifty acres of corn on another relative's allotment. Finally in 1914 and 1917, he obtained eighty-acre fee patents for his original allotment, selling the tracts quickly for $2,200 and $2,700. Proceeds from the 1917 sale were given to Ira Sankey, "an older brother" with whom Rowlodge's mother lived late in life.[9]

From 1915 to 1920, Rowlodge worked as the Geary district assistant farmer and farmer. He performed many duties: assisting members of that Arapaho community with leases, seeing that elderly people obtained money for living expenses, supervising purchase of farm stock, settling disputes between Arapahos and white neighbors and businessmen, delivering mortgage payments to local banks, encouraging people to work their land, and urging parents to send their children to school. After 1920, except for a few years during the 1930s when he was a Civilian Conservation Corps–Indian Department foreman, he no longer worked for the Indian service. As a district farmer, he became well acquainted with Geary district Arapahos whom he would later represent on tribal councils and after 1937 on the C&A business committee.[10]

Rowlodge did not marry until 1917, when he was thirty-three years old. His marriage to Carrie Lumpmouth, an Arapaho chief's daughter, was arranged by their families. Sons and daughters of Arapaho chiefs frequently married. According to Rowlodge, "[When I] grew up they had that girl [Carrie] picked out for me. So they had us get acquainted and she went to school, . . . then we got married." Carrie was seventeen. They were married by a Geary Baptist missionary, and during the next two days, their families exchanged feasts and presents, a marriage ceremony pattern for prominent Arapaho families who were at least nominally Christian. Carrie and Jesse's daughters received good educations; one became a federal civil service employee, another a primary school teacher, and the youngest was a senior in El Reno High School in 1972. After Carrie died, Rowlodge married Sarah Lucy Coolidge, whom he called "my half-breed Arapaho wife," the daughter of the Reverend Sherman Coolidge, a Northern Arapaho and a leader in Pan-Indian movements. Reverend Coolidge's wife was a wealthy white woman from whose estate Sarah received $480 monthly.[11]

Since Rowlodge had disposed of his land and inheritance, he and Carrie had made their home on her inherited land. They maintained a large garden and kept chickens, cattle, and hogs that she undoubtedly tended because of Rowlodge's frequent absence on tribal business. When feasts were given at dances honoring family members or for meetings of the Native American Church, Carrie and Jesse provided much of the food.[12]

In the 1920s, Rowlodge devoted himself to tribal politics. For the rest of his active public life, he became a key political intermediary between his tribe and federal officials. He had a secure base from which to operate. Trained by Row-of-Lodges, related to the influential Little Raven family, Arnold Woolworth and Theodore Haury, Arapaho chiefs, and supported by Haskell classmates, for more than three decades, Rowlodge fended off all challenges to his intermediary's role. Although he did not possess tribal ceremonial status, his attendance at Sun Dances and peyote ceremonies and his membership in a Christian church enabled him to mingle easily with Arapahos regardless of their religious orientation.[13]

During the mid-1920s, a vehicle began to emerge for Rowlodge's subsequent political activities. Until then, nonliterate Cheyenne and Arapaho chiefs dealt directly with U.S. officials and attorneys who represented the tribes for redress of financial inequities arising out of treaties and agreements. In 1911, they originated a claim to share with northern divisions of the tribes and the Teton Sioux any recovery awards for the U.S. government's unilateral action of 1877 that sheered off the Black Hills from the Great Sioux Reservation. Men educated in nonreservation schools at the outset of the twentieth century were limited to roles as interpreters for chiefs as they met with government officials or attorneys.[14]

For fifteen years, educated men struggled for greater influence in decisions affecting welfare of the tribes. Two rival organizations, the Cheyenne and Arapaho Wigwam Society and the Cheyenne and Arapaho Progressive Council, both led by returned students, unsuccessfully sought authorization between 1908 and 1923 from the BIA to retain legal counsel. Finally, Comm. C. H. Burke approved a contract for Daniel B. Henderson to become the tribes' claims attorney. Now the Oklahoma tribes could join their northern kinsmen in pursuing the Black Hills or other claims. Once approval was obtained, cooperation was vital between the leaders of both tribes and all agencies to effectively pursue tribal claims.[15]

In 1926, Rowlodge was a member of an intertribal delegation that traveled to Washington, D.C., for a meeting with Assistant Indian Commissioner E. B. Meritt. All three agencies were represented, but most of the delegates were from the C&A Agency, the largest of the three. The participation of educated men, some of whom were chiefs and headmen, was evident in this delegation. Nonliterate chiefs and headmen still outnumbered "schoolboys," and deference was paid to the oldest chiefs in attendance, but educated men with and without tribal rank offered their views on many subjects normally addressed only by the older chiefs. They sought a jurisdictional law allowing the tribes to sue the United States in the Court of Claims and for Henderson to fulfill his contract by working more vigorously on their claims. Clearly, Cheyennes and Arapahos were adapting their political leadership to meet new conditions and issues.[16]

For educated men, membership on tribal delegations was a means of entering into the tribes' decision-making bodies. They realized displacement of chiefs in federal relations was not feasible because people of the tribes respected their judgments. Resistance by Cheyenne leaders to change in the tribes' policymaking procedures was predictable, while Arapaho leaders were more likely to accept sharing of power with returned students. Indicative of the attitude of many Cheyenne leaders is that of Chief White Shield of the Hammon community. When the chief heard of another election of delegates, he wrote to Superintendent L. S. Bonnin, "Maybe the [school] boys wanted to go right ahead and leave [behind] the old Indians. Therefore I understand three boys will be delegates and I know old chiefs usually go to Washington but I think this will turn out different." Bonnin reassured White Shield that it was unimportant who became delegates as long as "good able young men" were given proper instructions. "You know," Bonnin continued, "most of the chiefs are now getting old and times have changed a great deal. . . . It is getting time for the younger men to begin to take hold of things."[17]

White Shield's perception about subsequent events was correct. On January 6, 1928, twenty-two Cheyenne and Arapaho representatives from eleven voting districts of the Cheyenne and Arapaho Agency met at El Reno. Eleven of the representatives were chiefs or headmen, only four of whom were without significant education; the others were returned students, and six of the representatives were mixed-bloods. The Cheyenne and Arapaho representatives each elected two delegates to meet with Henderson and BIA officials. The Arapahos selected Jesse Rowlodge and Arnold Woolworth, both chiefs, while the Cheyennes elected Robert Burns and Alfred Wilson, who were not chiefs or headmen. All were "schoolboys" within White Shield's definition, although Rowlodge and Wilson were in their forties, and Burns and Woolworth were in their sixties. With the election, Rowlodge became a political intermediary for the Arapahos.[18]

Several factors enabled Rowlodge and friends to continue their quest for a substantial role in tribal governance. After June 1927, the Cantonment and Seger agencies were consolidated with the Cheyenne and Arapaho Agency headquartered at Concho. Superintendent Bonnin, a Haskell classmate of Rowlodge's and others', was sympathetic to their aspirations. One rather than three delegations could now conduct all federal relations at the national capital or agency headquarters. A majority of returned students believed that the tribes' welfare depended on them rather than on older, uneducated chiefs and headmen. Probably with the concurrence of returned students, Bonnin asked John W. Block, who had presided at an earlier organizational meeting, to assist in creating a Cheyenne and Arapaho "General Council" to handle "in a businesslike manner all affairs pertaining to the tribe." Knowing Block planned to accept employment elsewhere, Bonnin asked him to convene a second meeting so that another "president" could be elected.[19]

Reassembling representatives from all agency districts required several months. The first attempt failed when older Cheyenne chiefs, piqued by not being included on the recent Washington delegation, refused to attend. On May 5, 1928, however, representatives from most districts met at DeForest Antelope's home near Watonga, with some influential Cheyenne and Arapaho chiefs present. John Fletcher, a Cheyenne mixed-blood, was elected president; Henry Rowlodge, vice-president; and Jesse Rowlodge, secretary and corresponding secretary. All were schoolboys. After the election, Jesse presented a report of the delegation's Washington meeting with BIA officials and Henderson. Bonnin later submitted to the Indian Office the names of those who were "the fully authorized and recognized officers of the tribal council."[20]

Dissent quickly emerged over the new general council. John Otterby, a Cheyenne mixed-blood headman educated at Haskell, complained to the Indian Office that older leaders did not understand what was transpiring and that some districts of the agency were not represented during the election of the general council's officers and delegates. Otterby denounced the officers as Native American Church defenders of "Payote [sic] & drinking and gambling," and his letter was sent to Bonnin for reply. Bonnin reminded Otterby that all circulars pertaining to the meetings had been sent to him, but he had been absent visiting Osage friends. To Commissioner Burke, Bonnin described Otterby as a person "of some education" who had been an agency employee, but presently "he had permitted his hair to grow out long and had reverted to wearing a blanket. . . . [Because he could speak and write English] he is able to put himself among the older type of Indians as a leader." Defending Jesse Rowlodge and other organizers of the general council, Bonnin explained that tribal business in the past had not been handled satisfactorily "by the so-called chiefs" so "the young ones and those who have been off to school are beginning to exert themselves."[21]

Chiefs from the Cheyenne Cantonment district also criticized the general council. Through Herbert Walker, a Haskell-trained headman, they inquired if a second lawyer could not be retained to pursue claims arising out of treaties and the tribes' cession agreement. "If we have to wait & wait for our attorney Mr. Henderson," Walker wrote, "we might lose our other claims." In response Bonnin informed Walker that Henderson had written a letter to Rowlodge explaining his work as tribal counsel. Bonnin thereby recognized the general council's officers as appropriate persons to conduct tribal business.[22]

The general council still needed a more formal political organization and tribal approval to sustain their participation in tribal business. In late May 1929, Cheyennes and Arapahos met in Clinton and approved a constitution establishing a continuing general council. Information about the Clinton assemblage is scanty, but Rowlodge was among those who worked out a crucial compromise assuring returned students a future role as intermediaries and decision makers. The constitution divided the agency into eight Cheyenne and six Arapaho election districts, each electing four members of the general council. By informal agreement, "two chiefs and two younger educated men" would be elected by local councils, assuring both groups of general council members.[23]

The 1929 constitution contained only four articles. It created a general council whose purpose was "to discuss all tribal matters and conditions" and to secure "to ourselves the rights of citizenship and justice to which we are entitled." Five officers were enumerated for two-year terms of office. The council president was empowered to call special council meetings and appoint members to standing committees. In practice, when the president was a Cheyenne, the vice-president was an Arapaho, and committee membership was divided between members of the two tribes. During the eight years of the general council's existence, Rowlodge served as corresponding secretary, council president (1933–35), or council member.[24]

Periodically, challenges arose to the council and to Washington delegations chosen only from council membership. Red Bird Black, a Cheyenne headman, implicitly criticized the new organization by calling for only chiefs to conduct all tribal business. DeForest Antelope, however, defended educated men sharing power with chiefs, asserting people "have gotten used to conducting our business in councils such as this meeting. I think our young men fit better in duties entrusted to them but [we] should recognize our older members." When another delegation was selected in December 1930, Turkey Legs and Whiteman, an Arapaho chief, both council members, were elected to accompany Jesse Rowlodge and Alfred Wilson, the council's president, to Washington.[25]

In 1931, when a U.S. Senate subcommittee visited Concho, only general council members offered testimony. Rowlodge, as the council's corresponding secretary, presented a written statement to the senators summarizing tribal needs, such as more adequate health care, extension of the agency boarding school through twelve grades, loans to assist Indians trying to farm, a home for the elderly, and more employment for younger tribal members.[26]

Cheyenne chiefs and headmen again in late 1931 challenged the growth of the council's prerogatives. They urged Comm. C. J. Rhoads "to again recognize the . . . rights of Chiefs and headmen in representing themselves. . . . Their rights have been taken away from them by a younger set of men." Their protest spilled over into a council meeting when some members were outspoken in their opposition to the council and its officers. Mack Haag, a Cheyenne mixed-blood, the council's president, and Rowlodge were particular targets of the critics, who called for their resignations. Rowlodge insisted that as long as a "majority of the districts express their desire to retain me" as corresponding secretary, he would not resign. He and the other officers were vindicated when they were reelected by a vote of twenty-six to three.[27]

Every election of Washington delegates resulted in conflict between factions within the general council. Early in 1932, a new contract with Henderson was necessary, so the council debated who should go to Washington. Some wanted to elect only chiefs; others desired only young, educated men as delegates. A compromise was reached: each tribe would send an older chief, a middle-aged chief, or a headman who could understand some English and a "well informed young man." Rowlodge was elected by the Arapahos, as were Chiefs Whiteman and Woolworth. After the Cheyennes elected their delegates, Cheyenne Chief Little Face exhorted the council to "unite, and as brothers encourage our young men and delegates. It is not good to pull apart or away."[28]

In late May 1932, Rowlodge and Wilson traveled to the nation's capital. They successfully lobbied the Oklahoma congressional delegation for another Cheyenne and Arapaho jurisdictional bill. With Henderson, they reviewed documents related to the Black Hills claim and the tribes' cession agreement. Commissioner Rhoads assisted Rowlodge and Wilson in writing and obtaining another contract for Henderson. Although their report revealed their competence to conduct tribal business, they delayed too long in reporting back to the tribal council.[29]

Even Arapaho chiefs who had supported the council temporarily joined its critics. In 1933 when another delegation was being formed, Sage wanted delegations to be composed of "older men of the Tribe and not young mixed bloods." Little Bird added, "Only full bloods [should] be used as Interpreters for any Delegation" because "mixed bloods are not always to be depended on." Cheyennes eliminated Wilson, but all the new delegates were either Carlisle or Haskell graduates, and one-half were mixed-bloods. At a later meeting with Superintendent Bonnin, Little Bird wondered "whether or not he . . . [was] a chief anymore" since he did not know what is going on in Washington conferences. Bonnin again staunchly defended the younger, educated men's representation of the tribes. Once a delegation was selected, Bonnin responded that it was "the lawful representative of the Cheyenne and Arapaho people" and that only the council could determine "what member of the tribe or [council] members should be elected as delegates."[30]

Rowlodge's election as president of the general council coincided with John Collier's appointment as commissioner of Indian affairs. The council quickly became enmeshed in Collier's proposed reform of Indian policy embodied in the Wheeler-Howard bill. One part of Collier's reform that called for Indians to "transfer control over their lands to an incorporated Indian community" caused consternation among Cheyennes and Arapahos who retained about one-third of the land originally allotted to tribal members. In a February 1934 meeting with Commissioner Collier, Rowlodge sought clarification of the Wheeler-Howard bill. He asked if landowners would be compelled to give up their land. Since the Cheyenne and Arapaho tribes lacked money to purchase sufficient land to establish colonies, how could additional funds be obtained? Collier's answers did not satisfy Cheyennes and Arapahos retaining trust land.[31]

A few months later, Rowlodge's testimony on the Wheeler-Howard bill before the Senate Indian Affairs Committee reflected the division of opinion among the tribes. About two-thirds of the tribes without trust land favored the bill, while trust landholders did not. When Rowlodge returned from Washington, gossip persisted that he favored landless people and that he had testified against landowners. Before the council, he vehemently denied favoring the landless. Tribal concern over the Wheeler-Howard bill ended when the Indian Reorganization Act (IRA) excluded Oklahoma tribes from its provisions.[32]

Collier, however, persisted for inclusion of Oklahoma tribes in his reform program. After a vigorous debate between Oklahoma Sen. Elmer Thomas, who had opposed inclusion of Oklahoma tribes in the IRA's provisions and one of Collier's assistants in October 1934 at Concho, the senator asked the council what the tribes wanted in the pending Thomas-Rogers bill that in 1936 became the Oklahoma Indian Welfare Act (OIWA). The holders of trust land, he was told, still feared Collier's colonization scheme. And the council again wrangled over who should travel to Washington. Finally, Rowlodge and John Fletcher, the council's secretary, were elected and testified in 1935 before the Senate Indian Affairs Committee. They supported most of the bill that would extend to Oklahoma tribes authority to adopt a constitution, elect a business committee, and incorporate under a federal charter for legal and financial purposes. Both objected to a provision, struck from the final bill, for competency commissions that would determine if an individual's property should remain in trust.[33]

In February 1937, Superintendent C. H. Berry initiated meetings to bring the tribes under the OIWA. Berry reported a "considerable percentage" of the tribes "more or less favorable" to the OIWA once they realized the tribes would not be required to adopt a charter of incorporation. The superintendent was, perhaps, too optimistic, because many Cheyenne and Arapaho leaders during a March 17 meeting in Weatherford opposed reorganization of the tribes. Even Woolworth, who assisted in steering the general council through several earlier crises, spoke against reorganization. Fletcher warned Morris Opler, an Indian service anthropologist, "You must understand the old Indians . . . don't trust the younger element." Berry agreed that leading chiefs feared defeat if offices were submitted to a popular vote enabling "the younger and better educated element . . . [to] be elected to positions of responsibility."[34]

Commissioner Collier informed Berry that the general council could write a new constitution. On May 4, 1937, he instructed the superintendent that "any duly authorized and elected council may and should be dealt with by the superintendent in the matter of tribal organization and incorporation" under OIWA. Four days later, the council empowered its president, Alfred Wilson, to appoint a committee that would bring a "tentative constitution" before the next council meeting for acceptance, amendment, or rejection.[35]

On May 17, 1937, President Wilson appointed his committee. It contained seven members from each tribe, only one of whom had not served on the council and only four or five of whom were not literate. With Rowlodge serving as secretary, the committee spent June 1 and 2 revising a draft constitution provided by Opler, and the final document was forwarded to the Indian commissioner for his comments. After several changes, Oscar L. Chapman, assistant secretary of the interior, on August 25, approved a revised constitution and by-laws for the Cheyenne-Arapaho Tribes of Oklahoma. The constitution provided for a twenty-eight member business committee equally divided between Cheyennes and Arapahos. The constitution continued the precedent of having a mix of appointed chiefs and headmen and elected members who presumably would be younger, educated tribal members.[36]

A tribal referendum was held on September 18, 1937, to ratify or reject the new constitution. The constitution was ratified by a vote of 542 (56.5 percent) to 417 (43.5 percent). Rowlodge's Geary district voted 71.2 percent in favor of ratification. The most intense opposition was centered in four predominantly Cheyenne districts and the Arapaho Cantonment district.[37]

Rowlodge was not elected to the first business committee, but he remained active in tribal business. In June 1939, he and Otterby met with Indian service officials arranging for a new tribal attorney, another jurisdictional bill, and restoration of unused agency and school lands to the tribes. He was, however, elected to the second business committee and became its chairman. During his tenure as chairman, several important ordinances were enacted. On January 3, 1940, the business committee adopted an ordinance requiring tribal members to marry and divorce according to civil laws, negating after August 21, 1941, marriages or divorces by tribal customs. In October 1941, the business committee was reduced by one-half, with its numbers still equally divided between the tribes. This action amending the 1937 constitution made no provision for the appointment of chiefs and headmen to the business committee, forcing them to seek election.[38]

While a business committee member during the 1940s and early 1950s, Rowlodge was one of the tribes' key representatives before congressional committees, and he met with Indian service officials and worked closely with tribal attorneys. He frequently chaired the business committee's legislative, claims, and resolutions committees. The claims committee became important after 1946 when Congress created the Indian Claims Commission. Thereafter, Rowlodge, described by another Arapaho chief as a person who "knew the ropes," assisted the tribes' attorney's preparation for the commission's hearings. Not everything Rowlodge sought for the tribes resulted in success. When the Fort Reno Military Reservation was abandoned as a cavalry remount station, he unsuccessfully argued before a congressional committee that the land should revert to the tribes.[39]

Rowlodge was elected in December 1951 to another term as chairman of the business committee. Much of his time was devoted to perfecting the tribes' presentation to the Indian Claims Commission and to a new, complex issue. A dam constructed by the U.S. Corps of Engineers near Canton flooded some allotments but created for recreational purposes valuable shoreline allotments and tribal land. The trust land, however, could not be leased legally for sufficient periods to justify private investments for recreational facilities. Again Rowlodge testified before congressional committees in support of a bill that became the 1955 Long Term Lease Act, which authorized renewable leases for recreational and other purposes.[40]

During 1954–55 a serious threat to the business committee's existence arose. Some Cheyenne chiefs and headmen still resented the necessity of being elected to the committee; others believed they alone should handle tribal business. Rowlodge's successor as chairman signed a few checks to pay tribal expenses with only informal consent of several committee members. Gossip spread that the chairman and a few individuals were profiting at the tribes' expense. Critics circulated a petition and acquired three hundred signatures calling for the dissolution of the business committee. At first the business committee merely tabled the petition, but when gossip persisted, the petition was sent to W. J. Pitner, director of the BIA Anadarko area office. Rowlodge tried to discredit those who circulated the petition, insisting that they had misinformed people about the petition's purpose. He also opposed an at-large election of the business committee's chairman, fearing, perhaps, that the more numerous Cheyennes would always elect one of their tribe as chairman.[41]

On June 1, 1955, Pitner met with the business committee, explaining that the committee could only be dissolved by vote of an annual meeting of the tribes or by a referendum of all eligible voters. Alfred Whiteman, an Arapaho who initiated the petition, continued to demand the committee's dissolution and restoration of chiefs' and headmen's control of tribal governance. An Arapaho chief, Dan Blackhorse, who had served previously on business committees, chided Whiteman for not first presenting his grievances to the Arapaho chiefs council. Rowlodge was even sharper than Blackhorse, asking "what is back of this [the petition] . . . and for one good reason" why the committee should be dissolved. Fi-

Jesse Rowlodge, 1958. Courtesy of the National Anthropological Archives, Smithsonian Institution.

nally, the committee decided to present the issue to a joint meeting of the committee and tribal members.[42]

The issue of the business committee's continuance was presented on October 15, 1955, to tribal members. Rowlodge reviewed adoption of the 1937 constitution and the accomplishments of the business committees. Undoubtedly knowing that most of the people in attendance supported the business committee, he moved for its dissolution, received a second from Richard Boynton, Sr., a pro-business committee Cheyenne. Whiteman continued his attack on the committee, impugning its administration of the tribal revolving loan fund and paying a tribal attorney large fees for accomplishing little. But Rowlodge had not erred; his motion failed by a vote of ten for to thirty-five against.[43]

At the age of seventy-three, Rowlodge did not stand for reelection to the business committee. He did not, however, abandon his interest in tribal governance. In the 1960s, he disapproved of several business committee candidates' methods of winning their seats, accusing them of buying votes with promises of favors, food, liquor, and transportation to polling places. He unjustly criticized two college graduates as unqualified to serve because they "did not know the old ways." He accused one 1960s business committee of being "high school smarties" and of bungling the final process leading to the $11,000,000 Indian Claims Commission award. Rowlodge did not like the committee's action setting aside money so that no one received their "full, complete, [per] capita share" of the award, hinting that he would use his influence to unseat some committee members.[44]

Rowlodge died on November 10, 1974, at the age of ninety. His ability to survive as political leader of and political intermediary for his people despite the turbulence of tribal factionalism was as remarkable as his longevity. During the thirty years he was active as a member and officer of the general tribal council and business committee, he made forty trips to Washington, D.C., on tribal business. He assisted tribal attorneys who attempted to obtain compensation for tribal lands lost by inequitable treaties and to restore a small fragment of those lands to tribal ownership. During his life, Moapie fulfilled his father's admonition that an Arapaho chief should be a "public hearted and public spirited" leader.[45]

CHAPTER 12

D'ARCY McNICKLE: LIVING A BROKER'S LIFE

DOROTHY R. PARKER

THE circumstances of D'Arcy McNickle's birth in 1904 created a potential for cultural brokerage that he did not realize for almost thirty years. In struggling to write his first novel, he found a new awareness of his mixed-blood heritage, and his work for the Bureau of Indian Affairs (BIA) in the seventeen years that followed provided a unique training ground for his subsequent writing and teaching. McNickle spent the rest of his life interpreting Indians to whites, whites to Indians, and even Indians to other Indians.[1]

McNickle was born on the Flathead reservation in western Montana, and he was barely a year old when he, his two sisters, and his mother were adopted into the Flathead tribe. His father's family was Irish, but his mother's people were métis, or French Canadian, descendants of earlier liaisons between French traders and Indian women. His maternal grandfather was Isidore Parenteau, a patriarch of one of the leading métis clans, and his grandmother was Judith Plante, whose family were well known as makers of the two-wheeled "Red River" carts used by the métis people on their travels across the northern prairies. Isidore, Judith, and their children had fled Canada in the aftermath of the Riel Rebellion of 1885, when D'Arcy's mother, Philomene, was three years old. Twenty years later, in 1905, she and her three children were adopted into the Flathead tribe, and the siblings were listed on tribal rolls as one-fourth Cree. Despite their Flathead affiliation, however, the children were raised in an English-speaking household. Neither parent wanted the children raised as Indians.

When McNickle was nine years old, his parents were divorced, and because the children were enrolled as tribal members, they were sent to Chemawa, an off-reservation Indian boarding school near Salem, Oregon. McNickle returned to Montana three years later and lived with his mother and her new husband, Gus Dahlberg, until his junior year at Montana State University. By that time he had decided to become a writer, and he had contributed some short stories and poetry to the college literary magazine.

By the early 1930s, McNickle had been to Europe, married his college sweetheart, and settled in New York City, where he began his first novel. Basing his narrative on a true event in recent Montana history, he told the story of Archilde, a mixed-blood youth caught between the Indian world of his mother and the non-Indian world of his father. Largely autobiographical, *The Surrounded* dramatically reflected the clash of cultures embedded in his memory of the reservation.[2]

The evolution of that first novel reflected McNickle's growing awareness of the Salish traditions that had marked the periphery of his childhood. The earliest extant version of the novel, "The Hungry Generations," which is preserved in McNickle's papers at the Newberry Library in Chicago, is an affirmation of mainstream American ideals of justice and the Puritan work ethic. In this early version, Archilde buys into the American dream. In the published work, however, he rejects that dream as he gradually discovers the traditional culture of his mother's people. As a result, he is "surrounded"—by the government, the church, and the values of the dominant society. The final scene of the novel holds little hope for Archilde's survival as an Indian.

McNickle himself, however, found such hope in John Collier's "Indian New Deal," during which he discovered his potential as a cultural broker. Collier was appointed commissioner of Indian affairs in 1933. Through the Indian Reorganization Act passed by Congress the following year, he attempted to restore Indian autonomy by establishing a constitutional basis for tribal government and by expanding the reservation land base. Collier hired McNickle as his administrative assistant in 1936 and assigned him to serve as liaison between the BIA and the various tribes that were voting to establish new tribal constitutions. Putting aside his dreams of becoming a novelist, McNickle committed himself totally to his new role.

McNickle's most enduring contribution as a cultural broker during the Collier years was his encouragement of dialogue among various Indian tribes. In 1944, he played a crucial role in founding the National Congress of American Indians (NCAI), which differed from earlier all-Indian organizations in that it preserved and projected a strong tribal emphasis rather than a more homogenized Pan-Indianism. At the same time, by bringing various tribal leaders together, McNickle and other NCAI leaders identified "Indian" issues that were common to all Indian people, thus creating a basis for future political action. During the 1940s, he continued to support Collier's program and worked his way up through the bureaucracy of the BIA, culminating in his appointment as director of tribal relations in 1951.

The most significant aspect of that program, in McNickle's opinion, was the commissioner's desire to use the insights of sociology and anthropology in developing Indian policy. Although most Indian bureau employees by this time held their positions through competitive Civil Service examinations, they still knew little or nothing about Indians. Collier had hoped to change that. He wanted to professionalize the bureau and to train its field personnel so that they might perform their duties with greater understanding of the people they served. He also believed that the social sciences, by providing insight into the dynamics of Indian personality and cultural change, could assist in the development of administrative policies that would encourage the Indians to adopt only those elements of mainstream society that would enable them to survive as Indian people. He labeled this, somewhat ambiguously, as "directed assimilation."

Collier's vision was valuable but limited.[3] While he believed in cultural pluralism, he also assumed that he and his associates knew what was best for the American Indians in the modern world. He was equally certain that if the Indians knew what he knew, they could not fail to agree with him. He believed that the process of social evolution was inevitable, but he also believed that cultural change could be directed toward goals whose desirability would be self-evident to all who were adequately informed.

D'Arcy McNickle. Photograph by Peter Weil. Courtesy of the Newberry Library, Chicago.

But Collier's goals were not desirable to many Indians, nor were they self-evident to those in Washington who held the reins of power and the federal purse strings. Collier's opponents continued to believe that Indian lands should be privatized rather than enlarged, and they viewed his program to restore the tribal land base as communistic. They also opposed strengthening the tribal governments, claiming that such actions would lead to greater isolation rather than to assimilation of Indian people. After Collier's resignation in 1945, opposition had become increasingly vocal, and one by one those who had supported his Indian New Deal transferred out of the bureau or retired from government service.

McNickle and other loyal supporters had stayed on, hoping to continue his program of tribal reorganization, but they became increasingly apprehensive when they learned of Dillon Myer's appointment as Indian commissioner in spring 1950. They had had some prior acquaintance with Myer during World War II, when he had directed the War Relocation Authority. One of the Japanese relocation centers had been administered briefly by the Indian bureau, and as BIA liaison, McNickle himself had maintained close contact with Myer during that eighteen-month period. It appeared to him now that Myer knew as little about Indians as he had known about the Japanese. Myer had been heard to say that Indian reservations were like those wartime relocation centers—they should be shut down as quickly as possible—and McNickle was understandably concerned about the new commissioner's appointment.

At this time McNickle agreed with Myer's desire to help the Indians move into mainstream society but only if that was what the Indians themselves wanted. Myer's immediate reorganization of the Indian bureau, however, removed Washington staff personnel, including McNickle, from direct contact with Indian tribes, thus reducing the Indians' opportunities for being heard, and McNickle became increasingly frustrated with Myer's myopic view of Indian people and policy. Myer enjoyed congressional support, however, and McNickle had little hope of effective resistance. Thus his own resignation became a distinct possibility.

For some months he cast about for a project that would use his practical expertise in the social sciences. While he had never received formal training in that field, his years with the Indian bureau had provided him with a broad background in cultural and social anthropology. He had worked closely with such well-known anthropologists as Dorothea Leighton and Alexander Leighton, Clyde Kluckhohn, Edward Spicer, Laura Thompson, and John Province. Learning from them all, he had received superb though informal training in cultural anthropology. Professional recognition had come in 1949, after the publication of his first narrative history,

They Came Here First, when he was elected a member of both the Society for Applied Anthropology and the American Anthropological Association. With his future in mind, although he was still with the Indian bureau, he decided to initiate a workshop program for "directed assimilation" as a study in cultural anthropology.

During the summer and fall of 1951, McNickle invited a number of Indian leaders to a series of BIA-sponsored community development workshops in Utah, Arizona, and Oklahoma. There the tribal leaders discussed their people's most immediate problems and shared remedies and solutions. McNickle's purpose, however, was not primarily to identify problems or to suggest remedies. His goal was to help tribal leaders discover what internal resources they and their people possessed that could be enlisted in dealing with those problems. He wanted them to become aware that they themselves could initiate changes on their reservations and that they were not totally powerless after all. The Indian office had so isolated the various tribes over the years that workshop participants were amazed to discover how many of their problems were shared by other tribes across the country.

The workshops were a step in the right direction, but their influence was brief and they failed to carry over into local action. McNickle's workshop plan, however, gradually evolved into a long-term project that was not subject either to bureaucratic whim or to the tyranny of budgetary constraints. Working through the NCAI, he obtained sufficient support for a two-year project, then applied for an extended leave of absence from the BIA. He was not quite ready to resign, as continuation of the project beyond those two years would depend on his ability to obtain renewed funding.

What followed from 1952 to 1960 was an intensive effort toward community development that continued to reflect McNickle's commitment to his role as cultural mediator. In describing his plans to potential donors, he made it very clear that he was not advocating programmatic changes in the life-style of the people he hoped to work with. "We wanted to discover," he wrote later, "in what manner and by what means we might help a community in decision-making without pre-empting the role of decision-makers. . . . If people of dependent status can be moved toward automacy [*sic*], then intervention by outsiders is justified; otherwise it is meddling."[4] He did not propose to meddle. Instead, he would try to initiate a process whereby the people themselves would learn to identify and solve their problems. The development of process, not program, was his goal.

His own role, while crucial, was to be one of low visibility. He intended to be involved as a catalyst rather than as a direct participant. While he would answer questions, facilitate contacts, and suggest options, decision making would remain with the people themselves. The funding he had obtained would cover his administrative costs, but the people themselves would have to raise money for whatever action they decided on.

Where to locate such an effort as McNickle envisioned was problematic, as almost any Indian community in the country could benefit from the kind of help he was prepared to offer. He finally selected the Navajo community of Crownpoint, New Mexico, because its location just outside the reservation had relegated it to a kind of administrative limbo. Crownpoint also had a small, deteriorating hospital, which was a significant consideration, as part of the project's funding was committed to health education. McNickle hoped to administer a limited program in health and hygiene as an adjunct to the community development work, and the hospital would provide a facility to support that effort.

There was another criterion in choosing a location, perhaps even more important than the presence of the hospital. The desire to solve community problems, as McNickle saw it, had to originate from within the tribal community; it could not be imposed effectively from without. Lasting development, therefore, would require at least the rudiments of indigenous leadership. McNickle hoped to find a group of older men and women who knew something about the outside world and who traditionally would have achieved status as tribal leaders. They might be former boarding school students or veterans of World War II. He believed that these people would be aware of a broader range of options and that they would provide greater motivation for change. But they also should have maintained their ties to traditional lifeways, so that any changes they attempted would be compatible with existing cultural patterns. Among the Navajos at Crownpoint, so he was told, there were a number of people who matched this description. In addition, the Navajo Tribal Council supported his efforts, especially at first.

McNickle was still developing the practical aspects of this program when he addressed a conference on American Indian assimilation sponsored by the Association on American Indian Affairs in May 1952.[5] In attempting to direct the assimilation process, he told his audience, policymakers must utilize the mechanics of culture change as social scientists were beginning to understand them. Indian people must be reached through the agencies of their own culture. This he would attempt to do. With private funding in hand, he intended to devote an extended period to exploring techniques that would encourage community development in ways that would not violate the integrity of the people involved.

For more than seven years, from mid-1953 through 1960, McNickle and Viola Pfrommer, whom he hired as health educator, maintained their program among the eastern Navajos at Crownpoint. They gathered together at Crownpoint a core group of community leaders who eventually represented all the chapters in the "checkerboard area" of northwestern New Mexico. Working together as the Navajo Development Committee, these leaders began to make a difference in the people's lives in a number of ways.

First, the committee reestablished strong ties with the tribal administration in Window Rock, ties that had become frayed because of Crownpoint's anomalous location outside the reservation boundaries. Then it brought local medicine men into a new and cooperative relationship with modern medical practice, which helped to improve communication with the people in matters of medicine and hygiene. Annie Dodge Wauneka, the first woman to serve on the Navajo Tribal Council and recently appointed chairman of the tribe's new Health Committee, received important technical assistance and support from Pfrommer. Wauneka became so effective in her fight against tuberculosis on the reservation that she later received the Medal of Freedom from President Lyndon Johnson.[6] Through their Navajo Development Committee, the eastern Navajos also found a capacity for decision making regarding public schools in the county and for resolving numerous livestock and fencing disputes.

The committee's building program provided more concrete evidence of the local people's increasing empowerment. The Navajo Development Committee refurbished one structure and built another, thereby providing overnight accommodations for families visiting patients in the hospital or students at the Crownpoint boarding school. In addition to comfortable cots, the buildings contained washing machines and showers, recreation facilities, and a large room to accommodate the committee's business meetings. People from the surrounding area provided money, labor, and materials, and they dedicated their new community houses with prayers and feasting.

McNickle's periodic reports of these changes reveal the techniques he developed in helping them become a reality.[7] After the Navajo Development Committee organized and began to meet regularly, he absented himself from the community while Pfrommer, whose work was more content specific, remained at Crownpoint. McNickle did not want to be too accessible when problems arose, as he wanted the people to have time and space to bring to fruition the goals they had set for themselves. He and his family had moved from Washington, D.C., to Boulder, Colorado, and that was close enough. He attended monthly meetings of the Navajo Development Committee, of course, and responded to the occasional crises that demanded his expertise. His project reports suggest long hours of committee meetings during which he fostered the traditional Indian process of working toward consensus. When asked, he supplied information about resources the committee might use, offered to make a particular contact, or responded to technical problems, but he refrained from making suggestions that would in any way preclude the Indians' own decisions.

The Crownpoint project thrived, and eventually McNickle received extended funding from the Emil Schwartzhaupt Foundation. In 1958, however, unanticipated problems began to surface. Navajo tribal income had risen suddenly and substantially because of new energy leases. Now, with unbudgeted new money at hand, the tribal council embarked on a chapter house building program that called into question the need for the committee's two community houses that had been built on federal, not tribal, land. Also in 1958, those on the tribal council who initially had supported the Crownpoint project were replaced by others who knew little about what the eastern Navajos had accomplished and who had other priorities. Shortly thereafter, the local leaders at Crownpoint split among themselves over the perennially quarrelsome issue of peyote. Then cultural attitudes toward money blocked the appointment of responsible management for the committee's new facilities. Through 1959 and into 1960, McNickle watched as these various elements overwhelmed the processes that earlier had produced such promising results.

As the project at Crownpoint began to unravel, McNickle wondered what he might have done differently. Perhaps he should have intervened at some point to save what had been accomplished. Perhaps he should have attended tribal council meetings in Window Rock and secured greater support from new council members, or perhaps he should have been more forceful in identifying and hiring qualified management for the new community houses. But such intervention would have violated his basic intention of supporting the people as they themselves dealt with their problems.

McNickle agonized over these and other questions as he and Pfrommer prepared to leave Crownpoint at the end of 1960. He had never planned to stay indefinitely, and the past seven years, he believed, should have been long enough to test his theory of how to direct or accelerate the processes of assimilation. Just what, he asked himself, had he accomplished toward that end? Perhaps it was too early to make a realistic assessment, but he was very discouraged.

In 1962, as he and Pfrommer wrote their final project report for the Emil Schwartzhaupt Foundation, they were still uncertain about its long-range impact. They had returned to Crownpoint several times, met with a few members of the almost defunct Navajo Development Committee, and found that little activity had been initiated since they left. The tribal council had built a new chapter house on land purchased by the tribe near Crownpoint, and the two buildings erected by the Navajo Development Committee had fallen into disuse.

But that was not really the end. When the Office of Navajo Economic Opportunity (ONEO) was established on the Navajo reservation during President Johnson's administration later in the 1960s, veterans of the Navajo Development Committee were among the leaders. They helped to establish community action committees, and their rhetoric echoed what the Navajo Development Committee had so often discussed about working together to meet community needs.[8] In addition, Navajos from the checkerboard area continued to provide leadership in local and tribal affairs. By this time, however, McNickle had become involved elsewhere. The project report was never published, and he seldom mentioned his Crownpoint experience.

McNickle's fieldwork in New Mexico was just one of a number of community development projects undertaken by cultural anthropologists in the 1950s. Several of those projects were funded by the Emil Schwartzhaupt Foundation, and others were underwritten by various foundations and universities. One project that was of particular interest to McNickle, directed by Allan Holmberg, was supported by Cornell University and endorsed by the U.S. State Department.[9] Like McNickle, Holmberg was interested in community revitalization, but he became much more involved personally in directing the decision-making process. Calling himself a participant-intervener, Holmberg brought about a small revolution in agricultural practices and landownership in an Indian community in Peru. However, a later effort to help another group of Indians in South America build a small hydroelectric plant was undertaken without the federal backing Holmberg had had for the Peruvian project. That project met with resistance from the local politicos and was unsuccessful. There seemed to be no simple solution to the problems of community development.

McNickle's nondirective approach to community development, with his emphasis on process rather than program, was obviously very different from Holmberg's, and McNickle himself was unsure which was the more effective professional methodology. Before World War II, anthropologists had worked primarily as observers and had avoided becoming personally involved in the various problems of the people they were studying. McNickle and Holmberg represented new approaches to professional fieldwork, the relative values of which continue to be discussed today. The question was whether, and how, anthropologists should become involved as brokers between their own world and that of their subjects. Some in the profession questioned whether anthropologists who became active participants could retain their professional objectivity.[10]

For McNickle, however, the crucial element of this professional debate had focused on the most effective method of bringing about so-called directed assimilation. While he remained skeptical about the value of Holmberg's "participant intervention," it was clear that both men shared Collier's view concerning the direction in which Indian people should move. Thus, when adverse cultural forces threatened the work of the Navajo Development Committee, it is not surprising that McNickle was disheartened. The people at Crownpoint had seemed to grow significantly in their problem-solving capabilities, yet their efforts appeared to have little lasting impact in moving the community toward permanent change.

His experience at Crownpoint having failed to answer definitively the question of how to be an effective intermediary, McNickle began to rethink the entire question of directed assimilation. Nevertheless, he continued to believe that selective adaptation was the key to Indian survival and that motivation for change must come from Indian people themselves. It also occurred to him that his reliance on traditional leadership at Crownpoint might have been misplaced, as newly elected tribal leaders were younger men who were less closely tied to cultural values.

While he was still involved at Crownpoint, therefore, he began a tentative association with a series of leadership training workshops designed to reach young Indian college students, the leaders of tomorrow. Initially invited in 1956 to participate as a guest speaker at the first workshop, in 1960 McNickle agreed to become director of the entire program. By that time he was ready to try a new approach. If Indian people chose to remain Indians—and history indicated that they did—they must have the inner resources to defend that choice in the face of outside pressures that pushed them toward assimilation.

The curriculum of the workshops was very much in keeping with this evolutionary turn of his own thinking. During each six-week summer session, young people who seemed destined to become future leaders acquired information about their own heritage and culture that had not been taught them in government and mission schools. They also learned about the motivations and practices of the non-Indian world and about areas of conflict that reflected the opposing values of the two cultures. The workshop staff was dismayed to discover how little the participants knew of their own tribal traditions and values, and they hoped to instill new pride in being Indian as they explained to the young people the dynamics of intercultural relationships. McNickle's willingness to direct the leadership training workshops indicated the profound shift in his thinking.

The annual summer workshops did not occupy all of his time, of course, and during the 1960s, McNickle undertook a variety of projects. In 1961, he became deeply involved with the American Indian Chicago Conference, which originated as a project in applied anthropology under Sol Tax at the University of Chicago. The conference, organized primarily by NCAI, further extended the reach of Indian self-awareness by including urban Indians and others who were not tribally affiliated and/or who opposed NCAI's approach to Indian affairs. McNickle, who chaired the steering committee, was the only one of NCAI's founders who was still alive and able to participate. Once again he had labored to bring Indian people together and helped them discover, through their unity, the political strength they had in dealing with the white world.[11]

During the next five years, McNickle kept his hand in Indian affairs while he cared for his aging mother. He wrote articles and book reviews and began the research for a biography of Oliver La Farge, longtime president of the Association on American Indian Affairs, which was published in 1971.[12] His work as a cultural anthropologist brought increasing recognition, and he was awarded an honorary doctorate by the University of Colorado in 1966. Subsequently, he was invited to chair the Department of Anthropology at the University of Saskatchewan in Regina, where he lived from 1966 to 1971. Retiring from this brief stint in academia, he turned his attention to the establishment of the Center for the History of the American Indian at the Newberry Library in Chicago, beginning a relationship that continued until his death in 1977.

Wind from an Enemy Sky, McNickle's third and last novel, which was published posthumously in 1978, reflected his continuing concern with questions of Indian-white relations and with the effectiveness of professional intervention.[13] Antoine, the novel's young hero, resembles Archilde of *The Surrounded* as he returns from boarding school in Oregon to learn traditional wisdom from his grandfather, Bull. The voices of John Collier, Oliver La Farge, Dillon Myer, and Allan Holmberg are all heard through such non-Indian characters as the Little Elk Agency doctor, the local missionary, the BIA agent, and Adam Pell, who as an amateur anthropologist claimed as his own the failed hydroelectric project in South America. The finely drawn Little Elk characters of Bull, his brother Henry Jim, the shaman Two Sleeps, and Son Child, the tribal policeman, represent both those who have resisted acculturation and those who have embraced it, while the young Antoine clearly embodies the future. The traditional life of the Little Elk people collides with the white man's technology at the new dam built on the reservation by Adam Pell, and it appears that the two peoples are following different "maps of the mind." They have traveled separate roads to that moment and are moving toward goals that are ultimately incompatible.

In 1952, McNickle had assumed that assimilation was a natural, indeed, an inevitable process and that the pertinent questions to be asked were whether it could or should be accelerated and channeled in a particular direction. Directed assimilation, at the heart of his Crownpoint project, had anticipated an eventual coming together as the two people moved toward common goals. But in this final novel, McNickle seems to say that this is not going to happen. Those who might have found a way of mutual accommodation are killed in the final tragic scene, and Antoine has no one to show him the way into the future. The novel ends bleakly with the observation that for the Little Elk people, "no meadowlarks sang, and the world fell apart."[14]

Whether the tragic ending of *Wind from an Enemy Sky* reflected McNickle's ultimate view of Indian-white relations or served only as a dramatic fictional device to conclude the story remains an open question. Although he had worked tirelessly, devoting his life to mediation, in his last novel he seems to suggest that Indians and whites still confront each other across an impassable abyss.

Although D'Arcy McNickle had assumed his role as a cultural broker during his thirties when he began to work for Collier, he carried the broker's mission in his blood: his mother's métis people had served for generations as interpreters and intermediaries between Indians and whites. Through his novels and his narrative histories, as well as his other activities, McNickle had tried to read both maps of the mind, to speak with understanding and compassion about the two worlds so as to link their divergent cultures. In the process, he became totally committed to the Indians' right to remain Indian. He believed that American society had an obligation to assure them the time and the space they needed to adapt to the non-Indian world in ways that would preserve their Indian identity.[15]

We are all finally catching up with D'Arcy McNickle. Indian people have found their collective voice not only through the National Congress of American Indians but in other Indian organizations, as well, and they continue to develop their political muscle. Indian and non-Indian historians alike are writing history from an Indian perspective, aided in large part by the D'Arcy McNickle Center for the History of the American Indian at the Newberry Library, which was renamed in his honor in 1983. More tribal young people are pursuing research into the culture and history of their people at the D'Arcy McNickle Center and at new tribal facilities such as the D'Arcy McNickle Library at the Salish Kootenai College on the Flathead reservation in Montana.

McNickle's novels, recently reprinted, are enjoying new critical acclaim, and his short stories will soon be available as well.[16] His writing is reaching new audiences, and his efforts as a cultural broker are providing new insights into the nation's dealings with its first citizens. McNickle would probably be amazed to learn that his countrymen, both red and white, are heeding more attentively than ever his appeal for understanding, tolerance, and goodwill. Somewhere out there, perhaps, and the meadowlark is still singing for those who will take the time to listen.

CHAPTER 13

SPEAKING THEIR LANGUAGE: ROBERT W. YOUNG AND THE NAVAJOS

PETER IVERSON

WRITING from Gallup, New Mexico, in fall 1940, the remarkable linguist John P. Harrington provided a reference for a colleague.

He has since graduating spent four entire years on the Navajo Reservation learning to actually talk the Navajo language, and perfectly and fluently, and also learning that first-hand ethnology with which book ethnology cannot compete. He is 27 years old, healthy, bright, good appearance, a good lecturer, and a hard worker. . . . He has a way about him which will make him liked by the public as well as by his inside employers.[1]

The twenty-seven-year-old was Robert W. Young, linguist, historian, scholar, intermediary, editor, government employee, observer, and friend. Since the 1930s, he has carried out these and other roles in the Indian Southwest. Currently an emeritus professor at the University of New Mexico and still deeply involved in the field of the Navajo language, Young has quietly established himself during the past half century as an extraordinary student of the largest Indian community in the United States.

Born on May 18, 1912, in Chicago, Illinois, Young was the son of a physician, who on completing medical school in the city moved westward in the state to establish his practice. Young grew up in Annawan and Geneseo, within twenty-five miles of the Mississippi River quad cities area of Bettendorf, Davenport, Rock Island, and Moline. Many immigrants came to the region, looking for work on the railroad or in local industries; Young heard languages other than English—Flemish and German, especially—in his early years.[2] And he heard and learned Spanish. Mexican Indians migrated north to work on the Rock Island railroad; children Young's age and their parents spoke with the curious seven-year-old from town. He also became interested in Nahuatl, spoken by some of the people. An old dictionary in the town library helped some, but he never studied Spanish in school. His knowledge did help him complete graduation credits by examination for the University of Illinois, to which he had transferred after a year at Augustana College in Rock Island.

Like many of his generation, Young found that his formal education was not expedited by the depression. Young did not have much money with which to go to school, as his father and his grandfather, a director of a bank, had lost considerable money in the stock market. He worked as a bill collector in the summers in the Geneseo area for doctors, dentists, and pharmacists; he tutored people in Spanish. Young clearly and unsentimentally recalled "the worst job I ever had": translating a Portuguese treaty. He could read what he termed "ordinary Portuguese," but the treaty language was different from the usual fare. Three weeks of struggle yielded ten dollars.

His father wanted him to be a doctor, and Young dutifully enrolled in premed courses. In time, the son had other ideas and eventually took a different direction, choosing that ancient and honorable major of history. Young studied some anthropology, took French and Greek, and lived in the Cosmopolitan Club, where he knew many foreign students and spoke a lot of Spanish.

He "knew damn little about Indians and had no deep interest in them" at the time of his graduation from the University of Illinois in 1935. But he had maintained an interest in Mexico from childhood, and he seriously considered attending the University of Mexico to study archaeology. This inexpensive route to further education was blocked when a friend wrote him and told him not to come. Riots had broken out at the university; it simply was not a good time to enroll.

Young "decided to come part of the way" and went to Albuquerque, where he enrolled in anthropology at the University of New Mexico in January 1936. Few Indians then attended the university.

Robert W. Young.

Several Navajos, however, numbered among the students. Young met Adolph Dodge Bitanny, who had worked with the prominent anthropologist Gladys Reichard. Through this acquaintance, he quickly became interested in the Navajos.

That spring he gained "what was euphemistically called a working fellowship" to study Navajo, courtesy of the School of American Research in Santa Fe. He thus spent the summer at Chaco Canyon, interpreting for Mexican workers and driving a truck up to the mountains above Cuba, New Mexico, where the Mexicans cut trees for vigas. Young mapped some ruins, went up various side canyons, and all in all, "very seldom saw any Navajos; they were smart enough to keep their distance."

He did, however, begin to meet people, slowly and deliberately as rural people will do. Because Tomasito Padilla, an old Navajo singer, "spoke pidgin Spanish," Young could communicate with him. Such a dialogue promptly proved useful, for Young sprained his ankle a long way from traditional Anglo medical care. Padilla made a poultice for Young of jimson weed, ashes, and mud. He predicted confidently and correctly that in four days the ankle would be fine.

In three months, Young "learned enough Navajo to be frustrated." He found the materials gathered by the Franciscans at St. Michael's only "useful up to a point." The information on nouns was helpful but that on verbs less so. "You couldn't inflect the verbs because you didn't know the next person." Nonetheless, from stories told by Monte Lope of Blanco Canyon he began to take a text and analyze it.[3]

At this point, Young met Smithsonian Institution ethnologist John P. Harrington, who had worked with Edgar L. Hewitt at the School of American Research and had been in touch with the school. Commissioner of Indian Affairs John Collier and his director of education, Willard Beatty, had contacted Harrington with regard to the goal of teaching the Navajos how to read and write their own language. Harrington therefore came to Navajo country to investigate the feasibility of this objective.

The idea of a written form of the Navajo language, to be sure, did not originate either with Collier or with Beatty. Earlier students of Navajo history and culture, as well as people who had worked with members of the tribe, had learned the language to varying degrees and had devised various forms of writing that language down to record their findings. Washington Matthews, a physician at Fort Wingate, New Mexico, pioneered in his extensive examination of

Navajo culture. The Franciscan fathers at St. Michael's, Arizona, followed his initiative in the first years of the twentieth century. As early as 1910, they had completed the *Ethnological Dictionary of the Navajo Language*; by 1912, they published the *Vocabulary of the Navajo Language*. Led by the tireless Father Berard Haile, the Franciscans "devised a phonemic alphabet that permitted accurate representation of the language, although like other students of the period, they failed to realize that fixed tone is a distinctive feature of Navajo requiring graphic representation."[4]

The major linguist, Edward Sapir, in Young's judgment, "improved their understanding of the language." He had worked on other Athapaskan languages and became interested in comparative linguistics. Sapir met Father Berard and took him east to his institution, the University of Chicago. Because of this influence, Father Berard and his colleagues modified their alphabet along the lines employed by Sapir, with diacritics now used "to mark tone."[5]

Unlike the Franciscans who were primarily concerned to publish for a non-Navajo public interested in Navajo culture, Protestant missionaries such as those of the Christian Reformed church and the Presbyterian church wanted to use written Navajo as a means for prospective converts to read the Bible and other church literature. Although they made some headway in this direction, it was not until the 1930s that federal interest encouraged the development of written Navajo to an unprecedented level. That transition provided the opportunity that altered the course of Young's life and career.

Gladys Reichard, Berard Haile, and John Harrington all figured in this process. Reichard, an anthropologist at Columbia University who wrote important books on Navajo religion and Navajo daily life, initiated in 1934 the Hogan School in Ganado, Arizona, under the aegis of the Bureau of Indian Affairs (BIA). The BIA wanted to encourage Navajo interpreters to be able to write in Navajo; it employed Reichard to teach them. Soon thereafter, Father Berard, again through BIA financial support, wrote Navajo texts for use by the Navajo language radio station in Window Rock, Arizona.

Neither Reichard nor Haile, however, had devised a written form of the Navajo language that Beatty and other BIA educators deemed satisfactory for this purpose. Beatty and his colleagues wanted Navajo children and adults to learn how to write in both English and Navajo. They reasoned that this task would be facilitated if the written form of Navajo, even allowing for its uniqueness, could appear similar to English. Sapir disagreed; such an approach was, as Young later put it, "anathema" to him. Haile and Reichard shared in his displeasure, but Collier and Beatty would not be deterred and turned to Harrington to develop a feasible alphabet and materials using that alphabet that the BIA could employ for teaching written Navajo.[6]

At one level, Harrington seemed an obvious and appropriate choice for the challenge. He surely was a gifted linguist, he was employed by the federal government, and he was not tied to any of the factions promoting their version of written Navajo over all others. However, Harrington lived in Washington, D.C., and he had not done much with Navajo or other Athapaskan languages. He needed help.

Through the Works Progress Administration, Young gained employment as an archaeological assistant in New Mexico. Despite the dust storms that raged—"for weeks we could not see the Sandias"—he was understandably grateful to have not only a job but a job that paid well. "I was paid seventy seven dollars a month. A fortune." And by the time the position ended in spring 1937, Harrington had learned of him through the School of American Research, and the two men had teamed up.[7]

That autumn he moved to Fort Wingate, where he continued work on developing the orthographic system for the language. Young also began a long-term, mutually beneficial collaboration with William Morgan, a 1936 graduate from Fort Wingate High School. Morgan was from Gallup. He had edited the school yearbook, *The Navajo Trail*, in which the senior class prophecy foresaw him as an honors engineering graduate from the University of Arizona, destined to dam up "arroyos on the Reservation."[8] Instead, he and Young both found jobs at the Southwestern Range and Sheep Breeding Laboratory at Fort Wingate. The two men would forge a partnership that has persisted to the present, with a variety of books resulting from their labors.

Although Young's position at the laboratory was designed in part to support his orthographic work, he also had other assignments as "a common laborer."[9] During Collier's term as commissioner, the

BIA attempted to impose a severe reduction of livestock held by the Navajos. This effort to cut the numbers of sheep, horses, cattle, and goats not only meant economic hardship for countless Navajos but also struck at the workings of the Navajo social system. Sheep, for example, fed the people who attended religious ceremonies and paid the singers who conducted these rituals. Thus, the destruction of livestock symbolized the destruction of the people themselves. "With our sheep we were created and that is why we weep and mourn," said Buck Austin.[10] Stung by the criticism of his program and desperately seeking an alternative to the Navajo dependence on the sheeps' wool for weaving, Collier came up with an idea that seems as bizarre today as it did in the 1930s.

"Collier had some unusual ideas," Young said, smiling at the recollection. "He loved dogs. And he knew that dogs had been in the Southwest for a long time. He thought perhaps the Navajos could use the hair from one kind of dog as well as wool for weaving purposes, somewhat like the chilkat blanket of the Northwest." Thus, Young received a pickup truck and a credit card for gas along with a singular assignment—to go out and look for dogs.

Harrington, as always, had a firm opinion. "Forget the damn dogs." However, the curious order permitted Young to try "every by-road of the Navajo reservation" and to get into some fairly inaccessible country. He would camp in the distant reaches of Navajo country, occasionally to be awakened by new sounds, such as coyotes chasing horses. As he came to know individuals and individual portions of that powerful land, from Jones Canyon to Navajo Mountain, Young "went from an academic interest to a personal interest." "This experience," he concluded, "shaped what would happen in subsequent years." "I wanted to do something constructive and I became interested in the people as well as the language."

Although a "great number of problems" were "evident" during the Indian New Deal, in part because of the "very autocratic" nature of federal-Navajo relations, Young portrayed Collier as a man "truly sympathetic to Indians and their cultures," as one who believed "Indian people should control their own destiny."[11] But both Collier and the Navajos were caught by the depression and the consequent demand for the conservation of natural resources and grazing controls in the Southwest. Young saw Navajo leader Jacob Morgan coming out to fan the fires of resentment; he realized how few Navajos spoke English and how few shared the Anglo value system. The whole program of livestock reduction thus caused a terrible and traumatic change in the socioeconomic order. The "precipitous" quality of the program undermined everything. "People had lived within the horizons set by Navajo culture. To conceive of a change in which you abruptly revolutionized the social system was ludicrous. It was far too short a period. The government attempted to accomplish in a few years what should have been carried out over one to two generations."

In late summer 1939, Young accompanied Harrington to Canada to work on the northern Athapaskan languages: Sarsi near Calgary, Chipewayan near Cold Lake, Beaver near Peace River, and Carrier at Fort Saint James. However, after a few months, travel within Canada became more difficult as the Second World War expanded. Young had trouble getting tickets, and people suspected him of being a spy. On a visit to Chicago to see his mother in spring 1940, he met Beatty, who spoke enthusiastically about the use of languages in forthcoming BIA bilingual education programs. When Beatty learned that Harrington had not been entirely forthcoming about Young's contributions, he asked Young if he would like to be involved with the Navajo program.

Beatty's desire to have personal control over the bilingual program led to a parting of the ways. Harrington concluded his involvement with the BIA and thus his association with Young. Young characterized his former colleague as "brilliant and a painstaking ethnologist." He could be "secretive," as he was "paranoic about people stealing his stuff." When asked, however, if the candid description of Harrington by Carobeth Laird in *Encounters with an Angry God* were essentially accurate, Young nodded his agreement.[12]

Young had intended to enroll at the University of California, Berkeley, or at the University of Southern California to write a dissertation on the Navajo language. Beatty's offer caused him to postpone those plans. He would work, he thought, for a while and save some money so that he could go back to school. Yet one thing led to another, and he never realized those educational goals. The University of New Mexico granted him an honorary doctorate in 1969.

Along with Edward A. Kennard, Young began in spring 1940 to

work for the BIA developing literature in written Navajo for use in the bilingual education program. Although Kennard moved on in the following year to Sioux and Hopi materials, Young stayed with the Navajos. In 1941, William Morgan joined in this effort. In addition to teaching written Navajo from 1940 to 1942 in different schools, Young traveled to Phoenix, site of the printing facility of the Phoenix Indian School. Here Young, Morgan, and Antonio Willetto translated materials for use in Navajo schools. Perhaps the best known example of this work came with the translation of the *Little Herder* (Na'nítkaadí Yázhí) series by Ann Nolan Clark.[13] Published in four installments, each correlated to a season of the year, the series was graced by the fine illustrations of the Navajo artist Hoke Denetsosie, twenty, who had been a student at the Phoenix Indian School.[14]

The Little Herder series is also noteworthy for Clark's clear, melodic prose. *The Little Herder in Summer* (Shįįgo Na'nítkaadí Yázhí) volume, for example, begins,

> Today
>> we leave by mother's hogan,
>> my mother's winter hogan.
> We leave the shelter of its
>> rounded walls.
> We leave its friendly center fire.
> We drive our sheep to the mountains.
> For the sheep,
>> there is grass and shade
>> and water,
>> flowing water
>> and water standing still,
>> in the mountains.
> There is no wind.
> There is no sand
>> up there.[15]

As Young said in 1990, such passages are "difficult to make into effective Navajo." He added, with his usual modesty, "The translations were the best we could do, but it was very difficult to come out with the same meter and for it to sound as pretty."[16] They translated the previous passage as follows.

Díí jí
    shimá bighandóó ńdii'náh,
    shimá haigo bighandóó.
Hooghan názbasgo nástł'inée
    bits'ą́ą́ ńdii'náh
Hooghan atníí'gi ko' yée
    bits'ą́ą́ ndii'náh.
Dziłgóó nihidibé dah dadíníilkaad.
Dibé tł'oh dóó chahash'oh
    dóó tó
    dóó tó danlínígíí
    dóó tó naazkánígíí bá hóló
    dziłtahgi.
'Áadi
    doo níyol da
    dóó séí 'ádin.[17]

These two passages were printed next to each other in the text. The Navajo child faced an impressive challenge in attempting to master both languages in written form, but at least he or she could read about a known and valued world. Young and his colleagues had succeeded in crafting an orthography, moreover, that worked for the purposes for which it was designed. As Beatty said in an afterward, the book used "with one exception . . . only the letters of the English alphabet, maintaining so far as possible comparable sound values. Diacritics have been reduced to indications of tone and nasalization. It may be reproduced on any typewriter or linotype." He noted that Young's residence on the Navajo reservation had resulted in a kind of familiarity with the Navajo language "so that these publications might represent a clearcut expression in the vernacular, of the story content." Beatty concluded, "They are the first publication in Navaho of anything save the Bible, religious tracts, and scientific monographs."[18]

By 1943, Young had played a major role in several other significant publications. With Morgan, he put together *The Navajo Language*, an introductory discussion of Navajo grammar as well as a bilingual dictionary. Even if he now calls it a "hasty" effort, it nonetheless represented the first step toward the definitive Navajo dictionary he and Morgan would later publish. He also translated a book about World War II by Charles T. McFarlane, entitling it, *Díí*

K'ad Anaa'ígíí Baa Hané (The Story of the Present War), so that Navajo students could learn more about the contemporary conflict.[19]

Concerned about Navajo access to information about the war and the employment of many of the people in off-reservation jobs, Young initiated *Ádahooníłgíí*, a monthly newspaper. Beginning in August 1945, *Ádahooníłgíí* provided important information about current events and filled a basic need at a time when few Navajos could read the *Gallup Independent* or other English-language papers; it continued to be published until 1957. Young went down to the shop at the Phoenix Indian School where the newspaper was printed and helped to set the type "personally, using two fingers." *Navajo Historical Selections* in 1954, edited by Young and Morgan, included selections from the newspaper on Navajo history, culture, livestock reduction, and current issues.[20]

The positive reception accorded the readers, the newspaper, and the dictionary spoke clearly to the value of his work. Young reflected in an article in *Indian Education*, an Indian Service newsletter edited by Beatty, that the debate over introducing written forms of Indian languages in addition to English had occurred before. "So also did the defenders of Latin argue against the proposed replacement of this 'most perfect language' by the crude and decadent speech of the people." Under the Collier administration, Indian languages finally had been recognized not as an encumbrance or an impediment to progress but as a natural aid in the educational process. Using an analogy that would be commonly employed in the 1960s, when many of the elements of bilingual, bicultural programs would be revived and expanded, Young asked how an Anglo child would fare if he were placed in a Syrian school and expected to immediately do satisfactory schoolwork in Arabic. Mastering English would take time, when starting from scratch; in the meantime, using Navajo would help to educate the child.

Young made several other critical points in the course of this extremely perceptive article. He reminded his audience that only through the introduction of writing were the classical works of literature from Greece and elsewhere preserved appropriately for posterity. The songs and legends of Indians "are certainly not less attractive," he contended, "nor are they greatly different from those songs, poems and legends of the Hellenes, the Hindus or the Semites." Use of written Indian languages would preserve them. Although Young concluded that "a thick book would be required to set down all the differences between Navaho and English," he sketched for his readers some of the basic ways in which the two languages differed, from sound to plurals to categories of verbal expression. If all of this seemed prohibitively complicated to his reader, then Young reminded his audience, "Is it not possible that the Navaho finds it equally hard to learn the English language?" Yet even though the fledgling Anglo student of the Navajo language inevitably would amuse the native Navajo speaker by unintended gaffes, a little study would go a long way. A teacher would gain insight into why his or her pupils would pronounce certain English words in certain ways as well as appreciate the kind of transition a Navajo child was making in tackling the English language.[21]

The Navajos gained lasting fame for their participation in the Second World War, especially as "codetalkers" in the Pacific campaign. Here, too, Young served as an intermediary. He joined the U.S. Marine Corps to recruit Navajos for what was termed a communications outfit. Stationed in Phoenix at the Marine Corps offices, he went to various communities on the reservation and interviewed promising prospective candidates who were truly bilingual.[22]

When the war ended, the Navajos faced difficult times. People who had served in the armed forces or who had worked elsewhere had to neglect their livestock. And the BIA clung to the idea that livestock reduction still needed to be carried out, despite all the attendant problems. From 1933 to 1947, the Navajos had been forced to reduce the number of their goats from 173,000 to about 56,000; their horses, from 44,000 to about 35,000, their cattle, from 21,000 to about 11,000; and their sheep, from 570,000 to about 358,600. Recently hired tribal attorney Norman Littell lobbied the secretary of the interior for a change in policy, and partially as a response to Littell, Julius Krug sent Lee Muck to study grazing regulations. Muck acknowledged continuing problems with soil erosion and an inability of the grazing resources to "support the large human population," yet urged a moratorium on further reduction while the Navajos developed regulations they could accept.[23]

Willie Morgan and Young decided there was a real need for the people to know what their alternatives were. Interpreters had often glossed over technical bureaucratic terms; the people were understandably confused about the current regulations. The "birds in the land division wanted me to use weasel wording like 'base preference number' and stuff like that," Young recalled, but he was determined to provide careful and full translations and explanations. Young added,

On the premise that the grazing resources of the reservation were the property of the tribe in its entirety, range technicians reasoned that each member of the tribe held claim to a pro rata share. This share was the base preference number, obtained by dividing the carrying capacity (the number of sheep units the range could support) by the number of Navajos. Knowing that such an arrangement would prove unpopular, range technicians wanted us to "weasel word" the translation—to purposely obscure its meaning in order to forestall protests by stockmen.

As one would anticipate, the Navajos were very upset when those translations began to appear.[24]

Thus, as the 1940s drew to a close, Young "got into it up to my neck." It seemed as though every Navajo community wanted him to explain grazing regulations. In summer 1949, he worked with tribal council delegates and appeared at meetings all over Navajo country. A deteriorating economic picture on the reservation had forced Krug in the previous year to issue recommendations for long-range planning for Navajo economic "rehabilitation." Passed by Congress in 1950, the Navajo-Hopi Long Range Rehabilitation Act prompted community meetings, where Young and Morgan again served as translators. Generally, the program "sounded good" to the people, except for the ill-advised scheme to relocate some of the Navajos on the Colorado River reservation.[25]

One wishes for a videotape of one of these meetings, attended sometimes by hundreds of people, even up to a thousand and where those assembled discussed a variety of topics. Young became closely associated with many individuals in the western Navajo country, including such leaders as Scott Preston, George Bancroft, and Maxwell Yazzie. He came to know Norman Littell well. Even at this time there was discussion about that Navajo perennial—a constitution. Littell frowned on any constitution that would limit his activities.

From 1950 to 1962, Young was assistant to the Navajo area director and had a front row seat to witness the birth of the modern Navajo nation. Revenue from oil resources and other income combined with changing circumstances to alter what the tribal government could do and how the people saw that government. In his role as a liaison between the BIA and the tribal government and by now as a respected veteran observer of Navajo affairs, he was involved in such innovations as the new ballot with photographs of the candidates and the election of judges for the courts of the Indian offenses instead of selection by the superintendent.

Thus, the 1950s "fostered interest in the tribal government by rural people who had felt the council had been dominated by the BIA and had been too removed from them." They now tried to get "people to go to Window Rock to look after their interests." Eighty-five percent of the people registered to vote in tribal elections. Young "attended council meetings as a resource person to promote popular understanding of issues and proposed solution." He took notes at the meetings and distributed them the next day to council members. He observed a shift in council membership, with a greater stress on bilingual abilities. And he watched the growth of interest in higher education while he was working with the executive secretary, Maurice McCabe, to develop a college scholarship program that the council approved.[26]

The Long Range Rehabilitation Act invested almost $90 million in the 1950s, with two-thirds of the funds directed toward road and school construction. Together with federal funds now available to establish and operate public schools, the face of reservation education was altered dramatically. New roads reduced dependence on local trading posts and broke down the insularity of many previously isolated communities. In a series of eight volumes entitled *The Navajo Yearbook*, Young recorded the impact of "a decade of progress."[27]

Volume 8, the final, cumulative volume published in 1961, remains an enormously valuable source not only for delineating the effects of the act but also for its review of Navajo religion and language and its survey of the development of Navajo education, government, and economy. The more extended perspective derived from Young's conviction that issues needed to be explained in detail, and he took pleasure in seeing council representatives carry the yearbook in their briefcases. He had not necessarily planned to write an eighty-page "sketch" of the Navajo language, but when an article in the *Arizona Republic* observed that the Navajo language did not have pronouns, it provoked him into a thorough response. In the yearbook, Young merely said diplomatically that the sketch "was provided largely for the purpose of providing basic information to teaching personnel in schools serving Navajo children, and to the interested public." Although he did not directly refer to the newspaper article, he added that the sketch was also "included for the purpose of dispelling the popular myths that commonly surround Indian languages."[28]

In the 1950s and again from 1962 to 1966, he was tribal operations officer in the Gallup area office, where he worked with Wade Head and in contact not only with the Navajos but with the Zunis, Mescalero Apaches, Southern Utes and Ute Mountain Utes; from 1966 to 1971, he worked with Walter Olson in the Albuquerque area office. During all of this period, he tried to interpret Indian attitudes to administrative personnel and administrative attitudes to Indians. Relocation, the workings of the judicial system, grazing control, various federal regulations, and health problems all demanded his time and energy.

This era did see greater understanding between Anglos and Navajos as well as continuing problems. Young recalled his association with the redoubtable Annie Wauneka and Dr. Fred Margolis on Navajo health issues in the 1950s. The living conditions of Navajo workers in off-reservation employment, such as the carrot fields near Grants, New Mexico, or for the Santa Fe railroad, were not always hygienic. Working with the tireless Wauneka, whom Young praised as "great to work with, very competent," Young played a role in improving such conditions and increasing cross-cultural communication about disease and healing. He served as a consultant for the Cornell University medical project at Many Farms, Arizona, where participants learned a great deal about the delivery of health care and community responses to that delivery.[29]

In 1971, Young retired from the government to become codirector with Bernard Spolsky of the Navajo Reading Study Program at the University of New Mexico. Then from 1974 to 1980, he served as director of the Navajo dictionary project, a University of New

Mexico program funded by the National Endowment for the Humanities. Undeterred by emeritus status granted by the university in the late 1970s, he has maintained an office in the linguistics department, working without pay on a number of projects and thus "staying out of the pool hall."[30]

In addition to his work in Navajo linguistics, he has written several important historical studies and generously listened to, advised, and instructed countless students of Navajo history and culture.[31] *The Role of the Navajo in the Southwestern Drama*, published by the *Gallup Independent* in 1968, the centennial year of the return from captivity at Fort Sumner, New Mexico, was "aimed at the periphery—the people from Gallup and elsewhere who did not know Navajo history."[32] In eight sweeping articles, Young took the Navajo story from early days to the present, hoping that the account would "help mold the image of the Navajo Indians as the hardy, resourceful and progressive people they are; that it will contribute to the feeling of pride that they can so justly take in their past; and that it will identify a few of the many leaders whose names and accomplishments should be remembered."[33] Although written for a general audience, the book is based on extensive research as well as Young's own involvement in Navajo life, and it remains an excellent introduction to Navajo history.

A decade later, *A Political History of the Navajo Tribe* appeared. Published by the Navajo Community College Press and illustrated by Hoke Denetsosie and Raymond Johnson, the book was designed for use in the schools. As Young notes in his foreword, the book traces "the emergence of the Navajo Tribe as an ethnopolitical entity and the metamorphosis of the Tribal Council from a beginning as medium for alien control of tribal affairs to its status, now, as an instrument for self-government."[34] Drawing again from personal observation as well as research, the book is especially strong in its treatment of the period Young knew so well, from the 1930s through the 1950s.

Two of his most useful articles were also published in the 1970s. "The Rise of the Navajo Tribe" is an exceptional synthesis of Navajo history included in *Plural Society in the Southwest*, edited by Edward H. Spicer and Raymond H. Thompson. "Written Navajo: A Brief History," in *Advances in the Creation and Revision of Writing Systems*, edited by Joshua A. Fishman, presents a concise yet thorough summary of the subject. They represent additional examples of Young's work to which students of Navajo history and culture refer and rely on as authoritative.[35]

The Navajo Language: A Grammar and Colloquial Dictionary, published in 1980 by the University of New Mexico Press and republished in revised form in 1987, is the culmination of the Young-Morgan collaboration. Its depth and breadth are astonishing. The portion devoted to grammar is 437 pages in length, followed by a Navajo-English, then English-Navajo dictionary of 1,069 pages. For good measure, the pages are set in small type and printed in two columns.

The grammar is appropriately technical, and discussion of such topics as mediopassive imperfective neuter verbs will be beyond the interest, let alone the grasp, of the casual reader. For Navajos eager to learn more about the structure of their language and for non-Navajo scholars with a shaky understanding of the elusive language, there is much to ponder. Among the appendices is a new comparative Athapaskan root inventory based on comparative linguistic data prepared by Michael E. Krauss and Jeffrey Leer at the Alaska Native Language Center, University of Alaska. In the same manner, the dictionary offers help to both serious and casual students. On the very first page, one learns the appropriate way to say in Navajo "yesterday playing football I made two touchdowns": 'Adą́ą́dą́ą́' jooł yitalígíí bee ndeii'néego naakidi 'aa'dii'ą́.[36] Only the most insensitive of readers will not be engaged at this point.

Young has been pleased with the "highly receptive" Navajo response to the volume, but predictably he has not rested on his laurels. Recently published is his *Analytical Lexicon of Navajo*, again the product of many years of work. He is glad to see the rise of formal interest in the language at the University of New Mexico, Navajo Community College, and elsewhere. Particularly gratifying is the involvement of many Navajos on different dimensions of *The Navajo Language* and the continuing scholarly efforts of Alice Neundorf and other Navajo linguists. He is heartened as well by the growth of work by Navajos and non-Navajos alike in a serious examination of the Navajo past. Among other things, "a knowledge of history is essential for successful work in the field of human problems, where the present can be fully understood only in terms of its antecedent past."[37]

In addition to an honorary doctorate from the University of New Mexico, Young has been accorded other professional recognition in the course of a long and distinguished career, including a distinguished service award from the Department of the Interior and awards for his work in bilingual education. One suspects what matters to him most is the kind of respect and affection he has earned through the years, so evident at gatherings such as the annual Navajo Studies Conference. For more than half a century, he has been a cultural translator of the first order, one who has truly eased misunderstanding, calmed fears, and allowed members of one culture to appreciate the complex realities of another. In his life as well as his work, Robert W. Young emerges as a cultural broker who leaves a lasting legacy.

CHAPTER 14

PABLITA VELARDE:
THE PUEBLO ARTIST AS CULTURAL
BROKER

SALLY HYER

SEVERAL years ago, a Hopi-Tewa woman told me of a mural representing a horned serpent that had been painted on the wall of the Indian Health Service Hospital at Keams Canyon, Arizona, close by her home in First Mesa. The serpent, an image of religious significance, often appears on Pueblo pottery, dance kilts, and walls. But, she said, at night in the hospital it slithered through the halls, frightening the doctors and causing such a disturbance that it had to be destroyed.

This story suggests the power of the Pueblo belief system, the special dangers associated with artistic representation, and the risks involved in crossing cultural boundaries. Fact or folklore, it demonstrates the potential for chaos that is created when powerful symbols are moved to new settings. The Hopi are renowned as painters; their ancient kiva murals and polychrome pottery are patterned with exquisite geometric designs and naturalistic figures. But those who commissioned the hospital mural were mistaken to consider such an image mere decoration. It defied their categories with an aggressive vitality.

The visual arts have become one of the main forms of intercultural communication between Native Americans and the non-native world. Among the Pueblos of New Mexico and Arizona, outsiders sometimes assume that noted artists represent their tribes or even are tribal spokespeople. The role of cultural intermediary has been embraced by some artists, forced on others, and rejected by still others. In this century, the first Pueblo artists to take on a cultural broker role were male easel painters. They were soon joined by women who were renowned potters. Through their art and as individuals, these artists linked worlds, helping outsiders understand and appreciate Pueblo culture.

Of the fifty Pueblo people who have pursued easel painting since the early 1900s, only six have been women: Tonita Peña of San Ildefonso, Eva Mirabal and Merina Lujan (Pop Chalee) of Taos, Geronima Cruz Montoya of San Juan, and Pablita Velarde of Santa Clara and her daughter, Helen Hardin.[1] Art historians have called Velarde the leading Indian women painter in the Southwest.[2] Perhaps equally important, she has acted as an interpreter of Pueblo culture to the non-Indian world during an era of increasing outside pressure. For almost sixty years, she has balanced her tribal identity and values with her individual artistic talents in an effort to work between cultures.

Velarde sees herself as a mediator between the Indian and white worlds, noting, "I was a kind of a go-between in telling one side this life, and telling this side the other life. I balanced it somehow."[3] Her story illuminates the role of the artist as a cultural broker in twentieth-century Pueblo life. This sketch traces her development within the context of Santa Clara Pueblo and the surrounding Anglo-American society and draws on oral history, anthropological sources, and archival research in addition to visual evidence. It attempts to compare the perspectives of both Indian and white worlds by evaluating the rewards and constraints imposed on those who mediate between tribal and mass cultures. It also examines the possibility of moving freely between worlds and the forces limiting allegiance to one or another.

Pablita Velarde was born on September 19, 1918, at Santa Clara Pueblo to Marianita and Herman Velarde. Given the Tewa name Tse Tsan, which she translates as Golden Dawn, it was several months before she would be given her Spanish baptismal name, Pablita, by the priest at the nearby Santa Cruz church.[4] She recalled that "the world didn't take any notice of my birth because my mother, with the assistance of my grandmother and father, had gone through this ordeal several times already. There were three other girls in the family and there were also some boys, but the boys did not live. My childhood was no different from that of hundreds of other Indian children in the village."[5]

Like all the other Santa Clara children at that time, Velarde spoke only Tewa. She was informally schooled in Pueblo values, skills, and attitudes. As she describes it, "The cultural life is always around you there. You just automatically learn it. You hear it, you see it, you feel it, and you do it."[6] When she was young, the elders still taught children through stories to know their strengths and weaknesses and to guard their inner selves from harm. She has said that her generation was the last to hear long winter evening storytelling around the fire from the precious elders known as "Old Father."[7]

Twenty miles north of Santa Fe, Santa Clara lies on the western bank of the Rio Grande surrounded by a reservation of about forty-six thousand acres. The pueblo was in a state of transition during Velarde's early years, with its population passing three hundred for the first time since 1790 and its economic system beginning to show the effects of the introduction of a money economy. Yet in the first thirty years of the century, pueblo residents continued to rely on subsistence agriculture of corn and other grains, beans, and squash, supplemented by home vegetable gardens, hunting, and livestock raising. Like the other eighteen pueblos in New Mexico, Santa Clara was a tightly woven society in which individuals were integrated into cohesive social, political, and religious organizations.

Flanked by Spanish settlements since the late 1600s, Santa Clara was long accustomed to outsiders. The village was introduced to Anglo-American missionaries, teachers, and government agents during the American occupation after 1848. The Denver and Rio Grande Railroad passed close by in 1881, bringing a flood of Anglo-American tourists and settlers to the territory which would irrevocably increase after statehood in 1912. These outside pressures, as well as internal controversies over the organization of the communal responsibilities of farming, harvesting, and irrigation, had disturbed the pueblo's political stability since at least 1894.

A series of tragedies marked the childhood of Pablita and her three sisters, Legoria (Standing Cloud), Rosita (Flower), and Jane (Little Turquoise Flower). In 1921, their mother died of tuberculosis, a disease that ravaged the pueblos in the 1920s. Soon after, both Pablita and Jane developed eye infections and temporarily lost their sight. It was two years before their infections were finally cured by the treatments of their grandmother, herbal healer Guadalupita Chavarria. "Temporary darkness made me want to see every-thing," remembers Velarde, who was changed by the experience. "I have trained myself to remember, to the smallest detail, everything I see."[8]

Although traditional education shaped children from birth on-ward within the pueblo, Santa Clara was also one of the first of the pueblos to acknowledge the usefulness of formal classroom educa-tion. As early as 1870, the pueblo hired its own instructor to teach students to read and write in Spanish. Twenty years later, govern-ment-sponsored American schools for Indians were burgeoning in northern New Mexico. Velarde's father, Herman, was an eighth-grade graduate of Santa Fe Indian School, a large federal boarding school in Santa Fe.

Velarde sent his three daughters to St. Catherine's Catholic board-ing school in Santa Fe when Pablita was six years old. Here she was first called by her Spanish baptismal name and learned a new lan-guage.

Since my sisters and I didn't speak a word of English, we didn't know what was said. All I remember is that I was afraid and I couldn't remember my name, so the sisters printed my name on a piece of paper and pinned it to my dress. Whenever I was called for something, one of the older girls would grab me and give me a shove towards where I was wanted. In a short time I learned my name and became less afraid. The sisters were very kind and patient and it seemed that they were especially nice to me. I grew to adolescence there, learning to speak English and [to do] the school work at the same time.[9]

Unlike children from other tribes who went to boarding schools in distant states, Pueblo children were able to go home in the sum-mer and in this way strengthen their traditional education and na-tive language. During the five years that she was at St. Catherine's, Velarde traveled the twenty-five miles to Santa Clara every summer. There her father dry-farmed beans on a mesa top a few miles from the pueblo, entertaining his daughters with stories about nearby Puye, the ancestral home of the Santa Claras, while they weeded the fields and played on the rocks. At a young age, Velarde pre-ferred the boys' chores of herding and irrigating to the domestic tasks of housework and food preparation. She sensed that the traditional women's role in the pueblo might be confining for her.[10]

In 1929, eleven-year-old Pablita and her sister Rosita transferred to Santa Fe Indian School. It was an overcrowded and underfunded institution with pervasive military discipline and a curriculum that emphasized manual labor. "I remember when I first went there they used to drill us. Drill us to the school, drill us to the dining room, and drill us back to the dormitory. . . . We were just like prisoners, marching everyplace. We had captains that had to count for us all the way there and all the way back. Then every afternoon we had to salute the flag!"[11]

Velarde's intuitions about women's work were reinforced at school, where courses and daily chores were strictly demarcated by gender. Boys were taught farming and trades; girls studied "domestic science," including sewing, cooking, housekeeping, nursing, and laundry. The goal of the curriculum was to train girls to be wives and homemakers, models of behavior for their future families. Much of the day was devoted to cleaning dorms, serving food, and mending socks, among other household chores. "They tried me in the kitchen—of course I was a horrible failure there. They tried me in the dining room—I guess I was a terrible waitress and table setter and dishwasher, so they threw me out of there. Even in the laundry I was a miserable failure and scorched everyone's clothes."[12] She remembers, "At that time my mind was up in the wild blue yonder."[13]

The 1929 girls' dorm adviser still recalls Pablita affectionately because of her independent spirit, humor, and mischievousness. Although Velarde describes herself as shy and timid, she could also be a difficult and perhaps troubled student. While she was away at school, her father was widowed a second time, married again, and began a new family. Like his grandfather and great-grandfather, both former leaders of the pueblo, Herman Velarde was deeply involved in the tumultuous and factionalized village politics and would later serve as a tribal official himself. His daughters felt unwelcome at home with their new stepmother.

About a year after Velarde started school, changes in the national political scene transformed federal Indian education and the life of the students in Santa Fe. Long-needed policy reforms were introduced by Herbert Hoover's appointees for Indian commissioner, Charles James Rhoads, and director of Indian education, Dr. W. Carson Ryan, Jr. Between 1929, when Velarde was eleven, and 1936, when she was eighteen, the school was converted from a repressive military institution to a national center for Indian arts and crafts and painting. Funding was increased, and as a result, students could be adequately fed, the campus remodeled, and the curriculum and staff upgraded for the first time since the early 1900s.

Chester E. Faris, the newly appointed superintendent at Santa Fe Indian School, saw arts, crafts, and agriculture as a basis for economic development among the Pueblos. He was also pressured by artists and anthropologists in Santa Fe and Taos who were determined to preserve the Indian arts they felt had deteriorated alarmingly since the turn of the century. Although higher-ups designated a non-Indian to direct the arts and crafts department, Faris was the first administrator to strive to involve the Indian community in the school, hiring native craftspeople to teach silversmithing, woodwork, embroidery, weaving, and pottery in the crafts program that opened in 1931.

Velarde's life was shaped by the personal contact she had at Santa Fe Indian School with an exceptional Pueblo woman, artist Tonita Peña. In 1932, Peña was the only woman in a group of artists from San Ildefonso and Zia pueblos to work on large mural panels at the school. Two years later, she and fifteen other painters and craftspeople were hired at the school under the federal Public Works of Art Project to create artwork for Indian service buildings in the Southwest. They were housed in the school dormitories. "That's how we got acquainted. She talked Tewa, and she used to tease and laugh and joke in Indian, and that was fun. Then she would be sitting in her room in the evening, just painting for herself. I'd watch her and talk to her."[14]

Among Native Americans nationwide, painting for sale to outsiders was predominantly a man's activity concentrated among the Pueblos and Plains tribes. Plains Indian warriors in prison at Fort Marion, Florida, in the 1870s had produced some of the earliest drawings and paintings for whites. Although the Pueblos had an ancient tradition of painting both secular and sacred subjects for private use within their own communities, they began to produce easel art for a commercial market in the early 1900s. This first generation of artists were men from San Ildefonso, Hopi, and Zia and one woman—Tonita Peña. Most painted individual dance figures, ceremonial groups, and village scenes and worked in watercolor, tempera, or ink on paper. They were self-taught but were also encouraged by government school teachers and intellectuals who gave them art supplies and bought their work.

At this time, the sphere of activity for women among the Pueblos was the home. Female responsibilities were housework, food preparation, gardening, and raising children. Acceptable avenues to higher status within the community included ability in pottery making, midwifery, or natural healing, but high status for women in the world outside the pueblo was unknown.[15] The first sign that women's roles were expanding came when female artists began to sign their work for sale to the non-Indian market. The groundbreakers for individual recognition outside the village were both Tewas from San Ildefonso. Peña began to sign her paintings before 1915, and Maria Martinez put her name on her pottery in the early 1920s.[16]

Born in 1893, Peña had lived most of her life at Cochiti. She was fully integrated into the life of the pueblo, where she raised a large family and participated in traditional women's activities. For her, painting was a supplementary activity, not a full-time job. Just as the male painters at San Ildefonso devoted their time to farming, pottery painting, and wage labor in addition to artwork, Peña baked bread, plastered adobe walls, made pottery, and danced in ceremonies. She deflected occasional criticism from Pueblo neighbors of her individualistic behavior by her exemplary conduct in the village and by not painting secret ceremonies. Although it was not possible for women to become tribal officials as many of the San Ildefonso male artists were in the 1930s, Peña was married to a governor of Cochiti, Epitacio Arquero.[17]

Peña was outstanding, not only because of the quality of her work, but also because she was the lone woman painter of her generation. She is also one of very few Pueblo easel painters who have faced no major conflicts between the culture of her home village and the white world of Santa Fe. As Velarde forged her identity as a young Pueblo woman, she recognized that "paintingwise there was only Tonita Peña. She was the rebellion way back in the early 1920s. She gave me the inner strength that I needed to dare the men to put me in my own place or let me go."[18]

Velarde was also influenced by a young Anglo-American teacher at Santa Fe Indian School, Dorothy Dunn. Hired in 1932, Dunn was armed with a degree from the Art Institute of Chicago and three years teaching experience on the Navajo reservation and at the conservative pueblo of Santo Domingo. Indian art collections at the Field Museum of Natural History and conversations with reformers in Santa Fe in 1928 had convinced her of her cultural mission to be a bridge between talented young people of native communities and white art collectors and museums. Commissioner Rhoads and Superintendent Faris included her in their plan to restructure the school program around the arts, offering her a job when she graduated from art school. Dunn taught drawing and painting and titled her program "the Studio."

"There was something about Dorothy Dunn that I liked," said Velarde, who transferred into painting class after some disagreements with the head of the crafts department. "We got along real good. I even stayed after school and did extra work."[19] Like Education Director W. Carson Ryan, a follower of John Dewey, Dunn was absorbed by the concepts of progressive education. She wanted students to feel pride in their cultural heritage, and she strove to bring their community life into the educational process with the same zeal with which it had been prohibited in government schools prior to 1930.

Because of her teaching experience, Dunn was well aware of the profound diversity of tribes and pueblos her students represented. She advised them to respect and maintain these differences. She believed that subject matter should be taken from memory, imagination, and research, not models, and encouraged the children to delve into their recollections of home and draw scenes from the past. Students emulated the techniques of ancient mural painters by gathering and grinding clay and sandstone pigments. Dunn urged them to use every available source of information on their tribes, ranging from Bureau of American Ethnology Reports and museum publications to photographs of the pueblos and conversations with relatives.

Although Velarde was only a child, Dunn's basic attitudes deeply impressed her. For example, Dunn explained that "sometimes a fragment of information will call to a child's mind a tale of old customs told to him by a grandparent and an idea for a painting grows as a result. Developments prove that a great amount of tribal culture is told from generation to generation. These children are trying to put their heritage down in a form which cannot be distorted or misconstrued by outsiders. They are doing it for their own people as well as for others."[20] The concept of the preservation and transmission of culture through art would become a recurring theme in Velarde's work.

Most of the painting students were boys from non-Pueblo tribes such as the Navajo, Sioux, Apache, and Kiowa. Velarde stood out. "I was the only girl in Dorothy Dunn's art class, and all the boys used to make fun of me. All they drew were boys and men horseback riding and dancing. They never showed women. So I drew nothing but women's activities." Dunn assumed that choice of subject matter was influenced by gender and that girls should concentrate on domestic and ceremonial themes. To Velarde, this demonstrated her teacher's sensitivity.

> In my own case, I wanted to tell with paint, brush, and paper the way of my people and not plants and birds or animals. I did not even know until later, but Miss Dunn sensed this many a time. When I came to class with my mind as blank as my paper, she asked, "What would the women be doing at Santa Clara on a day like this?" or "What kind of dances do they do?" Just ordinary questions and thoughts like this were always asked to make our imaginations work.[21]

Eventually other girls joined the studio, but according to Dunn, Velarde was always the star female pupil.[22] When she graduated in 1936 at eighteen, she had few vocational skills, but her artwork had already brought her public recognition in shows at the Museum of New Mexico and the Corcoran Gallery in Washington, D.C.

Few careers were open to young Pueblo women in the years before World War II. Velarde felt unprepared by her education. "[They] never stressed how awful it was going to be when you started out looking for work and then you were too dumb to do it. Because you weren't really educated to go out and find a good job. The only thing available at my time when I graduated was housework. So I did some housework."[23] A series of short-term jobs followed. She worked as a motel maid, was an assistant teacher at the government school at Santa Clara, and decided after a stint as a nurse that she could not bear to see people suffer. She later painted drums for tourists and worked as a switchboard operator for the Bureau of Indian Affairs.

Her experience of the world outside northern New Mexico was enlarged in the fall of 1938, when she was hired by Ernest Thompson Seton, naturalist and Indian lore popularizer, to care for his baby daughter during a three-month lecture tour. Traveling with the Setons by car to New England, down the East Coast, and back through the southern states was a rare experience for a twenty-year-old Pueblo woman who had never before been more than one hundred miles from Santa Clara. She enjoyed it but recalled later, "I wanted to kiss the ground of New Mexico when I got home."[24]

Although Velarde was still interested in painting, few buyers shared her teacher's enthusiasm for Indian subject matter. "Any young artist that was trying to paint was just a nothing. Who wants some kind of a painting that was done by a young Indian? Who wants it? They're not known and it wasn't any good, according to their opinion. In their taste for art, they like to see an apple on a plate better than they did the Indian dance figure." She resolved, "I'm not about to paint an apple on a plate. If they didn't like it, well, I'll get along somehow, maybe as a typist or a clerk."[25]

She began to get commissions from commercial and governmental sources. In 1939, she collaborated with other Studio school artists on a series of mural panels outside Maisel's Indian gift shop in Albuquerque. Her panel depicted Pueblo women in brightly patterned shawls standing by a row of black pottery storage jars. As part of a Civilian Conservation Corps project at Bandelier National Monument, she was hired to paint the ways of life, customs, and ceremonies of the Pueblo people. Her work at Bandelier consisted of eighty-four paintings completed between 1939 and 1945. The carefully researched works richly describe the social, political, and economic life of the pueblos.

The Bandelier paintings captured Pueblo life in the early 1900s. Through them, she began to define herself as an interpreter of Pueblo culture to a non-Indian audience. The paintings intricately detail Pueblo architecture, dress, and craft production. Some docu-

Dressing a Young Woman for Her First Ceremonial Dance, *ca. 1953, tempera, 14¹/₈ × 12⁵/₈ inches. This painting is typical of Velarde's "memory paintings" describing Pueblo life in intricate detail. Two women in patterned gingham dresses prepare a young woman for the dance by wrapping her high, deerskin moccasins and bringing her turquoise, shell, and coral beads to wear and a black apron to tie over her shoulders. The girl's embroidered black wool* manta *(dress) is fastened at one shoulder. and she wears a hand-woven belt of cotton twine and wool. Photograph by Ted Rice; neg. 24355-13. Museum of Indian Arts and Culture, Laboratory of Anthropology, Museum of New Mexico, Santa Fe.*

ment hunting and gathering; others compare men's and women's activities or describe daily activities. "If it wasn't for the Park Service," she declared, "I guess I still wouldn't have the nerve to keep [my art] up. [The paintings] have a lot of meaning, sincere meaning, and the early life, the way the old people lived."[26] To the artist, the significance of the paintings was that they preserved a way of life that had changed irreversibly.

Paradoxically, Velarde's artwork required a closer examination of Pueblo culture at the same time that her personal life drew her farther from it. Although the majority of Santa Claras found spouses within the pueblo, Velarde in 1942 married a man who was not Tewa, not Pueblo, and not even Indian—Anglo-American Bureau of Indian Affairs policeman Herbert Hardin. Marriage to outsiders, particularly of Santa Clara women to non-Pueblos, often met with disapproval in the pueblo. Although children of Santa Clara men who married non-Indians were accepted as members of the pueblo, children of Santa Clara women were generally not. It was customary for a woman to live with her husband's family.[27] After brief stays in Texas and California, the Hardins eventually settled in Albuquerque with their two children, Helen and Herbert.

During these years, Velarde began to win recognition for her work beyond the Pueblo world. Between 1946 and 1950, she was awarded prizes at the New Mexico State Fair and the Philbrook Art Center in Tulsa. In 1952, an article about her in *El Palacio* magazine by her former teacher, Dorothy Dunn, clinched her reputation as an important artist. During the 1950s and 1960s, her work was shown in annual exhibitions of Indian art where she regularly won top awards. She had one-woman shows in New Mexico, Florida, and California. In 1954, the French government honored her for excellence in art, and in 1960, her book, *Old Father, The Storyteller*, was selected as best southwestern book of the year.[28]

Velarde became known as the most prominent Indian woman easel painter in the nation. Still, painting was somewhat of an anomaly among Native American women. Clearly, the most renowned Indian woman artist of the century was potter Maria Martinez of San Ildefonso. While Velarde's Studio school classmates Pop Chalee (Taos) and Geronima Montoya (San Juan) continued to paint, women artists from tribes nationwide excelled not as painters but as potters, weavers, or basketmakers. Many remained relatively unknown, producing exquisite beadwork and quill work.

Two approaches have dominated the historiography of Native American painting in the twentieth century. The first, articulated by Dunn in her book *American Indian Painting* (1968), emphasizes the tribal identity of each artist and the continuity of "traditional" forms, styles, and techniques as defined by the author on the basis of her own research. Alternatively, revisionist J. J. Brody contends in *Indian Painters and White Patrons* (1971) that Indian easel painting was originally a paternalistic white invention, that it is logically impossible to expect tribal and individual creative expression to coexist, and that by definition, modern painting is innovative, individualistic, and nontribal. Dunn and Brody, both art historians, rely on formal and stylistic analyses of works of art to build their arguments and do not examine the points of view of contemporary Native Americans and tribal communities. The debate framed by these two scholars continues today.

Velarde accepted and enjoyed the role of public spokesperson for Pueblo culture in the non-Indian world. Her intelligence and dry humor were assets. She improved her speaking and writing skills by joining Toastmasters International and the National League of American Pen Women. Non-Indian individuals and institutions relied on her as an expert interpreter of native culture, and she generously accommodated them with her lectures and public appearances. By 1970, she had appeared on television, in three feature films, and in more than twenty newspaper and magazine articles. As she became more outspoken, she also became more competitive. She said, "Painting took me out of a shell—a shell of timidity and shyness. I've become—well, sort of brazen!"[29]

The 1950s and 1960s were marked by a struggle to balance the sometimes conflicting roles of artist, wife, mother, and Pueblo woman. As her success grew, her husband became resentful of the recognition that he felt took away from her responsibilities at home. In 1959, when their marriage ended after seventeen years, she began to pursue art even more seriously than before to support herself and her children. Thus, both her education and her marriage had removed her from Pueblo life while giving her the opportunity—and financial necessity—to develop as an artist.

While Velarde continued to paint Pueblo ceremonial and genre scenes in a documentary style, she also explored other subject matter and styles. Her artistic identity had been shaped by the Studio school approach, but she also sought to establish a unique personal vision. Her paintings became increasingly abstract as she began to incorporate pottery and petroglyph designs. Mural motifs from the site of Kawaika-a in northeastern Arizona near Hopi, excavated between 1935 and 1939, inspired her, and she enlarged the scope of her subject matter to include Navajo, Apache, and Zuni ceremonials.[31] For example, a letter to Dunn in 1959 describes a mural commission at the Western Skies Motel in Albuquerque. "I bet I'm the first self-made 'Navajo Medicine Woman' who ever painted a shooting chant of the 'Buffalo Who Never Dies.' I am very pleased with it for I think that I have shown with sincerity the true thoughts and meaning of symbolic painting—I have read a lot on Navajo sandpaintings and when they asked for [Yei] figures, I decided on the 'Buffalo Who Never Dies.'"[32]

Velarde strove to go beyond her early training in artistic techniques as well. Students at the Studio had experimented with mineral pigments, and Velarde later became celebrated for the use of "earth colors" that she gathered, pulverized on a grinding stone, and mixed and prepared herself. Pursuing individual uniqueness, she was still attracted to Dunn's precepts, which matched her own convictions about what art should be. As she tried to reconcile innovation and tradition in her work, she expressed her feelings in a 1953 letter to Dunn.

Maybe you can help me with a few ideas, something new that hasn't been shown every year. I always see one painting by some artist and then several others come along with the same idea and it seems that we all copy one another. I guess you know what I mean. Most horse painters now paint like [Quincy] Tahoma or Pop Chalee, you know that kind—those with the long silky mane and tail and very muscular. It may be good art but I have never seen a living horse like that, especially an Indian horse. Also the figures of people, Buffalo dancers for instance, all seem to have the same position. I do the same thing over and over. Maybe you can help me and suggest a few new ones.[33]

As Velarde searched for material for her paintings, she became interested in recording the legends, tales, and customs of her village. She was convinced that her generation was the last to experience traditional life in the pueblo and that it was her responsibility to record what she could for her children. In the mid-1950s, she began to visit her father to ask him about the stories he remembered the village grandfathers telling in the early 1900s. Her efforts to preserve those memories began with the painting *Old Father, The Storyteller*, which Dunn proclaimed would one day be recognized as a great American painting, one that revealed aspects of the Tewa world for the first time.[34]

Velarde decided to move back to Santa Clara in the 1960s, after being away more than twenty years, but the village had changed tremendously since her girlhood. It was no longer a closely knit pueblo dependent on subsistence agriculture but a more dispersed community tied into the state and national economy. The population had tripled; it was now 1,119. Conversely, the amount of irrigable land had declined by 64 percent to about eight hundred acres. The federal laboratories at Los Alamos, fifteen miles away, employed more than thirty Santa Claras. At least seventy people in the pueblo supplemented their income by making pottery. Santa Clara had a reputation among non-Indians for being progressive. It had adopted a constitutional form of government in 1935 and seemed better able to manage change than the more conservative Tewa pueblos.

Now in her midforties, she bought a new government-built house south of the plaza. She lived alone, unlike most of the families at the pueblo. The quick wit, gregariousness, and strong-willed personality that had helped her survive in the outside world were generally not viewed as appropriate female behavior at Santa Clara. She began to confront unexpected barriers to her homecoming. White friends who visited her after eight months observed, "We became keenly aware that some disturbing force in her life was making her physically ill. We were very alarmed. She [was] down to eighty-nine pounds and looked as though she were dying."[35] Velarde described her difficulties.

When I was up in Santa Clara and had all those spooky things happening to me, I got kind of lost there for a period of time when I began to lose so much weight. I was getting scared inside. Problems seemed to get much worse than they really were because of my imaginations, I guess. I used to hear things, sometimes even in the daytime, mostly at night-time. And living alone, it was kind of weird, too, to have this kind of thing happen to you. To hear people walking around outside, or sometimes even through your house even when you know that your doors were locked.[36]

Velarde's experiences were not unique. Pueblo artists who have painted for secular purposes have met with disapproval and ostracism since the days of the first easel painters at San Ildefonso. Velino Shije Herrera's paintings of ceremonies so upset people at Zia that he was afraid of being punished.[37] An Isleta man who provided the anthropologist Elsie Clews Parsons with one hundred watercolors of ceremonial activities between 1936 and 1941 told Parsons, "I don't want any soul to know as long as I live that I have drawn these pictures. . . . No one can see them but Indians who believe."[38] The anthropologist Leslie White noted in 1942 that "every pueblo Indian child is taught from childhood to guard the secrets of his people, to tell the white man nothing, and to keep the Indian ways concealed."[39] Although Velarde cherished her tribal identity and it was at the heart of her self-image, her chosen career put her in conflict with her people.

Many Pueblo people see cultural knowledge as both powerful and dangerous. Highly restricted, it is not equally accessible to all community members. Secrecy is enforced for two related reasons. According to a scholar from Santa Clara, the anthropologist Edward P. Dozier, it has enabled Pueblo people to survive centuries of outside domination and religious persecution.[40] For example, as recently as 1926, Pueblo parents who withdrew their children from school for religious instruction were imprisoned by the government. Elizabeth Brandt has argued, however, that secrecy is pervasive within the pueblos as well, where it is used by religious and political leaders to promote social order. Along with protecting against external opponents, prohibition of communication of secret knowledge to the outside world keeps this information from being reported back to the community.[41] The concept of maintaining a permanent record of Pueblo life is antithetical to the rule of secrecy. Recording culture, whether in a painting, a tape, or a book, may bring harm to the recorder and to the whole community.

Velarde claimed, "I was my own boss and nobody was going to tell me what to do. I was never one to sit back and say nothing. I guess it brought me a lot of problems. . . . I've been an independent woman all my life."[42] But independence and personal recognition may be threats to village harmony. Often the Pueblos place a higher value on cooperation and compatibility than they do on individual achievement. Individuality may be highly prized as well but only when it serves the tribe, not exclusively the individual. What is seen in the white world as a positive attribute is often viewed by the Pueblos as a self-serving effort that disrupts the well-being of the whole. Dozier explained the Pueblo ideal by quoting Ruth Bunzel.

In all social relations, whether within the family or outside, the most honored personality traits are a pleasing address, a yielding disposition, and a generous heart. All the sterner virtues—initiative, ambition, an uncompromising sense of honor and justice, intense personal loyalties—not only are not admired but are heartily deplored. The woman who cleaves to her husband through misfortune and family quarrels, the man who speaks his mind where flattery would be much more comfortable, the man, above all, who thirsts for power or knowledge, who wishes to be, as they scornfully phrase it, "a leader of his people," receives nothing but censure.[43]

Finally, the concept of cultural preservation that was fervently advocated by Dunn is rejected by many Pueblo people. Whites often mistrust spoken words while believing implicitly in what is written down; in many Pueblos' experience, oral traditions have proved far more trustworthy than documents. To them, if religion, history, and tradition are to remain dynamic and alive, they must be transmitted orally within the community. Culture is not something to be placed in storage. It is expressed through direct human interaction and is not sought in a library or viewed in a museum. Velarde's research into the past brought accusations that she was exploiting the culture for her own benefit. She explained, "It wasn't for profit that I was trying to do any research on our history and traditional life there. I told them I would give back whatever they wanted."[44]

Velarde moved back to Albuquerque. After two decades of experimentation, she abandoned her abstract work and returned to

"memory paintings," carefully researched portrayals of Pueblo life reminiscent of the early Bandelier commission. "I feel that I'm keeping the old art alive by painting the ancient way with my earth pigments and my traditional designs," she wrote to Dorothy Dunn. "I feel that I'm keeping them alive and they're keeping me alive."[45] These paintings contain complex visual images in which each pictorial element refers to an aspect of Pueblo myth and history that requires the artist's interpretation to fully understand.

Ultimately, Velarde's own culture has benefited from her stature in the non-Indian world. The Pueblo governors recognized her unique strengths as a spokeswoman and invited her to testify before Congress on tribal control of Indian education in 1979 and 1980. In recent years, she has donated her talents to tribally run institutions such as the Santa Clara Pueblo Senior Citizens' Center, the Santa Fe Indian School, and the Indian Pueblo Cultural Center.

Like Tonita Peña, she has begun to incorporate her own portrait in her work. Her first self-portrait, *Communicating with the Full Moon*, is a powerful expression of her struggle to balance a traditional Pueblo upbringing with an untraditional career and personal life. In a mural commissioned in 1977 by the Indian Pueblo Cultural Center, she portrays herself as the Buffalo Maiden in a winter dance at Santa Clara. A painting depicting the history of the Santa Fe Indian School includes a vignette of the artist in the company of important tribal leaders from Isleta, Santo Domingo, and Tesuque; San Ildefonso potter Maria Martinez; Jemez historian Joe Sando; Santo Domingo silversmith Santiago Coriz; and storytelling elders. These self-portraits help her come to terms with her identity as a Santa Clara woman and an artist; they reintegrate her symbolically in the world of her ancestors.

Communicating with the Full Moon, *1960s, casein, 23½ × 10 inches. This highly personal painting is a self-portrait of the artist in the 1960s after she had returned to Santa Clara to live. It is unique among Velarde's works. Velarde commented on the painting as follows: "I kind of got lost there for a period of time. . . . I made a self-portrait. That's the way my life was. It was kind of changing shape. The moon represents a symbol for healing, for strength, for peace of mind" (Hyer, "Woman's Work": The Art of Pablita Velarde, 17). Photograph by Herbert Lotz. Collection of Mr. and Mrs. B. W. Miller.*

In her many years as an artist, Pablita Velarde's intermediate position between cultures has won her both acclaim and censure. She has been an outsider and an insider in two worlds. Perhaps more than any other living Indian artist, she has faced a continuous struggle to balance her identity and goals as an Indian woman with the demands of her white audience. She has found that the values applauded in the outside world, such as independence, ambition, and candor, are precisely those disapproved of at home. While an artist's status in the larger society is based on communication, status in the pueblo is based on control of knowledge. Yet Velarde told a reporter in 1985, "I'm satisfied. Sure, it wasn't easy, but it has supported me. And it's opened a lot of doors I wouldn't have been able to walk through otherwise."[46] She remembers,

When I started to feed my soul with the old teachings, the old legends, and the old hearsays, and all the things that I learned at Bandelier, then I began to balance the two worlds a little bit more easy. . . . I was kind of a go-between in telling one side this life, and telling this side the other life. I balanced it somehow.

But now I'm at a point where I can pass some of my own expertise and some of my learning and my own feeling so that the people of the future, if they ever hear of me or read something about me, [they will] know that it's something that comes from my heart and from my own belief that I have accepted because the ancestors have taught it. I think that I have accomplished what God put me here on earth for. I'm satisfied with the work that I have done so far and this is the way I want to leave my world when I go back to Sandy Lake and become a Cloud Person. I want the earth to remember me through my work.[47]

As an artist, Velarde has worked at the intersection of two cultures. She learned brokering skills through the influence of her boarding school education; her powerful female mentors, Tonita Peña and Dorothy Dunn; and her marriage to a white man. Talent, opportunity, and economic necessity all shaped her career. Although her persistence as a painter distanced her from her Pueblo origins, her artwork is now being reclaimed by Santa Clara and other pueblos because it has come to represent the strength of Pueblo cultural identity. Her memory paintings are an irreplaceable visual resource to teach future generations about Pueblo life in the early 1900s.

The population of Santa Clara has quadrupled since Pablita Velarde was born in 1918. As the pueblo grows, more and more women have followed her lead and look to her as a role model. Several of the most prominent spokeswomen from Santa Clara today have married outside the pueblo and have been inspired by Velarde's outspoken advocacy of women's rights and her pursuit of a nontraditional career. Pueblo women are still potters, but now they are also easel painters, videographers, writers, and sculptors. Velarde has led the way for succeeding generations of Pueblo women and for Indian women of all tribes who aspire to be artists.

CONCLUSION

MARGARET CONNELL SZASZ

THE cultural brokers who have been discussed in this volume have offered some further insights into the general phenomenon of intermediaries. Through one means or another, they have all straddled the cultural divide. In this brief conclusion, I would like to look at three aspects of brokerage that these intermediaries have illuminated. The lives of these individuals suggest that brokers share certain common personality traits. In addition, while all of them have enjoyed some of the benefits of mediation, they have also experienced its detrimental effects. Finally, these intermediaries appear to fall into one of several patterns that shape the direction of their brokerage.

In response to Nancy Hagedorn's thesis that Andrew Montour's success as an interpreter depended in part on his personality, I have considered several characteristics of these intermediaries as integral to their position as border people. As a preface to any discussion of these traits, it should be noted that those who share these intermediary characteristics have also been favored by particular circumstances. Influential factors such as internal networks, mixed cultural heritage, and gender also predetermined who they would become. Jesse Rowlodge's connections through his mother, Owl, and his stepfather, Row-of-Lodges, ensured vital links for his political mediation. Helen Hunt Jackson's connections in the literary circles of the East provided the entrée for her brokerage. Others gravitated toward the cultural borders because they grew up within them. Montour's path to interpreting was smoothed by his French-

Oneida parentage. D'Arcy McNickle's childhood immersed him in a cultural mélange of métis, Salish-speaking Flathead, and Euramerican, which enabled him to move with sensitivity among different peoples. Tillie Kinnon Paul's youth reflected a mixed Tlingit-Scots heritage. Charlie Day absorbed Navajo ways while growing up at the family trading post. Sarah Dickinson moved from her Tlingit childhood into the world of multicultural skills with her marriage to an American fur trader. But even children of the same family reared in a multicultural heritage were affected by other limitations, such as gender. Montour's sister was a gifted linguist, but interpreting would have thrust her into competition with numerous skilled male interpreters who enjoyed a wider variety of opportunities to polish their talents. By contrast, Pablita Velarde recalled rebelling against traditional gender roles at Santa Clara as early as her childhood summers, when she chose the boys' tasks of herding and irrigating over housework and food preparation.

Given these conditions, intermediaries nonetheless exhibited characteristics that set them apart. All of the border people were curious about "the other side" of the cultural divide. The Cherokee students at the Brainerd boarding school moved even beyond the milieu of their "acculturating families" to acquire the values and skills of the non-Cherokee world. Their enthusiasm was contagious. The diligence with which Samson Occom devoted himself to his studies suggests a similar eagerness to learn about the other culture. Whether or not Crow intermediary A. B. Upshaw was forced to attend Carlisle Indian School, while there, he studied Euramerican ways carefully, gaining knowledge that served him well when he began to aid his own people. Helen Hunt Jackson found herself intensely interested in the other cultural world, but despite the historical circumstances that awakened her interest, curiosity alone did not guarantee her move into the border world.

Beyond their curiosity about other cultures, therefore, these intermediaries also demonstrated a receptiveness to what John Kessell has called "the ways and words of the other." William F. Cody dubbed it the harmonizing of the races. Dorothy Parker described the process as "trying to read both maps of the mind." Without this receptiveness, Occom would not have traveled to Lebanon to study with Eleazar Wheelock; Evan Jones would not have chosen to work with the fullblood Cherokees; Robert Young could not have explored the complex nuances of the Navajo language. By implication, those who were (and are) receptive to other cultural worlds acknowledged, either explicitly or implicitly, that those worlds offered something of value. Only when intermediaries retreated from this acknowledgment of inherent cultural worth, as William Clark did when he resorted "to advocating military action," did they lose a vital piece of the curious equation that formed their border world. I will return to this theme a little later.

If brokerage demanded curiosity and a receptiveness to the world beyond one's cultural borders, so, too, did it require determination. Montour offered the requisite determination in the form of aggression and ambition, but not all of these brokers were aggressive. Occom, for instance, might have benefited from a little more aggression in his relationship with Wheelock and other English ministers. Those who were not aggressive, like Occom, were, nonetheless, strong willed. Without her determination to be an educator, Fannie Willard would not have broken her engagement to pursue more schooling. Assessing this trait among the Southeast Alaska women, Victoria Wyatt noted that "their determination to ensure that their people survived is a testimony to cultural strength under adversity." This type of willpower, combined with aggression, lent a reservoir of strength to Jackson's campaign to win a permanent land base for the Mission Indians. It also enabled the Joneses to persist against innumerable odds in their alliance with the Cherokees.

Intermediaries who succeeded in this border world demonstrated that they were trustworthy. Late seventeenth-century Pueblo or Spanish intermediaries who failed this test usually paid the ultimate price, as Spaniard Diego Romero and Don Juan de Ye of Pecos learned. Montour's honesty and sincerity convinced both the Indians and the English. His brother Lewis was not as fortunate. Never fully trusted by the English, who suspected him of being "a Frenchman in his Heart," when he finally did gain their favor, it was cut short by his death in the Seven Years War. Honesty and trustworthiness were the sine qua non of those brokers who maintained the balance between conflicting cultural borders.

Those who succeeded in meeting these demands were, nonetheless, locked into the complexities of a position that offered rewards but often countered those rewards by immeasurable difficulties.

Many intermediaries bore the burden of responsibility with a conscientious forebearance. The Cherokee students at Brainerd carried even greater responsibilities than their counterparts in either non-Indian or Indian educational settings, yet their patience was amazing. Pondering the Navajo Community Development Project at Crownpoint, McNickle never resolved the question of what went wrong. It plagued him through his last years, appearing in the form of tragedy in his final novel, *Wind from an Enemy Sky*. Brokers like McNickle saw their commitment as total.

All too often intermediaries found themselves in awkward, sometimes precarious positions. By definition, the nature of mediation was that of a juggling act, and if the juggler did not suspend the apples and oranges in the air, one of the two sides or the juggler suffered the consequences. Tlingit Sarah Dickinson stepped into the chasm dividing cultures when the missionary S. Hall Young interfered with the practices of the Tlingit spiritual healers, the ixts. Aware of their power, when Dickinson translated Young's directives, she found herself caught on the knife edge of the cultural border. On the one hand, she could disobey the Christian; on the other, she might reap the retribution of witchcraft. The Franciscan missionary spared by the Zunis during the 1680 Pueblo Revolt could ill afford to persist in the juggling act that Dickinson maintained. Had he not donned Zuni attire and merged with these Pueblo people, Vargas might well have made a rather abrupt cultural choice for him. Juggling, therefore, involved a continuum of decision making necessary to preserve not only the balance between cultures but the survival of the juggler as well. It demanded a quick wit and a quicker eye, along with cross-cultural agility.

Crow intermediary A. B. Upshaw incurred the wrath of both sides of the cultural divide by marrying a white woman and also defending the Crow's land base, thereby demonstrating the wide-ranging burden borne by the brokers. In Kessell's words, "Brokers went too far and became part of the other, drew back disillusioned into their own culture, or found themselves ostracized by both." The risks were great, but so, too, were the rewards.

Even as the Cherokee students at Brainerd staggered under their complex mediation tasks of influencing families, teachers, Indians from other tribes, and non-Indians, they relied on small material rewards, such as books or tracts, and the sense of self-worth that came from guiding younger pupils at school, as well as their own families, to spur them toward their goals of selecting the finest from both cultures.

One of the strongest motives for brokering was the sense of power that it offered. As William Clark expanded his frontier domain, his mediation between Indian and non-Indian "relied on appeals to reason, order, and authority." Classifying Clark as a "power broker," James Ronda portrays him as a man who came to rely increasingly on a "real-life" chess game, moving tribes against other tribes to suit his needs and those of the federal government. In a similar fashion, Pueblo leaders who negotiated with Diego de Vargas wielded power both within their own pueblos and between their people and the Spaniards. After providing crucial military aid to Vargas's successful defeat of a Tewa/Tano revolt, the Pecos intermediary, Juan de Ye, thereafter "kept Vargas in his debt." Juan de Ye's successor, Don Felipe Chistoe, faced an internal challenge that he resolved by obtaining Vargas's assent and then destroying his opposition. In so doing, however, he also tore assunder the pueblo of Pecos. Surely no brokers dealt more shrewdly with power than the Joneses. Mediating between the federal government and the Cherokee Nation and among internal Cherokee rival groups in a deft display of juggling, Evan Jones and John Jones maintained a steady course despite the storms that plagued the Cherokees through the nineteenth century.

Beyond the anticipation of material reward and the pleasure obtained from power, cultural intermediaries also derived personal satisfaction. Often an intangible dimension of brokering, Peter Iverson's assessment of Robert Young's mediation with the Navajo clarifies this concept. "What matters to him [Young] most is the kind of respect and affection he has earned through the years." Surely Jesse Rowlodge would have echoed this sentiment. On his death at the age of ninety, he concluded a life dedicated to the ideal that his father had once expressed, "that an Arapaho chief should be a 'public hearted and public spirited' leader." In making forty trips to Washington, D.C., on tribal business, he had demonstrated his commitment to his people.

Each of the brokers discussed in this volume has followed a different path. In accordance with their historical and cultural circumstances, they have been interpreters, traders, and spiritual intermediaries; healers; government or education mediators; and brokers who have mediated through the humanities and arts and in performances. These were their routes to brokering, but to understand the stance they took as brokers, we need to assess the range of their responses to the border world.

They faced several choices. Those who determined to base their lives within their own cultures often moved into the pattern of accommodation. These intermediaries adapted selectively from other culture(s), and frequently they became teachers of their own people. But they were not necessarily formal educators. The show Indians exemplify this position. They were scarcely enchanted with all aspects of the non-Indian world. After too much of the East, American Horse commented, "I feel a wish sometimes to go out in the forest and cover my head with a blanket, so that I can see no more and have a chance to think over what I have seen." Nonetheless, the word that they brought back from their tours indicated that some adaptation was a necessity for their people. Despite the centuries that separated Occom from these Wild West performers, like them, he also believed in selective adaptation. The aggressiveness of Englishmen like David Jewett, Occom's nemesis armed with the "old musket," underlined the need for these Indians to retreat from Euramerican society. But the emigration to Brothertown did not signal Occom's disavowal of Christianity; it was interwoven into his world view.

On the reverse side of the cultural coin, a non-native intermediary like Helen Hunt Jackson was less concerned with selective adaptation from the native world than she was with teaching her own culture about that world. In a similar fashion, William Clark began to educate America about native people when he established his museum of Indian culture in St. Louis. Following yet another route, Pablita Velarde has relied on her painting to teach non-Pueblo America about her cultural heritage. All of these brokers have been message bearers; all have adapted selectively.

Clark, however, stands apart from most of the other intermediaries in this volume. As Ronda has argued, Clark virtually destroyed his position as broker when he resorted to force. But Ronda also suggests that Clark based his mediation with western Indians on the assumption that American geographic expansion was inevitable. Clark's "brokering was built not on equality but on presumption of dependency," Ronda concludes. Clark remains the major exception to the brokering experiences of these intermediaries. Even though he began within the accepted perimeters of the intermediary's role, attempting to "bridge the cultural divide," he "never transcended his own cultural and national loyalties." Clark's position vis-à-vis the other brokers would suggest that his was a failed brokerage, one that was destroyed by his own decision to resort to violence as a solution for the agonizing dilemma of Black Hawk and his people. A brokerage ensconced within the assumption of cultural superiority or paternalism was handicapped from the beginning.

If we return to the assessment of the broker's personality, it will be recalled that intermediaries were, by definition, receptive to other cultural worlds, and inherent in this receptivity was the belief that those cultures offered something of value. Taking this argument one step further, recognition of those cultures might also have implied that they were of intrinsic worth. If one considers the brokers included here, it appears that virtually all of them accepted this thesis except William Clark.

True, those who chose selective accommodation made the choice to live within their own cultural world, as Kessell has suggested. Still others, like Velarde, have directed their mediation from their own culture to the other side of the divide. As Hyer notes, Velarde "has been an outsider and insider in two worlds." Nonetheless, her painting has enabled her to spend her life as "a kind of go-between in telling one side this life, and telling this side the other life." Velarde concluded, "I balanced it somehow."

Like Velarde, the Joneses perceived balance as the nature of mediation. As William G. McLoughlin reminds us, for the Joneses, "God was not white. Nor was he red." Unlike many Christian missionaries, they accepted with grace the concept of syncretism as a natural form of spirituality that derives its being from several spiritual traditions. Ahead of their time, the Joneses demonstrated the power of self-determination in their reliance on Cherokees to complete the Cherokee/English Bible. The Joneses' determination to balance different cultural worlds through mediation reiterates once again Carl A. Hammerschlag's testimonial to the many dances. The cultural brokers discussed in this volume have mediated among the dancers with infinitely complex steps.

NOTES

INTRODUCTION

1. Carl A. Hammerschlag, M.D., *The Dancing Healers: A Doctor's Journey of Healing with Native Americans* (San Francisco: Harper & Row, 1988): 138.

2. William Simmons, "Culture Theory in Contemporary Ethnohistory," *Ethnohistory* 35 (Winter 1988): 2; James Axtell, *The European and the Indian: Essays in the Ethnohistory of Colonial North America* (New York and Oxford: Oxford University Press, 1981): 5; Marshall Sahlins, "Other Times, Other Customs: The Anthropology of History," *American Anthropologist* 85 (September 1983): 534.

3. Mary W. Helms, "Time, History, and the Future of Anthropology: Observations on Some Unresolved Issues," *Ethnohistory* 25 (Winter 1978): 5.

4. Bruce G. Trigger, "Ethnohistory: The Unfinished Edifice," *Ethnohistory* 33 (Summer 1986): 256.

5. Robert F. Berkhofer, Jr., "The Political Context of a New Indian History," *Pacific Historical Review* 40 (August 1971): 359; Francis Jennings, "A Growing Partnership: Historians, Anthropologists, and American Indian History," *Ethnohistory* 29, 1 (1972): 24.

6. Neal Salisbury, *Manitou and Providence: Indians, Europeans, and the Making of New England, 1500–1643* (New York and Oxford: Oxford University Press, 1982): 3.

7. Jennings, "A Growing Partnership," 22.

8. William Simmons, "Culture Theory in Contemporary Ethnology," 2.

9. Joan Mark, *A Stranger in Her Native Land: Alice Fletcher and the American Indians* (Lincoln: University of Nebraska Press, 1988): 144,

351–52. On La Flesche, also see Margot Liberty, "Francis La Flesche: The Osage Odyssey," in *American Indian Intellectuals*, ed. Margot Liberty, 44–59 (St. Paul: West, 1978); Michael C. Coleman, "The Mission Education of Francis La Flesche: An American Indian Response to the Presbyterian Boarding School in the 1860s," *American Studies in Scandinavia* 18 (1986): 67–82.

10. Margot Liberty, "Native American Informants: The Contributions of Francis La Flesche," in *American Anthropology: The Early Years*, ed. John V. Murra (St. Paul: West, 1978): 100.

11. Brumble criticizes the analysis of Gretchen Bataille and Kathleen Mullen Sands in *American Indian Women: Telling Their Lives* (Lincoln: University of Nebraska Press, 1984). He faults their assessment of certain "literary biographies" of Indian women because of their reliance on "a Western aesthetic and Western literary conventions." See H. David Brumble, *American Indian Autobiography* (Berkeley: University of California Press, 1988): 11, 14; also H. David Brumble, *An Annotated Bibliography of American Indian and Eskimo Autobiographies* (Lincoln: University of Nebraska Press, 1981).

12. Irving A. Hallowell, "American Indians, White and Black: The Phenomenon of Transculturalization," *Current Anthropology* 4 (December 1963): 520.

13. Ibid., 523. On colonials who became "Indianized," see Axtell, "The White Indians of Colonial America," in *The European and the Indian*, 168–206.

14. Theodore Stern, *The Klamath Tribe: A People and Their Reservation* (Seattle: University of Washington Press, 1965): 229–30. Elder is capitalized here as I have encountered it among native people; it denotes respect.

15. Ibid., 228.

16. Malcolm McFee, "The 150% Man, A Product of Blackfeet Acculturation," *American Anthropologist* 70 (1968): 1100, 1101. James Welch, a Blackfeet and Gros Ventre, has written on this theme in his novel *Fools Crow* (New York: Viking Penguin, Inc., 1986).

17. Stern, *The Klamath Tribe*, 100; McFee, "The 150% Man," 1101.

18. Robert Paine, "A Theory of Patronage and Brokerage," in Robert Paine, ed., *Patrons and Brokers in the East Arctic. Social and Economic Papers no. 2.* (Newfoundland: Memorial University of Newfoundland, University of Toronto Press, 1971): 8–21.

19. Vine Deloria, Jr., *Custer Died for Your Sins* (New York: Avon Books, 1971): 86.

20. Liberty, *American Indian Intellectuals*, 7–8.

21. Fenton, "'Aboriginally Yours,' Jesse J. Cornplanter, Hah-Yonh-Wonh-Ish, The Snipe," in ibid., 188–89.

22. Jennings, "Anthropological Foundations for American Indian History," *Reviews in American History* 7 (December 1979): 490–91.

23. Axtell, *The European and the Indian*, 5.

24. Francis Paul Prucha, ed., *A Bibliographical Guide to the History of Indian-White Relations in the United States* (Chicago: University of Chicago Press, 1977); *Indian-White Relations in the United States: A Bibliography of Works Published 1975–1980* (Lincoln: University of Nebraska Press, 1982). Dwight La Verne Smith, ed., *Indians of the United States and Canada: A Bibliography* (Santa Barbara, Calif.: ABC Clio, 1974). Donald L. Parman and Catherine Price, "A 'Work in Progress': The Emergence of Indian History as a Professional Field," *Western Historical Quarterly* 20 (May 1989): 188, 189 (n. 15), 191.

25. James Axtell, *The Invasion Within: The Contest of Cultures in Colonial North America* (New York and Oxford: Oxford University Press, 1985); Henry W. Bowden and James P. Ronda, eds., *John Eliot's Indian Dialogues: A Study in Cultural Interaction* (Westport, Conn.: Greenwood Press, 1985); Ronda, "Red and White at the Bench: Indians and the Law in Plymouth Colony, 1620–1691," *Essex Institute Historical Collections* 110 (July 1974): 200–15; Gary B. Nash, *Red, White and Black: The Peoples of Early America* (Englewood Cliffs, N.J.: Prentice Hall, 1974).

26. *Reflections on the Reservation System: Joshua Given—Kiowa Indian and Carlisle Alumnus* (n.p.: n.p., 1979). I am indebted to William T. Hagan for sending me a copy of this publication.

27. Alvin Josephy, *The Patriot Chiefs* (New York: Viking, 1971), xiv.

28. R. David Edmunds, ed., *Studies in Diversity: American Indian Leaders* (Lincoln: University of Nebraska Press, 1980), xiv; Berkhofer, "The Political Context of A New Indian History," 382.

29. L. G. Moses and Raymond Wilson, eds., *Indian Lives: Essays on Nineteenth- and Twentieth-Century Native American Leaders* (Albuquerque: University of New Mexico Press, 1985): 4. Brugge, "Henry Chee Dodge: From the Long Walk to Self-Determination," in *Essays on Native American Leaders*, ed. Moses and Wilson, 100; Hauptman, "Designing Woman, Minnie Kellog, Iroquois Woman," in *Essays on Native American Leaders*, ed. Moses and Wilson, 161.

30. Jacqueline Peterson and Jennifer S. H. Brown, eds., *The New Peoples: Being and Becoming Métis in North America*, (n.p.: University of Manitoba Press, 1985): 37.

31. J. Frederick Fausz, "'Middlemen in Peace and War': Virginia's Earliest Indian Interpreters, 1608–1632," *Virginia Magazine of History and Biography* 95 (January 1987): 45, 48, 62, 64.

32. Daniel K. Richter, "Cultural Brokers and Intercultural Politics: New York–Iroquois Relations, 1664–1701," *Journal of American History* 75 (June 1988): 40, 42, 67. Also see Richter, *Ordeal of the Longhouse: The*

People of the Iroquois League in the Era of European Colonization (Chapel Hill: University of North Carolina Press, 1992).

33. See Walter L. Williams, "Twentieth Century Indian Leaders: Brokers and Providers," *Journal of the West* 23 (July 1984): 3–6.

34. Nancy L. Hagedorn, "'A Friend To Go Between Them': The Interpreter as Cultural Broker During Anglo-Iroquois Councils, 1740–1770," *Ethnohistory* 35 (Winter 1988): 62.

35. James Clifton, ed., *Being and Becoming Indian: Biographical Studies of North American Frontiers* (Chicago: Dorsey Press, 1989): 25–26, 29–30.

36. Ibid., 24, 29–30.

37. Margaret B. Blackman, *Sadie Brower, Naekok: An Inupiaq Woman* (Seattle: University of Washington Press, 1989): 232; Joan Weibel-Orlando, *Indian Country, L.A.: Maintaining Ethnic Community in a Complex Society* (Urbana and Chicago: University of Illinois Press, 1991): 201, 220.

1. THE WAYS AND WORDS OF THE OTHER:
DIEGO DE VARGAS AND CULTURAL BROKERS
IN LATE SEVENTEENTH-CENTURY NEW MEXICO

I should like to thank my colleagues Margaret Connell Szasz, Meredith D. Dodge, Alison R. Freese, Suzanne B. Pasztor, and Rick Hendricks for helpful comments on this elusive theme.

1. Florence Hawley Ellis, collecting Zia oral tradition in support of the pueblo's land claim, described Ojeda as "the realistic Zia War Captain (probably Outside Chief) who saw cooperation with the conquerors as the only possibility of survival of his people." "Pueblo Boundaries and Their Markers," *Annual Report, Museum of Northern Arizona, Nineteen Hundred and Sixty-Five*, Supplement to *Plateau* 38, 4 (Spring 1966): 97–105.

2. Vargas's journal, 23–24 October 1692, in John L. Kessell and Rick Hendricks, eds., *By Force of Arms: The Journals of don Diego de Vargas, New Mexico, 1691–93* (Albuquerque: University of New Mexico Press, 1992): 517–20. An earlier translation appears in J. Manuel Espinosa, ed., *First Expedition of Vargas into New Mexico, 1692* (Albuquerque: University of New Mexico Press, 1940): 176–77.

3. Rick Hendricks, "Levels of Discourse in Early Modern Spanish: The Papers of Diego de Vargas, 1643–1704," *North Dakota Quarterly* 58 (Fall 1990): 124–39.

4. John L. Kessell, Rick Hendricks, Meredith D. Dodge, Larry D. Miller, and Eleanor B. Adams, eds., *Remote Beyond Compare: Letters of don Diego*

de Vargas to His Family from New Spain and New Mexico, 1675–1706 (Albuquerque: University of New Mexico Press, 1989): 128.

5. A continuous, three-phase Pueblo-Spanish War, 1680–1696, is suggested by John L. Kessell, "Spaniards and Pueblos: From Crusading Intolerance to Pragmatic Accommodation," in *Archaeological and Historical Perspectives on the Spanish Borderlands West*. Vol. 1., *Columbian Consequences*, ed. David Hurst Thomas (Washington, D.C.: Smithsonian Institution, 1989): 127–38. For the first phase, see Charles Wilson Hackett, ed., *Revolt of the Pueblo Indians of New Mexico and Otermín's Attempted Reconquest, 1680–1682* (Albuquerque: University of New Mexico Press, 1942); for the second, Vina Walz, "History of the El Paso Area, 1680–1692" (Ph.D. dissertation, University of New Mexico, 1950); and for the third, J. Manuel Espinosa, *Crusaders of the Río Grande: The Story of Don Diego de Vargas and the Reconquest and Refounding of New Mexico* (Chicago: Institute of Jesuit History, 1942).

6. Concerning the seventeenth-century New Mexico colony, the works of France V. Scholes, most of which appeared singly or serially in the *New Mexico Historical Review* (hereinafter *NMHR*), are still the most complete. A more recent, highly interpretive study is Ramón A. Gutiérrez, *When Jesus Came, the Corn Mothers Went Away: Marriage, Sexuality, and Power in New Mexico, 1500–1846* (Stanford: Stanford University Press, 1991).

7. See Florence Hawley Ellis, "Comments on Four Papers Pertaining to the Protohistoric Southwest," in *The Protohistoric Period in the North American Southwest, A.D. 1450–1700* (Tempe: Arizona State University, 1981): 378–433; and Alfonso Ortiz, *The Tewa World: Space, Time, Being, and Becoming in a Pueblo Society* (Chicago: University of Chicago Press, 1969). The most complete general work on the Pueblos is Alfonso Ortiz, ed., *Southwest*. Vol. 9. *Handbook of North American Indians* (Washington, D.C.: Smithsonian Institution, 1983). In this chapter, I have used "Pueblo" for the people and "pueblo" for the communities in which they lived and still do live.

8. John L. Kessell, "Diego Romero, the Plains Apaches, and the Inquisition," *American West* 15, 3 (May-June 1978): 12–16. Donald J. Blakeslee has identified the ritual Romero participated in among the Plains Apaches as a calumet ceremony. "The Origin and Spread of the Calumet Ceremony," *American Antiquity* 46 (October 1981): 761–62; John P. Wilson, personal communication, 13 December 1990.

9. Not enough historical archaeology has been conducted in seventeenth-century New Mexican domestic sites to assess the influence of such Indian servants—who functioned at some level as inadvertent cultural brokers—in Hispanic households. A suggestive study is Kathleen Deagan, *Spanish St. Augustine: The Archaeology of a Colonial Creole Community* (New York: Academic Press, 1983). See also Marc Simmons, *Witchcraft in*

the Southwest: Spanish and Indian Supernaturalism on the Rio Grande (Flagstaff: Northland Press, 1974).

10. The phenomenon of Europeans adopting the lifeways of Native Americans was by no means unique to Spanish America. See, e.g., James Axtell, "The White Indians of Colonial America," *William and Mary Quarterly* 32 (January 1975): 55–88, who deals almost exclusively with captives, not with noncaptive Europeans who ran away from European colonial society to join Indian society.

11. Frank Hamilton Cushing, "Outline of Zuni Creation Myths," in *Thirteenth Annual Report of the Bureau of Ethnology, 1891–92* (Washington, D.C.: Government Printing Office, 1896): 330–31; Frederick Webb Hodge, *History of Hawikuh, New Mexico* (Los Angeles: Southwest Museum, 1937): 102–105.

12. Fray Angélico Chávez, *Origins of New Mexico Families in the Spanish Colonial Period* (Santa Fe: Historical Society of New Mexico, 1954): 69. The idea of a mulatto leader of the Pueblo Revolt was proposed in Chávez, "Pohé-yemo's Representative and the Pueblo Revolt of 1680," *NMHR* 42 (April 1967): 85–126, and refined by Stefanie Beninato, "Popé, Pose-yemu, and Naranjo: A New Look at Leadership in the Pueblo Revolt of 1680," *NMHR* 65 (October 1990): 417–35.

13. John L. Kessell, "Esteban Clemente, Precursor of the Pueblo Revolt," *El Palacio* 86, 4 (Winter 1980–81): 16–17. Fray Angélico Chávez, "Pohé-yemo's Representative," 119, assumed that Clemente was a mixedblood. No one has explained where he got the family name Clemente, hardly known in colonial New Mexico. It would be interesting to have a comparative study of Hispanicized Indian leaders who put themselves at the head of nativistic uprisings in Spanish America, a phenomenon that seemed to increase in the later colonial period.

14. Pueblo Indian scholars do not agree on who Popé was. Alfonso Ortiz, "Popay's Leadership: A Pueblo Perspective," *El Palacio* 86, 4 (Winter 1980–81): 18–22, makes him the predominant spiritual leader, while Joe S. Sando, *Pueblo Nations: Eight Centuries of Pueblo Indian History* (Santa Fe: Clear Light, 1992): 177, stressing that Popé was only one of a number of leaders, thinks he was probably a war captain.

15. Fray Silvestre Vélez de Escalante, Extracto de noticias, c. 1778, Biblioteca Nacional, Mexico City, Archivo Franciscano, New Mexico Documents 3, 1 (19/397.1). Like Clemente, the family name Ojeda was a rarity in New Mexico.

16. Further details of the story—the debate by the Zia and Santa Ana people over accepting Catholicism, the Spaniards' ruse and abduction of Indian children, Bartolomé's care of the children in "Mexico," and the land-grants-for-conversion deal—may reflect Zia memory of the 1689 de-

feat and Ojeda's stay, with the other Keres captives, in El Paso. Ellis, "Pueblo Boundaries," 100–101.

17. Kessell et al., *By Force of Arms*; Espinosa, *First Expedition of Vargas*.

18. Espinosa, *Crusaders of the Río Grande*.

19. Ibid., 137, 145.

20. "General interpreter" Hidalgo, for whatever reasons, chose not to resettle in New Mexico in 1693 or later. Chávez, *New Mexico Families*, 47–48.

21. Ibid., 5, 33, 270.

22. John L. Kessell, *Kiva, Cross, and Crown: The Pecos Indians and New Mexico, 1540–1840* (Albuquerque: University of New Mexico Press, 1989): 243–53.

23. From Vargas's time on, Spanish men and women often served as godparents to Pueblo Indian children. The practice may also have been common before 1680, but the church records are missing. We do not have a study of what being compadres may have meant to Indians or Spanish colonists in religious, social, or economic terms in colonial New Mexico. For the more developed society of Peru, see Paul Charney, "The Implications of Godparental Ties between Indians and Spaniards in Colonial Lima," *The Americas* 47 (April 1991): 295–314.

24. Diego de Vargas to the king, Zacatecas, May 16, 1693, Archivo General de Indias, Seville, Spain, Audiencia de Guadalajara, 139: 5.

25. Kessell, *Kiva, Cross, and Crown*, 270.

26. Ibid., 254–70.

27. A frequently cited example, which seemed to combine intra-Pueblo hostility and opposition to the Spaniards, is the destruction of the Hopi community of Awatovi on Jeddito Mesa in 1700 or 1701 by Hopis from the other mesas. See Ross Gordon Montgomery, Watson Smith, and John Otis Brew, *Franciscan Awatovi* (Cambridge: Peabody Museum, 1949); John P. Wilson, "Awatovi—More Light on a Legend," *Plateau* 44, 3 (1972): 125–30; and Harold Courlander, ed., *Hopi Voices: Recollections, Traditions, and Narratives of the Hopi Indians* (Albuquerque: University of New Mexico Press, 1982): 55–60.

28. Kessell, *Kiva, Cross, and Crown*, 292.

29. Ibid., 229–30, 288–97. Some of the estranged Pecos evidently joined Apache groups, at least temporarily, while others scattered to various Pueblo communities. It is not known if any reestablished themselves at this early date among the Jemez, the only other Towa-speakers.

30. The last of the Pecos found refuge among the people of the pueblo of Jemez, where today their descendants number several hundred.

31. Agustín volunteered to show the Spaniards a shortcut from El Morro back to the ruined pueblo of Senecú on the Rio Grande. Diego de Vargas

to the Conde de Galve, El Paso, 8 January 1693, in Kessell and Hendricks, *By Force of Arms*, 606.

32. Although Spaniards in seventeenth-century New Mexico kept Indian servants, some slave and some free, and dealt often with cultural brokers, they evidently did not use the term "genízaro" for either. Concerning genízaros, see Fray Angélico Chávez, "Genízaros," in *Southwest*, ed. Alfonso Ortiz, 198–200. Vol. 9, *Handbook of North American Indians*; Robert Archibald, "Acculturation and Assimilation in Colonial New Mexico," *NMHR* 53 (1978): 210–14; Gutiérrez, *When Jesus Came*; and Suzanne B. Pasztor, "Between Cultures: The Genízaros of New Mexico," *Best Student Essays of the University of New Mexico* 1, 1 (1989): 26–32. Linked today by some to crypto-Jews or Penitentes, the genízaros deserve further study.

33. Accommodation between Pueblo and Hispanic neighbors began to come apart after the United States occupied New Mexico, especially when the federal government, having decided that the Pueblos were indeed Indians, moved in their behalf to protect their land and water rights. Kessell, "Spaniards and Pueblos," 134–35.

2. "FAITHFUL, KNOWING, AND PRUDENT":
ANDREW MONTOUR AS INTERPRETER AND
CULTURAL BROKER, 1740–1772

Research for this essay was supported in part by a short-term research fellowship at the Newberry Library in Chicago and a Kate B. and Hall J. Peterson Fellowship at the American Antiquarian Society in Worcester, Massachusetts.

The title of this chapter is taken from Samuel Hazard, ed., *Minutes of the Provincial Council of Pennsylvania, from the Organization to the Termination of the Proprietary Government* (spine title, *Colonial Records of Pennsylvania*), 10 vols. (Harrisburg: Theo. Fenn & Co., 1851–52) 5: 290. (Hereafter cited as *Pa. Col. Recs.*)

1. William A. Hunter, in the *Dictionary of Canadian Biography* ([Toronto, 1974] 3: 147), identified Madame Montour as Elizabeth Couc, born at Trois-Rivières in 1667 of a French father and Indian mother. I believe, however, that Elizabeth was probably her aunt. Witham Marshe, "Journal of the Treaty . . . at Lancaster in Pennsylvania, June 1744," Massachusetts Historical Society *Collections*, 1st ser., 4: 189–91; Governor Cornbury to Board of Trade, *Calendar of State Papers, Colonial Series, America and West Indies*, ed. W. Noel Sainsbury et al. (London: Her Majesty's Stationary Office, 1860–): 1708–09, item 107, 71; Charles A. Hanna, *The Wilderness Trail*, 2 vols. (New York: G. P. Putnam's Sons, 1911): 199–206; William M.

Darlington, "The Montours," *Pennsylvania Magazine of History and Biography* 4(1880): 218–25; and Howard Lewin, "A Frontier Diplomat: Andrew Montour," *Pennsylvania History* 33(April 1966): 155–56.

2. Colden's identification of Madame Montour as French, while technically ethnically incorrect, is understandable. Several colonials perceived her as French because she spoke that language fluently and tended to converse with them in French rather than English. *Cadwallader Colden Papers*, 9 vols., New York Historical Society *Collections* (vols. 50–56, 67–68), 68 (1876): 200; Charles A. Hanna, *Wilderness Trail*, 1: 199, n. 1, and 1: 201; and Pennsylvania History and Museum Commission, Pennsylvania Provincial Records, Vol. H: 28.

3. As Jacqueline Peterson has noted, "The people who are born and grow up at the interstices of two civilizations or nations are almost always in motion. . . . Over time, this group may begin to serve as a conduit for goods, services, and information and to see its function as a broker." Jacqueline Peterson, "Many Roads to Red River: Métis Genesis in the Great Lakes Region, 1680–1815," in *The New Peoples: Being and Becoming Métis in North America*, eds. Jacqueline Peterson and Jennifer H. Brown, Manitoba Studies in Native History 1 (Lincoln: University of Nebraska Press, 1985): 37.

4. Nancy L. Hagedorn, "'A Friend To Go Between Them': The Interpreter as Cultural Broker During Anglo-Iroquois Councils, 1740–1770," *Ethnohistory* 35 (Winter 1988): 60–80, quote on 61.

5. The best analysis of this group (called Mingos by their British contemporaries), their relationship to the Six Nations, and their motives and policies is Michael N. McConnell's, "Peoples 'In Between': The Iroquois and the Ohio Indians, 1720–1768," in *Beyond the Covenant Chain: The Iroquois and Their Neighbors in Indian North America, 1600–1800*, eds., Daniel K. Richter and James H. Merrell (Syracuse: Syracuse University Press, 1987): 93–112.

6. Howard Lewin, "A Frontier Diplomat: Andrew Montour," *Pennsylvania History* 33 (April 1966): 164–65; "Logs Town Treaty of 1752," Public Records Office, Kew, CO 5/1327, 595–96; "Thomas Cresap to Governor Dinwiddie, Oct. 1751," in *George Mercer Papers Relating to the Ohio Company of Virginia*, ed. Lois Mulkearn (Pittsburgh: University of Pittsburgh Press, 1954): 413–14. On another occasion, at Easton in October 1758, Montour's knowledge of protocol and sensitivity to Indian sensibilities avoided a breach in relations between the Six Nations, the Delaware, and The English. See *Minutes of a Conference at Easton, October 1758* (Philadelphia: B. Franklin & D. Hall, 1758): 12, in *Iroquois Indians: A Documentary History of the Diplomacy of the Six Nations and Their League*, eds. Francis Jennings et al. (Woodbridge, Conn.: Research Publications, 1984): reel 22, Oct. 7–26, 1758 (hereafter *Iroq. Inds.*; *Pa. Col. Recs.* 8: 189.

7. *Bethlehem Diary*, Trans. and ed. Kenneth G. Hamilton (Bethlehem: Archives of the Moravian Church, 1971): 97, 103; *Pa. Col. Recs.* 4: 641, 680; *Dictionary of Canadian Biography*, eds. George W. Brown et al. (Toronto: University of Toronto Press, 1966–): 3: 147; *Early Western Travels, 1748–1846*, ed. Reuben Gold Thwaites (Cleveland: Arthur H. Clark, 1904): 76.

8. *Pa. Col. Recs.* 7: 95–96.

9. *Pennsylvania Archives*, 9 ser., 138 vols. (Philadelphia and Harrisburg, 1852–1949), ser. 1, 2: 31; *Pa. Col. Recs.* 5: 455, 290, 441, 497, 520, 532, 707; *Early Western Travels*, 1: 56, 76; William M. Darlington, *Christopher Gist's Journals with Historical, Geographical, and Ethnological Notes and Biographies of His Contemporaries* (New York: Argonaut Press, 1966): 35, 161, 235; "Journal of Croghan & Montour, Proceedings at Logstown, May 1751," Penn MS, Indian Affairs 1: 6, Historical Society of Pennsylvania, Philadelphia, in *Iroq. Inds.* (14): May 18–30, 1751.

10. *Dictionary of Canadian Biography*, 6: 7.

11. "Washington to Dinwiddie, June 3, 1754," in *The Writings of George Washington from the Original Manuscript Sources, 1745–1799*, ed. John C. Fitzpatrick. 39 vols. (Washington, D.C.: Government Printing Office, 1932–1944), 1: 72; Darlington, *Gist's Journals*, 167; "Gov. Dinwiddie to Horatio Sharpe, Jan. 7, 1755," Emmet Collection, EM 47, Rare Books and Manuscripts Division, New York Public Library, in *Iroq. Inds.* (17): Jan. 7, 1755.

12. "Sharpe to Dinwiddie, Dec. 10, 1754," in *Archives of Maryland, Correspondence of Governor Horatio Sharpe, 1753–1757*, ed. William Hand Browne (Baltimore, 1888): 1: 139, 151.

13. Sir William Johnson, *The Papers of Sir William Johnson*, ed. Alexander C. Flick et al., 14 vols. (Albany: State University of New York, 1921–62): 4: 321, 412.

14. *Pa. Col. Recs.* 5: 290, 518, 540; Darlington, *Gist's Journals*, 163; and *Early Western Travels*, 1: 71.

15. *Pa. Col. Recs.* 8: 470; 5: 307–12, 677; William M. Beauchamp, *Life of Conrad Weiser as It Relates to His Services as Official Interpreter Between New York and Pennsylvania and as Envoy Between Philadelphia and the Onondaga Councils* (Syracuse: Onondaga Historical Association, 1925): 67; *Treaty with the Ohio Indians at Carlisle, Oct. 1753* (Philadelphia: Benjamin Franklin, 1753): 9–10.

16. "Logstown Treaty (copy c. 1774)," [Robert Dinwiddie?] Papers, 1744–1752, MS 4, V8194, D6197 al, 28, Virginia Historical Society, Richmond, Virginia, in *Iroq. Inds.* (15): May 28–June 13, 1752; *Pa. Col. Recs.* 5: 683; *Treaty at Carlisle, October 1753*, 12, in *Iroq. Inds.* (15): Oct. 1753; Darlington, *Gist's Journals*, 166.

17. *Pa. Col. Recs.* 5: 696, 497; *Johnson Papers*, 3: 183; "Moravian Martin

Mack's report of his visit with French Margaret, Aug. 28, 1753," cited in Hanna, *Wilderness Trail*, 1: 205; Darlington, *Gist's Journals*, 161.

18. "Richard Peters to the Proprietaries, Nov. 6, 1753," cited in Paul A. W. Wallace, *Conrad Weiser: Friend of Colonist and Mohawk* (Philadelphia: University of Pennsylvania Press, 1945): 345; "Richard Peters to [Thomas Penn]," Penn MS, Off. Corr., vol. 6, Hist. Soc. of Penn., in *Iroq. Inds.* (15): [Sept. 1753].

19. Darlington, *Gist's Journals*, 165; Beauchamp, *Life of Conrad Weiser*, 90–91; *Johnson Papers*, 2: 370; *Pa. Col. Recs.* 7: 12.

20. *Johnson Papers*, 2: 438; "Richard Peters to Thomas Penn, Philadelphia, April 25, 1756," Penn MS, Off. Corr., fol. 8, 75, Hist. Soc. of Penn., in *Iroq. Inds.* (18): Apr. 25, 1756.

21. *Pa. Col. Recs.* 7: 95; Darlington, *Gist's Journals*, 169; Hanna, *Wilderness Trail*, 1: 235, 237; *Johnson Papers*, 2: 427; *Pennsylvania Archives*, 2d ser., 6: 463.

22. "Proceedings of Indian Affairs," Public Archives of Canada, Ottawa, Federal Archives Division, Indian Records, RG10, vol. 1823: 67, in *Iroq. Inds.* (20): Apr. 29, 1757.

23. *Johnson Papers*, 5: 120; "Major Isaac Hamilton to General Thomas Gage, January 22, 1772," in *Correspondence of General Thomas Gage*, ed. C. E. Carter, 2 vols. (New Haven: Yale University Press, 1931–1933), cited in Lewin, "Frontier Diplomat," 186.

24. Darlington, *Gist's Journals*, 157; "Dinwiddie to Board of Trade, enclosed in William Trent's Journal to Ohio, July–Aug. 1753," Public Record Office, Kew, CO5/1328, in *Iroq. Inds.* (15): Nov. 17, 1753; *Pa. Col. Recs.* 5: 692, 6: 149; "Croghan to Peters, Feb. 3, 1754," *Pennsylvania Archives*, ser. 1, 2: 118.

25. *Pa. Col. Recs.* 5: 290, 566; Darlington, *Gist's Journals*, 164; "Weiser to Richard Peters, May 2, 1754," Penn MS, Indian Affairs, vol. 2, Hist. Soc. of Penn., in *Iroq. Inds.* (16): May 2, 1754; Hanna, *Wilderness Trail*, 1: 245; Thomas Penn Letterbook, 1752–1772, 55 and 69, American Antiquarian Society, Worchester, Mass.

26. "Weiser to Richard Peters, Lancaster, Aug. 4, 1748," *Pennsylvania Archives*, ser. 1, 2: 12, 31; Wilbur Jacobs, *Diplomacy and Indian Gifts: Anglo-French Rivalry Along the Ohio and Northwest Frontiers, 1748–1763* (Stanford: Stanford University Press, 1950): 105; Hanna, *Wilderness Trail*, 226; Darlington, *Gist's Journals*, 159.

27. Darlngton, *Gist's Journals*, 160, 163; *Pa. Col. Recs.* 5: 540; Hanna, *Wilderness Trail*, 1: 204, 241; *Johnson Papers*, 3: 329, 734, 877, 914; 10: 560, 637; 12: 642, 732, 804; Thomas Gage (1721–1787) Papers, 1754–1783, Warrants, 36 vols., William L. Clements Library, Ann Arbor, Mich., 9: 15, 85, 89; 10: 41; 14: 94; 17: 90; 23: 124; 27: 8, 14, 72; 29: 55; and 31: 49, 51.

28. *Pa. Col. Recs.* 5: 455, 6: 151; Hanna, *Wilderness Trail*, 1: 254;

"Sharpe to Dinwiddie, December 10, 1754," in *Maryland Archives, Sharpe's Correspondence*, 1: 139.

29. Sattelihu and Eghnisara were Montour's Indian names, the latter given to him on his elevation to the Ohio Six Nations Council. Darlington, *Gist's Journals*, 175; "Logstown Treaty (c. 1774 copy)," 28–29, in *Iroq. Inds.* (15): May 28–June 13, 1752.

30. Darlington, *Gist's Journal*, 175; *Memorials of the Moravian Church*, ed. William C. Reichel (Philadelphia: Lippincott, 1870): I: 95.

31. *Johnson Papers*, 2: 695, 9: 634, 10: 481; *Dictionary of Canadian Biography*, 6: 7.

32. "Peters to Richard Hockley, 1753," in "Notes and Queries," *Pennsylvania Magazine of History and Biography* 39 (1915): 239; "William Johnson to George Croghan, Ft. Johnson, May 14, 1760," Cadwallader Papers, 6 Croghan, Sect. 33, Misc. Docs., Hist. Soc. of Penn., in *Iroq. Inds.* (23): May 14, 1760; *Johnson Papers*, 5: 120. Another indication of Montour's indebtedness and inner confusion may be found, perhaps, in his adoption of the alias "Henry" Montour during the early 1750s. Lewin, "Frontier Diplomat," 168–69; Witham Marshe, *Lancaster in 1744*, ed. William H. Egle (Lancaster: New Era Steam Book and Job Print, 1884): 28–29.

33. Wallace, *Conrad Weiser*, 371.

34. Ibid.; Hanna, *Wilderness Trail*, 1: 232.

35. *Johnson Papers*, 3: 4, 7: 685, 11: 873; "Major Isaac Hamilton to General Thomas Gage, January 22, 1772," cited in Lewin, "Frontier Diplomat," 186.

3. SAMSON OCCOM: MOHEGAN AS SPIRITUAL INTERMEDIARY

1. Works on Occom include William DeLoss Love, *Samson Occom and the Christian Indians of New England* (Boston: Pilgrim Press, 1899); Harold Blodgett, *Samson Occom* (Hanover: Dartmouth College, 1935); Leon Burr Richardson, *An Indian Preacher in England* ([1933] Reprint. Hanover: Dartmouth College Publications, 1939); Margaret Connell Szasz, *Indian Education in the American Colonies, 1607–1783* (Albuquerque: University of New Mexico Press, 1988): chaps. 8–10; David Murray, *Forked Tongues: Speech Writing and Representation in North American Indian Texts* (Bloomington and Indianapolis: Indiana University Press, 1991): 44–47, 53–57.

2. Transcript of Samson Occom's Journal [Diary], 3 vols., Dartmouth College Archives, Hanover (hereafter cited as DCA). September 17, 1768, 1: 82 (hereafter cited as Occom Diary). On natives of this region see Bert Salwen, "Indians of Southern New England and Long Island: Early Period,"

in *Handbook of North American Indians, Northeast*, vol. 15, ed. by Bruce G. Trigger (Washington, D.C., Smithsonian Institution, 1978), 160–176.

3. September 17, 1768, Occom Diary, 1: 84. On Wheelock, see David McClure and Elijah Parish, *Memoirs of the Rev. Eleazar Wheelock* (Newburyport, Mass.: Edward Norris and Co., 1811); James Dow McCallum, *Eleazar Wheelock, Founder of Dartmouth College* (Hanover: Dartmouth College Publications, 1939); McCallum, *The Letters of Eleazar Wheelock's Indians* (Hanover: Dartmouth College Publications, 1932); James Axtell, "Dr. Wheelock's Little Red School," in Axtell, *The European and the Indian: Essays in the Ethnohistory of Colonial North America* (New York and Oxford: Oxford University Press, 1981); Szasz, *Indian Education in the American Colonies*, chaps. 8–10.

4. The Rev. Samuell Buell, who preached Occom's ordination sermon, said that had Occom's failing eyes not prevented him from enrolling in Yale, he would have entered as a second-year student. Love, *Samson Occom*, 40–41.

5. September 17, 1768, Occom Diary, 1: 86, 87.

6. Love, *Samson Occom*, 93.

7. Wheelock to Dennys de Berdt, November 16, 1761, 761616 DCA.

8. Samuel Hopkins to Wheelock, September 30, 1761, 761530 DCA.

9. Wheelock to George Whitefield, September 16, 1762, 7651516 DCA; Love, *Samson Occom*, 98.

10. Wheelock to Whitefield, September 16, 1764, 764526.2 DCA.

11. Occom to Wheelock, September 8, 1764, 764508.3 DCA.

12. Wheelock to Whitefield, September 26, 1764, 764526.2 DCA.

13. September 17, 1768, Occom Diary, 1: 91–92. In this context, David Murray suggests that "we need to be aware of the extent to which Occom may be utilizing the complex situation of Indians talking to each other, but being overheard and stage-managed by whites, and turning it, if only marginally, to his own purposes." Murray, *Forked Tongues*, 47.

14. On the Mason Case see William Kellaway, *The New England Company, 1649–1776* (London: Longman, Green & Co., 1961), 253–255; Szasz, *Indian Education in The American Colonies*, 186–87, 196.

15. Love, *Samson Occom*, 120–21; McCallum, *Eleazar Wheelock*, 152.

16. Wheelock to Whitefield, May 4, 1765, 765304 DCA; Wheelock to John Brainerd, January 14, 1765, 765114.3 DCA.

17. Love, *Samson Occom*, 123.

18. Saturday, November 23, 1765, Occom Diary, 1: 62. John Hancock, part owner of the ship Occom and Whitaker sailed in, helped to pay for their passage. Love, *Samson Occom*, 136.

19. September 17, 1768, Occom Diary, 1: 82. Without the pressures that forced this narrative, inserted into his diary as a recollection, history would have little record of Occom's childhood.

20. Richardson, *An Indian Preacher in England*, 15.

21. Thursday, February 13, 1766, Occom Diary, 1: 64.

22. Occom is quoted in William B. Sprague, *Annals* of the American Pulpit, Presbyterian Print (New York: Arno Press, 1969): III: 194.

23. Peter Jilliard to Wheelock, March 2, 1767, quoted in Richardson, *An Indian Preacher in England*, 227.

24. Saturday, February 22, 1766, Occom Diary, 1: 75.

25. Wheelock to Occom, April 9, 1766, 766259 DCA; Wheelock to Whitaker, November 28, 1767, in Richardson, *An Indian Preacher in England*, 321. These references to pride may be the outcome of Occom's independent stand during the Mohegan land issue, a source of annoyance to Wheelock.

26. David McClure to Wheelock, May 21, 1770, 770321 DCA. On the founding of Dartmouth, see Leon Burr Richardson, *History of Dartmouth College*, 2 vols. (Hanover: Dartmouth College Publications, 1932); Frederick Chase, *A History of Dartmouth College and the Town of Hanover, New Hampshire (to 1815)*, 2d ed. (Brattleboro: Vermont Printing Co., 1929): 1; Jere Daniell, "Eleazar Wheelock and the Dartmouth College Charter," *Historical New Hampshire* 24 (Winter 1969): 3–44.

27. A list of Mohegans compiled in 1782 includes only 141 names. Indians, Ser. 1, vol. 2: 328-a, b, c, d. Connecticut State Archives, Hartford [hereafter cited as CA].

28. Occom to Wheelock, March 17, 1769, 769217.2 DCA.

29. William Stillhouse (?) to the Honorable, The Government and Council of his majesties colony of Connecticut, May, 1769. Indians, Ser. 1, vol. 2: 286-a. Stillhouse wrote that the Indians' absence made it "almost impossible" to carry the coffin for burial at the "usual Burying place" in Norwich, so it was buried at "Mohegan on their own Land."

30. At least four copies of the hymnal are in collections, including the Congregational Library in Boston and the New London Library (Conn.). Love, *Samson Occom*, 180.

31. Love, *Samson Occom*, 179–87.

32. Monday, October 24 [1785], Occom Diary, 2: 162.

33. Sabb: September 3 [1786], ibid., 235.

34. Occom to Wheelock, July 1, 1769, 769041 DCA.

35. On Brothertown, see Love, *Samson Occom*, 247–315; Blodgett, *Samson Occom*, 172–214. On Stockbridge, see Patrick Frazier, *The Mohicans of Stockbridge* (Lincoln: University of Nebraska Press, 1992).

36. Sabbath, July 24 [1774], Occom Diary, 1: 97.

37. Ibid.

38. Occom Sermons, no. 13, 2–3, DCA.

39. Friday, June 15 [1787], Occom Diary, 3: 297.

40. Monday, August 4 [1788], ibid., 371.

4. RED-HEAD'S DOMAIN: WILLIAM CLARK'S INDIAN BROKERAGE

1. Clark to Jefferson, St. Louis, December 15, 1825, Jefferson Papers, Library of Congress, Washington, D.C.

2. Robert Reynolds et al., "Recommendation of William Clark as Governor," April 29, 1809, Clarence E. Carter, ed., *The Territorial Papers of the United States: The Territory of Illinois, 1809–1814* (Washington, D.C.: Government Printing Office, 1948): 16: 32.

3. Thomas Forsyth, "Memoirs of the Sauk and Foxes," in *The Indian Tribes of the Upper Mississippi Valley and Region of the Great Lakes,* ed. Emma H. Blair, 2 vols. (Cleveland: Arthur H. Clark Co., 1911): 2: 189.

4. Clark to McKenney, St. Louis, December 10, 1827, HR 20, Doc. 283 (1838): 4.

5. Clark, "A Report of the Names and Probable Numbers of the Tribes of Indians. . . . St. Louis, November 4, 1816," Letters Received, War Department, RG 75, National Archives, Washington, D.C. Hereafter cited as DNA.

6. Clark to Crawford, St. Louis, December 11, 1915, *Territorial Papers: Missouri* 15: 95–96.

7. Ibid., 15: 96.

8. For typical examples, see Charles J. Kappler, comp., *Indian Treaties 1778–1883* (New York: Interland Publishing Co., 1972): 111–23.

9. Clark to Crawford, St. Louis, October 1, 1815, *American State Papers, Indian Affairs,* 2 vols. (Washington, D.C.: Gales and Seaton, 1789–1838): 2: 77.

10. Ibid.

11. Kappler, ed., *Indian Treaties,* 217–21, 222–25.

12. Clark to Barbour, Washington, D.C., March 1, 1826, *American State Papers, Indian Affairs,* 2: 653–54.

13. Clark to Robb, St. Louis, September 26, 1832, Ellen M. Whitney, ed., *The Black Hawk War,* 3 vols. (Springfield: Illinois State Historical Library, 1970–1978) 2, pt. 2, 672.

14. Minnie Clare Yarbrough, ed., *The Reminiscences of William C. Preston* (Chapel Hill: University of North Carolina Press, 1933): 16.

15. Henry Rowe Schoolcraft, *A View of the Lead Mines of Missouri* (New York: Charles Wiley, 1819): 241.

16. Harlin M. Fuller and LeRoy R. Hafen, eds., *The Journal of Captain John R. Bell* (Glendale, Calif.: Arthur H. Clark Co., 1973): 58.

17. Paxton's *St. Louis Directory of 1821,* quoted in John C. Ewers, "William Clark's Indian Museum in St. Louis, 1816–1838," in *A Cabinet of Curiosities: Five Episodes in the Evolution of American Museums,* ed. Walter Muir Whitehill (Charlottesville: University of Virginia Press, 1967): 56.

18. William Clark and Meriwether Lewis Clark, "Catalogue of Indian

Curiosities in William Clark's Museum," William Clark Papers, Missouri Historical Society, St. Louis.

19. Clark to Jefferson, St. Louis, December 15, 1825, Jefferson Papers, Library of Congress, Washington, D.C.; Clark to McKenney, St. Louis, December 10, 1827, HR 20, Doc. 283 (1838), 2: 189.

20. The Black Hawk War has generated a considerable body of historical scholarship. The best general treatment remains William T. Hagan, *The Sac and Fox Indians* (Norman: University of Oklahoma Press, 1958): chaps. 2–15; Anthony F. C. Wallace, "Prelude to Disaster: The Course of Indian-White Relations Which Led to the Black Hawk War of 1832," in *Black Hawk War*, 1: 1–51.

21. Kappler, *Indian Treaties*, 74–77.

22. Richard P. Metcalf, "Who Shall Rule at Home? Native American Politics and Indian-White Relations," *Journal of American History* 61 (December 1974): 657–61.

23. Forsyth to Clark, Rock Island, May 24, 1827, Thomas Forsyth Papers, Draper Manuscripts, 6T, State Historical Society of Wisconsin, Madison. (Hereafter cited as Forsyth-Draper.)

24. Edwards to Clark, May 25, 1828; Edwards to Clark, May 29, 1828. E. B. Washburne, ed., *The Edwards Papers*, 3 vols. (Chicago: Chicago Historical Society, 1884): 3: 338–40.

25. Forsyth to Clark, Rock Island, May 24, 1828. Bureau of Indian Affairs, Letters Received, Illinois RG 75, DNA.

26. Forsyth to Clark, Rock Island, June 16, 1828.

27. Peter B. Porter to Edwards, Washington, July 7, 1828; Porter to Edwards, Washington, July 22, 1828. Evarts B. Greene and Clarence W. Alvord, eds., *The Governor's Letterbooks* (Springfield: Illinois State Historical Library, 1909): 1: 139.

28. Forsyth to Clark, Rock Island, May 22–23, 1829, ibid., 1: 144–46.

29. Clark to Forsyth, St. Louis, July 4, 1829, ibid., 1: 148.

30. Forsyth to Clark, Ft. Armstrong, October 1, 1829, Forsyth-Draper, 6T.

31. Forsyth to Clark, Rock Island, April 28, 1830, Forsyth–Draper, 6T. The description of the Winnebago Prophet is in Forsyth to Clark, Rock Island, June 10, 1828, ibid.

32. Clark to Eaton, St. Louis, April 6, 1830; "Minutes of a Council Held by William Clark With the Sacs and Foxes, March 26, 1830," Bureau of Indian Affairs, Letters Received, St. Louis, RG 75, DNA.

33. Clark, "Sac and Fox talk at St. Louis, May 24, 1830," Bureau of Indian Affairs, Treaties, Talks, and Councils, RG 75, DNA.

34. Clark to Thomas McKenney, St. Louis, June 16, 19, 1830, Bureau of Indian Affairs, Letters Received, St. Louis, RG 75, DNA.

35. Kappler, *Indian Treaties*, 305–10.

36. St. Vrain to Clark, Rock Island, October 4, 1830, Bureau of Indian Affairs, Letters Received, St. Louis, RG 75, DNA.

37. St. Vrain to Clark, Rock Island, May 15, 1831, *Black Hawk War* 2, pt. 1, 8.

38. Reynolds to Clark, Rock Island, May 15, 1831, *Black Hawk War* 2, pt. 1, 8.

39. Clark to Eaton, St. Louis, May 30, 1831, *Black Hawk War* 2, pt. 1, 24.

40. Clark to Eaton, St. Louis, June 29, 1831, ibid., 2, pt. 1, 83.

41. Reynolds to Cass, Belleville, April 17, 1832, ibid., 2, pt. 1, 83.

42. Clark to Cass, St. Louis, April 20, 1832, ibid., 2, pt. 1, 283.

43. Clark to Cass, St. Louis, April 20, 1832, ibid., 2, pt. 1, 283.

44. Street to Clark, Prairie du Chien, August 3, 1832, ibid., 2, pt. 2, 926.

45. Meriwether Lewis Clark to Clark, Blue Mounds, July 25, 1832, ibid., 2, pt. 2, 878.

46. Campbell to Jackson, Galena, July 13, 1832, ibid., 2, pt. 2, 788.

47. Forsyth to George Davenport, St. Louis, July 10, 1831, ibid., 2, pt. 1, 107.

48. Forsyth to Davenport, St. Louis, May 23, 1832, ibid., 2, pt. 1, 413–14.

5. AN ALTERNATIVE MISSIONARY STYLE:
EVAN JONES AND JOHN B. JONES AMONG THE CHEROKEES

1. Robert F. Berkhofer, *Salvation and the Savage* (New York: Atheneum, 1976): 152.

2. Ibid., 10.

3. For a full biography of the Joneses, see William G. McLoughlin, *Champions of the Cherokees* (Princeton: Princeton University Press, 1989). Evan Jones was born in Brecknockshire, Wales, in 1788 and was a schoolteacher and linen draper in London until he emigrated to Philadelphia in 1821.

4. See William G. McLoughlin, *Cherokees and Missionaries, 1789–1839* (New Haven: Yale University, 1984): chap. 9.

5. Cyrus Kingsbury to Dr. S. A. Worcester, December 19, 1816, in the papers of the American Board of Commissioners for Foreign Missions, Houghton Library, Harvard University. (Hereafter cited as ABCFM Papers.)

6. McLoughlin, *Champions*, 67.

7. Ibid., 38.

8. Ibid., 64. See also Berkhofer, *Salvation*, 48.

9. Ibid., 37.

10. Ibid., 323.

11. For slavery among the Cherokees, see Theda Perdue, *Slavery and the Evolution of Cherokee Society, 1540–1866* (Knoxville: University of

Tennessee Press, 1979); and Rudi Halliburton, *Red Over Black* (Westport, Conn.: Greenwood Press, 1977).
12. McLoughlin, *Champions*, 372.
13. Daniel F. Littlefield, Jr., *The Cherokee Freedmen* (Westport, Conn.: Greenwood Press, 1978): 78–80.
14. McLoughlin, *Champions*, 449.
15. Ibid., 449–452.
16. See the following letters in the ABCFM Papers: D. S. Butrick to David Greene, June 21, 1842; D. S. Butrick to David Greene, April 15, 1842; Timothy Ranney to S. B. Treat, July 30, 1857.
17. For these and other statistics, see the tables in McLoughlin, *Champions*.

6. AMERICAN INDIAN SCHOOL PUPILS AS
CULTURAL BROKERS: CHEROKEE GIRLS AT
BRAINERD MISSION, 1828–1829

I wish to thank the D'Arcy McNickle Center for the History of the American Indian, Newberry Library, Chicago, for the short-term fellowship that allowed me to research this chapter; Miami University, Oxford, Ohio, for a part-time visiting professorship in American studies (1988–89); the University of Jyväskylä, Finland, for a leave of absence on partial salary; and John Aubrey, Sirkka Coleman, Frederick Hoxie, Cynthia Kasee, the late William G. McLoughlin, Jay Miller, Theda Perdue, Steven Saletta, Margaret Connell Szasz, William H. A. Williams, and Allan Winkler.
1. Margaret Connell Szasz, *Indian Education in the American Colonies, 1607–1783* (Albuquerque: University of New Mexico Press, 1988): 23. Also, on cultural brokers see, James A. Clifton, ed., *Being and Becoming Indian: Biographical Studies of North American Frontiers* (Chicago: Dorsey Press, 1989); L. G. Moses and Raymond Wilson, eds., *Indian Lives: Essays on Nineteenth- and Twentieth-Century Native American Leaders* (Albuquerque: University of New Mexico Press, 1985); Daniel K. Richter, "Cultural Brokers and Intercultural Politics: New York–Iroquois Relations, 1664–1701," *Journal of American History* 75 (June 1988): 40–67; Nancy L. Hagedorn, "'A Friend To Go Between Them': The Interpreter as Cultural Broker During the Anglo–Iroquois Councils, 1740–70," *Ethnohistory* 35 (Winter 1988): 60–80.
2. See, however, Richard C. Trexler, "From the Mouths of Babes: Christianization by Children in Sixteenth-Century New Spain," in *Religious Organization and Religious Experience*, ed. J. Davis (London: Academy Press, 1982): 115–35; Szasz, *Indian Education*, esp. 196–200; Michael C.

Coleman, *American Indian Children and the School, 1850–1930* (Jackson: University Press of Mississippi, 1993): esp. chap. 7.

3. Sketch of Cherokee history and culture based on, especially, William L. Anderson, ed., *Cherokee Removal: Before and After* (Athens: University of Georgia Press, 1991); William G. McLoughlin, *Cherokee Renascence in the New Republic* (Princeton: Princeton University Press, 1986); William G. McLoughlin, *Champions of the Cherokees: Evan and John B. Jones* (Princeton: Princeton University Press, 1990); *Cherokees and Missionaries, 1789–1839* (New Haven: Yale University Press, 1984); William G. McLoughlin and Walter H. Conser, Jr., "The Cherokees in Transition: A Statistical Analysis of the Federal Cherokee Census of 1835," *Journal of American History* 64 (December 1977): 678–703; *Georgia Historical Quarterly* 73 (Fall 1989). Special issue commemorating the sesquicentennial of Cherokee removal, 1838–39. Theda Perdue, *Slavery and the Evolution of Cherokee Society, 1540–1866* (Knoxville: University of Tennessee Press, 1979); Gary E. Moulton, *John Ross: Cherokee Chief* (Athens: University of Georgia Press, 1978); Mary Young, "The Cherokee Nation: Mirror of the Republic," *American Quarterly* 33 (Winter 1981): 502–24; Charles Hudson, *The Southeastern Indians* (Knoxville: University of Tennessee Press, 1976); James Mooney, *Historical Sketch of the Cherokees* ([1900] Reprint Chicago: Aldine, 1975); Fred Gearing, *Priests and Warriors: Social Structures for Cherokee Politics in the Eighteenth Century* (Menasha, Wis.: American Anthropological Association memoir 93, 1962); William N. Fenton and John Gulick, eds., *Symposium on Cherokee and Iroquois Culture* (Washington, D.C.: Smithsonian Institution, Bureau of American Ethnology bulletin 180, 1961); ABCFM, *First Ten Annual Reports of the American Board of Commissioners for Foreign Missions . . . 1810–1820* (Boston: ABCFM, 1834); and *Annual Report of the American Board of Commissioners for Foreign Missions* (Boston: ABCFM, 1821–40). Title changes; hereafter, ABCFM, *AR*, date and page; accounts by the "civilized" Cherokee: John Ridge to Hon. Albret Gallitin, Feb. 27, 1826, John Howard Payne Papers, 8: 103–15 (hereafter JHPP, 8, followed by page number), Newberry Library, Chicago; Elias Boudinott, *An Address to the Whites* (Philadelphia: Gedden, 1826), Hill Library, Miami University, Ohio.

4. McLoughlin, *Cherokee Renascence*, 358–59; *Cherokees and Missionaries*, 18–19. Also, Gearing, *Priests and Warriors*, esp. chaps. 2 and 3; Hudson, *Southeastern Indians*, chaps. 3 and 6.

5. Quotations: John R. Finger, *The Eastern Band of the Cherokees, 1819–1900* (Knoxville: University of Tennessee Press, 1984): 4; McLoughlin, *Cherokee Renascence*, 4.

6. McLoughlin, *Cherokee Renascence*; ABCFM, *AR* (1827): 111 (misprint: 109); Constitution of the Cherokee Nation (1827), in Emmett Starr,

History of the Cherokee Indians and Their Legends and Folklore ([1921] Reprint New York: Kraus, 1969): 55–63.

7. Ridge to Gallitin, JHPP, 8: 115. Ridge later became a member of the Cherokee group which accepted removal.

8. ABCFM, *AR* (1823): 56; McLoughlin, *Cherokees and Missionaries*, chap. 5.

9. ABCFM, *AR* (1817): 153–58; *AR* (1819): 236; *AR* (1821): 49; Robert Sparks Walker, *Torchlights to the Cherokee: The Brainerd Mission* (New York: Macmillan, 1931); Althea Bass, *Cherokee Messenger* (Norman: University of Oklahoma Press, 1936).

10. This is a major theme of McLoughlin's studies. See, e.g., *Cherokee Renascence*, 357–60.

11. McLoughlin, *Cherokees and Missionaries*, 132 (quotation), 138–40; ABCFM, *AR* (1827): 103–04; *AR* (1828): 64–73. The ABCFM also ran two schools among the emigrant Cherokees in Arkansas, 84–89; Report of Samuel Worcester (1827), in Bass, *Cherokee Messenger*, 44–49; many of the pupil letters (n. 12, below), systematically list curriculum and vocational duties.

12. JHPP, 8: 1–62. I examined the "originals" but cite verbatim from typed copies. Some letters lack a full date, but apparently all were written from 1828 to 1829, so I omit dates in citations below. McLoughlin, *Cherokees and Missionaries*, 141, n. 37, alerted me to the letters. See also Theda Perdue, ed., "Letters from Brainerd," *Journal of Cherokee Studies* (Winter 1979): 4–8. Mary Ann Vail (a white pupil) claimed that Miss Ames requested pupils "to write with as much freedom on the subject of religion as they would speak to their parents," to Jeremiah Everts (15–typed page number in JHPP, 8). These girls' enthusiasm for the Christian civilization was like that of adults John Ridge and Elias Boudinot, cited in n. 3, above. ABCFM teacher Sophia Sawyer claimed authorship of a student's letter, which reads more like an adult's than those on which this chapter is based; Bass, *Cherokee Messenger*, 119–21. On Lucy Ames, ABCFM, *AR* (1828): 66.

13. Most of these girls were probably from the acculturating "middle class," as only the Taylor name appears in McLoughlin and Conser's list of the forty-two elite families in 1835; the great majority of full-blood Cherokees constituted the third "class," see "Cherokees in Transition," esp. 680, 696. In July 1828, Nancy Reece claimed that six of twenty-one Brainerd girls were "what is called full Cherokees," to Elizabeth Preston (12). Quotation, Sally Reece is Respected Sir (45).

14. Elizabeth Taylor to Miss Abigail Parker (13–14).

15. Elizabeth Taylor to Miss Abigail Parker (14). See also Lucy A. Campbell to Miss Sarah Reece (61).

16. Nancy Reece to Dear Madam (1), and to Respected Sir (25–26); Lucy McPherson to Mrs. Conner (41).

17. McLoughlin, *Cherokees and Missionaries*, 141–42; Nancy Reece to Mrs. Conner (10), and to Miss Electa Steele (17): "I fear I shall not say anything that will be interesting to you. I do not know much about the world"; Elizabeth Taylor to Miss Abigail Parker (13).

18. Lucy McPherson to Rev. Fayette Shepherd (48). See McLoughlin, *Cherokee Renascence*, 360–62.

19. Lucy McPherson to Jack and Susan McPherson (36); Nancy Reece to Rev'd Fayette Shepherd (22). On Lancastrian method, ABCFM, *AR* (1818): 193; McLoughlin, *Cherokees and Missionaries*, 132, 155.

20. Lucy A. Campbell to Miss Jane Speaker (49); Nancy Reece to Rev'd Fayette Shepherd (22); Lucy McPherson to Jack and Susan McPherson (36); Cherokee respect for age: Gearing, *Priests and Warriors*, 60, and Pt. I, passim; McLoughlin, *Cherokee Renascence*, 110–11.

21. Polly Wilson to Master John Wilson (43).

22. Susan Taylor to Jeremiah Everts (55); also Elizabeth Taylor to Miss Flora McDonald (3).

23. Lucy A. C. Reece to the young Choctaw acquaintances of Col. Laflore (33–34); Nancy Reece to Mrs. Thankful Holton (29); and to Respected Sir (25–26); Lucy A. Campbell to Mr. Jeremiah Everts (52).

24. Nancy Reece to Rev'd John Johnston (23); to Mrs. Burnham (30); to Mrs. Eunice Ames (18); to Elizabeth Ames, n.d., (19). Also, Elizabeth Taylor to Miss D. Gould (9).

25. Lucy A. Campbell to Miss Sarah Perry (61); Nancy Reece to Rev'd Fayette Shepherd (21). Also Elizabeth Taylor to Mrs. Louisa Sanborn (7).

26. Lucy Reece to the young Choctaw acquaintances of Col. LaFlore (33–34).

27. Christiana McPherson to the President (31).

28. Ann Bush to Jeremiah Everts (50). Under the pseudonym William Penn, Everts published essays defending the Cherokees. McLoughlin, *Cherokee Renascence*, 434; Nancy Reece to Rev'd Fayette Shepherd (21–22). Also, Susan Taylor to Jeremiah Everts (55).

29. Nancy Reece to Mrs. Elizabeth Preston (12–13).

30. Ann Bush to Rev. Mr. Patter (44).

31. Art. VI, sec. 10, in Starr, *History*, 63; Lucy McPherson to Miss Mary Coe (42); Sally Reece to Respected Sir (45); on Charles Reece, Nancy Reece to Rev'd John Johnston (24); Elizabeth Taylor to Miss Flora McDonald (3); Theda Perdue, "Southern Indians and the Cult of True Womanhood," in *The Web of Southern Social Relations: Women, Family, and Education*, eds. Walter J. Fraser, et al. (Athens: University of Georgia Press, 1985), 35–51.

32. Lucy A. Campbell to Miss Sarah Perry (61); Nancy Reece to Mrs. Eunice Ames (18). On same page: "I think more than I can talk."

33. Rewards: Nancy Reece to Mrs. Thankful Holton (28); peer dynamics, Lucy McPherson to Jeremiah Everts (53).

34. Nancy Reece to Dear Madam (1), to Miss Abigail Williams (8), to Electa Steele (17); James A. Clifton, "Alternative Identities and Cultural Frontiers," in *Being and Becoming Indian*, 29–31. Clifton utilizes Malcolm McFee's concept of the bicultural person as "the 150% man." See Moses and Wilson, Indians lived not in two worlds but in *one* "complex world of multiple loyalties," *Indian Lives*, 3–4.

35. Nancy Reece to Miss Sarah Gilbreath and Miss Jane Speaker (20–21).

36. ABCFM, *AR* (1823): 57; ABCFM, *AR* (1828): 67.

37. Coleman, *American Indian Children*, esp. chap. 7. Based on 100 autobiographical accounts by Indians from about thirty tribal groups (about one-third by women), this book shows widespread mediating—some voluntary, some at the behest of authorities—by Indian pupils at missionary and federal government schools from 1850 to 1930. The book also shows greater pupil resistance to or even rejection of schooling than emerges in the Brainerd letters.

7. HELEN HUNT JACKSON AS POWER BROKER

1. Jackson to Grover Cleveland, 8 August 1885 (Helen Hunt Jackson Papers), General Manuscripts [Miscellaneous], Special Collections, Princeton University Library, Princeton, N.J.

2. Thomas Wentworth Higginson, "Helen Jackson," *The Critic* n.s. 4 (August 22, 1885): 86.

3. For more information see, e.g., Ruth Odell, *Helen Hunt Jackson (H. H.)* (New York: D. Appleton-Century, 1939); and Valerie Sherer Mathes, *Helen Hunt Jackson and Her Indian Reform Legacy* (Austin: University of Texas Press, 1990).

4. Jackson to Warner, 21 December 1879, Charles Dudley Warner Collection, Watkinson Library, Trinity College, Hartford, Conn.

5. Thomas Wentworth Higginson, "Mrs. Helen Jackson ("H. H."), *Century Magazine* 31, n.s. (November 1885): 254.

6. See Thomas Henry Tibbles, *The Ponca Chiefs: An Account of the Trial of Standing Bear*, ed. Kay Graber (Lincoln: University of Nebraska Press, 1972); and Mathes, *Jackson and Her Indian Reform Legacy*, 21–37.

7. Higginson, "Mrs. Helen Jackson," *Century Magazine*, 254.

8. Jackson to Warner, 18 November 1879 and 15 January 1880, Watkinson Library.

9. Jackson to Conway, 25 July 1880, Moncure D. Conway Papers, Rare

Book and Manuscript Library, Butler Library, Columbia University, New York, N.Y.

10. Jackson to Warner, 15 January 1880, Watkinson Library.

11. "H. H.," "The Indian Problem: Questions for the American People," *New York Daily Tribune*, 15 December 1879, 4.

12. Jackson to William Hayes Ward, 20 December 1879 (HM 13977), Jackson manuscripts, Huntington Library.

13. Jackson to Warner, n.d. [probably written at the end of February 1881], Watkinson Library.

14. Jackson to Mr. Abbott, 11 December 1880, Chapin-Kiley Manuscripts, Special Collections, Amherst College Library, Amherst, Mass.

15. Jackson to Mr. Payne, 15 December 1880, Henry W. and Albert A. Berg Collection, New York Public Library, Astor, Lenox and Tilden Foundations, New York, N.Y.

16. Jackson to Warner, 6 December 1880, Watkinson Library.

17. Jackson to Longfellow, Henry Wadsworth Longfellow Papers, and to Holmes, Oliver Wendell Holmes Papers, 2 March 1881, Houghton Library, Harvard University, Cambridge, Mass.

18. Jackson to Dawes, 10 December 1880, Henry L. Dawes Papers (Box 24), Library of Congress, Washington, D.C.

19. "H. H.," "A Small Matter to Murder an Indian: "H. H." Scores Another Point," *New York Daily Tribune*, 25 January 1880, 5.

20. H. H., "Justifiable Homicide in Southern California," *New York Independent*, 27 September 1883, 2.

21. "H. H.," "The Starving Utes: More Questions for the People by 'H. H.' What White men have done and are doing to Indians in Colorado," *New York Daily Tribune*, 5 February 1880, 5.

22. "H. H.," "The Sand Creek Massacre: A Slaughter of Friendly Indians," *New York Daily Tribune*, 24 February 1880, 2.

23. Jackson to Ward, 1880 [probably April or May], (HM 13992), Jackson manuscripts, Huntington Library.

24. Jackson to Warner, 21 December 1879, Watkinson Library.

25. Jackson, "The Present Condition of the Mission Indians in Southern California," *Glimpses of Three Coasts* (Boston: Roberts Brothers, 1886): 84, 86. For her California work, see Mathes, *Jackson and Her Indian Reform Legacy*, 38–94.

26. Jackson to Warner, 31 October 1882, Watkinson Library.

27. Jackson to Henry Teller, 11 June 1882, and Teller to Hiram Price, 30 June 1882, National Archives, Record Group 75, Office of Indian Affairs, Letters Received [hereinafter cited as NA, RG 75, OIA, LR], 11819 [11429 and 11701]–1882.

28. Jackson to Aldrich, 4 May 1883, Thomas Bailey Aldrich Papers, Houghton Library, Harvard University.

29. See Lawson to Price, 1 June 1884, NA, RG 75, OIA, SC 31, LR, 10808–1883, included in 10049–1883, and Lawson to Jackson, 7 June 1883, Jackson Papers, Colorado College Library.

30. Jackson to Aldrich, 4 May 1883, Houghton Library.

31. Jackson to Amelia Stone Quinton, 2 April 1884, Pierpoint Morgan Library (MA 4571), New York, N.Y.

32. Higginson, "How Ramona Was Written," *Atlantic Monthly* 86 (November 1900): 712–14.

33. "Helen Hunt Jackson's Life and Writings," *Literary News* (Baltimore: Cushings & Bailey Booksellers and Stationers, April 1887): 100.

34. George Wharton James, *Through Ramona's Country* (Boston: Little, Brown, 1913): 318.

35. Jackson to William Sharpless Jackson, 29 March [1885], Pt. I, box 1, folder 5, William S. Jackson Family Papers, Colorado College Library.

36. Jackson to Higginson, 27 July 1885, in Thomas Wentworth Higginson, "Helen Hunt Jackson," *Nation* 41 (August 20, 1885): 151.

37. William T. Hagan, *American Indians* (Chicago: University of Chicago Press, 1961): 123. For more on *Ramona*, see Mathes, *Jackson and Her Indian Reform Legacy*, 76–94.

38. "Albert K. Smiley and General E. Whittlesey to Clinton B. Fisk, Chairman, BIC, May 1, 1884," *Sixteenth Annual Report of the Board of Indian Commissioners, 1884* (Washington, D.C.: Government Printing Office, 1885): 18–19.

39. Charles C. Painter, *A Visit to the Mission Indians of Southern California and Other Western Tribes* (Philadelphia: Office of the Indian Rights Association, 1886): 11.

40. Charles C. Painter to Joshua W. Davis, 30 June 1887, Reel 2, *Indian Rights Association Papers* (Glen Rock, N.J.: Microfilming Corporation of America, 1973).

41. "M. Byrnes v. A Alas–Copy Findings" and "M. Byrnes v. A Alas et al.—Copy Judgment," included with J. M. Dodge to Leland Stanford, 7 August 1886, NA, RG 75, OIA, SC 31, box 24, LR, 6885–1886.

42. *Milwaukee Sentinel*, 9 August 1885, enclosed with Mrs. John Hiles to Pres. Grover Cleveland, 12 August 1885, NA, RG 75, OIA, LR, 19236–1885.

43. Francis Paul Prucha, "A 'Friend of the Indian' in Milwaukee: Mrs. O. J. Hiles and the Wisconsin Indian Association," *Indian Policy in the United States: Historical Essays* (Lincoln: University of Nebraska Press, 1981): 214–228.

44. "Through Southern California: Letter Number Seven," *Indian's Friend* 4 (October 1891): 5.

45. Quinton to Weinland, July 1889, box 7, William H. Weinland Collection, Huntington Library.

46. For the transfer of Potrero, see Quinton to Weinland, 3 May 1890; for Cahuilla, see Quinton to Weinland, 6 June 1896 and 15 April 1898; and for Agua Caliente, see Quinton to Weinland, 6 July 1898 and 1 August 1898, box 7, Huntington Library.

8. INTERPRETING THE WILD WEST, 1883–1914

1. These phrases appeared often in the advertisements for Cody's Wild West show, and many of his competitors borrowed them. See, e.g., the Boston *Daily Advertiser*, May 13, 1911, 5.

2. See, e.g., the liner notes to Michael P. Malone and Richard W. Etulain, *The American West: A Twentieth-Century History* (Lincoln and London: University of Nebraska Press, 1989).

3. Newspaper clipping: The Aberdeen (Scotland) *Evening Gazette*, August 27, 1904, Buffalo Bill Cody Scrapbook, 1891–1922, 76, William Frederick Cody Papers, 1887–1919, State Historical Society of Colorado (CHS), Denver. (Cited hereafter as Cody Scrapbook, CHS.) Actually, the scrapbook was put together by Robert "Pony Bob" Haslam, a longtime member of Cody's troupe.

4. See L. G. Moses, "Wild West Shows, Reformers, and the Image of the American Indian, 1887–1914," *South Dakota History* 14, no. 3 (Fall 1984): 193–221.

5. This is what Rayna Green describes as "playing Indian." The Wild West show in Europe, assisted by the German writer Karl May, creates the enduring image. She likewise, however, does not see the Wild West show as solely responsible for creating the Plains image of the quintessential American Indian. See Rayna Green, "The Tribe Called Wannabee: Playing Indian in America and Europe," *Folklore* 99, no. 1 (1988): 38.

6. On the images of Indians in film and television, consult Jon Tuska, *The American West in Film: Critical Approaches to the Westerns* (Westport, Conn.: Greenwood Press, 1985); Ralph E. Friar and Natasha A. Friar, *The Only Good Indian: The Hollywood Gospel* (New York: Drama Book Specialists, 1972); Gretchen M. Bataille and Charles L. P. Silet, *The Pretend Indians: Images of Native Americans in the Movies* (Ames: Iowa State University Press, 1980); Kevin Brownlow, *The War, the West and the Wilderness* (New York: Alfred A. Knopf, 1979); and Wayne Michael Sarf, *God Bless You, Buffalo Bill: A Layman's Guide to History and the Western Film* (New York: Associated University Press, 1983).

7. Newspaper clipping: Aberdeen *Evening Gazette*, August 27, 1904, in Cody Scrapbook, CHS, 76.

8. 1883 Program, William F. Cody Collection, Denver Public Library, Western History Department, Denver, Colo.

9. Sarah J. Blackstone, *Buckskin, Bullets, and Business: A History of Buffalo Bill's Wild West* (Westport, Conn.: Greenwood Press, 1986): 19; and Joseph G. Rosa and Robin May, *Buffalo Bill and His Wild West* (Lawrence: University Press of Kansas, 1989): 92.

10. In 1879, the federal court acknowledged on behalf of the Ponca leader Standing Bear the right of a "peaceful Indian to come and go as he wishes with the same freedom accorded to a white man." This ruling, however, was often ignored. See Arrell Morgan Gibson, *The American Indian: Prehistory to the Present* (Lexington, Mass.: D. C. Heath, 1980): 465; and Francis Paul Prucha, *American Indian Policy in Crisis: Christian Reformers and the Indian, 1865–1900* (Norman: University of Oklahoma Press, 1976): 321.

11. Noble to Morgan, January 30, 1890, Records of the Bureau of Indian Affairs, Letters Received (LR) 1881–1907, Land, no. 1890–3013, Record Group 75 (RG 75), National Archives and Records Service (NARS), Washington, D.C.

12. CIA to Dawes, April 15, 1889, Henry L. Dawes Papers, Library of Congress Manuscripts Division, Washington, D.C. Commissioner Oberly, as Francis Paul Prucha has written, recognized the reformers' dilemma. They agitated against government action when they thought it was oppressive or inequitable, yet they advocated government force when they considered such action to be in the Indians' best interest. See Francis Paul Prucha, *American Indian Policy in Crisis*, 321. See also Moses, "Wild West Shows," 203.

13. The shows, according to Ralph Friar and Natasha Friar, did nothing more than reinforce the "classic clichés about Native Americans." Stereotypes derived from the Wild West show in time contributed to the "filmic cultural genocide" of American Indians. See Friar and Friar, *The Only Good Indian*, 57, 70. Raymond Stedman has read the history of Indian images as decline, holding Indians themselves partially accountable for their own degradation. "Indians whose ancestors did not wear the familiar plains attire," he has written, "should think twice about disregarding traditional dress patterns and selling out to the Wild West crowd." Real Indians therefore should eschew the nontraditional, whether in dress or in employment. Passing muster under the discerning eye of the ethnologist, however, is hardly the criterion for establishing genuine Indianness. See Raymond William Stedman, *Shadows of the Indians: Stereotypes in American Culture* (Norman: University of Oklahoma Press, 1982): 79–80. Others have held Buffalo Bill almost personally responsible for the denigration of Indian images. In Cody's Wild West show career, two historians have written, "The Indians were firmly established as figures of entertainment like the stage Irishman and the comic Jew." See Bataille and Silet, eds., *Pretend Indians*, xxii. Another critic has written that as entertainers, Indians be-

came "the first clear-cut victims of media bias." Once Hollywood absorbed whatever was usable of the Indian stereotype from the Wild West shows, history, according to Donald Kaufman, dismissed the Indians as a "shaping force in American experience. White paternalism, in league with the new media of the twentieth century, became the red man's burden." See Donald L. Kaufman, "The Indians as Media Hand-Me-Down," in Bataille and Silets, eds., *Pretend Indians*, 22. The film historian John Tuska has expressed the hope that "we may once and for all put to rest that killing 'mythical' Indians is only so much 'newspeak' for enjoying genocide and that the western film as it has been made deserves the strongest censure which can be brought to bear for the lies it has told." What the filmmakers embraced was presumably the Wild West show version of American Indians. See Tuska, *The American West in Film*, 260. Michael Dorris (Modoc) has written that for the last five hundred years, "Indians have competed against a fantasy over which they have had no controls." They have been compared to beings who never really were. And finally, "flesh and blood Native Americans" have neither participated to any great extent in the creation of "imaginary Indians" nor benefited materially. Rocky Bear, Red Shirt, and a host of others might disagree. See Michael Dorris, "Indians on the Shelf," in Calvin Martin, ed., *The American Indian and the Problem of History* (New York: Oxford University Press, 1987): 99.

14. John Burke to Commissioner of Indian Affairs, n.d. (ca. 1886), Land, LR, no. 1886–5564, NARS.

15. Cody Scrapbook, CHS, 76. Cody continued to employ continually those leaders who became "stars." What is more, other Wild West shows hired veterans of Cody's tours.

16. See Blackstone, *Buckskins, Bullets, and Business*, 18–21.

17. G. H. Bates to Secretary of the Interior, January 11, 1887, Records of the Bureau of Indian Affairs, LR, no. 1887–1124, RG 75, NARS.

18. Stanley Vestal, *Sitting Bull: Champion of the Sioux* (Norman: University of Oklahoma Press, 1957): 251. Cody, to his credit, never identified Sitting Bull as Custer's murderer. See Robert M. Utley, *The Lance and The Shield: The Life and Times of Sitting Bull* (New York: Henry Holt and Co., 1993): 265–66.

19. Quoted in Richard J. Walsh, *The Making of Buffalo Bill* (Indianapolis: Bobbs-Merrill Co., 1928): 256.

20. Louis Pfaller, "Enemies in '76, Friends in '85—Sitting Bull and Buffalo Bill," *Prologue* 1, no. 2 (Fall 1969): 26.

21. McLaughlin to Burke, April 16, 1886, Maj. James McLaughlin Papers, Correspondence and Miscellaneous Papers, 1855–1937, microfilm ed., roll 20, frames 479–80, Assumption Abbey Archives (AAA), Richardton, N.D. (Cited hereafter as McLaughlin Papers, AAA.) Microfilm ed. courtesy of the South Dakota Historical Research Center, Pierre.

22. Announcement: "Buffalo Bill's Wild West," Cody Scrapbook, CHS, n.p.

23. Quoted in Walsh, *The Making of Buffalo Bill*, 257.

24. Ibid.

25. Quoted in ibid., 264–65.

26. *Sheffield Leader*, 5 May 1887, quoted in Rita G. Napier, "Across the Big Water: American Indians' Perceptions of Europe and Europeans, 1887–1906," in *Indians and Europe: An Interdisciplinary Collection of Essays*, ed. Christian F. Feest, 383. (Aachen, the Netherlands: Rader Verlag, 1987).

27. Quoted in Henry Blackman Sell and Victor Weybright, *Buffalo Bill and the Wild West* (Basin, Wyo.: Big Horn Books, 1979): 166.

28. See, Raymond J. DeMallie, ed., *The Sixth Grandfather: Black Elk's Teachings Given to John G. Neihardt* (Lincoln and London: University of Nebraska Press, 1984): 248.

29. Napier, "Across the Big Water," 385. Black Elk's quotation appears in John G. Neihardt, *Black Elk Speaks* (Lincoln: University of Nebraska Press, 1961): 221.

30. DeMallie, ed., *The Sixth Grandfather*, 246.

31. Rayna Green also alludes to what "Black Elk and others must have felt about the shows." She quotes from the preposterous dialogue in Arthur Kopit's play, *Indians* (New York: Hill and Wang, 1969), where the ghost of Sitting Bull declaims to Cody that the showman allowed Indians to imitate their glory. It was humiliating, Sitting Bull muses. Sometimes the Indian participants could almost imagine it was real. See Green, "The Tribe Called Wannabee," 38. When Sitting Bull is allowed to speak for himself, he usually praises Cody and laments the fact that he was not allowed to travel with Cody following the 1885 season.

32. See Agent D. F. Royer, Pine Ridge, S.D., to Morgan, January 10, 1891, LR, Land, no. 1891–3186, RG 75, NARS.

33. Moses, "Wild West Shows," 208–11.

34. Nate Salsbury to Capt. Charles G. Penny, Acting U.S. Indian Agent, Pine Ridge, S.D., May 8, 1891, Buffalo Bill's Wild West Show Contracts (1891, 1895), General Records, Pine Ridge Reservation, Main Decimal Files, 047, box 162, RG 75, Federal Archives and Records Center, Kansas City, Mo.

35. "Examination of the Indians Traveling with Cody and Salsbury's Wild West Show by the Acting Commissioner of Indian Affairs, R. V. Belt," in Acting Commissioner of Indian Affairs to Secretary of the Interior, December 20, 1890, Correspondence Land Division, vol. 104, November 11, 1890–December 20, 1890, Letter Books 207–208, 196–97, RG 75, NARS.

36. Ibid., 200–201.

9. FEMALE NATIVE TEACHERS IN SOUTHEAST ALASKA: SARAH DICKINSON, TILLIE PAUL, AND FRANCES WILLARD

1. Mary Lee Davis, *We Are Alaskans* (Boston: W. A. Wilde Co., 1931): 246.

2. S. Hall Young, *Hall Young of Alaska, "The Mushing Parson," The Autobiography of S. Hall Young* (New York and Chicago: Fleming H. Revell Co., 1927): 92.

3. Correspondence, Caroline Willard to friends, August 23, 1881, in Eva McClintock, ed., *Life in Alaska: Letters of Mrs. Eugene S. Willard* (Philadelphia: Presbyterian Board of Education, 1884): 49.

4. Correspondence, Mrs. A. R. McFarland to Sheldon Jackson, September 10, 1877, in Sheldon Jackson, *Alaska and Missions on the North Pacific Coast* (New York: Dodd, Mead & Co., 1880): 151.

5. Young, *Hall Young of Alaska*, 92.

6. Correspondence, Caroline Willard to friends, August 23, 1881, in McClintock, ed., *Life in Alaska*, 49.

7. For a detailed account of these developments from Sheldon Jackson's point of view, see his description in Jackson, *Alaska*, 128–47.

8. Jackson, *Alaska*, 144.

9. Correspondence, Mrs. A. R. McFarland to Sheldon Jackson, September 10, 1877, in Jackson, *Alaska*, 148–51.

10. Young, *Hall Young of Alaska*, 92–93.

11. Ibid., 165.

12. Correspondence, Amanda McFarland to Sheldon Jackson, April 6, 1879, in Sheldon Jackson Correspondence, Presbyterian Historical Society, Philadelphia, Pa.; and Jackson, *Alaska*, 219. These accounts differ both in chronology and in details and may describe two different episodes. Young and McFarland wanted girls placed in the residence so they would not become concubines of non-native miners.

13. Young, *Hall Young of Alaska*, 130–31.

14. Ibid., 150.

15. L. A. Beardslee, Reports of Captain L. A. Beardslee, U.S. Navy Relative to Affairs in Alaska, and the Operations of the USS *Jamestown* under His Command, while in the Waters of that Territory. January 24, 1882. 47th Cong., 1st sess., 1882, Sen. Ex. Doc. 71, 181.

16. William T. Hagan, *Indian Police and Judges: Experiments in Acculturation and Control* (Lincoln: University of Nebraska Press, 1966): 72–74.

17. Correspondence, Caroline Willard to friends, August 23, 1881, in McClintock, ed., *Life in Alaska*, 49.

18. Correspondence, Caroline Willard to friends, August 23, 1881, ibid., 57.

19. Correspondence, Caroline Willard to the Little Mission Band of the

Second Presbyterian Church, New Castle, Pennsylvania, February 3, 1882, in McClintock, ed., *Life in Alaska*, 158–59.

20. Correspondence, Caroline Willard to Sheldon Jackson, September 26, 1882, in McClintock, ed., *Life in Alaska*, 93.

21. Correspondence, Caroline Willard to parents, August 14, 1882, in McClintock, ed., *Life in Alaska*, 231–32.

22. Correspondence, Caroline Willard to the Sabbath-School of the Presbyterian Church of East Springfield, New York, November 17, 1882, in McClintock, ed., *Life in Alaska*, 248.

23. Correspondence, Caroline Willard to the Sabbath-School of the Presbyterian Church of East Springfield, New York, May 8, 1883, in McClintock, ed., *Life in Alaska*, 300–305.

24. *North Star*, Sitka, Alaska, vol. 4, no. 11 (October 1891): 4. (As reproduced in facsimile by the Shorey Book Store, *The North Star: A Monthly Publication in the Interests of Schools and Missions in Alaska, The Complete Issues from December 1887–December 1892* [Seattle: Shorey Book Store, 1973]: 188.)

25. Sheldon Jackson, Report of the General Agent, Office of the General Agent of Education in Alaska, Sitka, June 30, 1887, to the Territorial Board of Education. Schools in Alaska. In Bureau of Education, Report of the Commissioner for 1886–1887. 50th Cong., 1st sess., H.R. Ex. Doc. 1, pt. 5, v. 2, serial 2545.

26. Carrie M. Willard, "Native Sabbath School Teachers," *North Star*, vol. 1, no. 9 (August 1888): 4 (reproduced in Shorey, 36).

27. Davis, *We Are Alaskans*, 224.

28. Ibid., 240–45.

29. Ibid., 245–46.

30. Correspondence, Maggie J. Dunbar to Sheldon Jackson, November 29, 1879, in Jackson, *Alaska*, 250–51.

31. Davis, *We Are Alaskans*, 247–48.

32. Florence Hayes, *A Land of Challenge: Alaska* (New York: Board of National Missions of the Presbyterian Church of the United States of America, 1940): 16.

33. Correspondence, Caroline Willard to Sheldon Jackson, May 24 and June 1, 1882, in McClintock, ed., *Life in Alaska*, 215–17; and Correspondence, Caroline Willard to friends, June 30, 1883, ibid., 317–18.

34. Davis, *We Are Alaskans*, 252–53.

35. Clipping of unidentified newspaper article written by Louis Paul from Chilkat mission, probably in 1882. In Jackson Scrapbook Collection, vol. 5, Presbyterian Historical Society.

36. Davis, *We Are Alaskans*, 254.

37. Julia McNair Wright, *Among the Alaskans* (Philadelphia: Presbyterian Board of Home Missions, 1893): 342.

38. Correspondence, Caroline Willard to friends, July 16, 1882, in McClintock, ed., *Life in Alaska*, 318.

39. Davis, *We Are Alaskans*, 254–55.

40. Ibid., 256.

41. Tillie Paul, "My First Trip," in *North Star*, vol. 3, no. 7 (June 1890): 3 (reproduced in Shorey, 123).

42. *North Star*, vol. 3, no. 12 (November 1890): 4 (reproduced in Shorey, 144).

43. *North Star*, vol. 3, no. 1 (December 1889): 2 (reproduced in Shorey, 98).

44. *North Star*, vol. 2, no. 5 (April 1889): 2 (reproduced in Shorey, 66).

45. *North Star*, vol. 2, no. 9 (August 1889): 3 (reproduced in Shorey, 83).

46. Paul, "My First Trip."

47. *North Star*, vol. 3, no. 6 (May 1890): 1 (reproduced in Shorey, 117); ibid., vol. 4, no. 3 (February 1891): 2 (reproduced in Shorey, 154).

48. *North Star*, vol. 3, no. 10 (September 1890): 3 (reproduced in Shorey, 135).

49. *North Star*, vol. 4, no. 1 (December 1890): 4 (reproduced in Shorey, 148); ibid., vol. 4, no. 2 (January 1891): 4 (reproduced in Shorey, 152).

50. *North Star*, vol. 4, no. 4 (March 1891): 2 (reproduced in Shorey, 158).

51. Sheldon Jackson, Education in Alaska, 1890–91. Reprint of chap. 25, Bureau of Education, Report of the Commissioner of Education for 1890–1891. Washington, D.C.: U.S. Government Printing Office, 1893. [Also in 52nd Cong., 1st sess., H.R. Ex. Doc. 1, pt. 5, v. 5, pt. 2, serial 2939.]

52. *North Star*, vol. 2, no. 4 (March 1889): 4 (reproduced in Shorey, 64); ibid., vol. 2, no. 5 (April 1889): 2–3 (reproduced in Shorey, 66–67).

53. Sheldon Jackson, Education in Alaska, 1890–91.

54. *North Star*, vol. 3, no. 6 (May 1890): 2 (reproduced in Shorey, 118).

55. Davis, *We Are Alaskans*, 262ff.

56. Ibid., 273ff.

57. *North Star*, vol. 4, no. 5 (April 1891): 1 (reproduced in Shorey, 161); ibid., vol. 3, no. 10 (September 1890): 2 (reproduced in Shorey, 134).

58. *North Star*, vol. 3, no. 10 (September 1890): 2 (reproduced in Shorey, 134).

59. *North Star*, vol. 4, no. 2 (January 1891): 4 (reproduced in Shorey, 152).

60. Ibid.

61. *North Star*, vol. 4, no. 5 (April 1891): 1 (reproduced in Shorey, 161).

62. *North Star*, vol. 4, no. 12 (November 1891): 2–3 (reproduced in Shorey, 190–91).

63. *North Star*, vol. 5, no. 3 (February 1892): 4 (reproduced in Shorey, 204).

64. As quoted in *North Star*, vol. 5, no. 5 (April 1892): 1 (reproduced in Shorey, 209).

65. *North Star*, vol. 3, no. 1 (December 1889): 2 (reproduced in Shorey, 98); ibid., vol. 4, no. 4 (March 1891): 3 (reproduced in Shorey, 159). For a biography of Edward Marsden, see William Gilbert Beattie, *Marsden of Alaska, A Modern Indian: Minister, Missionary, Musician, Engineer, Pilot, Boat Builder and Church Builder* (New York: Vintage Press, 1955).

66. Correspondence, Fannie Willard to Sheldon Jackson, May 23, 1898, Sheldon Jackson Correspondence, Alaska State Historical Library, Juneau, Alaska.

67. Sheldon Jackson, "Alaska," in Lake Mohonk Conference, Friends of the Indian, Report of the 20th Annual Meeting (Philadelphia: 1902): 31–38.

68. Undated obituary, John Green Brady Papers, Beinecke Rare Book and Manuscript Library, Yale University, New Haven, Conn.

69. Sheldon Jackson, Education in Alaska, 1896–97, reprint of chap. 35, Bureau of Education, Report of the Commissioner for 1896–1897 (Washington, D.C.: U.S. Government Printing Office, 1898): 1608 [also in 55th Cong., 2d sess., H.R. Doc. 5, pt. 2, serial 3650]; *Assembly Herald* 6 (June 1902): 240.

70. David Waggoner, "In the land of the Hydahs," *Assembly Herald* 13 (June 1907): 252–54.

71. Charles Replogle, *Among the Indians of Alaska* (London: Headley Bros., 1904): 144–49, 177–78; Arthur O. Roberts, *Tomorrow Is Growing Old: Stories of the Quakers in Alaska* (Newberg, Ore.: Barclay Press, 1978): 43, 48–53, 60–66, 81.

72. Sallie Chesham, *Born to Battle: The Salvation Army in America* (New York: Rand McNally, 1965): 105–07, 197; and Arch R. Wiggins, *The History of the Salvation Army* 4: 1886–1904 (London: T. & A. Constable, 1964): 90.

10. THREE CULTURAL BROKERS IN THE CONTEXT OF EDWARD S. CURTIS'S THE NORTH AMERICAN INDIAN

1. Edward S. Curtis, *The North American Indian*, ed. Frederick Webb Hodge. (Cambridge and Norwood, Conn.: University Press and Plimpton Press, 1907–30; hereafter cited as *NAI*).

2. Information on the North American Indian project—as supplemented by research in primary documents—from Florence Curtis Graybill and Victor Boesen, *Edward Sheriff Curtis: Visions of a Vanishing Race* (New York: Thomas Crowell, 1976); Bill Holm and George I. Quimby, *Edward S.*

Curtis in the Land of the War Canoes (Seattle: University of Washington Press, 1980); Christopher M. Lyman, *The Vanishing Race and Other Illusions: Photographs of Indians by Edward S. Curtis* (Washington, D.C.: Smithsonian Institution Press, 1982); Mick Gidley, "The Vanishing Race in Sight and Sound: Edward S. Curtis' Musicale of North American Indian Life," in Jack Salzman, ed., *Prospects: An Annual of American Cultural Studies*, no. 12 (New York: Cambridge University Press, 1987): 59–87.

3. See Brian Dippie, *The Vanishing American: White Attitudes and U.S. Indian Policy* (Middletown: Wesleyan University Press, 1982); Lyman, *Vanishing Race*; and Mick Gidley, "The Repeated Return of the Vanishing Indian," in *American Studies: Essays in Honour of Marcus Cunliffe*, ed. Brian Holden Reid and John White (London: Macmillan, 1991): 189–209.

4. Information on Day from Clifford E. Trafzer, "Sam Day and His Boys: Good Neighbors to the Navajos," *Journal of Arizona History* 18 (Spring 1977): 1–22. On Hunt, from Ronald P. Rohner, "Franz Boas: Ethnographer of the Northwest Coast," in *Pioneers of American Anthropology: The Uses of Biography*, ed. June Helm (Seattle: University of Washington Press, 1966): 149–222; and letter to author, December 7, 1976; introduction to Helen Codere, ed., *Kwakiutl Ethnography* by Franz Boas (Chicago: University of Chicago Press, 1966). On Upshaw, from items cited below.

5. C. Hart Merriam, "Journal of Harriman Alaska," vol. I: 233, C. Hart Merriam Papers, Manuscript Division, Library of Congress.

6. Curtis to Candelario, October 31, 1905, Candelario Collection, Museum of New Mexico, Santa Fe; see also Curtis letters of October 7 and 19, 1905. A laudatory piece by Adolf Muhr in *Photo-Era* spoke of the studio as "the home of Mr. Curtis and of the Curtis Indian" ("E. S. Curtis and His Work," *Photo-Era* [July 1907]: 9–13). Curtis photos were often sold with a notice on the verso of the frame calling his studio "the home of the American Indian."

7. Curtis to Bowditch, January 10 and January 21, 1913, E. S. Curtis File, Manuscript Collection, Museum of Northern Arizona, Flagstaff.

8. Curtis, untitled typescript from the *NAI* materials, Los Angeles County Museum of Natural History; this extract and variations on it were probably composed for the 1911 musicale tour.

9. See Clifford, "Histories of the Tribal and the Modern" and other essays in *The Predicament of Culture* (Cambridge and London: Harvard University Press, 1988); and Jeanette Greenfield, *The Return of Cultural Treasures* (Cambridge and New York: Cambridge University Press, 1989), a book that, though it does not deal with "internal" expropriation, contains much pertinent commentary.

10. See William H. Goetzmann and Kay Sloan, *Looking Far North: The Harriman Expedition to Alaska 1899* (Princeton: Princeton University Press, 1982): 161–68.

11. See Curtis to Hubbell, August 20 and December 7, 1906; February 1, April 1, April 5, May 27, July 14, and October 4, 1907; and April 19 and June 2, 1909, Hubbell Papers, Special Collections, University of Arizona, Tucson.

12. Information from Trafzer, "Sam Day and His Boys," passim. The Samuel Edward Day Collection of manuscript material is in the Library of Northern Arizona University, Flagstaff, and Day's photographs are at the Museum of Northern Arizona, Flagstaff. See also Curtis to Charlie Day, November 19, 1908, Day Collection.

13. See Trafzer, "Sam Day and His Boys," 16–18 and, for the full context, the same author's edition of one of the protest letters: "An Indian Trader's Plea for Justice, 1906," *New Mexico Historical Review* 47 (July 1972): 239–56.

14. See Day to Curtis, February 10, 1905, enclosed with Curtis to Leupp, March 15, 1905, Letters to the Commissioner of Indian Affairs, Record Group 75, National Archives, Washington, D.C.

15. Curtis to Leupp, March 15, 1905.

16. For Curtis family lore, see, e.g., Ralph W. Andrews, *Curtis' Western Indians* (Seattle: Superior, 1962): 26–27; and Graybill and Boesen, *Edward Sheriff Curtis*, 25–26. Curtis to Day, December 20, 1904, Day Collection.

17. See "A Seattle Man's Triumph," *Seattle Times* May 4, 1904, clipping in the Pacific Northwest Collection fully reproduced in Lyman, *Vanishing Race*, 65–69.

18. Stevenson to Walcott, November 17, 1908, Matilda Coxe Stevenson Papers, National Anthropological Archives, Washington, D.C. Stevenson was generally a Curtis supporter, as her letters to Curtis of February 21 and May 5, 1907, and April 9, 1908, indicate. For her bossiness, see Nancy Oestereich Lurie, "Women in Early American Anthropology," in Helm, ed., *Pioneers of American Anthropology*, esp. 53–54, 60–62, 233 n. 41, 234 n. 53.

19. Curtis to Leitch, March 3, 1951, E. S. Curtis File, History Department, Seattle Public Library.

20. For material on Hunt, see Rohner, "Franz Boas: Ethnographer on the Northwest Coast"; Codere, ed., *Kwakiutl Ethnography*; Ira Jacknis, "Franz Boas and Photography," *Studies in Visual Communication* 10, no. 1 (Winter 1984): 2–60; and Irving Goldman, *The Mouth of Heaven: An Introduction to Kwakiutl Religious Thought* (New York and London: John Wiley, 1975): esp. 9–12. Brief theoretical commentary on the relationship between Hunt and Boas in the constitution of a representation of Northwest Coast culture may be found in David Murray, *Forked Tongues: Speech, Writing and Representation in North American Indian Texts* (London: Pinter, 1991): 100–04.

21. See Holm and Quimby, *Edward S. Curtis*, esp. 66–69; and for

Hunt's changeableness, Graybill and Boesen, *Edward Sheriff Curtis*, 61–65.

22. For a full account of this enterprise, see Holm and Quimby, *Edward S. Curtis*, esp. 127–8.

23. "Grotesque Indian Mask in Curtis Collection," *Seattle Times*, November 10, 1912, clipping in the Curtis Biography File, Pacific Northwest Collection.

24. The Curtis memoir, probably written in the 1930s, was one of a number kept by the Curtis family and is fully reproduced in Graybill and Boesen, *Edward S. Curtis*, 64–67.

25. See Rohner, "Franz Boas: Ethnographer of the Northwest Coast," esp. 172; and Marie Mauzé, "Le destin d'un Sanctnaire," *Gradhiva*, 10 (1992): 11–25, the revised version of a paper on the reconstruction of a Nootka whaling shrine, delivered at the Tenth European American Indian Workshop, Vienna, April 1989.

26. There is ample evidence of average practice; with reference to Hunt, see Rohner, "Franz Boas," esp. 191–211; and for Curtis project, see letter from E. W. Gifford to Curtis's principal ethnologist, William E. Myers, September 12, 1915, Museum Archives, University Archives, Bancroft Library, University of California, Berkeley.

27. Phillips, "Beside an Old Chief's Resting Plot," typescript of a memoir probably written in 1911, 9 pp., private collection. Phillips's field notes of the visit to Nespelem survive in the *NAI* materials at Los Angeles County Museum of Natural History.

28. Phillips, "Through the Country of the Crows," typescript, 10 pp., private collection; subsequent quotations are from this piece. Interestingly, anthropologist Robert Lowie, in writing about his primary informant on the Crow reservation, Jim Carpenter, recorded that Carpenter, when first encountered in 1910, was also viewed at the agency as a shiftless troublemaker but turned out to be, in Lowie's view, concerned for his people, proud, and outspoken; see "My Crow Interpreter," in Joseph B. Casagrande, ed., *In the Company of Man: Twenty Portraits of Anthropological Informants* (New York: Harper Torchbook, 1964): 427–37.

29. Some of Upshaw's father's deeds are recorded in *NAI*, 4 (1909): 18–20. Information on Upshaw himself came from Daniel F. Littlefield and James W. Parins, *A Bio-bibliography of Native American Authors, 1772–1924* (Metuchen, N. J., and London: Scarecrow, 1981): 170 and 303, from his own, "What Indians Owe to the United States Government," *Red Man* 14 (April 1897): 8, from Phillips, and from interviews with Curtis's son, Harold P. Curtis, January 1977, and with his daughter, Florence Curtis Graybill, December 1976, who remembered her father speaking of his death.

30. See "Six Weeks Among the Indians," a 1905 newspaper clipping in

Clarence Bagley scrapbook no. 5, 110, Pacific Northwest Collection. The surviving manuscripts of *NAI* at the Los Angeles County Museum of Natural History include a wealth of handwritten notes, typed materials, vocabularies, and so on. There is much evidence of contributions by Upshaw. Most impressively, in a particular file labeled "Blackfeet," there are two copies of material entitled "Upshaw Notes," and typescripts of interviews and histories, and in one carton of typed material on the Apsaroke (Crow) and Hidatsa peoples, the typed and indexed volumes of field notes cite Upshaw's name, as might be expected, frequently. A brief note on Upshaw's White House visit appeared in the *Washington Post*, March 26, 1909 (reproduced in a Curtis publicity brochure, *The North American Indian*, n.d. [ca. 1911], author's collection).

31. Typescript reminiscence by Curtis, probably written in the midthirties, quoted very fully in Andrews, *Curtis' Western Indians*, 39–42.

32. Interview with Fritz Dalby, Edwin Dalby's son, August 1978.

33. File 389/1911, Crow 311, National Archives, Letters to the Commissioner of Indian Affairs, Record Group 75.

34. File 41014-08-321 Crow, Record Group 75; Curtis's letter is dated February 3, 1909.

35. Curtis to Leupp, March 15, 1905.

36. "Edward S. Curtis: Photo-Historian of the North American Indian," *Seattle Sunday Times*, Magazine Section, November 15, 1903, clipping in Curtis Biography File, Pacific Northwest Collection.

37. Information supplied by William B. Lee, then of the Los Angeles County Museum of Natural History, in an interview, August 1980; Lee's evidence is also fully reported in Lyman, *Vanishing Race*, 69. Similar experience with Navajos and the film footage was communicated by Trafzer in discussions during spring 1985.

11. JESSE ROWLODGE: SOUTHERN ARAPAHO AS POLITICAL INTERMEDIARY

1. Indian Oral History Collection, Western History Collections, University of Oklahoma Library, Norman, Tape 41, 4 (hereafter cited as IOHC, tape number and page); *Indian Leader* (Lawrence, Kans.), September 6, 1910.

2. Cheyenne and Arapaho census files are available on microfilm from the National Archives, Washington, D.C., and Oklahoma Historical Society, Oklahoma City, Oklahoma. IOHC, OU, T41, 2, 15; T158, 5; T159, 7; T174, 18; T235, 16–17; T239, 20; T352, 20. E. B. White to G. W. H. Stouch, February 19, 1906, contains the deposition of Owl, dated March 5, 1906, Estates File, Henry Rowlodge to W. B. Freer, June 3, 1910, Land Sales File,

Cheyenne and Arapaho Agency Records, Division of Archives and Manuscripts, Oklahoma Historical Society, Oklahoma City, (hereafter cited as file, C&A, OHS).

3. IOHC, OU, T41, 3–4, 15; T125, 10.

4. IOHC, OU, T235, 12–15; T240, 2; T352, 1, 5–6, 12–13, 29. Alfred L. Kroeber, *The Arapaho*, foreword by Fred Eggan (Lincoln: University of Nebraska Press, 1983): 153–55, 181–82.

5. IOHC, OU, T41, 20, 26; T159, 4; T169, 5; T172, 32; T265, 25; T352, 28. *Indian Leader*, April 9 and September 17, 1909, September 9, 1910.

6. IOHC, OU, T41, 13; T265, 25. H. B. Peairs to C. E. Shell, October 3, 1906, and August 1, 1907, Haskell Institute File, C&A, OHS.

7. IOHC, OU, T352, 11–12. Schedule showing names . . . [of] Cheyenne and Arapaho Indians in Oklahoma, for their pro rata shares of tribal trust funds . . . February 2, 1909, Per Capita File, C&A, OHS.

8. Jesse Rowlodge to [C. E. Shell], April 4, 1908, Haskell Institute File; Rowlodge to Shell, July 29, September 8, November 16, 1909; Shell to Rowlodge, November 23, 1909, with statement of J. H. Geeslin, November 16, 1909, C&A Patents File, C&A, OHS.

9. Jesse Rowlodge to W. B. Freer, April 19, 1911, Freer, Report on Application for Patent in Fee, n.d. [1911], J. W. Ijams to Freer, n.d. [1911], Fee Patents issued to Cheyenne and Arapaho Allottee (or their heirs) of the Cheyenne and Arapaho Indian Agency, Concho, Oklahoma [1905–26], n.d., Patents File, C&A, OHS; IOHC, OU, T352, 17–19, 39.

10. IOHC, OU, T352, 1–2; W. W. Scott to Jesse Rowlodge, October 29, 1918, Rowlodge to Scott, November 29, 1919, Rowlodge to C. W. Ruckman, April 27, 1920, Ruckman to Rowlodge, May 4, 1920, Farmers File, C&A, OHS; IOHC, OU, T352, 1–2; *Messenger* (Canton, Okla.), vol. 9, no. 9 (September 9, 1934): 2.

11. IOHC, OU, T41, 3; T235, 32; T174, 16–17; T191, 1. Loretta Fowler, *Arapahoe Politics, 1851–1978: Symbols in Crises of Authority* (Lincoln: University of Nebraska Press, 1982): 85. Virginia Cole Trenholm, *The Arapahoes: Our People* (Norman: University of Oklahoma Press, 1970): 233, 278.

12. IOHC, OU, T248, 23; T352, 39.

13. IOHC, OU, T141, 14; T235, 16; T352, 19, 29; T680, 10.

14. Transcripts of meetings between Cheyenne and Arapaho chiefs and headmen and government officials and some correspondence with attorneys after 1907 are found in Central Classified File 056, Cheyenne and Arapaho, Cantonment, Seger and Red Moon agencies, Records of the Bureau of Indian Affairs, Record Group 75, National Archives, Washington, D.C. (hereafter cited as agency file number, NAW); Central Classified Files 064 and 066, Records of the Cheyenne and Arapaho Agency, National Archives-Southwest Region, Fort Worth, Tex. (hereafter cited as File, C&A,

NASW); and Federal Relations and Claims Against the Government files, C&A, OHS.

Rowlodge's political career from 1926 to 1938 is also found in D. J. Berthrong, "Struggle for Power: The Impact of Southern Cheyenne and Arapaho 'Schoolboys' on Tribal Politics," *American Indian Quarterly* 16 (Winter 1992): 1–24, portions of which are used here with permission.

15. Cato Sells to R. E. Richardson, March 24, 1915, E. B. Meritt to Jesse Rowlodge, June 7, 1916, Meritt to Paul Boynton, December 6, 1916, L. S. Bonnin to Chief Turkey Legs, March 11, 1921, C. H. Burke to Bonnin, October 3, 1921, Claims Against the Government File, C&A, OHS; F. E. Perkins to Commissioner of Indian Affairs (CIA), March 21, 1923, Henderson's contract, approved June 13, 1924, CF 269, box 52, C&A, NASW.

16. Hearings Held before E. B. Meritt, Assistant Commissioner of Indian Affairs, February 15, 1926, CF 1828-1926-056, C&A, NAW; L. S. Bonnin to CIA, January 8, 1926, C&A, CF 066, box 31, C&A, NASW. Rowlodge's role in tribal politics, 1926–37, is more fully described in Berthrong, "Struggle for Power." Pp. 1–24 are used in part with permission of the *American Indian Quarterly*.

17. Chief White Shield to Mr. [L. S.] Bonnin, December 31, 1927, Bonnin to White Shield, January 4, 1928, CF 066, box 31, C&A, NASW.

18. *Watonga* (Oklahoma) *Republican*, February 2, 1929; L. S. Bonnin to John Otterby, May 23, 1928, CF 066, box 31, C&A, NASW.

19. L. S. Bonnin to John W. Block, March 28, 1928, CF 064, box 25, C&A, NASW. Block was a mixed-blood Cheyenne and a Haskell graduate.

20. Hearings in Commissioner's Office, March 2, 1928, CF 064, L. S. Bonnin to Farmers, Circular 119, April 4, 1928, Circular 123, April 21, 1928, CF 102, no box number, Bonnin to John Otterby, May 23, 1928, CF 066, box 31, C&A, NASW. DeForest Antelope was a grandson of White Antelope, killed at the 1864 Sand Creek massacre, and Carlisle trained. John Fletcher was educated at Hampton Institute.

21. John Otterby to CIA, May 4, 1928, L. S. Bonnin to CIA, May 13, 1928, Bonnin to Otterby, May 23, 1928, CF 066, box 31, C&A, NASW. Otterby was the son of Charlie Otterby, an employee at Bent's Fort, and Picking Bones Woman, a Cheyenne.

22. D. B. Henderson to Jesse Rowlodge, November 7, 1928, Herbert Walker to L. S. Bonnin, December 7, 1928, Bonnin to Walker, December 11, 1928, CF 066, box 31, C&A, NASW.

23. The constitution, ratified on May 25, 1929, is in CF 064, box 26, Jesse Rowlodge to L. S. Bonnin, January 18, 1932, CF 064, box 25, C&A, NASW.

24. Constitution, May 25, 1929, CF 064, box 26, C&A, NASW; 49 U.S. Statutes 1967–68.

25. Cheyenne and Arapaho (C&A) Tribal Council Minutes, December

22, 1930, Resolution, Southern Cheyenne and Arapaho Tribal Council . . . held at Concho, Oklahoma, on the 22nd day of December, 1930, CF 064, C&A, NASW.

26. Tribal Corresponding Secretary [Jesse Rowlodge] to Honorable Chairman and Gentlemen of the Subcommittee of the Committee on Indian Affairs, n.d., CF 064, box 25, C&A, NASW; Survey of Conditions of Indians of the United States, Hearings before Subcommittee of the Committee on Indian Affairs, U.S. Senate, 70th Cong. to the 78th Cong., pt. 15, 7211–7229, 7235, 7238–7239, 7243.

27. Little Hand et al. to C. H. [sic] Rhoads, December 12, 1931, CF 064, box 25, C&A Tribal Council Minutes, December 15, 1931, CF Organization and Circulars, box 27, C&A, NASW.

28. C&A Tribal Council Minutes, January 27, 1932, CF Organization and Circulars, box 27, C&A, NASW.

29. Henderson's new contracts are in CF 060.1, box 25, C&A, NASW. Oklahoma Sen. Elmer Thomas introduced a Cheyenne and Arapaho jurisdictional bill, but it was not reported out of committee, see Congressional Record, June 6, 1932. Jesse's and Wilson's report was received at the agency office on July 19, 1932, but not by the general council until November 25, 1932; see Report to the Cheyenne and Arapaho Tribal Council with C&A Tribal Council Minutes, November 25, 1932, CF 064, box 25, C&A, NASW.

30. Notes for the Arapaho Meeting with Superintendent Bonnin by C. W. Ruckman, November 9, 1932, C & A Tribal Council Minutes, November 25, 1932, Transcript of Chiefs' Statements and Bonnin's Responses, March 14, 1933, CF 064, box 25, C&A, NASW.

31. C&A Tribal Council Minutes, February 2, 16, 24, 1934, Transcript of February 16, 1934, Cheyenne and Arapaho Council Meeting, CF Miscellaneous, box 5, C&A Tribal Council Minutes, March 24, 1934, CF 011, box 2, C&A, NASW.

32. To Grant to Indians Living Under Federal Tutelage the Freedom to Organize for the Purpose of Local Self-Government and Economic Enterprise, Hearings before the Committee on Indian Affairs, U.S. Senate, 73d Cong., 2d sess., on S. 2755 and S. 3645 (1934), 107–110; C&A Tribal Council Minutes [May–June 1934], CF 011, box 3, C&A, NASW; 48 U.S. Statutes 984–88.

33. Transcript of Meeting Held at Concho, Oklahoma, October 22, 1934, CF Miscellaneous, box 26, C&A Tribal Council Minutes, December 8, 1934, CF Organization, box 25, C&A, NASW; To Promote the General Welfare of the Indians of Oklahoma, Hearings before the Committee on Indian Affairs, U.S. Senate 74th Cong., 1st sess., on S. 2074 . . . April 8, 9, 10, 11, 96–99; 49 U.S. Statutes 1967–68.

34. C. H. Berry, Notice to Cheyenne and Arapaho Indians, February 25,

1937, CF 171, box 27, Berry to Cheyenne and Arapaho Indians, March 15, 1937, Berry to Alfred Wilson, March 13, 1937, Berry to John Collier, March 18, 1937, Informal Meeting Minutes, March 17, 1937, CF 064, box 26, C&A, NASW.

35. John Collier to C. H. Berry, May 4, 1937, M. E. Opler to Alfred Wilson, May 1, 1937, CF 064, C&A Tribal Council Minutes, May 8, 1937, CF Tribal Council "M," box 26, C&A, NASW.

36. C. H. Berry to CIA, May 10, June 25, 1937, Berry to Alfred Wilson, May 17, 1937, M. E. Opler to Berry, June 7, 1937, Members of Special Committee on Revision to Secretary of the Interior, June 21, 1937, Wilson to William Zimmerman, Jr., July 12, 1937, Constitution and By-Laws of the Cheyenne and Arapaho Tribes of Oklahoma, CF 064, box 26, John Collier to Berry, June 17, 1937, CF Organization and Circulars, box 27, C&A, NASW.

37. Certificates of Adoption [of the Constitution], n.d., to which is appended Cheyenne and Arapaho Election Report, September 18, 1937, CF 064, box 26, C&A, NASW. Rowlodge served as secretary of the election board.

38. F. H. Daiker to Ed Burns, John Otterby, Jesse Rowlodge, and Theodore Haury, June 30, 1939, CF 067.4, box 31, F. M. Goodwin to John Fletcher, January 31, 1941, CF Organization and Circulars, box 27, W. L. Gray to Jesse Rowlodge, April 30, 1941, CF 060.1, box 25, C&A, NASW; Council Meetings of Major American Indian Tribes, 1907–1971 (microfilm, Frederick, Md.: University Publications of America, 1981): Pt. 1, Sec. I, reel 13, Minutes of the Cheyenne and Arapaho Business Committee Held December 6, 1939, at Concho, Oklahoma, and those of January and April 1940 and October 1, 1941 (hereafter cited as C&A Business Committee Minutes, UPA).

39. C&A Business Committee Minutes, April 11, 1942, February 16, 1943, February 12, 1944, March 28, April 4, 1945, UPA; Lands on the Fort Reno Military Reservation, Oklahoma, Congressional Hearings on Disposition of Fort Reno Lands . . . on the 24th Day of April, 1954, House of Representatives, 74–76.

40. C&A Business Committee Minutes, December 5, 26, 1951, December 3, 1952, CF 17127-1940-054, Pt. I, December 1, 1954, April 26 and October 14, 1955, C&A, NAW; 25 U.S. Code 415.

41. C&A Business Committee Minutes, November 3, December 1, 1954, CF 17127-1946-054, pt. 2, C&A, NAW.

42. C&A Business Committee Minutes, June 1, 1955, CF 17127-1946-054, pt. 2, C&A, NAW.

43. C&A Business Committee Minutes and Annual Meeting of Tribal Council, October 14, 1955, CF 17127-1946-054, pt. 2, C&A, NAW.

44. Indian Claims Commission, *Arapaho-Cheyenne Indians* (New York: Garland Publishing, 1974): 227–343; IOHC, OU, T-158, 1–3.

45. *Clinton* (Oklahoma) *Daily News*, November 11, 1974; Oklahoma City *Daily Oklahoman*, November 12, 1974; *Geary* (Okla.) *Star*, November 14, 1974.

12. D'ARCY McNICKLE: LIVING A BROKER'S LIFE

1. My book *Singing an Indian Song: A Biography of D'Arcy McNickle* was published by the University of Nebraska Press in 1992. The biographical material in this chapter derives primarily from research for the biography.

2. D'Arcy McNickle, *The Surrounded* (New York: Dodd, Mead, 1936; reprint ed. with an afterword by Lawrence W. Towner, Albuquerque: University of New Mexico Press, 1978).

3. D'Arcy McNickle, "The Surfacing of Native Leadership," *The Patterns of Amerindian Identity, Symposium, Montmorency, Quebec, Canada, October 1974* (Quebec: Les Presses de l'Université Laval, 1976): 11.

4. D'Arcy McNickle and Viola Pfrommer, "Dine Txah," 24. This unpublished manuscript of the Crownpoint Report is in the McNickle Papers at the Newberry Library, Chicago.

5. D'Arcy McNickle, "A Battle Yet to Wage." A copy of this unpublished address is in the papers of the National Congress of American Indians, Smithsonian Institution, Washington, D.C.

6. John Adair, Kurt Deuschle, and Clifford Barnett, *The People's Health: Anthropology and Medicine in a Navajo Community* (Albuquerque: University of New Mexico Press, 1988): 33, 244 nn. 3, 4.

7. For a description of McNickle's Crownpoint project and others funded by the Emil Schwartzhaupt Foundation, see Carl Tjerandson, *Education for Citizenship: A Foundation's Experience* (Santa Cruz, Calif.: Emil Schwartzhaupt Foundation, 1980).

8. See transcribed Doris Duke Tapes 303, 309, 311, Navajo Tribe, Special Collections, Zimmerman Library, University of New Mexico, Albuquerque.

9. Allan Holmberg, "Participant Intervention in the Field," *Human Organization* 14 (Spring 1955): 23–26; Allan Holmberg, "The Research and Development Approach to the Study of Change," *Human Organization* 17 (Spring 1958): 12–16. According to McNickle, Richard Adams directed the hydroelectric project in the Andean village of Muquiyauyo. McNickle to Douglas Latimer, July 6, 1976, General Correspondence, McNickle Papers, Newberry Library.

10. Wilcomb E. Washburn, "Ethical Perspectives in North American

Ethnology," in *Social Contexts of American Ethnology, 1840–1984* (Washington, D.C.: American Anthropological Association, 1985): 50–64.

11. Hazel Hertzberg, *The Search for an American Indian Identity: Modern Pan-Indian Movements* (Syracuse: Syracuse University Press, 1971): 289–92; Nancy Oestreich Lurie, "The Contemporary American Indian Scene," in *North American Indians in Historical Perspective*, eds. Eleanor Burke Leacock and Nancy Oestreich Lurie (New York: Random House, 1971): 453, 462–63; Peter Iverson, "Building Toward Self-Determination: Plains and Southwestern Indians in the 1940s and 1950s," *Western Historical Quarterly* 16 (April 1985): 163–73.

12. D'Arcy McNickle, *Indian Man: A Life of Oliver La Farge* (Bloomington: Indiana University Press, 1971). The latest biography of Oliver La Farge, by Robert A. Hecht, *Oliver La Farge and the American Indian: A Biography* (Metuchen, N.J.: Scarecrow Press, 1991), offers an interesting comparative study. Like McNickle, La Farge also experienced a shift in his understanding of adaptation/acculturation/assimilation of the Native Americans into mainstream society (Hecht, *Oliver La Farge*, 194–200).

13. D'Arcy McNickle, *Wind from an Enemy Sky* (New York: Harper and Row, 1978; reprint ed. with an afterword by Louis Owens, Albuquerque: University of New Mexico Press, 1988).

14. Ibid., 256.

15. D'Arcy McNickle, "Process or Compulsion: The Search for a Policy of Administration in Indian Affairs," *American Indigena*, (July 1957).

16. See D'Arcy McNickle, *The Hawk Is Hungry and Other Stories*, ed. by Birgit Hans (Tucson: University of Arizona Press, 1992); John Lloyd Purdy, *Word Ways: The Novels of D'Arcy McNickle* (Tucson: University of Arizona Press, 1990); and Bernd Peyer's *The Singing Spirit: Early Short Stories by Native American Indians* (Tucson: University of Arizona Press, 1990), for McNickle's short stories. See also Dorothy R. Parker, "D'Arcy McNickle: An Annotated Bibliography of His Published Articles and Book Reviews in a Biographical Context," *American Indian Culture and Research Journal* 14 (1990): 55–75.

13. SPEAKING THEIR LANGUAGE:
ROBERT W. YOUNG AND THE NAVAJOS

1. John P. Harrington to M. W. Stirling, October 28, 1940. John P. Harrington Papers, National Anthropological Archives, Smithsonian Institution. Thanks to Dorothy R. Parker for a copy of this letter.

2. Robert W. Young, personal interview, June 2, 1990. Unless otherwise noted, all quotations from Young are taken from this extended interview, conducted in his office in the linguistics department at the University of New Mexico.

3. Ibid.

4. Ibid; Robert W. Young, "Written Navajo: A Brief History," in *Advances in the Creation and Revision of Writing Systems*, ed. Joshua A. Fishman (The Hague: Mouton, 1977): 460–61.

5. Ibid.

6. Young interview; Young, "Written Navajo," 461–63.

7. Young interview.

8. *The Navajo Trail*, 13, 15. My copy of the yearbook was given to me by my grandfather, principal of the school in 1936.

9. Young interview.

10. Buck Austin, "We Have Lived on Livestock a Long Time," in *Navajo Historical Selections*, ed. Robert W. Young and William Morgan (Phoenix: Bureau of Indian Affairs, 1954): 62.

11. Young interview.

12. Ibid. Carobeth Laird was married to Harrington before marrying a Chemehuevi Indian, George Laird. See *Encounters with an Angry God: Recollections of My Life with John Peabody Harrington* (New York: Ballantine, 1977).

13. Clark contributed to other Indian-language series as well. See, e.g., *Singing Sioux Cowboy* (Lawrence, Kans.: Bureau of Indian Affairs, 1954).

14. Young interview; Young, "Written Navajo," 465–66.

15. Ann Clark, *Little Herder in Summer* (Shįįgo Na'nikkaadi' Yázhi) (Phoenix: Office of Indian Affairs, 1942): 5–6.

16. Young interview.

17. Clark, *Little Herder*, 5–6.

18. Willard Beatty, "Bilingual Readers," in Clark, *Little Herder*, 118–19. *Navaho* is the alternative spelling, more commonly employed fifty years ago than it is today. *Navajo* is the spelling generally used today.

19. Young interview; Young, "Written Navajo," 466.

20. Young interview; Young, "Written Navajo," 466–68.

21. Robert W. Young, "Two Languages Better Than One," in *Education for Action*, ed. Willard W. Beatty (Chilocco, Okla.: U.S. Indian Service, 1944): 254–57.

22. Young interview.

23. Peter Iverson, *The Navajo Nation* (Albuquerque: University of New Mexico Press, 1983): 54; Lee Muck, "Survey of the Range Resources and Livestock Economy of the Navajo Indian Reservation," mimeographed (Washington, D.C.: Department of the Interior, 1948): 30–32; Young interview.

24. Young interview.

25. Iverson, *Navajo Nation*, 56–68; Young interview.

26. Young interview.

27. Robert W. Young, ed., *The Navajo Yearbook* (Window Rock: Bureau of Indian Affairs, 1961): vol. 8.

28. Young, *Navajo Yearbook*, 430; Young interview.

29. Young interview. For a full discussion, see John Adair, Kurt W. Deuschle, and Clifford R. Barnett, *The People's Health: Anthropology and Medicine in a Navajo Community* (Albuquerque: University of New Mexico Press, 1988), rev. and expanded ed.

30. Young interview.

31. For example, I interviewed Young in 1974, as I was completing research on my dissertation.

32. Young interview.

33. Robert W. Young, *The Role of the Navajo in the Southwestern Drama* (Gallup, New Mex.: *Gallup Independent*, 1968): iii.

34. Robert W. Young, *A Political History of the Navajo Tribe* (Tsaile, Ariz.: Navajo Community College Press, 1978): xi.

35. Robert W. Young, "The Rise of the Navajo Tribe," in *Plural Society in the Southwest*, ed. Edward H. Spicer and Raymond H. Thompson (New York: Weatherhead Foundation, 1972): 167–237; Robert W. Young, "Written History."

36. Robert W. Young and William Morgan, *The Navajo Language: A Grammar and Colloquial Dictionary* (Albuquerque: University of New Mexico Press, 1987): 1.

37. Young interview.

14. PABLITA VELARDE: THE PUEBLO ARTIST
AS CULTURAL BROKER

1. J. J. Brody, *Indian Painters and White Patrons* (Albuquerque: University of New Mexico Press, 1971): 210–13.

2. Clara Lee Tanner, *Southwest Indian Painting: A Changing Art*, 2d ed. (Tucson: University of Arizona Press, 1973): 176.

3. Pablita Velarde, *Pablita Velarde: An Artist and Her People*, produced by the National Park Service, 20 min., n.d., videocassette.

4. Mary Carroll Nelson, *Pablita Velarde* (Minneapolis: Dillon Press, 1971): 1–2.

5. Dorothy Dunn, Personal Papers, Private Collection.

6. Pablita Velarde, interview by Margaret Connell Szasz, February 9, 1972, Albuquerque. Tape Recording 853, American Indian History Research Project Files, Special Collections, Zimmerman Library, University of New Mexico, Albuquerque.

7. Pablita Velarde, *Old Father, The Storyteller* (Globe, Ariz.: Dale Stuart King, 1960): 17.

8. Jeanne O. Snodgrass, *American Indian Painters: A Biographical Directory*, contributions from the Museum of the American Indian, Heye Foundation, vol. 21, pt. 1 (New York: Museum of the American Indian, 1968): 202.

9. Dunn Papers.

10. Pablita Velarde, *The Enchanted Arts*, produced and directed by Irene-Aimee Depke, 25 min., KRGW, Las Cruces, New Mex., 1979, videocassette.

11. Sally Hyer, *One House, One Voice, One Heart: Native American Education at the Santa Fe Indian School* (Santa Fe: Museum of New Mexico Press, 1990): 11.

12. Velarde, Connell Szasz interview.

13. Pablita Velarde, Interview, October 2, 1986. Tape Recording 22, Santa Fe Indian School First One Hundred Years Project, Santa Fe Indian School Archives, Santa Fe, N.M.

14. Hyer, *One House*, 42.

15. H. H. Hill, *An Ethnography of Santa Clara Pueblo, New Mexico*, edited and annotated by Charles H. Lange (Albuquerque: University of New Mexico Press, 1982): 164, 169–70.

16. Samuel L. Gray, *Tonita Peña: Quah Ah, 1893–1949* (Albuquerque: Avanyu Publishing, 1990): 65; Robert Ritzenthaler, "From Folk Art to Fine Art: The Emergence of the Name Artist Among the Southwest Indians," in *The Visual Arts: Plastic and Graphic*, ed. Justine Cordwell (The Hague: Mouton, 1979), 431–38.

17. Gray, *Tonita Peña*, 17–20.

18. Velarde, *An Artist and Her People*.

19. Velarde, Connell Szasz interview.

20. Dunn Papers.

21. Ibid.

22. Ibid.

23. Hyer, *One House*, 53.

24. Velarde, *Enchanted Arts*.

25. Velarde, Connell Szasz interview.

26. Ibid.

27. The number of women marrying outside the pueblo has increased since the 1940s, and the tribe's enrollment policy has been disputed by some Santa Claras. In 1972, a lawsuit was filed in federal court against the pueblo by Julia Martinez, who argued that the policy violated the 1968 Civil Rights Act and that her children were denied certain rights because their father was not Santa Clara. The Supreme Court ruled in favor of the tribe.

28. This 1960 publication has been reissued as Pablita Velarde, *Old Father, Story Teller* (Santa Fe: Clear Light Publishers, 1989).

29. Kim Anderson, "Earth Yields a Harvest of Colors, Textures For Traditional Artist," *Albuquerque Journal*, 29 September 1985, 1(E).

30. Dunn Papers.

31. Watson Smith, *Kiva Mural Decorations at Awatovi and Kawaika-a* (Cambridge: Papers of the Peabody Museum of American Archaeology and Ethnology, Harvard University, vol. 37, 1952), fig. 60, color pl. D, 106–51.

32. Dunn Papers.

33. Ibid.

34. Dorothy Dunn, "The Art of Pablita Velarde," *El Palacio* 64 (July-August 1957): 231–32.

35. Velarde, *Enchanted Arts*.

36. Ibid.

37. Florence Hawley, "The Keresan Holy Rollers: An Adaptation to American Individualism," *Social Forces* 26 (1948): 272–80.

38. Elsie Clews Parsons, *Isleta Paintings*, ed. Esther Goldfrank (Washington, D.C.: Smithsonian Institution, 1962): 1.

39. Leslie A. White, *The Pueblo of Santa Ana, New Mexico* (Menasha, Wis.: Memoirs of the American Anthropological Association 60, 1942): 9.

40. Edward P. Dozier, *The Pueblo Indians of North America* (New York: Holt, Rinehart and Winston, 1970): 4–5.

41. Elizabeth Brandt, "On Secrecy and the Control of Knowledge: Taos Pueblo," in *Secrecy: A Cross-Cultural Perspective*, ed. Stanton Tefft (New York: Human Sciences Press, 1980): 123–46.

42. Dunn Papers.

43. Dozier, *The Pueblo Indians*, 180.

44. Dunn Papers.

45. Ibid.

46. Anderson, "Earth Yields a Harvest," 1(E).

47. Velarde, *An Artist and Her People*.

BIBLIOGRAPHY

Adair, John, Kurt W. Deuschle, and Clifford R. Barnett. *The People's Health: Anthropology and Medicine in a Navajo Community*. Revised and expanded ed. Albuquerque: University of New Mexico Press, 1988.

American Baptist Mission Union Papers. "Papers of Evan and John B. Jones," Rochester, N.Y.: American Baptist Historical Society.

American Board of Commissioners for Foreign Missions. Houghton Library, Harvard University, Cambridge, Mass.

_____. *Annual Report of the American Board of Commissioners for Foreign Missions*. Boston: American Board of Commissioners for Foreign Missions, 1821–40.

_____. *First Ten Annual Reports of the American Board of Commissioners for Foreign Missions*. Boston: American Board of Commissioners for Foreign Missions, 1834.

Anderson, Kim. "Earth Yields a Harvest of Colors, Textures for Traditional Artist." *Albuquerque Journal,* 29 September 1985, 1(E).

Andrews, Ralph W. *Curtis' Western Indians*. Seattle: Superior, 1962.

Archibald, Robert. "Acculturation and Assimilation in Colonial New Mexico." *New Mexico Historical Review* 53 (1978): 205–17.

Assembly Herald 6 (June 1902).

Austin, Buck. "We Have Lived on Livestock a Long Time." In *Navajo Historical Selections*, edited by Robert W. Young and William Morgan, editors, 62. Phoenix: Bureau of Indian Affairs, 1954.

Axtell, James, "The White Indians of Colonial America." *William and Mary Quarterly* 32 (January 1975): 55–88.

_____. *The European and the Indian: Essays in the Ethnohistory of Colonial North America.* New York: Oxford: Oxford University Press, 1981.

_____. *The Invasion Within: The Contest of Cultures in Colonial North America*. New York and Oxford: Oxford University Press, 1985.

Bass, Althea. *Cherokee Messenger*. Norman: University of Oklahoma Press, 1936.

Bataille, Gretchen M., and Kathleen Mullen Sands. *American Indian Women Telling Their Lives*. Lincoln: University of Nebraska Press, 1984

Bataille, Gretchen M., and Charles L. P. Silet. *The Pretend Indians: Images of Native Americans in the Movies*. Ames: Iowa State University Press, 1980.

Beardslee, L. A. Reports of Captain L. A. Beardslee, U.S. Navy Relative to Affairs in Alaska, and the Operations of the U.S.S. *Jamestown* under His Command, while in the Waters of that Territory. January 24, 1882. 47th Cong., 1st sess., 1882, Sen. Ex. Doc. No. 71.

Beattie, William Gilbert. *Marsden of Alaska, A Modern Indian: Minister, Missionary, Musician, Engineer, Pilot, Boat Builder and Church Builder*. New York: Vintage Press, 1955.

Beauchamp, William M. *Life of Conrad Weiser as It Relates to his Services as Official Interpreter Between New York and Pennsylvania and as Envoy Between Philadelphia and the Onondaga Councils*. Syracuse: Onondaga Historical Association, 1925.

Beninato, Stefanie. "Popé, Pose-yemu, and Naranjo: A New Look at Leadership in the Pueblo Revolt of 1680." *New Mexico Historical Review* 65 (October 1990): 417–35.

Berkhofer, Jr., Robert F. "The Political Context of a New Indian History." *Pacific Historical Review* 40 (August 1971): 357–82.

_____. *Salvation and the Savage*. New York: Atheneum Press, 1976.

Berthong, D. J. "Struggle for Power: The Impact of Southern Cheyenne and Arapaho 'Schoolboys' on Tribal Politics." *American Indian Quarterly* 16 (Winter 1992): 1–24.

Blackman, Margaret B. *Sadie Brower, Naekok: An Inupiaq Woman*. Seattle: University of Washington Press, 1989.

Blackstone, Sarah J. *Buckskin, Bullets, and Business: A History of Buffalo Bill's Wild West*. Westport, Conn.: Greenwood Press, 1986.

Blakeslee, Donald J. "The Origin and Spread of the Calumet Ceremony." *American Antiquity* 46 (October 1981): 761–62.

Blair, Emma H., ed. *The Indian Tribes of the Upper Mississippi Valley and Region of the Great Lakes*. 2 vols. Cleveland: Arthur H. Clark, 1911.

Blodgett, Harold. *Samson Occom*. Hanover: Dartmouth College Publications, 1935.

Boudinot, Elias. *An Address to the Whites*. Philadelphia: Gedden, 1826.

Bowden, Henry W., and James P. Ronda, eds. *John Eliot's Indian Dia-*

logues: A Study in Cultural Interaction. Westport, Conn.: Greenwood Press, 1985.

Brady, John Green, Papers, Beinecke Rare Book and Manuscript Library, Yale University, New Haven, Conn.

Brandt, Elizabeth. "On Secrecy and the Control of Knowledge: Taos Pueblo." In *Secrecy: A Cross-Cultural Perspective,* edited by Stanton Tefft, 123–46. New York: Human Sciences Press, 1980.

Brody, J. J. *Indian Painters and White Patrons.* Albuquerque: University of New Mexico Press, 1971.

Brownlow, Kevin. *The War, the West and the Wilderness.* New York: Alfred A. Knopf, 1979.

Brumble, H. David. *An Annotated Bibliography of American Indian and Eskimo Autobiographies.* Lincoln: University of Nebraska Press, 1981.

––––––. *American Indian Autobiography.* Berkeley and Los Angeles: University of California Press, 1988.

Carter, Clarence E., ed. *The Territorial Papers of the United States: The Territory of Illinois, 1809–1814.* Washington, D.C.: Government Printing Office, 1948.

––––––. *The Territorial Papers of the United States: The Territory of Missouri, 1815–1821.* Washington, D.C.: Government Printing Office, 1951.

Charney, Paul. "The Implications of Godparental Ties Between Indians and Spaniards in Colonial Lima." *The Americas* 47 (April 1991): 295–314.

Chase, Frederick. *A History of Dartmouth College and the Town of Hanover, New Hampshire (to 1815).* 2d ed. Vol. 1. Brattleboro: Vermont Printing Co., 1929.

Chávez, Fray Angélico. *Origins of New Mexico Families in the Spanish Colonial Period.* Santa Fe: Historical Society of New Mexico, 1954.

––––––. "Pohé-yemo's Representative and the Pueblo Revolt of 1680." *New Mexico Historical Review* 42 (April 1967): 85–126.

––––––. "Genízaros." In *Southwest.* Vol. 9, *Handbook of North American Indians.* Edited by Alfonso Ortiz, 198–200. Washington, D.C.: Smithsonian Institution, 1979.

Chesham, Sallie. *Born to Battle: The Salvation Army in America.* New York: Rand McNally & Co., 1965.

Chona, Maria. *Papago Woman.* Edited by Ruth Underhill. New York: Holt, Rinehart and Winston, 1979. (Reprinted from *Memoirs of the American Anthropological Association,* number 46 (1936) under the title *The Autobiography of a Papago Woman.*)

Clark, Ann Nolan. *Little Herder in Summer* (Shį́įgo Na'nikkaadi' Yazhi). Phoenix: Bureau of Indian Affairs, 1942.

_____. *Singing Sioux Cowboy*. Lawrence, Kans.: Bureau of Indian Affairs, 1954.

Clifford, James. "Histories of the Tribal and the Modern" and other essays. In *The Predicament of Culture*. Cambridge and London: Harvard University Press, 1988.

Clifton, James A., ed. *Being and Becoming Indian: Biographical Studies of North American Frontiers*. Chicago: Dorsey Press, 1989.

Codere, Helen. Introduction in Franz Boas, *Kwakiutl Ethnography*, edited by Helen Codere. Chicago: University of Chicago Press, 1966.

Colden, Cadwallader. Papers. 9 vols. New York Historical Society *Collections*, vols. 50–56, 67–68. New York: Printed for the New York Historical Society, 1917–23, 1937.

Coleman, Michael C. "Western Education, American Indian and African Children: A Comparative Study of Pupil Motivation Through Published Reminiscences, 1860s–1960s. *Canadian and International Education* 18 (1989): 36–53.

_____. *American Indian Children at School, 1850–1930*. Jackson: University Press of Mississippi, 1993.

Courlander, Harold, ed. *Hopi Voices: Recollections, Traditions, and Narratives of the Hopi Indians*. Albuquerque: University of New Mexico Press, 1982.

Curtis, Edward S. *The North American Indian*. Edited by Frederick Webb Hodge. 20 vols., 20 portfolios. Cambridge and Norwood, Conn.: University Press and Plimpton Press, 1907–30.

Cushing, Frank Hamilton. "Outline of Zuni Creation Myths." In *Thirteenth Annual Report of the Bureau of Ethnology, 1891–92*. Washington, D.C.: Government Printing Office, 1896.

Daniell, Jere. "Eleazar Wheelock and the Dartmouth College Charter." *Historical New Hampshire* 24 (Winter 1969): 3–44.

Darlington, William M. "The Montours." *Pennsylvania Magazine of History and Biography* 4 (1880): 218–25.

_____. *Christopher Gist's Journals with Historical, Geographical, and Ethnological Notes and Biographies of His Contemporaries*. New York: Argonaut Press, 1966.

Davis, Mary Lee. *We Are Alaskans*. Boston: W. A. Wilde Co., 1931.

Deagan, Kathleen. *Spanish St. Augustine: The Archaeology of a Colonial Creole Community*. New York: Academic Press, 1983.

Deloria, Jr., Vine. *Custer Died for Your Sins*. 1969. New York: Avon Books, 1971.

DeMallie, Raymond J., ed. *The Sixth Grandfather: Black Elk's Teachings Given to John G. Neihardt*. Lincoln and London: University of Nebraska Press, 1984.

Dictionary of Canadian Biography. Edited by George W. Brown et al. Toronto: University of Toronto Press, 1966– .

Dippie, Brian. *The Vanishing American: White Attitudes and U.S. Indian Policy*. Middletown: Wesleyan University Press, 1982.

Dozier, Edward P. *The Pueblo Indians of North America*. New York: Holt, Rinehart and Winston, 1970.

Duke, Doris, Tapes, Navajo Tribe, Special Collections, Zimmerman Library, University of New Mexico, Albuquerque.

Dunn, Dorothy. Personal Papers. Private Collection, Santa Fe, New Mex.

_____. "The Art of Pablita Velarde." *El Palacio* 64 (July-August 1957): 231–32.

Edmunds, R. David, ed. *Studies in Diversity, American Indian Leaders*. Lincoln: University of Nebraska Press, 1980.

Ellis, Florence Hawley. "Pueblo Boundaries and Their Markers." *Annual Report, Museum of Northern Arizona, Nineteen Hundred and Sixty-Five*. Supplement to *Plateau* 38, 4 (Spring 1966): 97–105.

_____. "Comments on Four Papers Pertaining to the Protohistoric Southwest." In *The Protohistoric Period in the North American Southwest*, A.D. *1450–1700*, 378–433. Tempe: Arizona State University, 1981.

Espinosa, J. Manuel. *Crusaders of the Río Grande: The Story of Don Diego de Vargas and the Reconquest and Refounding of New Mexico*. Chicago: Institute of Jesuit History, 1942.

_____. ed. *First Expedition of Vargas into New Mexico, 1692*. Albuquerque: University of New Mexico Press, 1940.

Ewers, John C. "William Clark's Indian Museum in St. Louis, 1816–1838." In *A Cabinet of Curiosities: Five Episodes in the Evolution of American Museums,* edited by Walter Muir Whitehill. Charlottesville: University of Virginia Press, 1967.

Fausz, J. Frederick. "'Middlemen in Peace and War': Virginia's Earliest Indian Interpreters, 1608–1632." *Journal of American History* 75 (June 1988): 41–64.

Feest, Christian F., ed. *Indians and Europe: An Interdisciplinary Collection of Essays*. Aachen, Germany: Rader Verlag, 1987.

Fenton, William N., and John Gulick, eds. *Symposium on Cherokee and Iroquois Culture*. Washington, D.C.: Smithsonian Institution, Bureau of American Ethnology, bulletin 180, 1961.

Finger, John R. *The Eastern Band of the Cherokees, 1819–1900*. Knoxville: University of Tennessee Press, 1984.

Fletcher, Alice, *The Omaha Tribe*. With Francis La Flesche. Smithsonian Institution, Bureau of American Ethnology, 27th Annual Report, 1905–1906, Washington, D.C., 1911.

Fowler, Loretta. *Arapahoe Politics, 1851–1978: Symbols in Crises of Authority.* Lincoln: University of Nebraska Press, 1982.

Frazier, Patrick. *The Mohicans of Stockbridge.* Lincoln: University of Nebraska Press, 1992.

Friar, Ralph E., and Natasha A. Friar, *The Only Good Indian: The Hollywood Gospel.* New York: Drama Book Specialists, 1972.

Fuller, Harlin M., and Leroy R. Hafen, eds. *The Journal of Captain John R. Bell.* Glendale: Arthur H. Clark, 1973.

Gearing, Fred. *Priests and Warriors: Social Structures for Cherokee Politics in the 18th Century.* Menasha, Wis.: American Anthropological Association, memoir 93, 1962.

Georgia Historical Quarterly 73 (Fall 1989). Special Issue Commemorating the Sesquicentennial of Cherokee Removal, 1838–39.

Gibson, Arrell Morgan. *The American Indian: Prehistory to the Present.* Lexington: D. C. Heath & Co., 1980.

Gidley, Mick. "The Vanishing Race in Sight and Sound: Edward S. Curtis' Musicale of North American Indian Life." In *Prospects: An Annual of American Cultural Studies,* no. 12, edited by Jack Salzman, 59–87. New York: Cambridge University Press, 1987.

————. "The Repeated Return of the Vanishing Indian." In *American Studies: Essays in Honour of Marcus Cunliffe,* edited by Brian Holden Reid and John White, 189–209. London: Macmillan, 1991.

Goetzmann, William H., and Kay Sloan. *Looking Far North: The Harriman Alaska Expedition, 1899.* Princeton: Princeton University Press, 1982.

Goldman, Irving. *The Mouth of Heaven: An Introduction to Kwakiutl Religious Thought.* New York and London: John Wiley, 1975.

Gray, Samuel L. *Tonita Peña: Quah Ah, 1893–1949.* Albuquerque: Avanyu Publishing, 1990.

Graybill, Florence Curtis, and Victor Boesen. *Edward Sheriff Curtis: Visions of a Vanishing Race.* New York: Crowell, 1976.

Green, Rayna. "The Tribe Called Wannabee: Playing Indian in America and Europe." *Folklore* 99, no. 1 (Winter 1988): 30–55.

Greene, Evarts B., and Clarence W. Alvord, eds. *The Governor's Letterbooks, 1818–1834.* Springfield: Illinois State Historical Library, 1909.

Greenfield, Jeanette. *The Return of Cultural Treasures.* Cambridge and New York: Cambridge University Press, 1989.

Gutiérrez, Ramón A. *When Jesus Came, the Corn Mothers Went Away: Marriage, Sexuality, And Power in New Mexico, 1500–1846.* Stanford: Stanford University Press, 1991.

Hackett, Charles Wilson, ed. *Revolt of the Pueblo Indians of New Mexico and Otermín's Attempted Reconquest, 1680–1682.* Translated by

Carmon Clair Shelby. Albuquerque: University of New Mexico Press, 1942.

Hagan, William T. *The Sac and Fox Indians.* Norman: University of Oklahoma Press, 1958.

_____. *Indian Police and Judges: Experiments in Acculturation and Control.* Lincoln: University of Nebraska Press, 1966.

_____. *Reflections on the Reservation System; Joshua Given: Kiowa Indian and Carlisle Alumnus.* N.p.: N.p., 1979.

_____. *American Indians.* Chicago: University of Chicago Press, 1961.

Hagedorn, Nancy L. "'A Friend To Go Between Them': The Interpreter as Cultural Broker During Anglo-Iroquois Councils, 1740-1770." *Ethnohistory* 35 (Winter 1988): 60-80.

Halliburton, R. *Red Over Black.* Westport, Conn.: Greenwood Press, 1978.

Hallowell, Irving A. "American Indians, White and Black: The Phenomenon of Transculturalization." *Current Anthropology* 4 (December 1963): 519-29.

Hamilton, Kenneth G., trans. and ed. *Bethlehem Diary.* Bethlehem, Pa.: Archives of the Moravian Church, 1971.

Hammerschlag, Carl A. *The Dancing Healers: A Doctor's Journey of Healing with Native Americans.* San Francisco: Harper & Row, 1988.

Hanna, Charles A. *The Wilderness Trail.* 2 vols. New York: G. P. Putnam's Sons, 1911.

Harrington, John P., to M. W. Stirling, October 28, 1940. John P. Harrington Papers, National Anthropological Archives, Smithsonian Institution.

Hawley, Florence. "The Keresan Holy Rollers: An Adaptation to American Individualism." *Social Forces* 26 (1948): 272-80.

Hayes, Florence. *A Land of Challenge: Alaska.* New York: Board of National Missions of the Presbyterian Church of the United States of America, 1940.

Hazard, Samuel, ed. *Minutes of the Provincial Council of Pennsylvania, from the Organization to the Termination of the Proprietary Government* (spine title *Colonial Records of Pennsylvania*). 10 vols. Harrisburg, Pa.: Theo. Fenn & Co., 1851–1852.

Hecht, Robert A. *Oliver La Farge and the American Indian: Biography.* Metuchen, N.J.: Scarecrow Press, 1991.

"Helen Hunt Jackson's Life and Writings." *Literary News.* Baltimore: Cushings & Bailey Booksellers and Stationers, April 1887.

Helm, June, ed. *Pioneers of American Anthropology: The Uses of Biography.* Seattle: University of Washington Press, 1966. Especially the essays by Nancy Oestereich Lurie and Ronald P. Rohner on women in early American anthropology and Franz Boas, respectively.

Helms, Mary W. "Time, History, and the Future of Anthropology: Observations on Some Unresolved Issues." *Ethnohistory* 25 (Winter 1978): 1–13.

Hendricks, Rick. "Levels of Discourse in Early Modern Spanish: The Papers of Diego de Vargas, 1643–1704." *North Dakota Quarterly* 58 (Fall 1990): 124–39.

Hertzberg, Hazel. *The Search for an American Indian Identity: Modern Pan-Indian Movements.* Syracuse: Syracuse University Press, 1971.

Higginson, Thomas Wentworth. "Helen Hunt Jackson." *Nation* 41 (August 20, 1885): 151.

———. "Helen Jackson." *The Critic,* N.S. 4 (August 22, 1885): 86.

———. "Mrs. Helen Jackson ("H. H.")." *Century Magazine* 31, N.S. (November 1885): 254.

———. "How Ramona Was Written." *Atlantic Monthly* 86 (November 1900): 712–14.

Hill, W. W. *An Ethnography of Santa Clara Pueblo, New Mexico.* Edited and annotated by Charles H. Lange. Albuquerque: University of New Mexico Press, 1982.

Hodge, Frank Webb. *History of Hawikuh, New Mexico.* Los Angeles: Southwest Museum, 1937.

Holm, Bill, and George I. Quimby. *Edward S. Curtis in the Land of the War Canoes: A Pioneer Cinematographer in the Pacific Northwest.* Seattle and London: University of Washington Press, 1980.

Holmberg, Allan. "Participant Intervention in the Field." *Human Organization* 14 (Spring 1955): 23–26.

———. "The Research and Development Approach to the Study of Change." *Human Organization* 17 (Spring 1958): 12–16.

Hudson, Charles. *The Southeastern Indians.* Knoxville: University of Tennessee Press, 1976.

Hyer, Sally. *One House, One Voice, One Heart: Native American Education at the Santa Fe Indian School.* Santa Fe: Museum of New Mexico Press, 1990.

———. *"Woman's Work": The Art of Pablita Velarde.* Santa Fe: Wheelwright Museum of the American Indian, 1993.

Indian Claims Commission. *Arapaho-Cheyenne Indians.* New York: Garland Publishing, 1974.

Iverson, Peter. *The Navajo Nation.* Albuquerque: University of New Mexico Press, 1983.

———. "Building Toward Self-Determination: Plains and Southwestern Indians in the 1940s and 1950s." *Western Historical Quarterly* 16 (April 1985): 163–73.

Jacknis, Ira. "Franz Boas and Photography." *Studies in Visual Communication* 10, no.1 (Winter 1984): 2–60.

Jackson, Helen Hunt. *Glimpses of Three Coasts.* Boston: Roberts Brothers, 1886.

———. [H. H., pseud.]. "The Indian Problem: Questions for the American People." *New York Daily Tribune,* 15 December 1879, 4.

———. "A Small Matter to Murder an Indian: 'H.H.' Scores Another Point." *New York Daily Tribune,* 25 January 1880, 5.

———. "The Starving Utes: More Questions for the People by 'H.H.' What White men have done and are doing to Indians in Colorado." *New York Daily Tribune,* 5 February 1880, 5.

———. "The Sand Creek Massacre: A Slaughter of Friendly Indians." *New York Daily Tribune,* 24 February 1880, 2.

———. "Justifiable Homicide in Southern California." *New York Independent,* 27 September 1883, 2.

Jackson, Sheldon. *Alaska and Missions on the North Pacific Coast.* New York: Dodd, Mead & Co., 1880.

———. Report of the General Agent, Office of the General Agent of Education in Alaska, Sitka, June 30, 1887, to the Territorial Board of Education. Schools in Alaska. In Bureau of Education, Report of the Commissioner for 1886–1887. 50th Cong., 1st sess., H.R. Ex. Doc. 1, pt. 5, v. 2, serial 2545.

———. Education in Alaska, 1890–1891. Reprint of chap. 25, Bureau of Education, Report of the Commissioner of Education for 1890–91. Washington, D.C.: U.S. Government Printing Office, 1893. [Also in 52d Cong., 1st sess., H.R. Ex. Doc. 1, pt. 5, v. 5, pt. 2, serial 2939.]

———. Education in Alaska, 1896–1897. reprint of chap. 35, Bureau of Education, Report of the Commissioner for 1896–97. Washington, D.C.: U.S. Government Printing Office, 1898 [Also in 55th Cong., 2d sess., H.R. Doc. 5, pt. 2, serial 3650.]

———. "Alaska." In *Lake Mohonk Conference, Friends of the Indian, Report of the 20th Annual Meeting, 1902* (Philadelphia, 1902): 31–38.

———. Correspondence, Alaska State Historical Library, Juneau, Alaska.

———. Correspondence, Presbyterian Historical Society, Philadelphia.

———. Scrapbook Collection. Vol. 5. Presbyterian Historical Society.

Jacobs, Wilbur. *Diplomacy and Indian Gifts: Anglo-French Rivalry Along the Ohio and Northwest Frontiers, 1748–1763.* Stanford: Stanford University Press, 1950.

James, George Wharton. *Through Ramona's Country.* Boston: Little Brown and Company, 1913.

Jennings, Francis. "A Growing Partnership: Historians, Anthropologists, and American Indian History." *Ethnohistory* 29, 1 (1971): 21–34.

Jennings, Francis, et al., eds. *Iroquois Indians: A Documentary History of the Diplomacy of the Six Nations and Their League.* Woodbridge, Conn.: Research Publications, 1984. Microfilm.

Johnson, Sir William. *The Papers of Sir William Johnson.* 14 vols. Edited by Alexander C. Flick et al. Albany: State University of New York, 1921–62.

Josephy, Alvin. *The Patriot Chiefs.* New York: Viking Press, 1971.

Kappler, Charles J., comp. *Indians Treaties, 1778–1883.* New York: Interland Publishing Company, 1972.

Kellaway, William. *The New England Company, 1649–1776.* London: Longman, Green & Co., 1961.

Kessell, John L. "Diego Romero, the Plains Apaches, and the Inquisition." *American West* 15, 3 (May–June 1978): 12–16.

――――. "Esteban Clemente, Precursor of the Pueblo Revolt." *El Palacio* 86, 4 (Winter 1980–81): 16–17.

――――. *Kiva, Cross, and Crown: The Pecos Indians and New Mexico, 1540–1840.* Albuquerque: University of New Mexico Press, 1989.

――――. "Spaniards and Pueblos: From Crusading Intolerance to Pragmatic Accommodation." In *Archaeological and Historical Perspectives on the Spanish Boderlands West.* Vol. 1, *Columbian Consequences,* edited by David Hurst Thomas, 127–38. Washington, D.C.: Smithsonian Institution, 1989.

Kessell, John L., and Rick Hendricks, eds. *By Force of Arms: The Journals of don Diego de Vargas, New Mexico, 1691-93.* Albuquerque: University of New Mexico Press, 1992.

Kessell, John L., Rick Hendricks, Meredith D. Dodge, Larry D. Miller, and Eleanore B. Adams, eds. *Remote Beyond Compare: Letters of don Diego de Vargas to His Family from New Spain and New Mexico, 1675–1706.* Albuquerque: University of New Mexico Press, 1989.

Kroeber, Alfred L. *The Arapaho.* Foreword by Fred Eggan. Lincoln: University of Nebraska Press, 1983.

La Flesche, Francis. *The Osage Tribe,* Part One. "Role of the Chief, Sayings of the Ancient Men." Smithsonian Institution, Bureau of American Ethnology, 36th Annual Report, 1914–15. Washington, D.C., 1921, pp. 43–497.

――――. *The Osage Tribe,* Part Two. "The Rite of Vigil. Smithsonian Institution, Bureau of American Ethnology, 39th Annual Report, 1917–18. Washington, D.C., 1925, pp. 37–630.

――――. *The Osage Tribe,* Part Three. "Two Versions of the Child-Naming Rite." Smithsonian Institution, Bureau of American Ethnology, 43rd Annual Report, 1925–26. Washington, D.C., 1928, pp. 29–820.

_____. *The Osage Tribe*, Part Four. "Rite of the Wa-xo'-be and Shrine Degree." Smithsonian Institution, Bureau of American Ethnology, 45th Annual Report, 1927–28. Washington, D.C., 1930, pp. 529–833.

Laird, Carobeth. *Encounters with an Angry God: Recollections of My Life with John Peabody Harrington.* New York: Ballantine, 1977.

Lewin, Howard. "A Frontier Diplomat: Andrew Montour." *Pennsylvania History* 33 (April 1966): 153–86.

Liberty, Margot, ed. *American Indian Intellectuals.* St. Paul: West, 1978.

Littlefield, Jr., Daniel F. *The Cherokee Freedmen.* Westport, Conn.: Greenwood Press, 1978.

Littlefield, Jr., Daniel F., and James W. Parins. *A Bio-bibliography of Native American Authors, 1772–1924.* Metuchen, N.J., and London: Scarecrow, 1981.

Love, William DeLoss. *Samson Occom and the Christian Indians of New England.* Boston: Pilgrim Press, 1899.

Lowie, Robert E. "My Crow Interpreter." In *In the Company of Man: Twenty Portraits of Anthropological Informants*, edited by Joseph B. Casagrande, 427–37. New York: Harper Torchbook, 1964.

Lurie, Nancy Oestreich. "The Contemporary American Indian Scene." In *North American Indians in Historical Perspective*, edited by Eleanor Burke Leacock and Nancy Oestreich Lurie, 418–80. New York: Random House, 1971.

_____. ed., *Mountain Wolf Woman, Sister of Crashing Thunder, The Autobiography of a Winnebago Indian.* 1961. Ann Arbor: University of Michigan Press, 1974.

Lyman, Christopher M. *The Vanishing Race and Other Illusions: Photographs of Indians by Edward S. Curtis.* Washington, D.C.: Smithsonian Institution Press, 1982.

Malone, Michael P., and Richard W. Etulain. *The American West: A Twentieth-Century History.* Lincoln: University of Nebraska Press, 1989.

Mark, Joan. *A Stranger in Her Native Land, Alice Fletcher and the American Indians.* Lincoln: University of Nebraska Press, 1988.

Marshe, Witham. "Journal of the Treaty . . . at Lancaster in Pennsylvania, June 1744." Massachusetts Historical Society *Collections,* 1st ser., vol. 7, 171–201. Reprinted as *Lancaster in 1744.* Edited by William H. Egle. Lancaster, Pa.: New Era Steam Book & Job Print, 1884.

Martin, Calvin. *The American Indian and the Problem of History.* New York: Oxford University Press, 1987.

Mathes, Valerie Sherer. *Helen Hunt Jackson and Her Indian Reform Legacy.* Austin: University of Texas Press, 1990.

McCallum, James Dow. *The Letters of Eleazar Wheelock's Indians.* Hanover: Dartmouth College Publications, 1932.

_____. *Eleazar Wheelock, Founder of Dartmouth College.* Hanover: Dartmouth College Publications, 1939.

McClintock, Eva, ed. *Life in Alaska: Letters of Mrs. Eugene S. Willard.* Philadelphia: Presbyterian Board of Education, 1884.

McClure, David, and Elijah Parish. *Memoirs of the Rev. Eleazar Wheelock.* Newburyport, Mass.: Edward Norris and Co., 1811.

McConnell, Michael N. "Peoples 'In Between': The Iroquois and the Ohio Indians, 1720–1768." In *Beyond the Covenant Chain: The Iroquois and Their Neighbors in Indian North America, 1600–1800,* edited by Daniel K. Richter and James H. Merrell. Syracuse: Syracuse University Press, 1987.

McFee, Malcolm. "The 150% Man, A Product of Blackfeet Acculturation." *American Anthropologist* 70 (1968): 1096–1103.

McLoughlin, William G. *Cherokees and Missionaries, 1789–1839.* New Haven: Yale University Press, 1984.

_____. *Cherokee Renascence in the New Republic.* Princeton: Princeton University Press, 1986.

_____. *Champions of the Cherokees: Evan and John B. Jones.* Princeton: Princeton University Press, 1989.

McLoughlin, William G., and Walter H. Conser, Jr. "The Cherokees in Transition: A Statistical Analysis of the Federal Cherokee Census of 1835." *Journal of American History* 64 (December 1977): 678–703.

McNickle, D'Arcy. "Process or Compulsion: The Search for a Policy of Administration in Indian Affairs." In *American Indigena* (July 1957).

_____. "The Surfacing of Native Leadership." *In Patterns of Amerindian Identity, Symposium, Montmorency, Quebec, October 1974.* Quebec: Les Presses de l'Université Laval, 1976.

_____. *The Surrounded.* New York: Dodd, Mead, 1936; reprint ed. with an afterword by Lawrence W. Towner. Albuquerque: University of New Mexico Press, 1978.

_____. *Wind from an Enemy Sky.* New York: Harper & Row, 1978; reprint ed. with an afterword by Louis Owens. Albuquerque: University of New Mexico Press, 1988.

_____. *Indian Man: A Life of Oliver La Farge.* Bloomington: Indiana University Press, 1991.

_____. *The Hawk Is Hungry and Other Stories.* Edited by Birgit Hans. Tucson: University of Arizona Press, 1992.

_____. "A Battle Yet to Wage." In Papers of the National Congress of American Indians, Smithsonian Institution.

McNickle, D'Arcy, and Viola Pfrommer. "Dine Txah." In McNickle Papers, Newberry Library, Chicago.

Mercer, George. *Papers Relating to the Ohio Company of Virginia.* Edited by Lois Mulkearn. Pittsburgh: University of Pittsburgh Press, 1954.

Metcalf, Richard P. "Who Shall Rule at Home? Native American Politics and Indian-White Relations." *Journal of American History* 61 (December 1974): 651–65.

Montgomery, Ross Gordon, Watson Smith, and John Otis Brew. *Franciscan Awatovi.* Cambridge: Peabody Museum, 1949.

Mooney, James. *Historical Sketch of the Cherokee.* 1900. Reprint. Chicago: Aldine, 1975.

Moses, L. G. "Wild West Shows, Reformers, and the Image of the American Indian, 1887–1914." *South Dakota History* 14 (Fall 1984): 193–221.

_____. "Indians on the Midway: Wild West Shows and the Indian Bureau at World's Fairs, 1893–1904." *South Dakota History* 21 (Fall 1991): 205–29.

Moses, L. G., and Raymond Wilson, eds. *Indian Lives: Essays on Nineteenth- and Twentieth-Century Native American Leaders.* Albuquerque: University of New Mexico Press, 1985.

Moulton, Gary E. *John Ross: Cherokee Chief.* Athens: University of Georgia Press, 1978.

Muck, Lee. "Survey of the Resources and Livestock Economy of the Navajo Indian Reservation." Mimeograph. Washington, D.C.: Department of the Interior, 1948. 30–32.

Muhr, Adolf. "E. S. Curtis and His Work." *Photo-Era* (July 1907): 9–13.

Murra, John V., ed. *American Anthropology: The Early Years.* St. Paul: West, 1978.

Murray, David. *Forked Tongues: Speech, Writing and Representation in North American Indian Texts.* Bloomington and Indianapolis: Indiana University Press, 1991.

Nash, Gary B. *Red, White and Black: The Peoples of Early America.* Englewood Cliffs, N.J.: Prentice-Hall, 1974.

The Navajo Trail. Yearbook of Charles Burke School (Fort Wingate High School), Fort Wingate, New Mex., 1936. Copy in the possession of Peter Iverson.

Neihardt, John G. *Black Elk Speaks.* Lincoln: University of Nebraska Press, 1961.

Nelson, Mary Carroll. *Pablita Velarde.* Minneapolis: Dillon Press, 1971.

North Star (Sitka, Alaska): Vol. 2, no. 4 (March 1889), no. 5 (April 1889), no. 9 (August 1889); vol. 3, no. 1 (December 1889), no. 6 (May 1890), no. 10 (September 1890), no. 12 (November 1890); vol. 4, no. 1 (December 1890), no. 2 (January 1891), no. 3 (February

1891), no. 4 (March 1891), no. 5 (April 1891), no. 11 (October 1891), no. 12 (November 1891); vol. 5, no. 3 (February 1892), no. 5 (April 1892).

Occom, Samson. Diary. Dartmouth College Archives, Hanover, N.H.

Odell, Ruth. *Helen Hunt Jackson (H. H.)*. New York: D. Appleton-Century Company, 1939.

Opler, Morris E. *Apache Odyssey, a Journey Between Two Worlds*. New York: Holt, Rinehart and Winston, 1969.

Ortiz, Alfonso. *The Tewa World: Space, Time, Being, and Becoming in a Pueblo Society*. Chicago: University of Chicago Press, 1969.

———. "Popay's Leadership: A Pueblo Perspective." *El Palacio* 86, 4 (Winter 1980-81): 18–22.

———, ed. *Southwest*. Vol. 9, *Handbook of North American Indians*. Washington, D.C.: Smithsonian Institution, 1983.

Paine, Robert, ed. *Patrons and Brokers in the East Arctic*. Newfoundland Social and Economic papers no.2. Memorial University of Newfoundland. N.p.: University of Toronto Press, 1971.

Painter, Charles C. *A Visit to the Mission Indians of Southern California and Other Western Tribes*. Philadelphia: Office of the Indian Rights Association, 1886.

Parker, Dorothy R. "D'Arcy McNickle: An Annotated Bibliography of His Published Articles and Book Reviews in a Biographical Context." *American Indian Culture and Research Journal* 14 (1990): 55–75.

———. *Singing an Indian Song: A Biography of D'Arcy McNickle*. Lincoln: University of Nebraska Press, 1992.

Parman, Donald L., and Catherine Price. "'A Work in Progress': The Emergence of Indian History as a Professional Field." *Western Historical Quarterly* 20 (May 1989): 184–96.

Parsons, Elsie Clews. *Isleta Paintings*. Edited by Esther Goldfrank. Washington, D.C.: Smithsonian Institution, 1962.

Pasztor, Suzanne B. "Between Cultures: The Genízaros of New Mexico." *Best Student Essays of the University of New Mexico* 1, 1 (1989): 26–32.

Paul, Tillie. "My First Trip." *North Star* 3, no. 7 (June 1890): 3.

Payne, John Howard. Papers. Vol. 8. Newberry Library, Chicago.

Pennsylvania Archives. 9 series. 138 vols. Philadelphia and Harrisburg, 1852–1949.

Perdue, Theda. *Slavery and the Evolution of Cherokee Society, 1540–1866*. Knoxville: University of Tennessee Press, 1979.

———. "Southern Indians and the Cult of True Womanhood." In *The Web of Southern Social Relations: Women, Family, and Education*, edited by Walter J. Fraser, Jr., et al., 35–51. Athens: University of Georgia Press, 1985.

———, ed. "Letters from Brainerd." *Journal of Cherokee Studies* (Winter 1979): 4–8.

Peterson, Jacqueline. "Many Roads to Red River: Métis Genesis in the Great Lakes Region, 1680–1815." In *Being and Becoming Métis in North America,* edited by Jacqueline Peterson and Jennifer S. H. Brown. Manitoba Studies in Native History 1. Lincoln: University of Nebraska Press, 1985.

Peterson, Jacqueline, and Jennifer S. H. Brown, eds. *The New Peoples: Being and Becoming Métis in North America.* N.p.: University of Manitoba Press, 1985.

Peyer, Bernd. *The Singing Spirit: Early Short Stories by Native American Indians.* Tucson: University of Arizona Press, 1990.

Pfaller, Louis. "Enemies in '76, Friends in '85." *Prologue* 1 (Fall 1969): 17–31.

Prucha, Francis Paul. *American Indian Policy in Crisis: Christian Reformers and the Indian, 1865–1900.* Norman: University of Oklahoma Press, 1976.

———. "A 'Friend of the Indian' in Milwaukee: Mrs. O. J. Hiles and the Wisconsin Indian Association." *Indian Policy in the United States: Historical Essays.* Lincoln: University of Nebraska Press, 1981.

———. *Indian-White Relations in the United States: A Bibliography of Works Published 1975–1980.* Lincoln: University of Nebraska Press, 1982.

———, ed. *A Bibliographical Guide to the History of Indian-White Relations in the United States.* Chicago: University of Chicago Press, 1977.

Purdy, John Lloyd. *Word Ways: The Novels of D'Arcy McNickle.* Tucson: University of Arizona Press, 1990.

Radin, Paul, ed. *Crashing Thunder, the Autobiography of an American Indian.* 1926. Lincoln: University of Nebraska Press, 1983.

Reichel, William C., ed. *Memorials of the Moravian Church.* Philadelphia: Lippincott, 1870.

Replogle, Charles. *Among the Indians of Alaska.* London: Headley Bros., 1904.

Richardson, Leon Burr. *An Indian Preacher in England.* 1933. Reprint. Hanover: Dartmouth College Publications, 1939.

Richter, Daniel K. "Cultural Brokers and Intercultural Politics: New York–Iroquois Relations, 1664–1701." *Journal of American History* 75 (June 1988): 40–67.

———. *Ordeal of the Longhouse: The People of the Iroquois League in the Era of European Colonization.* Chapel Hill: University of North Carolina Press, 1992.

Ritzenthaler, Robert. "From Folk Art to Fine Art: The Emergence of the

Name Artist among the Southwest Indians." In *The Visual Arts: Plastic and Graphic,* edited by Justine Cordwell, 431–38. The Hague: Mouton, 1979.

Roberts, Arthur O. *Tomorrow Is Growing Old: Stories of the Quakers in Alaska.* Newberg, Ore.: Barclay Press, 1978.

Ronda, James P. "Red and White at the Bench: Indians and the Law in Plymouth Colony, 1620–1691." *Essex Institute Historical Collections* 110 (July 1974): 200–15.

Rosa, Joseph G., and Robin May. *Buffalo Bill and His Wild West.* Lawrence: University Press of Kansas, 1989.

Sahlins, Marshall. "Other Times, Other Customs; The Anthropology of History." *American Anthropologist* 85 (September 1983): 517–44.

Sainsbury, Noel, et al., eds. *Calendar of State Papers, Colonial Series, America and West Indies.* London: Her Majesty's Stationery Office, 1860– .

Salisbury, Neal. *Manitou and Providence, Indians, Europeans, and the Making of New England, 1500–1643.* New York and Oxford: Oxford University Press, 1982.

Salwen, Bert. "Indians of Southern New England and Long Island: Early Period." In *Handbook of North American Indians.* Vol. 15, *Northeast,* ed. by Bruce G. Trigger, 160–76. Washington, D.C.: Smithsonian Institution, 1978.

Sando, Joe S. *Pueblo Nations: Eight Centuries of Pueblo Indian History.* Santa Fe: Clear Light, 1992.

Sarf, Wayne Michael. *God Bless You, Buffalo Bill: A Layman's Guide to History and the Western Film.* New York: Associated University Press, 1983.

Schoolcraft, Henry Rowe. *A View of the Lead Mines of Missouri.* New York: Charles Wiley, 1819.

Sell, Henry Blackman, and Victor Weybright. *Buffalo Bill and the Wild West.* Basin, Wyo.: Big Horn Books, 1979.

Sharpe, Horatio. *Archives of Maryland, Correspondence of Governor Horatio Sharpe, 1753–1757,* edited by William Hand Browne. Baltimore: Maryland Historical Society, 1888.

Shorey Book Store. The North Star: *A Monthly Publication in the Interests of Schools and Missions in Alaska, the Complete Issues from December 1887 – December 1892.* Seattle: Shorey Book Store, 1973.

Simmons, Marc. *Witchcraft in the Southwest: Spanish and Indian Supernaturalism on the Rio Grande.* Flagstaff: Northland Press, 1974.

Simmons, William. "Culture Theory in Contemporary Ethnohistory." *Ethnohistory* 35 (Winter 1988): 1–14.

Sixteenth Annual Report of the Board of Indian Commissioners, 1884. Washington, D.C.: Government Printing Office, 1885.

Smith, Dwight La Verne, ed. *Indians of the United States and Canada: A Bibliography.* Santa Barbara: ABC Clio, 1974.

Smith, Watson. "Kiva Mural Decorations at Awatovi and Kawaika-a." *Papers of the Peabody Museum of American Archaeology and Ethnology, Harvard University* 37 (1952): 106–51.

Snodgrass, Jeanne O. *American Indian Painters: A Biographical Directory.* Contributions from the Museum of the American Indian, Heye Foundation. vol. 21, pt. 1. New York: Museum of the American Indian, 1968.

Starr, Emmett. *History of the Cherokee Indians and Their Legends and Folklore.* 1921. Reprint. New York: Kraus, 1969.

Stedman, Raymond William. *Shadows of the Indians: Stereotypes in American Culture.* Norman: University of Oklahoma Press, 1982.

Stern, Theodore. *The Klamath Tribe: A People and Their Reservation.* Seattle: University of Washington Press, 1965.

Szasz, Margaret Connell. *Indian Education in the American Colonies, 1607–1783.* Albuquerque: University of New Mexico Press, 1988.

Talayesva, Don C. *Sun Chief, the Autobiography of an American Indian.* Edited by Leo W. Simmons. New Haven: Yale University Press, 1942. Revised ed. 1963.

Tanner, Clara Lee. *Southwest Indian Painting: A Changing Art.* 2d ed. Tucson: University of Arizona Press, 1973.

Thwaites, Reuben Gold, ed. *Early Western Travels.* Cleveland: Arthur H. Clark Co., 1904.

Tibbles, Thomas Henry. *The Ponca Chiefs: An Account of the Trial of Standing Bear.* Edited by Kay Graber. Lincoln: University of Nebraska Press, 1972.

Tjerandson, Carl. *Education for Citizenship: A Foundation's Experience.* Santa Cruz, Calif.: Emil Schwartzhaupt Foundation, 1980.

Trafzer, Clifford E. "An Indian Trader's Plea for Justice, 1906." *New Mexico Historical Review* 47 (July 1972): 239–56.

———. "Sam Day and His Boys: Good Neighbors to the Navajos." The *Journal of Arizona History* 18 (Spring 1977): 1–22.

Trenholm, Virginia Cole. *The Arapahoes: Our People.* Norman: University of Oklahoma Press, 1970.

Trexler, Richard C. "From the Mouths of Babes: Christianization by Children in Sixteenth Century New Spain." In *Religious Organization and Religious Experience,* edited by J. Davis, 115–35. London: Academy Press, 1982.

Trigger, Bruce G. "Ethnohistory: The Unifinished Edifice." *Ethnohistory* 33 (Summer 1986): 253–67.

Tuska, John. *The American West in Film: Critical Approaches to the Westerns.* Westport, Conn.: Greenwood Press, 1985.

Upshaw, A. B. "What the Indians Owe to the United States Government." *Red Man and Helper* 14 (April 1897): 8.

Utley, Robert M. *The Lance and the Shield: The Life and Times of Sitting Bull.* New York: Henry Holt and Co., 1993.

Velarde, Pablita. Interview by Margaret Connell Szasz, 9 February 1972, Albuquerque. Tape recording 853. American Indian History Research Project Files, Special Collections, Center for Southwest Research, Zimmerman Library, University of New Mexico, Albuquerque.

_____. *The Enchanted Arts.* Produced and directed by Irene-Aimee Depke. KRGW, Las Cruces, New Mex., 1979. Videocassette.

_____. Interview, 2 October 1986. Tape recording 22, transcript. Santa Fe Indian School First One Hundred Years Project, Santa Fe Indian School Library Media Center, Santa Fe, New Mex.

_____. *Old Father, the Storyteller.* Globe, Ariz.: Dale Stuart King, 1960. Reprint. Santa Fe: Clear Light, 1989.

_____. *Pablita Velarde: An Artist and Her People.* Produced by the National Park Service. N.d. Videocassette.

Vestal, Stanley. *Sitting Bull: Champion of the Sioux.* Norman: University of Oklahoma Press, 1957.

Waggoner, David. "In the Land of the Hydahs." *Assembly Herald* 13 (June 1907): 252–54.

Walker, Robert Sparks. *Torchlights to the Cherokees: The Brainerd Mission.* New York: Macmillan, 1931.

Walsh, Richard J. *The Making of Buffalo Bill.* Indianapolis: Bobbs-Merrill Co., 1928.

Walz, Vina. "History of the El Paso Area, 1680–1692." Ph.D. dissertation, University of New Mexico, 1950.

Washburn, Wilcomb E. "Ethical Perspectives in North American Ethnology." In *Social Contexts of American Ethnology, 1840–1984,* 50-64. Washington, D.C.: American Anthropological Association, 1985.

Washburne, E. B., ed. *The Edwards Papers.* 3 vols. Chicago: Chicago Historical Society, 1884.

Washington, George. *The Writings of George Washington from the Original Manuscript Sources, 1745-1799.* 39 vols. Edited by John C. Fitzpatrick. Washington, D.C.: Government Printing Office, 1932-1944.

Weibel-Orlando, Joan. *Indian Country, L.A., Maintaining Ethnic Community in a Complex Society.* Urbana and Chicago: University of Illinois Press, 1991.

Welch, James. *Fools Crow.* New York: Viking Penguin, 1986.

White, Leslie A. *The Pueblo of Santa Ana, New Mexico.* Memoirs,

American Anthropological Association, n.s., no. 60. Menasha, Wis.: American Anthropological Association, 1942.

White, Richard, *The Middle Ground: Indians, Empires and Republics in the Great Lakes Region, 1650–1815*. Cambridge: Cambridge University Press, 1992.

Whitney, Ellen M., ed. *The Black Hawk War.* 3 vols. Springfield: Illinois State Historical Library, 1970–1978.

Wiggins, Arch R. *The History of the Salvation Army.* Vol.IV: 1886–1904. London: T. and A. Constable, 1964.

Willard, Carrie M. "Native Sabbath School Teachers." the *North Star* 1, no. 9, August 1888.

Williams, Walter L. "Twentieth Century Indian Leaders: Brokers and Providers." *Journal of the West* 23 (July 1984): 3–6.

Wilson, John P. "Awatovi—More Light on a Legend." *Plateau* 44, 3 (1972): 125–30.

Wright, Julia McNair. *Among the Alaskans.* Philadelphia: Presbyterian Board of Home Missions, 1893.

Yarborough, Minnie Clare, ed. *The Reminiscences of William C. Preston.* Chapel Hill: University of North Carolina Press, 1933.

Young, Mary. "The Cherokee Nation: Mirror of the Republic." *American Quarterly* 33 (Winter 1981): 502–24.

Young, Robert W. "Two Languages Better Than One." In *Education for Action*, edited by Willard W. Beatty, 254–57. Chilocco, Okla.: U.S. Indian Service, 1944.

———. *The Role of the Navajo in the Southwestern Drama.* Gallup: *Gallup Independent*, 1968.

———. "The Rise of the Navajo Tribe." In *Plural Society in the Southwest*, edited by Edward H. Spicer and Raymond H. Thompson, 167–237. New York: Weatherhead Foundation, 1972.

———. "Written Navajo: A Brief History." In *Advances in the Creation and Revision of Writing Systems* edited by Joshua Fishman, 460–63. The Hague: Mouton, 1977.

———. *A Political History of the Navajo Tribe.* Tsaile, Ariz.: Navajo Community College Press, 1978.

———. Personal interview with Peter Iverson, June 2, 1990, in Albuquerque, New Mex.

———. ed. *The Navajo Yearbook.* Vol. 8. Window Rock, Ariz.: Bureau of Indian Affairs, 1961.

Young, Robert W., and William Morgan. *The Navajo Language: A Grammar and Colloquial Dictionary.* Albuquerque: University of New Mexico Press, 1987.

Young, S. Hall. *Hall Young of Alaska, "The Mushing Parson": The Autobiography of S. Hall Young.* New York and Chicago: Fleming H. Revell Co., 1927.

THE CONTRIBUTORS

Donald J. **Berthrong** *is the author of* The Southern Cheyennes, The Cheyenne and Arapaho Ordeal: Reservation and Agency Life in the Indian Territory, 1875–1907, *and a number of journal articles on the Cheyenne and Arapaho tribes of Oklahoma. Before retirement in 1991 he taught western and American Indian history at the University of Oklahoma and Purdue University. He served as a consultant and expert witness for the Cheyenne and Arapaho tribes before the Indian Claims Commission and federal courts.*

Michael C. **Coleman** *is a lecturer in the Department of English, a docent in the Department of History, and director of the North American Studies Program at the University of Jyväskylä, Finland. He graduated with a B.A. from University College, Dublin, in 1970 and with a Ph.D. from the University of Pennsylvania in 1977. He is the author of* American Indian Children at School, 1850–1930 *and* Presbyterian Missionary Attitudes Toward American Indians, 1837–1893. *His articles and reviews have appeared in academic journals in the United States, Canada, Scandinavia, and India. In 1988–1989, he was a visiting professor of American studies at Miami University, Ohio. Born in Dublin in 1946, Coleman is a citizen of Ireland. He is married and has three children.*

Mick Gidley *is director of the Centre for American and Commonwealth Arts and Studies at the University of Exeter, England. He has been awarded fellowships by the American Council of Learned Societies, the British Academy, and The Netherlands Institute for Advanced Study. His publications include* With One Sky above Us: Life on an Indian Reservation at the Turn of the Century, Kopet: A Documentary

Narrative of Chief Joseph's Last Years, American Photography, *and, as editor or co-editor,* The Vanishing Race: Selections from Edward S. Curtis' "The North American Indian," Views of American Landscapes, Locating the Shakers, Representing Others: White Views of Indigenous Peoples, and Modern American Culture: An Introduction. *He has also written articles on American literary and cultural history, and is associate editor of the* European Reviews of Native American Studies.

Nancy L. Hagedorn *was born in Cincinnati, Ohio, and attended the University of Cincinnati, where she received her B.A. in history in 1981. She is currently a doctoral candidate in early American history at the College of William and Mary, and holds the position of curatorial fellow and research associate with the Colonial Williamsburg Foundation. She was a Kate B. Hall J. Peterson fellow at the American Antiquarian Society in Worcester, Massachusetts, and a short-term fellow at the Newberry Library in Chicago. Her publications include "'A Friend To Go Between Them': The Interpreter as Cultural Broker during Anglo-Iroquois Councils, 1740–1770" and as coauthor,* Tools: Working Wood in Eighteenth-Century America.

Sally Hyer *was a guest curator of "'Women's Work': The Art of Pablita Velarde" at the Wheelwright Museum of the American Indian in Santa Fe, New Mexico, in 1993. She is the author of* One House, One Voice, One Heart: Native American Education at the Santa Fe Indian School, *an oral history sponsored by the nineteen pueblos of New Mexico. She worked for the All Indian Pueblo Council and the tribally operated Santa Fe Indian School for ten years as a planner, writer, and researcher. A former Fulbright scholar to Peru, she has master's degrees in community planning and art history.*

Peter Iverson *is professor of history at Arizona State University. His publications include* The Navajo Nation, Carlos Montezuma and the Changing World of American Indians, The Navajos, *and, as editor or co-editor,* The Plains Indians of the Twentieth Century *and* Major Problems in American Indian History. *Iverson has taught at Navajo Community College and serves currently on the National Advisory Council for the Newberry Library's D'Arcy McNickle Center for the History of the American Indian. He has held fellowships through the Newberry Library, the National Endowment for the Humanities, and the W. K. Kellogg Foundation.*

Editor of the Vargas Project at the University of New Mexico, **John L. Kessell** *specializes in the Southwest during the Spanish colonial period. Among his publications are* Kiva, Cross, and Crown: The

Pecos Indians and New Mexico, 1540–1840 *and* Remote Beyond Compare: Letters of don Diego de Vargas to His Family from New Spain and New Mexico, 1675–1706.

Valerie Sherer Mathes *received her B.A. and M.A. from the University of New Mexico and her Ph.D. from Arizona State University. She has been teaching the history of the American West, Indian history, and United States history at City College of San Francisco since 1967. She is the author of numerous scholarly articles, appearing in such quarterlies as* Montana The Magazine of Western History, South Dakota History, American West, American Indian Quarterly, North Dakota History, Nebraska History, *and* Arizona and the West. *She received a Spur Award for best western nonfiction from Western Writers of America for her article on Helen Hunt Jackson in* Montana *and for her book* Helen Hunt Jackson and Her Indian Reform Legacy.

William G. McLoughlin *received his A.B. from Princeton University and his A.M. and Ph.D. from Harvard University. He joined the faculty of Brown University in 1954 and was the Annie McClelland and Willard Prescott Smith Professor of History and Religion from 1981 until his death in 1992. He published numerous books and articles on American Indians, evangelicalism, and the Baptists. His books currently in print include* New England Dissent, 1630–1833: The Baptists and the Separation of Church and State; Revivals, Awakening, and Reform: An Essay on Religion and Social Change in America, 1607–1977; *and* Cherokee Renascence in the New Republic.

L. G. Moses, *professor of history at Oklahoma State University, teaches America Indian history and the history of the American West. He is the author of* The Indian Man: A Biography of James Mooney *and co-editor of* Indian Lives: Essays on Nineteenth- and Twentieth-Century Native American Leaders.

Dorothy R. Parker *received her B.A. from the University of California at Berkeley in 1969 and her M.A. from California State University, Hayward, the following year. She completed her doctorate in history at the University of New Mexico in 1988. Her book* Singing an Indian Song: A Biography of D'Arcy McNickle *received the Gaspar Perez de Villagra Award from the Historical Society of New Mexico in 1993. In addition, she has published numerous articles and book reviews. She is currently teaching history at Eastern New Mexico University in Portales.*

James P. Ronda *is the H. G. Barnard Professor of Western American History at the University of Tulsa. His area of specialty is the exploration* *of the American West. He is the author of six books, including* Lewis and Clark among the Indians *and* Astoria and Empire *(both of which were nominated for the Pulitzer Prize in American history) and* The Exploration of North America, *one of four majors works commissioned by the American Historical Association for the 1492–1992 Columbian quincentenary. He is a member of* the *editorial boards of the* Western Historical Quarterly *and* Montana The Magazine of Western History *and serves on advisory boards for the Center for Columbia River History, the Maximillian Journals Project, the West film project, and the Gilcrease Museum.*

Margaret Connell Szasz *teaches courses in American Indian history at the University of New Mexico. The first recipient of the Snead Wertheim Lectureship in History and Anthropology at this institution, she also has held a University of New Mexico Regent's Lectureship. In 1991–92 she was a Senior Lecturer at the University of Aberdeen, Scotland. Her publications include* Education and the American Indian: The Road to Self-Determination since 1928 *and* Indian Education in the American Colonies: 1607–1783.

Victoria Wyatt *is associate professor in the Department of History in Art at the University of Victoria in Canada. A historian focusing on native history and arts, she is the author of* Images from the Inside Passage: An Alaskan Portrait by Winter and Pond, Shapes of Their Thoughts: Reflections of Culture and Contact in Northwest Coast Indian Art, *and several articles and anthology chapters.*

INDEX

A Century of Dishonor (Jackson),
141, 147, 154, 157
"'A Friend To Go Between
Them': The Interpreter as Cul-
tural Broker During Anglo-Iro-
quois Councils, 1740–1770,"
18
*A Political History of the Navajo
Tribe* (Young), 270
Abenaki, 10
Abó (pueblo), 32
Abolition, 109–12, 144
Acculturation, 10–11, 104, 116,
125, 126–29, 166, 170, 177
Act for the Relief of the Mission
Indians in the State of Califor-
nia, 152
Adahooníłgíí, 265
Adaptation, selective (adoption,
selective), 57, 59, 78, 251,
299, 300
*Advances in the Creation and
Revision of Writing Systems*
(ed. Fishman), 270
Agents to the tribes, 44, 81, 90,
94, 105, 114, 146, 152, 168,
201

Agriculture, 86, 87, 103, 104,
115, 123, 148, 150, 163–65,
224, 226, 227, 275
Ainse, Sarah, 48, 58
Alabama, 123
Alaska, 179
Alaska Native Language Center,
271
Alaska-Yukon-Pacific Exposition,
Seattle, 200
Albuquerque, N.M., 269, 282,
284, 289
Allen, Henry B., 213
Alliances, 91
Allotment, 163, 213, 225
American Anthropological Asso-
ciation, 13, 245
American Board of Commission-
ers for Foreign Missions
(ABCFM), 105, 110, 120,
122–25, 132, 136
American Fur Company, 84
American Horse (the younger),
170
American Indian Chicago Con-
ference, 252

American Indian Intellectuals
(Liberty), 13
American Indian Painting
(Dunn), 285
American Museum of Natural
History, 208
American Revolution, 102, 123
American Society for Ethnohistory, 8, 14
Ames, Lucy, 126, 128, 130–31,
132, 134
Analytical Lexicon of Navajo
(Young), 271
Anaya Almazán, Cristóbal de, 36
Antelope, DeForest, 230, 232
Anthropology, 244, 250, 252
Apache, 159, 199
Apache (Mescalero), 269
Apache (Mescalero-Chiricahua),
9
Apache Odyssey, a Journey Between Two Worlds (ed. Opler),
9
Apodaca, Juana de, 36
Arapaho, 146, 223–24, 227–39
Arikara, 212
Arizona, 159
Arquero, Epitacio, 279
Art Institute of Chicago, 280
Artists, native, 263, 273, 282,
284–85; historiography of Native American painting, 285
Assimilation, the policy of, 82,
86, 100, 163, 164, 211, 247,
250–51, 253; "directed assimilation," 242, 245, 251, 253
Association of American Indian
Affairs, 247, 252
Astor, John Jacob, 84, 86
Astor Library, New York City,
144, 147
Athapaskans, 262, 271
Atkinson, Henry, 95, 96
Aughwick conference, 58
Austin, Buck, 261
Autobiographies, native, 9

The Autobiography of a Hopi Indian (Talayesva), 9
Autonomy, 100, 113, 116–17,
241, 245
Axtell, James, 7, 8, 13, 14

Bad Thunder, 91
Bancroft, George, 267
Bandelier National Monument,
282
Banning reservation, 157
Baptist Church, 106–11, 114,
118–120, 227
Barbour, James, 87
Barrett, Samuel M., 198
Bates, George H., 165, 166
Bear Man, 223, 226
Beardslee, L., 184
Beatty, Willard, 258, 262, 264,
265
*Being and Becoming Indian:
Biographical Studies of North
American Frontiers* (ed. Clifton), 18
Bell, John R., 88
Bella Coola, 204
Benson, William, 195
Berkhofer, Robert F., 98, 99
Berkhofer, Robert F., Jr., 7, 15
Berry, C. H., 235
Bible, translated into Cherokee,
108
Bibliographies, 14
Biographies, native, 12–19
Bitanny, Adolph Dodge, 257
Black, Red Bird, 232
Black Elk, 164, 172, 174
Black Hawk, 90–92, 94–96
Black Hawk War, 82, 87, 89–96
Black Heart, 175
Black Hills (Dakota territory),
228, 233
Black Kettle, 146
Blackfoot (Blackfeet), 11, 212
Blackhorse, Dan, 237

Blackman, Margaret B., 19
Block, John W., 230
Blue Lodge, 111
Board of Indian Commissioners, 154
Boarding schools. *See separately by name*
Boas, Franz, 7, 198, 204, 207
Bonnin, L. S., 229, 230, 231, 233
Boston Board of Commissioners of the New England Company, 63–65, 67, 68
Boston Indian Citizenship Committee, 144
Boudinot, Elias, 106
Boulder, Colo., 248
Bowditch, Charlotte, 199
Boynton, Richard, Sr., 239
Brainerd school, 122, 125–36
Brandt, Elizabeth, 288
Brant, Joseph, 64
British Band, the, 90, 91, 92, 94, 95
British Columbia, Can., 182
British Isles, natives touring the, 68–69
Brody, J. J., 285
Brothertown movement, 75–77
Brugge, David M., 16
Brumble, H. David, 9
Brunson and Wells (law firm), 151, 154, 156
Bunzel, Ruth, 289
Bureau of American Ethnology, 203, 208
Bureau of Indian Affairs (BIA), 201, 225, 228, 241–45, 259, 263, 284; livestock reduction policy of the, 261, 266–67. *See also* Indian affairs, United States; Indian bureau
Burke, C. H., 228, 231
Burke, John ("Arizona John"), 164, 170
Burns, Robert, 230
Bush, Ann, 132, 133

Butler, Thomas, 52
Byers, William N., 147
Byrnes v. the San Jacinto Indians, 156

Cáceres, Juan Ruiz de, 30
Cahuilla, 146, 152, 156
California, 146–56
California Mission Indian Commission, 154, 155
Calvinism, 127
Campbell, Lucy A., 129, 131, 134
Campbell, William, 96
Canada, 11, 182, 240, 262
Candelario, J. S., 199
Cañon de Chelly, 201
Captives: French-Indian, 44; Pueblo-Spanish, 36, 41
Caripicado, 41
Carlisle Indian School, 14, 198, 211, 224–25, 295
Carondawana, 44, 45
Cass, Lewis, 95
Catholic Church, 157
Catití, Alonso, 32
Cattlemen and cattle grazing, 114–15, 214
Century Magazine, 148, 151
Chapman, Oscar L., 235
Chavarria, Guadalupita, 275–76
Cherokee Messenger, 109
Cherokee, 98–121, 124, 133; "Southern party" of, 117
Cheyenne, 146, 147, 229, 230–37, 239
Cheyenne-Arapaho: Clinton assemblage (1929), 231; general council, 230–39; Progressive Council, 228; reservation (C&A Agency), 223, 225, 227, 228, 230
Chicago, Ill., 255
Chief Joseph, 208
Chinle, Ariz., 201
Chippewa, 91

Chistoe, Felipe, 30, 39, 41
Chivington, John M., 146
Choctaw, 125, 130
Choice Collection of Hymns (Occom), 73, 74
Chona, Maria, 9
Chouteau, Auguste P., 83
Christian Reformed Church, 259
Christian Union, 153
Christianity, 163. *See also separately by church*
Citizenship for Indians, 163, 164
Civil War, 112–13
Civilian Conservation Corps, 282
Civilian Conservation Corps–Indian Department, 227
Clah, (Tsimshian minister), 182
Clark, Ann Nolan, 263
Clark, Meriwether (son of William), 96
Clark, William, 81–97, 299; his Indian Museum, 87–89, 97
Clemente, Esteban, 32–33
Cleveland, Grover, 141
Clifford, James, 200
Clifton, James A., 18–19, 135
Cochiti (pueblo), 279
Codetalkers, 266
Cody, William Frederick ("Buffalo Bill"), 158–78
Colden, Cadwallader, 45
Collier, John, 234, 235, 241–44, 251, 258, 261; his "Indian New Deal," 241
Colorado Springs, Colo., 142
Columbia University, 259
Communicating with the Full Moon (Velarde), 291
Community development, 245–52
Compadrazgo, 36–37
Conflict, dealing with, 51, 65, 67, 89–97, 183–84, 201–202, 214, 247, 251, 267, 279, 287, 288–89, 291–92. *See also* Factionalism

Congregational New Light Church, 63
Congress. *See* United States Congress
Congress of Rough Riders of the World, 165
Connecticut, 61–78 passim
Connecticut Board of Correspondents, 65, 68
Conway, Moncure D., 144
Coolidge, Sarah Lucy, 227
Coolidge, Sherman, 227
Corcoran Gallery, Washington, D.C., 281
Coriz, Santiago, 291
Cornell University, 250, 269
Cornplanter, Jesse, 13
Coronado, Francisco Vázquez de, 27
Couc, Catherine, 44
Cowart, Robert, 112
Craig, Vincent, 19
Crashing Thunder, the Autobiography of An American Indian (ed. Radin), 9
Crawford, William H., 83
Crazy Pend D'Oreille, 211
Cree, 240
Croghan, George, 48, 51, 52
Crook, George, 142, 146
Crow, 198, 209, 211, 212
Crownpoint, N.M., 246–51
Cruzate, Domingo Jironza Petrís de, 33, 34
Cultural broker: classification of roles, 11–12; personality of, 294–300; the term, 17–19
"Cultural Brokers and Intercultural Politics: New York-Iroquois Relations, 1664–1701" (Richter), 17
Culture, preserving native, 7, 73, 87, 133, 158–78, 190, 192, 201, 202, 204, 207, 215, 224, 225, 246, 251–54, 265, 270, 278, 280–81, 285, 287–89, 291

Curtis, Edward S., 197–215; the collection of, 198–207
Cushing, Frank Hamilton, 31
Custer battlefield, 212
Custer Died for Your Sins (Deloria), 13

D'Arcy McNickle Center for the Study of the American Indian, 14
Dahlberg, Gus, 241
Dalby, Edwin J., 213
The Dancing Healers (Hammerschlag), 3
Dartmouth College, 71
Davis, Mary Lee, 187, 188, 190
Davis, Samuel, 195
Davis, W. W. H., 31
Dawes, Henry L., 144, 146, 163
Dawes Severalty Act, 163, 213
Day, Bill, 201
Day, Charlie, 198, 200, 214
Day, Sam, Jr., 201
Day, Samuel Edward Day, Sr., 200
Delaware (tribe), 45, 46, 47, 49, 50
Deloria, Vine, Jr., 12–13
Demmert, George, 195
Denetsosie, Hoke, 263, 270
Department of Indian Affairs, British Northern, 52, 55
Dependency, 86, 97
Determination, 296, 297. *See also* Culture, preserving native
Detribalization, 116–17. *See also* Assimilation
Dewey, John, 280
Dickinson, Billy, 183
Dickinson, George, 182
Dickinson, Sarah, 180, 181–86, 194–95
Diego, Juan, 146
Díí K'ad Anaa'ígíí Baa Hané (McFarlane), 264–65
Dinwiddie, Robert, 48

Diplomacy, roles in, 53, 83, 84
Dippie, Brian W., 198
Dodge, Henry Chee, 16
Downing, Lewis, 117
Dozier, Edward P., 288, 289
Duncan, William, 182, 193
Dundy, Elmer S., 144
Dunn, Dorothy, 280, 281, 284, 285, 286, 287, 291

Eaton, John H., 94
Economics, 84, 278. *See also* Agriculture
Edmonds, R. David, 15
Education, bilingual, 100, 108, 109
Education, cross-cultural, 14–15, 32, 33, 46, 50, 63, 74, 86, 104, 116, 118, 122, 125–36, 145, 156, 163, 165, 178–79, 180, 182, 187, 190, 193, 194, 198, 211, 223–25, 228–33, 240, 241, 251, 260, 276, 277. *See also* Educators, native
Education, Lancastrian system of, 128, 134
Educators, native, 63, 74, 109, 128–29, 179–96, 211, 278; training of, 186
Edwards, Ninian, 90
Eghnisara, 51, 57
Emigration, 75–78, 107
Emil Schwartzhaupt Foundation, 248, 249, 250
Employment, 45, 49–52, 55, 59, 63, 65, 67, 82, 83, 115, 147–48, 161–63, 172, 174, 178, 180–81, 184, 190, 204, 208, 211, 213, 225–27, 241–45, 252, 255, 256, 258, 260–262, 268, 269, 281–84
Encounters with an Angry God (Laird), 262
Environment, cross-cultural, 102, 103, 107, 294–95. *See also* Education, cross-cultural

Environment, native, and the pattern of accommodation, 299
Ethnography, 203
Ethnohistory, 6–19
Ethnological Dictionary of the Navajo Language, 259
Ethnology, 198–200, 212, 215
Everts, Jeremiah, 132

Factionalism, 35, 39, 41, 67–68, 78, 90–92, 104–106, 110–11, 116–18, 124, 224, 228–39, 248, 277
Factory trading system, 83, 84, 86
Faris, Chester E., 278, 280
Fausz, J. Frederick, 16
Fenton, William N., 13
Field, George, 195
Fishman, Joshua A., 270
Five Nations, 17
Flathead, 240
Fletcher, Alice, 9
Fletcher, John, 230, 234, 235
Forsyth, Thomas, 81, 90–92, 96
Fort Armstrong, Ill., 91
Fort Defiance, Ariz., 201
Fort Marion, Fla., 278
Fort Omaha, Nebr., 142
Fort Reno Military Reservation, Okla., 236
Fort Wingate, N. M., 258, 260
Fowler, David, 64–65, 74, 75
Fowler, Jacob, 75
Fowler, Mary, 64
Fox (tribe), 89–93
Franciscans (religious order), 27, 31, 32, 33, 34, 36, 37, 148, 201, 258, 259
Franklin, Benjamin, 147
Freer, W. B., 226
Friends Church, 195

Gaines, Edmund, 94, 95
Galloway, Colin G., 18

Gallup Independent, 270
Gallup, N.M., 255, 269
Ganado, Ariz., 200, 259
Gender and roles, 53, 123, 125, 133, 144, 180, 276–78, 281
Genízaro, 41
Genoa, Neb., 211
Georgia, 104, 123, 124
Ghost Dance, 174
Girty, Simon, 18
Gist, Christopher, 46
Given, Joshua, 14–15
Goddard, Delano, 144
Godoy, Francisco Lucero de, 30
Goldman, Irving, 204
Government, tribal constitutional, 235–36, 241, 268
Grant, Ulysses S., 114
Great Awakening, 63
Great Sioux Reservation, 142, 228
Gunnock, Charles, 195

Haag, Mack, 232
Hagan, William T., 13, 14, 154
Hagedorn, Nancy L., 18
Haida, 179, 180
Haile, Berard, Father, 259
Haines Mission, Alaska, 184
Hallowell, Irving A., 10, 12
Hamilton, Isaac, 53, 56
Hammerschlag, Carl A., 3
Hardin, Helen, 274
Hardin, Herbert, 284
Harriman Alaska Expedition, 198, 200
Harrington, John P., 255, 258, 260, 262
Harris, Henry, 146
Harris, Robert, 195
Harrison administration, 162
Hartford Courant, 142, 144
Haskell Institute, Kans., 225, 230, 231
Hauptman, Lawrence C., 16
Haury, Theodore, 228

Hayes, Rutherford B., 146
Head, Wade, 269
Henderson, Daniel B., 228, 231, 233
Herrera, Velino Shije, 288
Hewitt, Edgar L., 258
Hidalgo, Pedro, 30, 35
Higginson, Thomas Wentworth, 141, 142, 153
Hiles, Osia Joslyn, Mrs., 156
Hogan School, 259
Holmberg, Allan, 250
Holmes, Oliver Wendell, 145
Home Mission Monthly, 192, 193
Hoover, Herbert, 277
Hopi, 201, 273, 279
Howard, John, 195
Hubbell, Lorenzo, 200
Hudson River Valley, 76
Hudson's Bay Company, 186, 198
"The Hungry Generations" (McNickle), 241
Hunkpapa, 167
Hunt, Edward Bissell, 142
Hunt, George, 198, 204, 205, 207
Hunter, Robert, 45
Hymns, 73–74

Identity, the question of, 18, 23, 127–28, 219–21. *See also* Culture, preserving native; Status, tribal
Ihowai, 91
Illinois, 89, 90–92, 94–95
Imagery of American Indians, 159, 163–70, 198, 206
In the Land of the Head-Hunters (Curtis), 204, 205
Indian affairs, English/British, 44, 48
Indian affairs, United States, 82, 90, 93, 102, 105, 106, 114, 152; critics of, 141, 145–47, 154, 201

Indian bureau: *Annual Report* (1880), 145; and Show Indians, 161
Indian Claims Commission, 7, 236, 239
Indian Country, L.A.: Maintaining Ethnic Community in a Complex Society (Weibel-Orlando), 19
Indian Lives: Essays on Nineteenth- and Twentieth-Century Native American Leaders (ed. Moses and Wilson), 15
Indian Painters and White Patrons (Brody), 285
An Indian Preacher in England (Richardson), 69
Indian Reorganization Act (IRA), 234, 241
Indian Rights Association (IRA), 141, 154–56, 161
Indians, urban, 19, 252
Indios ladinos, 30
Informant, the role of, 204, 212
Inquisition, the, 31
Intermarriage. *See* Mixed ancestry/mixed blood
Interpreter, role of, 35, 44–47, 49, 53, 55, 106, 128–29, 159, 166, 171, 181–84, 187, 189, 209, 213, 228, 258, 259, 267, 274, 282
Inuit, 18
Iowa, 91
Iroquois, 44, 50, 52, 64–66
Iroquois (Ohio), 46, 51
Isleta (pueblo), 288

Jackson administration, 90, 95
Jackson, Andrew, 96, 104, 132
Jackson, Helen Hunt, 141–57
Jackson, Sheldon, 182, 189, 190, 193
Jackson, William Sharpless, 142
Jackson/Kinney report, 152, 157

James, Darwin Rush, 165
Jefferson, Thomas, 81, 84, 86
Jemez (pueblo), 291
Jennings, Francis, 7, 8, 13, 14
Jewett, David, 65, 67, 72
Jilliard, Peter, 69
Johnson, Joseph, 74, 75
Johnson, Lyndon, 247, 249
Johnson, Raymond, 270
Johnson, William, 44, 47, 52, 53, 59, 64, 83
Jones, Evan, 98–121
Jones, John B., 107, 109–21
Josephy, Alvin, 15
Journal of American History, 17
Juneau, Alaska, 186

Kansa, 86
Kansas, 112, 113, 225
Keetoowah Society, 111–12, 114, 117
Kellog, Minnie, 16
Kelly, William, 190
Kennard, Edward A., 262, 263
Kentucky, 123
Keokuk, 90–95
Keres, 34
Kickapoo, 91
Kinney, Abbot, 150–54
Kinnon, Tillie, 187, 188. *See also* Paul, Tillie Kinnon
Kinship, 50, 77, 104, 123, 180. *See also* Status, tribal
Kiowa, 14
Klamath, 10–11
Kluckhohn, Clyde, 244
Knights of the Golden Circle, 111
Krauss, Michael E., and Jeffrey Leer, 271
Krug, Julius, 266, 267
Kwakiutl, 198, 204, 207
Kwakiutl Texts (ed. Boas and Hunt), 204

La Farge, Oliver, 252

La Flesche, Francis, 9
Laird, Carobeth, 262
Lake Mohonk Conference, 141, 154, 156
Lake Mohonk Mission Indian Committee, 156
Lakota, 168
Lancaster conference, 50
Land, claims cases on, 67
Land cession, 86, 93, 95
Land ownership: communal, 102; Mexican grant, 148, 150, 156; native/tribal, 141, 150–51, 154, 211, 213, 214, 226, 228, 234–35, 237, 242, and a brief on Indian land rights, 147; private, 114, 117, or individual trust, 234
Languages, using native, 45, 47, 50, 106–108, 124, 181, 182, 190, 200–201, 258–68, 271, 278
Lawson, S. S., 152
Leighton, Alexander, 244
Leighton, Dorothea, 244
Leupp, Francis E., 202, 214
Lewis and Clark Expedition, 83, 87
Liberty, Margot, 13
Lincoln, Abraham, 112, 113
Linguistics, comparative, 271
Lisa, Manuel, 83
Littell, Norman, 266, 267
Little Bird, 233
Little Face Chief, 233
Little Herder in Summer (Clark), 263
Little Raven, Chief, 224, 228
Logstown treaty conference, 46
Long, John D., 144
Long, Stephen H., 88
Long Term Lease Act, 237
Longfellow, Henry Wadsworth, 144, 145
Lope, Monte, 258
Lujan, Merina, 274

Lumpmouth, Carrie, 227
Lurie, Nancy Oestreich, 9

McCabe, Maurice, 268
McElroy, Ann, 18
McFarland, Amanda R., 182, 187
McFarlane, Charles T., 264
McFee, Malcolm, 11, 12, 19
Mackaye, Steele, 165, 170
McKenney, Thomas, 82
McLaughlin, James, 168
McLoughlin, William G., 123, 127
McNickle, D'Arcy, 240–54
McPherson, Christiana, 132
McPherson, Lucy, 127, 128, 129, 133
Mandan, 212
Many Farms, Ariz., 269
"Many Roads to Red River: Métis Genesis in the Great Lakes Region, 1618–1815" (Peterson), 16
Margolis, Fred, 269
Mark, Joan, 9
Maroh, Juana, 34
Márquez, Diego, 32
Marsden, Edward, 193, 195
Martinez, María, 279, 284, 291
Mason Case, 67
Mason, John, 67
Massacres, 146, 147
Matthews, Washington, 258
Medal of Freedom, 247
Medical care (among the Navajo), 247
Meeker, Nathan, 146
Menominee, 91, 93
Meritt, E. B., 228
Merriam, C. Hart, 198
Methodist Church, 106, 120, 187
Métis, 16, 56
Miami (Indians), 46, 50
The Middle Ground: Indians, Empires and Republics in the Great Lakes Region, 1650–1815 (White), 20

"'Middlemen in Peace and War': Virginia's Earliest Indian Interpreters, 1608–1632" (Fausz), 16
Military: negotiator for the, 34, 37; diplomat, 48–52, 55
Ministries, native religious, 100, 118–20. See also Missionaries, native
Mirabel, Eva, 274
Mission Indian bill, 152, 154, 157
Mission Indian reservations, 150
Mission Indians, 142, 148–57
Missionaries, native (native clergy), 63–73, 182, 191
Missionary escort, 45
Missionary, role of, 86, 98–121, 180, 181, 186. See also Missionaries, native
Mitchell, Daniel Holmes, 201
Mixed ancestry/mixed blood, 32, 34, 36, 41, 44, 56, 102–104, 124, 125, 186, 188, 198, 211, 227, 240, 284
Mohawk, 46
Mohegan, 61–65, 67, 72, 74
Montana, 11, 209, 211, 240, 254
Montana State University, 241
Montauk, 63, 64
Montezuma, Carlos, 15
Montour, Andrew, 44–60; as Indian officer, 49–52, 55, 59; Six Nations Council member, 51
Montour, Lewis, 45, 53
Montour, Madame, 44, 45, 47
Montoya, Geronima Cruz, 274, 284
Moor's Indian Charity School, 64, 65, 66, 74
Moore, Frederick, 195
Moravian church, 45, 106, 108, 156, 157
Morgan, J. Pierpont, 197
Morgan, Jacob, 261
Morgan, Thomas Jefferson, 162, 174

Morgan, William, 260, 263, 264
Moses, L. G., and Raymond Wilson, 16
Motivation, 22–23, 35, 297–98. *See also* Employment
Mountain Wolf Woman, Sister of Crashing Thunder, the Autobiography of a Winnebago Indian (ed. Lurie), 9
Muck, Lee, 266
Muir, John, 200
Museum of New Mexico, 281
Myer, Dillon, 244
Myers, William E., 204, 211

Naranjo, 32
Nash, Gary B., 14
National Congress of American Indians (NCAI), 242, 245, 252, 254
National Endowment for the Humanities, 270
National League of American Pen Women, 285
Nationalism, questions of, 93
Native American Church, 228, 231
Native American studies, 14
"Native Sabbath School Teachers" (Willard), 186
Navajo, 19, 198, 203, 246, 257, 259, 261, 266
Navajo Development Committee, 247–49
Navajo dictionary project, 269
Navajo Historical Selections (ed. Young and Morgan), 265
Navajo language, 255–72
The Navajo Language: A Grammar and Colloquial Dictionary (Young and Morgan), 264, 271
Navajo Nation, 268
Navajo Reading Study Program, 269

Navajo reservation, 198, 200, 215, 280
Navajo Tribal Council, 246, 247
The Navajo Yearbook (Young), 268
Navajo-Hopi Long Range Rehabilitation Act, 267, 268
Nawtwaig, 91
Nebraska, 142, 144
Negotiator, military, 34, 37
Neundorf, Alice, 271
New Echota treaty, 104
New Mexico, 25–43, 159, 275; reconquest of, 34–41
New York, 44–45, 47, 52, 55, 75–78, 165
New York City, N.Y., 144, 153, 200, 208, 241
New York Daily Tribune, 144–46
New York Independent, 145, 148
Newberry Library, Chicago, 241, 252, 254
Newton, James, Mr. and Mrs., 195
Nez Perce, 147, 208
Niantic, 63, 65
Niebur, Reinhold, 98
Noble, John, 162
Nootka, 204, 207
The North American Inc., 197
The North American Indian (Curtis), 197, 202, 211
North Carolina, 104, 107, 123
North Star (Sitka, Alaska), 189, 190, 191, 192, 194
Northern Baptist church, 110
Northwest Coast, 204

Oakley, Annie, 167
Oberly, John H., 163
Occom, Mary Fowler, 78
Occom, Samson, 61–78
Occom, Tabitha, 74
Office of Indian Affairs, 162. *See also* Bureau of Indian Affairs

Office of Navajo Economic Opportunity (ONEO), 249
Oglala, 172, 175
Ohio Company, 46
Ohio (tribe), 48, 51
Ohio (state), 95
Ohio Valley Historic Indian Conference, 8
Ojeda, Bartolomé de, 25, 30, 33–34
Ojibwa, 18
Oklahoma, 104, 112, 114, 116, 124, 223, 224, 228, 233, 234
Oklahoma Indian Welfare Act (OIWA), 234, 235
Old Father, The Storyteller (Velarde), 284, 287
Olson, Walter, 269
Olumapies, 47
Omaha Committee, 144
Omaha exposition, 209
Omaha reservation, 142
The Omaha Tribe (Mark), 9
Oñate, Juan de, 27
Oneida, 16, 44–45, 48, 50, 51, 64–65, 74, 75
Oneida colony, 75–78
Opler, Morris E., 9, 12, 235
Oregon, 10, 189
Osage, 83, 86
The Osage Tribe (La Flesche), 9
Ottawa, 91
Otterby, John, 230, 236
Owl (mother of Jesse Rowlodge), 223, 224, 226

Pachanga Canyon, Calif., 148, 152
Pacheco, Francisco, 38
Packs Wolf, 212
Padilla, Tomasito, 258
Paine, Robert, 11
Painter, Charles C., 154–55
Pala Valley, Calif., 148
Pan-Indianism, 130, 227

Papago Woman (Chona, ed. Underhill), 9
Parenteau, Isidore, 240
Parsons, Elsie Clews, 288
Participant-intervener, 250, 251
The Patriot Chiefs (Josephy), 15
Patriotism, 128, 132, 135, 211. *See also* Status, tribal
Patton, James, 46
Paul, Louis (son of Louis Francis Paul), 189
Paul, Louis Francis, 188
Paul, Moses, 73
Paul, Samuel, 188
Paul, Tillie Kinnon, 180, 186–91, 194–95
Paul, William, 188
Peairs, H. B., 225
Pecos (pueblo), 35–37, 39
Peña, Tonita, 274, 278, 279
Penn, Thomas, 51
Pennsylvania, 44–52, 55, 57, 198
Pequot, 63
Pérez, Gaspar, 30
Perry, Reuben, 201
Peters, Richard, 51, 58
Peterson, Jacqueline, 16
Pfrommer, Viola, 247–49
Philbrook Art Center, Tulsa, 284
Phillips, W. W., 208, 209, 211, 213
Phoenix Indian School, 263, 265
Pitner, W. J., 237
Plains Indians, 30–32, 37, 159, 278. *See also separately by tribe*
Plante, Judith, 240
Plural Society in the Southwest (ed. Spicer and Thompson), 270
Policemen, native, 184
Policy, federal Indian. *See* Indian Affairs, United States; Office of Indian Affairs

Politics, intermediary role in, 223, 228–32, 236
Ponca, 141–46
Pontiac's uprising, 48, 52, 55, 65
Pop Chalee, 274, 284
Popé, 15, 27, 33
Portage des Sioux, 83
Potawatomie, 91
Prairie du Chien, 92–93
"Presbygational" church, 124
Presbyterian Church, 181–84, 188, 191, 195, 259
Prestige, reciprocal responsibility of, 55–58
Preston, Scott, 267
Preston, William C., 88
Price, Hiram, 150, 152
Prince, Frederick O., 144
Princess Angeline, 204
Private property, 87. *See also* Land ownership, private
Privilege, burden of, 134
Protocol, conveyer of, 46, 49, 131
Province, John, 244
Prucha, Francis Paul, 14
Public Works of Art Project, 278
Pueblo Indians, 25–43, 273–93; language groups of, 29. *See also separately by pueblo name*
Pueblo Revolt, 25
Pueblo-Spanish War, 27, 30–43

Quinton, Amelia Stone, 153, 156

Radin, Paul, 9
Railroads, 115, 142, 275
Ramona (Jackson), 141, 142, 146, 153, 154, 156, 157
Receptiveness, 295, 300. *See also* Education, cross-cultural
Reconstruction, tribal (revitalization/revival), 87, 100, 102, 114, 123, 181

Recruiter, tribal, 225
Red Shirt (Ogilasa), 171
Reece, Charles, 133
Reece, Lucy A. C., 130, 131
Reece, Nancy, 125–35
Reece, Sally, 126, 133
Reformers, Indian policy, 142, 154–56, 162–63, 175, 234, 280
Regina, Saskatchewan, 252
Reichard, Gladys, 257, 259
Reid, Whitelaw, 144
Religion, 75, 123. *See also* Syncretism, religious
Removal, policies of, 87, 90–94, 104–107, 124, 132, 142, 146, 148, 150
Reservations, 162. *See also separately by name*
Response, the Indian, 50, 51, 65, 73, 85, 102, 106–108, 110, 113, 126, 167, 170, 171
Rewards, 71, 134, 135. *See also* Employment
Reynolds, John, 94, 95
Rhoads, Charles James, 232, 233, 278, 280
Richardson, Leon Burr, 69
Richter, Daniel K., 17, 19
Ridge, John, 124
Riel Rebellion, 240
"The Rise of the Navajo Tribe" (Young), 270
Robb, John, 87
Rocky Bear, 174
Rocky Mountain News, 147
Rodríguez, Sebastián, 36, 37
Rohner, Ronald P., 198
The Role of the Navajo in the Southwestern Drama (Young), 270
Roles for brokers, general and listed, 41, 44, 46, 48, 56–59, 61, 67, 81, 82, 106, 114, 116, 118–19, 125–33, 165, 174, 183–85, 187, 189, 191–92,

201–203, 245–46, 252, 266, 279, 280, 285, 291
Roman Catholic Church, 25–41, 157
Romero, Diego, 30–31
Ronda, James P., 14
Roosevelt, Theodore, 201
Rosas, Luis de, 32
Ross, John, Chief, 100, 105–107, 109–14
Ross, William Potter, 117
Row-of-Lodges, Chief, 223, 224
Rowlodge, Henry, 224, 230
Rowlodge, Jesse, 223–39
Ryan, W. Carson, Jr., 278, 280

Saboba, Calif., 150, 151, 156
Sac, 89–93
Sadie Brower, Naekok: An In-upiaq Woman (Blackman), 19
Sage, Chief, 233
Sahlins, Marshall, 7
St. Louis, Mo., 84
St. Vrain, Felix, 94
Salem, Ore., 241
Salisbury, Neal, 8, 14
Salish, 241
Salish Kootenai College, 254
Salvation Army, 195
San Ildefonso (pueblo), 274, 278, 279
San Juan (pueblo), 35, 36, 274
San Luis Rey de Francia Mission, Calif., 148
San Pasqual Valley, Calif., 148
Sand Creek Massacre, 147
Sandham, Henry, 150, 151
Sando, Joe, 291
Sankey, Ira, 227
Santa Clara (pueblo), 274, 275, 276, 284, 287, 293
Santa Fe, N.M., 275, 276
Santa Fe Indian School, 277, 278, 280, 291
Santo Domingo (pueblo), 280, 291

Sapir, Edward, 259, 260
Satank, 14
Sattelihu, 57
Saxman, Mrs., 189
Saxman, Samuel, 188
Scarouady, 50, 51, 52
School of American Research, Santa Fe, 258, 260
Schoolcraft, Henry Rowe, 88
Schooling. See Education, cross-cultural
Schurz, Carl, 142, 145, 147
Scott, Winfield, 107
Scout, role of, 48
Scribner's Monthly, 147
Seattle, Chief, 204
Seattle, Wash., 200
Second Great Awakening, 124
Self-awareness, 252. See also Culture, preservation of
Seneca, 13, 46
Sequoyah, Chief, 108, 124
Seton, Ernest Thompson, 282
Seven Years War, 48, 52
Shamans, 183–84, 188
Sharpe, Horatio, 49, 56
Shawnee, 45, 46, 49, 50
Sheldon Jackson Institute, 189
Shell, C. E., 225, 226
Sheriff, Mary, 151, 157
Shoshone (Wind River), 15
Show Indians, 158–78
Simmons, Leo W., 9
Simmons, William S., 7, 8
Sioux, 92, 93, 142, 212
Sioux (Plains), 161, 169, 171, 174
Sioux (Standing Rock), 12
Sioux (Teton), 228
Sitka Industrial Training School, 189–91, 193, 195
Sitting Bull, 167–68, 170
Six Nations Indians, 45, 46, 50, 51, 52
Slavery, 103, 105, 109–14
Smiley, Albert K., 154
Smith, Dick, 195

Smith, Dwight L., 14
Smithsonian Institution, 203, 258
Social Organization and Secret Societies of the Kwakiutl Indians (Boas), 204
Society for Applied Anthropology, 245
Society in Scotland for Propagating Christian Knowledge, 64, 65
South America, 250
South Carolina, 123
South Dakota, 142
Speaker for Indians, 50. *See also* Interpreters
Spicer, Edward, 244; and Raymond H. Thompson, 270
Spolsky, Bernard, 269
Standing Bear, 141, 142, 144
Standing Bear v. Crook, 144, 162
Standing Rock Agency, 167, 168
Star Lodge, 224
Status, tribal, 47, 50, 63–64, 72, 73, 113, 168, 187, 188, 211, 223, 224, 228, 229, 236, 240, 247, 279, 291–92
Stern, Theodore, 10–11, 12
Stevenson, Matilda Coxe, 203
Street, Joseph M., 96
Studies in Diversity: American Indian Leaders (ed. Edmonds), 15
The Surrounded (McNickle), 241
Syncretism, cultural, 10–11
Syncretism, religious (spiritual syncretism), 77, 99, 112, 118–21
Szasz, Margaret Connell, 122

Talayesva, Don C., 9
Tallaferro, Lawrence, 89
Tamaree, William, 191
Tanos, 34–35, 37
Taos (pueblo), 37–39, 274
Tapia, Pedro de, 34
Tax, Sol, 252

Taylor, Elizabeth (Cherokee schoolgirl), 126, 128, 133
Taylor, Susan, 125, 130
Teller, Henry, 150
Temecula Valley, Calif., 148
Temple, Sam, 146
Tennessee, 106, 123, 125
Tewa, 15, 34–35, 37, 274, 279, 287
Texas, 225
Thayendanegea, 64
They Came Here First (McNickle), 245
Third Colorado Volunteers, 146
Thomas, Elmer, 234
Thomas-Rogers bill, 234
Thompson, Laura, 244
Thwing, Clarence, 189
Tibbles, Thomas Henry, 144, 146
Tlinglit, 179, 180, 182, 186–88, 190, 191, 195, 198
Tlingit (Chilkat), 184, 188
Toastmasters International, 285
Tohono O'odham, 9
Tongass, 188
Traders, 32, 44, 47, 84, 86, 182, 198–200, 201, 203, 206, 214
Treaties, Clark's, 83–84, 86, 92, 93
Treaty of 1804, land cession, 89–92
Treaty of 1866, railroad, 115
Treaty of Prairie du Chien, 93
Trigger, Bruce G., 7, 13
Trustworthiness, 296. *See also* Status, tribal
Tsimshian, 182, 190, 193
Tupatú, Luis, 35
Turkey Legs, 232
Tutoring, 256. *See also* Educators, native

Ubach, Anthony D., 148
Umbiro, Diego, 39
Uncas, Ben, 67, 72
Underhill, Ruth, 9

Unitarian church, 144
United States Congress, 146, 147, 152, 236, 267, 291
United States Corps of Engineers, 237
United States Marine Corps, 266
United States National Museum, 204
United States State Department, 250
University of Alaska, 271
University of Chicago, 252, 259
University of Colorado, 252
University of Illinois, 256
University of New Mexico, 255, 256, 262, 269–70
University of Saskatchewan, 252
Upshaw, Alexander B., 198, 209–13
Utes (Southern), 269
Utes (Ute Mountain), 269
Utes (White River), 145, 146, 147

Vancouver Island, Can., 204
Vargas, Diego de, 25–26, 30–41
Velarde, Herman, 276, 277
Velarde, Jane, 275
Velarde, Legoria, 275
Velarde, Pablita, 273–93
Velarde, Rosita, 275, 277
Vestal, Stanley, 167
Virginia, 16–17, 46, 47, 55, 123
Vocabulary of the Navajo Language, 259

Walcott, Charles D., 203
Walker, Herbert, 231
Wapello, 91
War of 1812, 83, 90
Ward, William Hayes, 145, 147, 156
"The Wards of the United States Government" (Jackson), 147
Warner, Charles Dudley, 142, 144, 147, 150

Warner, Glenn S. ("Pop"), 225
Warner, Wynkoop, 93
Warner Incident, 93
Washakie, 15
Washington, D.C., 145, 167, 228, 232–35, 281
Washington, George, 48
Watts, Isaac, 73
Wauneka, Annie Dodge, 247, 269
Weibel-Orlando, Joan, 19
Weinland, William H., 156
Weiser, Conrad, 44–48, 55, 56, 58
Wells, G. Wiley, 156
Wesley, Samuel, 73
Whaling, 207
Wheeler-Howard bill, 234
Wheelock, Eleazar, 63–66, 68, 71, 72, 74
Whishcobaugh, 91
Whitaker, Nathaniel, 68
White, Leslie, 288
White, Richard, 20
White Path's Rebellion, 104, 111
White Shield, Chief, 229
Whitefield, George, 65–66, 69
Whiteman, Alfred, 237
Whiteman, Chief, 232, 233
Whittlesey, E., 154
Wigwam Society, 228
Wild West show: in England, 170; goals of the, 159; program of the, 161
Willard, Caroline, 185, 186, 188
Willard, E. S., Reverend and Mrs., 184
Willard, Frances, 180, 190, 191–94, 195
Willetto, Antonio, 263
Williams, Roger, 118
Williams, Sam, 195
Wilson, Alfred, 230, 232, 233, 235
Wilson, Polly, 129
Winchester conference, 48

Wind from an Enemy Sky (McNickle), 252–53
Wind River reservation, Wyo., 224
Window Rock, Ariz., 247, 259
Winnebago, 9, 146
Winnebago War, 90
Wisconsin, 18, 78
Wisconsin Indian Association, 156
Women's Christian Temperance Union, 191
Women's National Indian Association (WNIA), 141, 153, 156, 157
Wool, John, 106
Woolworth, Arnold, Chief, 224, 228, 229–30, 233, 235
Worcester, Samuel A., 105–106, 110, 112
Works Progress Administration, 260

World War I, 158
World War II, 264, 266
Wrangell, Alaska, 182, 187, 188, 191
Wright, Julia McNair, 188
Wright, Peter M., 15
"Written Navajo: A Brief History" (Young), 270
Wyandot, 46
Wyoming, 224

Yavapai, 15
Yazzie, Maxwell, 267
Ye, Juan de, 30, 35–39
Young, Robert W., 255–72
Young, S. Hall, 181–84, 187

Zia (pueblo), 25, 33–34, 278, 279, 288
Zinzendorf, Nicolaus Ludwig von, 45, 57
Zuni, 31–32, 269